The Image of God in Man

The circle shape, representing God, is reflected like a mirror. It is God's image reflected in man.

Sin

This diamond represents sin and its absolute corruption. The sharp edges and corners contrast the perfect wholeness of the circle.

Justification

These triangles are perfectly matched, which speaks to the idea of being made complete only by God's righteousness in us.

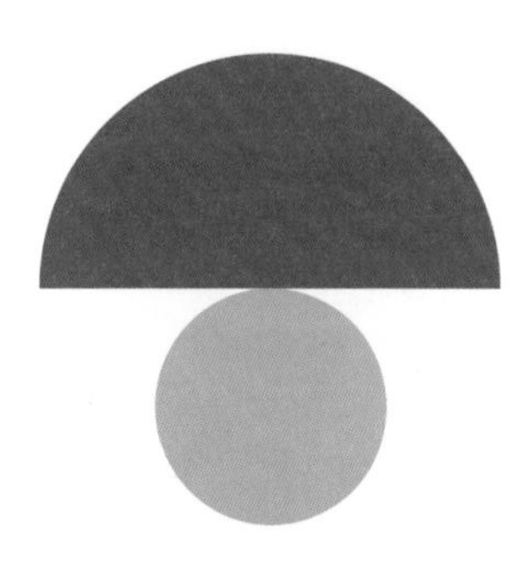

Sanctification

The circle here represents the Spirit of God, which supports the half circle that symbolizes mankind becoming more and more like God.

Perseverance and Glorification

The quarter circles represent the saints glorifying God. They are united, mirroring the circle that represents God.

Eternity

This ring shape represents eternity because it has no beginning and no end. It is infinite.

"In this useful and searching book, Paul Tripp does what we have come to count on him to do—take the great and glorious truths of the Christian faith and funnel them into our actual, real-time lives. This book makes wonderfully unavoidable what theology is *for*—buoyancy and hope and energy in my life today."

Dane Ortlund, Senior Pastor, Naperville Presbyterian Church; author, *Gentle and Lowly* and *Deeper*

"'The Bible is a life book given for life purposes,' Paul Tripp contends. Based on this premise, Tripp provides a fresh treatment of twelve major doctrines—many of them related to God and his character and work—and connects each of them to life. The connection between biblical doctrine and real life makes this a valuable, practical tool for the pursuit of greater godliness. Highly recommended!"

Andreas J. Köstenberger, Director, Center for Biblical Studies and Research; Research Professor of New Testament and Biblical Theology, Midwestern Baptist Theological Seminary; Founder, Biblical Foundations

"Many people believe that biblical illiteracy is the primary cause of the church's weakness today. And while learning more about the Bible is indeed good, merely knowing right doctrine isn't enough. The remedy we need will be found only when we take God's truth into our hearts and ask it to confront and transform us. It is meant to be ingested and lived out, not just studied and examined, and Paul David Tripp knows exactly how to help you do that. *Do You Believe?* will show you how the great doctrines of the Bible are meant not only to inform us but also to quench our thirst, direct our course, and invigorate us. I strongly recommend it!"

Elyse Fitzpatrick, author, *Worthy: Celebrating the Value of Women*

"Here is a book that stretches our minds and hearts to embrace big truths—and to secure those truths like a great tent sheltering us as we live and love, here and now. These chapters keep reminding us to look up and worship the God who is there—and so to better see what's right in front of our eyes. In his honest, companionable, and still-awed voice of experience, Paul Tripp covers huge doctrinal ground with Jesus and the gospel at front and center. And, on this ground, we find our next small step more solid and sure."

Kathleen Nielson, author; speaker

"One reason skeptics don't take Christianity seriously is the disconnect they see between the beliefs and behavior of so many Christians. Do we really believe the doctrines we say we believe? If so, why are our lives so often unchanged—so often indistinguishable from the lives of unbelievers? Paul Tripp tackles this problem compellingly in *Do You Believe?* For twelve central Christian doctrines, he lays out not only what the doctrine is but how we should live in light of it. Doctrine is not just about knowing information, he says. It's about transformation. This is an urgent and essential book—a treasure trove of wisdom for any Christian willing to take seriously the implications of belief for everyday life."

Brett McCracken, Senior Editor, The Gospel Coalition; author, *The Wisdom Pyramid* and *Uncomfortable*

"Doctrine comes from God, teaches us about God, and leads us back to God in worship. That is precisely what this book helps us to do—to know God that we might authentically love and worship God in all of life. This book is sure to become a widely used resource for discipleship in churches throughout the world. For far too long, doctrine and the application of doctrine have been separated, and this book rightly brings them back together. Doctrine is about knowing God and living for God in all of life. In this book, Paul Tripp beautifully shows us how to experience the joy of knowing God and living out that knowledge every day of our lives."

Burk Parsons, Senior Pastor, Saint Andrew's Chapel, Sanford, Florida; Editor, *Tabletalk*

"In this important book, Paul Tripp puts his finger on a live nerve in the body of Christ. He addresses the dangerous disconnect that often exists between sound doctrine and sound living. Tripp sounds the needed warning that knowing truth is never an end in itself but only a means to a far greater end. He reminds us that the goal of biblical instruction must be personal transformation. Here is made the inseparable connection between biblical indicatives and practical imperatives. What God has joined together, let no man separate."

Steven Lawson, President, OnePassion Ministries; Professor of Preaching, The Master's Seminary; Teaching Fellow, Ligonier Ministries

"How horrible would it be to hear the charge, 'You profess to know Christ but deny him by your actions'? The apostle Paul saw it in the Cretans to whom he sent Titus, and no doubt he could spy such gaps, whether tiny or glaring, in all of our lives. I desperately want to close those gaps. Hopefully, you do as well. This is a remarkable resource for doing precisely that, by the grace of God: minding the gaps between what we profess to believe and how we live in tangible, everyday moments. Few in our day can speak so compellingly and accessibly on this topic as Paul Tripp. Let him win you back to the critical importance of what we in Christ believe, and how we who believe then live."

David Mathis, Senior Teacher and Executive Editor, desiringGod.org; author, *Habits of Grace*

"Whenever a fresh article or book by Paul David Tripp is released, I take note. I am an avid follower of his counsel, for no matter how many others might cut me slack—I am, after all, a lifelong quadriplegic—I know Paul David Tripp will insist that I interpret my difficult circumstances, as well as my response to them, solely through the lens of Scripture. Although we rarely cross paths, my friend knows my heart, and how prone I am to wander. It's why I am especially excited about his new work, *Do You Believe?* Our life in Christ thrives only when we are rooted in the great doctrines of the faith, and Paul David Tripp does a stellar job of presenting the fundamentals. Whether you already have a grasp on Christian doctrine or are just getting started, this should be your next read!"

Joni Eareckson Tada, Founder, Joni and Friends International Disability Center

Do You Believe?

Other Books by Paul David Tripp

A Quest for More: Living for Something Bigger Than You

Age of Opportunity: A Biblical Guide for Parenting Teens (Resources for Changing Lives)

Awe: Why It Matters for Everything We Think, Say, and Do

Broken-Down House: Living Productively in a World Gone Bad

Come, Let Us Adore Him: A Daily Advent Devotional

Dangerous Calling: Confronting the Unique Challenges of Pastoral Ministry

Forever: Why You Can't Live without It

Grief: Finding Hope Again

How People Change (with Timothy S. Lane)

Instruments in the Redeemer's Hands: People in Need of Change Helping People in Need of Change (Resources for Changing Lives)

Journey to the Cross: A 40-Day Lenten Devotional

Lead: 12 Gospel Principles for Leadership in the Church

Lost in the Middle: Midlife and the Grace of God

Marriage: 6 Gospel Commitments Every Couple Needs to Make

My Heart Cries Out: Gospel Meditations for Everyday Life

New Morning Mercies: A Daily Gospel Devotional

Parenting: 14 Gospel Principles That Can Radically Change Your Family

Redeeming Money: How God Reveals and Reorients Our Hearts

Sex in a Broken World: How Christ Redeems What Sin Distorts

Shelter in the Time of Storm: Meditations on God and Trouble

Suffering: Eternity Makes a Difference (Resources for Changing Lives)

Suffering: Gospel Hope When Life Doesn't Make Sense

Teens and Sex: How Should We Teach Them? (Resources for Changing Lives)

War of Words: Getting to the Heart of Your Communication Struggles (Resources for Changing Lives)

Whiter Than Snow: Meditations on Sin and Mercy

Do You Believe?

12 Historic Doctrines to Change
Your Everyday Life

Paul David Tripp

Foreword by David Platt

WHEATON, ILLINOIS

Do You Believe: 12 Historic Doctrines to Change Your Everyday Life

Published by Crossway
1300 Crescent Street
Wheaton, Illinois 60187

Cover design: Ordinary Folk, ordinaryfolk.co

First printing 2021

Printed in China

All emphases in Scripture quotations have been added by the author.

Hardcover ISBN: 978-1-4335-6771-1
ePub ISBN: 978-1-4335-6774-2
PDF ISBN: 978-1-4335-6772-8
Mobipocket ISBN: 978-1-4335-6773-5

Library of Congress Cataloging-in-Publication Data

Names: Tripp, Paul David, 1950– author.
Title: Do you believe? : 12 historic doctrines to change your everyday life / Paul David Tripp.
Description: Wheaton, Illinois : Crossway, [2021] | Includes bibliographical references and indexes.
Identifiers: LCCN 2021006798 (print) | LCCN 2021006799 (ebook) | ISBN 9781433567711 (hardcover) | ISBN 9781433567728 (pdf) | ISBN 9781433567735 (mobi) | ISBN 9781433567742 (epub)
Subjects: LCSH: Theology, Doctrinal—Popular works. | Christian Life—Biblical teaching.
Classification: LCC BT77 .T765 2021 (print) | LCC BT77 (ebook) | DDC 230—dc23
LC record available at https://lccn.loc.gov/2021006798
LC ebook record available at https://lccn.loc.gov/2021006799

Crossway is a publishing ministry of Good News Publishers.

RRDS 31 30 29 28 27 26 25 24 23 22
15 14 13 12 11 10 9 8 7 6 5 4 3

Luella, you have always been my muse, but with this book you became a partner. Those morning and afternoon discussions about chapter after chapter have been a major contributor to what this book has become. I am blessed to have you as my life companion and my best friend.

Contents

Foreword

I REMEMBER EXACTLY where I was sitting. I also remember thinking that I shouldn't be sitting.

It was a theology class in seminary, and my professor was teaching on the doctrine of God. As he spoke about God's holiness in all, his sovereignty over all, and his glory above all, I sat in awe. And I thought, "I shouldn't just be sitting here taking notes. I should be bowing down on my knees. Truth like this is not mere information to be learned; truth like this is revelation that completely changes the posture of my life."

I share this memory because it's exactly how I felt as I read this book. I couldn't just sit there as my eyes scrolled across each page. Not when those eyes at times were filled with tears that drove me to my knees in worship. Not when my heart at other times was so filled with joy that I stood to my feet and started to sing. Not when my soul was overwhelmingly moved to pray for my life, my family, the church, and billions of people who have never even heard this truth.

Now don't misunderstand: this book is filled with information to be learned. I think I underlined half of the sentences I read! But far more important, this book is filled with revelation that will completely change the posture of your life—if you will let it.

I make the statement above only because this book is filled with truth from God's word. To be clear, the Bible alone is supernaturally inspired to transform your heart, mind, and life (you'll read about this in the first two chapters). But God has gifted the church with servants who help us understand God's word and apply it to our lives. Paul Tripp is one such servant, and he has given us an invaluable gift in this book.

For this book takes truth that is all too often reserved for select students in theology classes and makes it available, accessible, and applicable to every single follower of Jesus. No matter how young or old you are, and regardless of whether you have been a Christian for a day or fifty years, this book is for you. It takes the cardinal doctrines of the Christian faith that we all need to know and brings them to bear on the everyday struggles, trials, temptations, and pleasures of students and senior adults, singles and married couples, children and parents, men and women in every age and stage of life.

In sum, I can say without hesitation or reservation that this book will become a staple resource that I walk through with my wife, my children, my church, and anyone else I am helping to grow in Christ. For this reason, I gladly and wholeheartedly commend it to you. May reading the pages ahead lead you to fall on your knees in worship and then rise to your feet with zeal to love God with everything you have and to live for the spread of his glory everywhere you go.

David Platt

Preface

WRITING THIS BOOK has been one of the greatest privileges of my life. That I have been able to spend month after month meditating on the most amazing body of truth the human mind could ever consider leaves me in awe of God's goodness. As is true with every book I write, I write what I need, knowing that if I need it, then others do too. I wrote this book to awaken us out of our street-level theological thoughtlessness. I wrote it to narrow that troublesome gap between what we say we believe and how we actually live. Without ever intending to, many of us live theologically contradictory lives. We say we believe that God is both sovereign and good, but when trouble comes, we panic as if no one is in control or we allow ourselves to question God's goodness and love. We say we believe in the necessity and power of divine grace, but when confronted, we argue for our righteousness, and in so doing, resist the very grace we say we believe in. We say we believe in eternity but get caught up in expending our time, energy, and money on the temporary pleasures of the moment.

I confess that there are still gaps between what I profess to believe in my life and how I live in given moments, and I am sure there are some in your life as well. My prayer is that God would open our eyes to those gaps and that he will use this book to help us understand more clearly what it looks like to live out of what God has declared and we have affirmed to be true.

I want to explain something about this book. My goal wasn't to write a comprehensive systematic theology; many fine ones have been written. This book doesn't cover every doctrine of the Christian faith, but rather focuses on twelve of its core doctrines. These are doctrines that should be known and familiar to any Bible believer. There are two chapters dedicated to each doctrine. The first chapter defines and explains the doctrine being considered, and the second chapter considers what it looks like to live in light of that particular truth.

My goal in the twelve application chapters is not to make direct application to every area of life, but to help you to understand that there is a particular culture or lifestyle that flows out of each doctrine. Truth that does not form your lifestyle is probably not truth that is believed in the biblical sense of what faith actually is. In this book I am asking how our lives should be shaped by the doctrines of God's omnipotence, the doctrine of creation, the doctrine of justification, the doctrine of eternity, and so on. My goal is that thinking of biblical truth as a lifestyle will become more and more natural as you read through this book.

So rather than being an exhaustive consideration of the theology of Scripture, this book is meant to be a training manual on what it looks like to carry what you believe into the situations, locations, and relationships of your daily life. I haven't covered every doctrine and I haven't traced out all of the implications of the doctrines that I do cover, but my hope is that this book will help you to think of the theology of God's word in new and practical ways. And my prayer is that the result would be less of a lifestyle of theological forgetfulness and more of an everyday culture in your life that is shaped and directed by the precious truths that God has so lovingly revealed to you and that you have come to hold dear.

Paul David Tripp
12/1/2020

Introduction

The Dangerous Dichotomy

I FOUND MYSELF in yet another frustrating conversation with one of the most theologically knowledgeable men I have known. There was no theological hallway I could walk down with him that he hadn't traversed again and again. He was confident, defensive, and ready for the next debate. The problem was that I was not there to debate him; I was there to help him. But he was nearly impossible to help. I was his counselor, and the reason he needed counsel was that there was a huge, dysfunction-producing gap between what he knew so well and the way he lived. His marriage was crumbling, none of his children respected him, and his friends found him more than hard to handle.

In his home, this master of the theology of God's grace was a man of ungrace. He was known more for impatient criticism than patient mercy. He could exegete and explain the doctrine of God's sovereignty, but in the situations and relationships of his daily life, he had to be in control. He had an airtight Christology, but unlike Christ, he did not love well, serve well, or forgive well. His wife had asked if I would counsel them because their marriage was imploding. He made it very clear that he didn't think he needed to be counseled. To say that there was a contrast between the gorgeous theology he had spent so much time studying and the way he lived would surely be an understatement.

• • •

Salina loved the gospel, never missed her morning devotional reading, and had Alexa belting Christian music throughout her house all day long. If the doors of her church building were open, she was there. If a Christian conference or concert came to her city, she'd probably go. On the surface everything looked fine with Salina. But Salina lived in constant fear. She was so afraid of what people would think of her that she would frenetically replay conversations over and over again in her head, regretting what she said and fretting about what the hearer now thought of her. She was afraid of her boss and constantly convinced that she was about to lose her job. Over the years she had become a bit of a hypochondriac, fretting over any small sign of physical abnormality. Somehow the big, transforming gospel that she consumed every day hadn't freed her from her bondage to fear.

• • •

Brad led one of the small groups in his church. He was asked to do so because he was biblically literate and on the surface seemed mature. He was good at leading this small group, and they studied and discussed God's word together. He had recently been asked to participate in elder training and seemed eager to do so. The people in his small group appreciated him and his leadership. But Mindy, Brad's wife, had a different experience of Brad and those small group meetings. Every time they met, Mindy struggled with the difference between the "public" Brad, the well-liked small group leader, and the "private" Brad, the man she was married to.

At home, Brad did not act like a mature Christian man. With Mindy, Brad was often angry, cynical, and demeaning. He would argue Mindy into a corner over the smallest of things, leaving her wondering what had happened to the man she thought she was marrying. As Mindy sat with her small group friends, she was often tempted to blurt out, "Brad's not who you think he is and we need help," but she knew she never would. She loved Brad and pleaded to God for help, but she just didn't know what to do.

• • •

I could give example after example of a dichotomy that exists in so many of us (and still exists in some places in my own life) between what we say we believe and the way we live. And I am persuaded that the gap between the doctrine we say we believe and the way we actually live is a workroom for the enemy. What I am going to say next may surprise you, but I think it needs to be said and considered. The enemy of your soul will gladly give you your formal theology, if in your real daily life he can control the thoughts and motives of your heart and, in so doing, control the way you act, react, and respond.

This dichotomy is the reason for this book. It has convicted me when I look at my own life and saddened me as I've seen it in so many others. As we begin, I want to first look at the importance of doctrine and then examine what the Bible has to say about this dichotomy.

The Importance of Doctrine

"Daddy, did God make telephone poles?" It seemed like one of those endless unimportant questions that, near the end of a long day, can make a parent a bit insane. We had been teaching our children that God created the world and everything in it, and our son had been mulling that deep thought in his little brain. In fact, as we drove to Burger King, he was thinking about it quietly in the back seat as he looked out the window at the string of telephone poles that lined the street. It was a deeply theological question asked by the little philosopher strapped into the child's seat in the back of the car. He couldn't help thinking, because he couldn't help being human. He was doing what God designed humans made in his image to do. Sometimes his questions made us laugh, sometimes they made us wonder what was rattling around in his cranium, and other times his constant questions just made us wish he would stop asking us questions. But he wouldn't ever stop because he was doing what every human being does.[1]

Little children never seem to quit asking why, teenagers obsess about what's fair and unfair, husbands and wives argue because they have interpreted a particular situation differently, and the elderly person looks back over the years trying to make sense of it all. We all do it all the time, and most of the time we don't realize that we're doing it and we fail to understand the profound significance of what we're doing. It's a deeply and uniquely human thing that we're doing. It gets to the heart of how God wired us to operate, yet its life-shaping importance doesn't tend to get the play that it should. Every day at some time and in some way we all work to make sense out of our lives. We dig through the mound of the artifacts of the old civilization that was our past and try to understand our journey and what it means. We endlessly toss around the current events and relationships of our little worlds, trying to decide how we should respond to the situations and relationships around us. We peer into the future, hoping we can somehow divine what is to come and prepare ourselves for it. We just never leave our lives alone, and we never stop thinking, even when we are asleep.

It's important that we all become more conscious of the vibrant mental activity that so influences the choices we make, the words we say, and the things we do. You may be a plumber, a homemaker, a musician, a dad, a teacher, a student, an accountant, a gardener, or an athlete, but you are also a thinker. If you are human, you think (although some of us show it more than others). You may think improperly or inconsistently, but you think. None of us have ever had a thoughtless day. All of us have constructed a superstructure of life assumptions that functions as the instrument we use to make sense out of life. So, all of us are

1 Much of this section first appeared in my article "The Importance of Doctrine," Paul Tripp website, July 2, 2018, www.paultripp.com/.

theologians, all of us are philosophers, all of us are counselors, and all of us are archeologists who dig through the past to understand what was. And here's what is vital to understand: *your thoughts always precede and determine your activity*. Stop and reread the previous sentence because it is very, very important. You don't do what you do because of what you are experiencing at the moment. No, you do what you do because of the way you have thought about and interpreted what you are experiencing.

We know that you can put three people in the very same situation, experiencing the very same thing, and all three will have remarkably different reactions. Why? Because they interpret that situation differently. A variance in interpretation will always lead to a difference in response.

Now what does this have to do with the purpose of the doctrines that are revealed in the word of God? Well, everything! The God who hardwired you to be a thinker is also the God who inspired the writers of the Old and New Testaments to pen his truths so that we would have them at our disposal. The Bible is the result of a loving Creator unpacking what is true for his creatures so that they will know how properly to make sense out of life. Without his loving revelation, we wouldn't know how to know, we wouldn't know for sure what we know, and we would have no way to know if what we think we know is true or not. In the Bible, God, the meaning-giver, explains foundational truths to the meaning-makers he created. Every person who has ever lived has desperately needed the unfolded mysteries found in Scripture. The Bible is not so much a religious book, left to be relegated to the hallowed and separate corridors of institutional religion. No, the Bible is a life book given for life purposes, so that the creatures to whom it is given would look for life in the only place where life can be found. The doctrines of the Bible are not so much ideology as they are living and divine tools of salvation, transformation, identity, and guidance.

Before we look at how the doctrine of the Bible is an instrument of these four things, we want to think through what the Bible is and how it works. If you have spent any time reading or studying God's word, you know that the Bible isn't arranged by topic. If we're honest, that frustrates some of us. We wish the Bible were arranged by topic and had subject tabs on the edge of the page so we could quickly go to our topic of interest. But the Bible is arranged the way it is by divine intention. Your Bible has been carefully designed by your Lord to operate in a particular way that is for your good and his glory.

The Bible is essentially a grand redemptive story, a narrative. Or we could say that the Bible is a theologically annotated story. It is the sweeping story of God's plan and purpose of redemption accompanied by God's essential explanatory and applicatory notes. This means you cannot treat your Bible like an encyclopedia; it doesn't work that way. For example, if you only go to verses with the word *parent* in them to understand parenting, you will omit the majority of the things the Bible has to say about this significant human calling. To the degree that every passage tells me things I need to know about God, things I need to know about myself, things I need to know about life in the fallen world, things I need to know about the disaster of sin, and things I need to know about the operation of grace, to that degree every passage tells me something I need to know about every area of my life. I will say much more about this in the chapter to follow.

So, what role does doctrine play? First, the doctrines of Scripture provide a helpful shorthand for the grand redemptive story. Every doctrine captures something about God, his work, and our need, allowing us to summarize vast amounts of content and historical activity in one word. For example, the doctrine of justification captures a set of things that God did to secure our right standing with him. Because of this doctrine we have a summary term to use when speaking of God's grace that is shorthand for all the things God did to secure our position as his children. We can use the term *justification* without having to retell the story, with all of its detail, again. Every doctrine in Scripture provides a summary or shorthand for things God knows are vital for us to know and understand.

Second, every doctrine is an explanation. We would not fully understand, for example, the implications of the fall of Adam and Eve, the calling of Abraham, the righteous life of Jesus, the cross, the empty tomb, the ascension, or the establishment of the church if it were not for the explanatory doctrines of God's word. Through them, God helps us to understand how we have acted in our sin and how he has acted toward us and for us in his grace. We are saved not so much by the doctrine, but by the historical things God has willingly and graciously done on our behalf. The doctrines explain those things to us so that we can admit our need and reach out for God's help.

Now carefully consider this: God never intended the doctrines of the Bible to be ends in themselves, but rather means to an end. The doctrines God has revealed have a greater purpose than to give you a big theological brain. They are meant to provide more than an outline and a theological confession. Perhaps the best word picture for what the doctrines of the Bible were intended to do is found in Isaiah 55:10–13. Isaiah describes the truths in the Bible being like rain or snow that falls and waters the earth. What is the result?

> Instead of the thorn shall come up the cypress;
> instead of the brier shall come up the myrtle;
> and it shall make a name for the LORD,
> an everlasting sign that shall not be cut off. (Isa. 55:13)

We must admit that this is one of the strangest word pictures in all of the Bible. If you had a thornbush in your backyard, you wouldn't say, "You know, if it keeps raining, that thornbush will turn into a cypress tree." If you did say that, the person next to you would think you were a bit insane. You would never think that a well-watered brier would somehow morph into a myrtle. What is the prophet trying to communicate by stretching our botanical understanding? What does this metaphor tell us about what God intends the truths (doctrines) of his word to produce?

Isaiah's strange word picture paints a picture of radical, organic transformation. The plant that is being watered becomes an entirely different plant. So it is with the doctrines of the word of God. Their primary purpose is not *information* but *transformation*. The informative function of the truths of Scripture is not the goal of those truths but a necessary means to the goal of those truths, which is radical personal transformation. God's plan is that when the rain of biblical doctrine falls on us, it would change us—not that we would become better renditions of ourselves but that we would become spiritually different than we were before. As the rain of truth falls, angry people become peacemakers, greedy people become givers, demanding people become servants, lustful people become pure, faithless people become believers, proud people become humble, rebels become obedient people, and idolaters become worshipers of God.

The doctrines of the word of God were not intended just to lay claim on your brain, but also to capture your heart and transform the way you live. Those doctrines are meant to turn you inside out and your world upside down. Biblical doctrine is much more than an outline you give confessional assent to. Doctrine is something you live in even the smallest and most mundane moments of your life. Biblical doctrine is meant to transform your identity, alter your relationships, and reshape your finances. It's meant to change the way you think and talk, how you approach your job, how you conduct yourself in time of leisure, how you act in your marriage, and the things you do as a parent. It's meant to change the way you think about your past, interpret the present, and view the future.

The doctrines of the word of God are a beautiful gift to us from a God of amazing grace. They are not burdensome, life-constricting beliefs. No, they impart new life and new freedom. They quiet your soul and give courage to your heart. They make you wiser than you had the natural potential to be, and they replace your complaining heart with one that worships with joy. God unfolds these mysteries to you because he loves you. He is the giver of life, and every doctrine in his word plants seeds of life in your heart. And as those seeds take root and grow, you too grow and change.

God isn't just after your mind; he's after your heart. And he's not just after your heart; he's after everything that makes up you. His truths (doctrines) are the ecosystem in which the garden of personal transformation grows.

No passage captures this better than 2 Timothy 3:16–17: "All Scripture is breathed out by God and profitable for teaching, for reproof, for correction, and for training in righteousness, that the man of God may be complete, equipped for every good work." This passage is so important for understanding how the truths (doctrines) of Scripture are meant to function in our lives. It gives us not only four ways that Scripture (and each of its doctrines) is meant to function in our lives but, more importantly, it provides a process by which Scripture is meant to function. Here are the four steps in the process.

1. Teaching: the standard. The truths of the Bible are God's ultimate standard. They establish for us who God is, who we are, what our lives were designed to be, what is true and what is not, why we do the things we do, how change takes place, what in the world has gone wrong, and how in the world it will ever get corrected. The doctrines of the word of God provide the standard, lovingly revealed to us by our Creator, by which we can know, with surety, what we would never know without them.

Everyone looks to some kind of standard because we all want to know, and we all want to know that what we know is true. So everyone carries a "bible" around with them, either one of his or her own making or the perfect standard handed down by the one who is truth.

2. Reproof: comparison to the standard. Reproof is the process by which you are compared to a standard and in some way found lacking. This word clues us in to what we are meant to do with the truths revealed in God's word. Every truth is meant to function as a mirror into which we look to see what is revealed about us in light of that truth. If you look into the mirror of God's perfection, you are immediately confronted with the reality that you are far from perfection. If you look into the mirror of the doctrine of sin, you see that you, too, are a sinner. No truth is meant to live in abstract, impersonal separation from us. Every truth is a measuring stick to which we compare our thoughts, desires, words, choices, motivations, relationships, worship, and hopes. Knowledge of doctrine should produce not only knowledge of God, but a penetratingly humbling knowledge of self.

Theological study should produce not only praise and worship of God, but also heartfelt grief, confession, and repentance. Truth that does not reprove (confront) is truth not properly handled. It is possible and tempting to handle biblical doctrine unbiblically by omitting or resisting its reproving function.

3. Correction: closing the gap between where I am and where God wants me to be. The doctrines of Scripture are meant to correct us. Correction is a process where what has been revealed to be wrong or lacking is brought closer to the standard. In the face of every truth in Scripture our question should be, "What does this truth reveal about me that needs to be corrected, and how will that correction take place in a way that is consistent with who God is, how he has revealed change takes place, and in light of what he has provided for me in the person and work of the Lord Jesus?"

Progressive sanctification, which is God's redeeming work in us between our conversion and our homegoing, is a continual process of comparison-correction, comparison-correction, driven by the truths of his word and empowered by the work of his Spirit.

4. Training: faithfully putting God's standard into practice. In the face of every teaching of Scripture we should ask, "What new thing is God calling me to put into regular practice in my thoughts, desires, words, and actions?" You train to do better what you haven't done well or haven't done at all. Embedded in every doctrine of the word of God is a call to brand-new ways of living. So, believing in the indwelling presence of the Holy Spirit and the inexhaustible resources of his grace, we submit to his call to live in a new way.

Second Timothy 3:16–17 calls us to handle the truths of Scripture in a way that results in a constant pattern of personal self-examination that leads to honest and humble confession, which produces a commitment to repentance, resulting in a life of increasing spiritual maturity and joyful obedience. Not just your thinking is being changed, but every area of your life is being brought into greater and greater conformity to the will of the one who created you and recreated you in Christ Jesus.

Now, let's be honest. This is not always the way that we relate to and respond to the truths of God's word. In all of us, somewhere, gaps still exist between what we say we believe and how we actually live. Many of us are willing to live with functional inconsistency between the truths that we declare we believe and how we choose to live. So it must be said that the truths you actually believe are the truths that you live, because faith is never just intellectual assent. More importantly, biblical faith is a commitment of the heart that radically alters the way you live. Truth not lived is truth not believed.

This dichotomy I am describing is a dangerous, God-dishonoring, spiritually debilitating, idolatry-producing, moral-resolve-weakening, relationship-damaging, and body-of-Christ-weakening spiritual dynamic that gives the devil a huge opportunity in our hearts and lives. Some of us don't see the gaps in our lives. Some of us confess and repent when we see the gaps. And some of us have learned to live with the gaps for so long that they don't bother us anymore.

This gap jumps off the pages of Scripture in two specific accounts. The stories of these two characters are well known to us. They have been retained for us, by the God of grace, because they are about people who are just like us and God does not want us to fall into the same traps they did.

The first character is Jonah. God called Jonah to preach warnings of judgment to the evil city of Nineveh. The very thought of taking God's message to these despicable people was repulsive to Jonah, so rather than heeding God's call, he booked himself on a boat heading in the opposite direction as far as he could go. But God wasn't done with Jonah.

God sent a terrifying storm. The crew of the boat, trying to figure out why this storm had been inflicted upon them, cast lots, and the lot fell on Jonah. So they asked Jonah who he was and where he was from. Jonah's answer should get your attention: "I am a Hebrew, and I fear the Lord, the God of heaven" (Jonah 1:9). Take time to examine and think through Jonah's answer. "I am a Hebrew." Well, that's true. "I fear the Lord, the God of heaven." What? There appears to be no fear of God whatsoever in this man. He had no problem with looking God in the face and saying, "I will not do what you have asked me to do." He had no problem with taking his life into his own hands and doing the opposite of what God had called him to do.

A huge gap exists between the cultural confession of this Hebrew man and the reality of how he responded to God and chose to live his life. The "fear" he is talking about is a cultural abstraction that bears little resemblance to the way he chooses to live his life. It may be a distant, impersonal item of intellectual assent, but it falls short of the transforming power of true belief the Bible describes. True belief always results in a willing submission to God and a joyful obedience to his calling. God wants more from Jonah than a cultural identity. God will settle for nothing less than the allegiance of Jonah's heart and the submission of himself to the holy will of God.

The second incident is equally as striking. Here is the apostle Paul's account of what happened.

> But when Cephas came to Antioch, I opposed him to his face, because he stood condemned. For before certain men came from James, he was eating with the Gentiles; but when they came he drew back and separated himself, fearing the circumcision party. And the rest of the Jews acted hypocritically along with him, so that even Barnabas was led astray by their hypocrisy. But when I saw that their conduct was not in step with the truth of the gospel, I said to Cephas before them all, "If you, though a Jew, live like a Gentile and not like a Jew, how can you force the Gentiles to live like Jews?" (Gal. 2:11–14)

It is one of the most dramatic moments in the New Testament church. Paul confronts Peter face-to-face. How high must the stakes have been for this encounter to have taken place? The answer is, very high. At stake was the very character and purity of the gospel and faithful allegiance to God's revelation. We know from Acts 10 that

God had made it clear to Peter that Gentiles were included in his plan of redemption, and they were not to be excluded in any way or to be treated as second-class citizens. But Peter, who had been in open fellowship with the Gentiles, withdrew from the Gentiles when a Jewish circumcision group showed up. In so doing, he acted in direct contradiction to the gospel doctrines he had been taught and had professed to believe. This striking moment makes it clear how dangerous the dichotomy between doctrine and life can be.

It is important to note that what happened here was not the result of Peter changing his doctrinal position. The problem was not first theological; it was moral. Fear of man was a more powerful motivator in Peter's heart than what God had taught him was right and true. This is why we must always shine the light of the doctrines of Scripture on the thoughts, desires, motivations, and craving of our hearts.

Do we think as the doctrines of God's word have taught us to think?

Do we value what these doctrines have taught us to value?

Do we love what these doctrines have taught us to love?

Do we accept whom these doctrines have declared us to be?

Do we desire what these doctrines have taught us to desire?

Do we make choices that these doctrines would direct us to make?

Do we act, react, and respond in light of what these doctrines have taught us?

Where in our hearts is there a war of allegiance between what these doctrines call us to and what we want for ourselves?

Are there places where we have become comfortable with a dichotomy between what we say we believe and the way we live?

It is these questions that are the motivation for this book. My prayer is that this book would be one of God's tools to help you, by his illuminating and enabling grace, to close the gap between your confessional theology and your functional theology, and by closing the gap, give the enemy less opportunity to do his evil work.

My intention is not to give you an exhaustive systematic theology with applicatory insights, but rather to look at twelve cardinal gospel doctrines and ask, "What does it look like to live as an individual, citizen, parent, spouse, or child in light of these doctrines?" May God meet you with his rescuing and renewing grace as you take this walk with me through the beautiful garden of the doctrines of his word.

1

The Doctrine of Scripture

ALTHOUGH OUR CONSCIENCE and God's creation beautifully display his goodness, wisdom, and power, and therefore leave us without excuse, their message is not enough to give us the knowledge of God and his will, which is necessary for salvation. So God, in his wisdom and grace, at various times and in a variety of ways, revealed himself, declared his will, preserved and proclaimed his truth, and protected the church against corruption and the deceits of Satan and the world by committing his truth to writing. This makes Scripture (the Bible, Old and New Testaments) necessary and essential.

The authority of Scripture, that it is to be believed and obeyed, does not depend on the testimony of any person, but completely on God, the author. It is to be joyfully received because it is the word of God.

The testimony of the church along with Scripture's doctrine, its majestic style, the agreement of all its parts, the fact that every part gives glory to God and reveals the only way of our salvation, and its overall perfection together argue that it is the very word of God. All things necessary for God's own glory and for our salvation, faith, and life, have either clearly been set down by God in Scripture or can properly be deduced from Scripture, so nothing needs to be or ever should be added by new revelations or any new human insights or traditions.

One final thing must be said. All Scripture, every book in the Old and New Testaments, penned by some forty authors and encompassing Biblical Literature, Narrative, History, Poetry, Wisdom, Prophecy, Gospels, Epistles, and Apocalypse, was written under and directed by the inspiration of God. See Ps. 19:1–3; Prov. 22:19–21; Isa. 8:20; Luke 16:29, 31; 24:27, 44; John 16:13–14; Acts 15:15; Rom. 1:19–21; 2:14–15; 3:2; 15:4; 1 Cor. 2:10–12; Eph. 2:20; 2 Thess. 2:13; 2 Tim. 3:15–17; Heb. 1:1; 2 Pet. 1:19–20; 1 John 2:20, 27; 1 John 5:9.[1]

Understanding the Doctrine of Scripture

> For the wrath of God is revealed from heaven against all ungodliness and unrighteousness of men, who by their unrighteousness suppress the truth. For what can be known about God is plain to them, because God has shown it to them. For his invisible attributes, namely, his eternal power and divine nature, have been clearly perceived, ever since the creation of the world, in the things that have been made. So they are without excuse. (Rom. 1:18–20)

God created the world not only to bring us pleasure through its beauty and sustain us through its resources but also to serve a significant moral purpose. Everything God made is designed to confront us with God's existence and nature and, in so doing, confront our delusions of autonomy and self-sufficiency. Every morning when we get up, we bump into God and come face-to-face with his existence. He is revealed in the wind and the rain, in the bird and the flower, in the rock and the tree, in the sun and the moon, in the grass and the clouds, in sights, smells, touches, and tastes. Everything that exists is a finger that points to God's existence and glory. The cycle of the seasons points to his wisdom and faithfulness. The fact that we all see creation's beauty and are warmed

1 Author's paraphrase of the doctrine of Scripture as found in parts of the Westminster Confession of Faith, chap. 1.

by its sun and drenched by its rain points us to his love and mercy. The thunderous storms, with crashes of lightning and violent winds, point to the immensity of his power. The created world is a surround-sound, Technicolor display of the existence and attributes of the one who created it all. The message of the created natural, physical world is so all-encompassing and clear to everyone that you have to fight to suppress, deny, and resist its message.

How good God is to build into creation reminders of himself, so that we, image bearers created for relationship with him, would be reminded of him again and again simply by looking at the world he created, which surrounds us everywhere we look.

But God in his infinite wisdom knew that the general revelation of creation, which confronts us with his existence and glory, could not impart to us the kind of knowledge of him, the necessary knowledge of ourselves, an understanding of the meaning and purpose of life, and an awareness of the disaster of sin and of the falleness of the surrounding world that could rescue us from us, propel us to him for his saving grace, and provide us a plan for how we should then live as children of that same grace. And so he gave us the wonderful and amazing gift of his word.

It is important to never stop giving thanks that God guided and directed the writing of every portion of his word and carefully ruled the process by which the various books of the Bible were protected, collected together, and preserved, so that we could hold the very words of God himself in our hands and be assured that what we are reading is, in fact, all that God knew would be essential for us to know and understand.

As we think about the doctrine of Scripture, it is impossible to overstate the importance of what we are now considering. The existence, inspiration, authority, and trustworthiness of Scripture is the doctrinal foundation upon which every other doctrine stands. If there is no such thing as a God-breathed Scripture, if it does not reveal to me the truths that are essential for a knowledge of God, knowledge of self, and the way of salvation, then I have no right or authority to say what is true to myself or anyone else. If there is no inspired, authoritative, and trustworthy word of God, then I am left to myself to decide, by my own experience, personal insight, or collective research with others, what is true.

This would mean, then, that there is no unified, God-given standard to which we all can appeal. Every person must discover what he or she thinks is true, and then we all must do what we think is right in our own eyes. There can be no way of being sure that what you think and believe is right, so you have no right to argue for what you believe to another; no authoritative system of truth exists that can provide a unified standard of belief and moral behavior. We are left in a world (with its fingers pointing to God) without any way of knowing for certain what the word, passed down from the Creator himself, would provide for us. No one has any basis for delineating doctrines, declaring that they are true, and teaching that they should provide the framework to guide our thinking, desires, decisions, words, and actions.

As we consider Scripture as a gift of God's grace, we must think about one other thing. One of the devastating results of sin is that it reduces all of us to fools. A fool looks at truth and sees falsehood. A fool looks at bad and sees good. A fool ignores God and inserts himself into God's position. A fool rebels against God's wise and loving law and writes his own moral code. A fool thinks he can live independently of help. A fool will not think as he was designed to think, desire what he was created to desire, or do what he has been called to do. But here is what is deadly about all of this: a fool doesn't know he is a fool. If a fool isn't given eyes to see his foolishness, then he will continue to think he is wise. So God, in the beauty of his grace, did not turn his back on our foolishness and walk away. God looked on foolish humanity with a heart of compassion and not only sent his Son to recue fools from themselves, but also gave us the wonderful gift of his word so that fools would not only recognize their foolishness, but would also have a tool by which they could progressively become wise.

I have thought many times that I would not know how to live without the wisdom of God's word. I would not know how to be a responsible man without the wisdom of God's word. I would not know how to be a husband, a father, a neighbor, a friend, a member of the body of Christ, a citizen, or a worker without the Bible. Without Scripture, I would not know right from wrong. Without the truths of the word, I would not to know how to understand and respond to suffering. Without Scripture, I would be confused about who I am and what the purpose of my life is. Without my Bible, I would not know about sin or understand true righteousness. Without God's word, I would not know how to handle sex, money, success, power, or acclaim. Without Scripture, I would have no understanding of origins and no concept of eternity. Without the word, I would ask people and material things to do for me what they have no power to do. Without God's word, I would have no idea of my need for rescue, reconciliation, and restoration. Without my Bible, I would have no understanding of what it means to love or what it is that I should hate. Apart from God's word, I would have no wise and holy law to follow and no amazing grace to give me hope.

The way I understand everything in my life has been shaped by the body of wisdom that is found only between the first chapter of Genesis and the last chapter of Revelation.

True confession: I have written more than twenty books on a variety of topics, but none would have been written apart from the gift of God's word to me. If it were not for Scripture, I would have no wisdom of any worth to share. And if I were so bold as to attempt to write something, I would have no confidence in the truthfulness and helpfulness of what I wrote, if it were not for God's word. My Bible is my lifelong friend and companion. My Bible is my wisest and most faithful teacher. My Bible is my mentor and my guide. My Bible confronts me when I am wrong and comforts me when I am struggling. The word of God turned me into a willing student, and I will never quit studying until I am in my final home. Because I am a fool who has been rescued by Wisdom and given by him the gift of the wisdom of his word, my Bible is my most treasured physical possession. I know that as long as sin still lives in me, there will be pottery shards of that old foolishness still lying around that will need to be dug up and replaced with divine wisdom, so I approach my Bible every day as a needy and thankful man. I cannot boast in any wisdom that I have because it is all from my Lord, written into the pages of his word.

The apostle Paul speaks to the foolishness of sin and the rescuing wisdom of God's word:

> For the word of the cross is folly to those who are perishing, but to us who are being saved it is the power of God. For it is written,
>
> > "I will destroy the wisdom of the wise,
> > and the discernment of the discerning I will thwart."
>
> Where is the one who is wise? Where is the scribe? Where is the debater of this age? Has not God made foolish the wisdom of the world? For since, in the wisdom of God, the world did not know God through wisdom, it pleased God through the folly of what we preach to save those who believe. For Jews demand signs and Greeks seek wisdom, but we preach Christ crucified, a stumbling block to Jews and folly to Gentiles, but to those who are called, both Jews and Greeks, Christ the power of God and the wisdom of God. For the foolishness of God is wiser than men, and the weakness of God is stronger than men.
>
> For consider your calling, brothers: not many of you were wise according to worldly standards, not many were powerful, not many were of noble birth. But God chose what is foolish in the world to shame the wise; God chose what is weak in the world to shame the strong; God chose what is low and despised in the world, even things that are not, to bring to nothing things that are, so that no human being might boast in the presence of God. And because of him you are in Christ Jesus, who became to us wisdom from God, righteousness and sanctification and redemption, so that, as it is written, "Let the one who boasts, boast in the Lord." (1 Cor. 1:18–31)

As he writes this powerful contrast between human wisdom and the wisdom of God, Paul is talking about Scripture, with its core message being the gospel of Jesus Christ. Paul's words echo David's in Psalm 119, where we see the wisdom of God's law. There is hope for fools because there is wisdom to be found—not first in the university classroom, on the pages of a research paper, on a popular podcast, or on the *New York Times* bestseller list, but in the pages of God's word. You can be highly trained and still be a fool. You can be a well-educated and gifted communicator and still be a fool. You can be successful and prominent and be a fool. You can have social media dominance and still be a fool. You can be a person that people look to for guidance and still be a fool. But no one is hopelessly trapped in their foolishness, because God, who is the source of all true wisdom, is a God of tender, forgiving, and rescuing grace. To all who confess their foolishness and run to him for wisdom, he offers mercy and grace in their time of need.

I want to note one more thing. Although the Old Testament was originally written in Hebrew and the New Testament in Greek, God, in the wisdom of his sovereignty and the tenderness of his grace, has ordained and guided the translation of his word into the common languages of peoples around the world, so that the truths revealed only in his word would be available to all who would desire to know them and live in light of them. And he has called generations of gifted, trained, and godly scholars to participate in the ongoing translation of his book, so that no one anywhere would be left without the gift of God's word.

Not only do we have the gift of God's word, but we also have the gift of the Holy Spirit, who guides us, teaches us, and illumines the word for us so that we can know, understand, confess, and repent. I not only need the content of God's word, but I also need the help of the Holy Spirit to enable me to understand it, to assist me to apply it, to empower me to live it, and to equip me to take its message to others. God rescues me from my foolishness not just by handing me a book, but also by giving me himself to open the wisdom of that book to me. I don't do this as an author. I write a book and move on. It is then up to the reader to make sense of what I have written. I don't travel to reader after reader, sitting with them as long as it takes, shining light on the things I have written, making sure they understand, and helping them to apply the content of the book to their everyday lives. But that is exactly what God does. He goes everywhere his word goes. He patiently sits with readers every time they open his book. He teaches them out of his word. God is not only the author of his word, but he is also its primary teacher. When you get the word of God, you also get the God of the word, and that is a beautiful thing.

2

Scripture in Everyday Life

WHAT DOES IT LOOK LIKE to live in light of the inspiration, authority, and sufficiency of the word of God? Well, if you really believe that the Bible is the word of God, preserved by God for you, wouldn't it be the most valuable, esteemed, treasured, and well-used possession in your life? Would you not love the moments when you could sit with it, read it carefully, study its content, and meditate on its implications? Wouldn't you commit yourself to be an avid reader and a lifelong student of the word of God? Wouldn't you work to be sure that you have understood and interpreted it correctly? Wouldn't you treasure the teachers and preachers whom God has raised up to walk you through his word? Wouldn't you want to make sure that everything you desire, think, say, and do was done in a joyful submission and careful obedience to the word of God? Wouldn't you want to apply it to every area of your life? Wouldn't you run to its comfort and heed its call? Wouldn't it have more influence over your decisions than your friends, Google, or the voices on Twitter? Wouldn't biblical literacy and theological knowledge be your life-long quest? Wouldn't you be looking for every opportunity to share its glorious message with others? And wouldn't you grieve those moments when you have to confess that you ignored or resisted its message? Wouldn't it be the thing that shapes the way you approach every area of your life? Wouldn't that quiet time, when you separate yourself from other people and other responsibilities and it is just you, your Lord, and his word, be your favorite part of your day? Wouldn't you give God heartfelt praise for the amazing gift of his word every day?

If the Bible that we have in our houses and can hold in our hands is the word of God, shouldn't what I have described above be true of all of us? But sadly, it isn't. Many of us do not spend daily time in our Bibles. Many of us have a low level of biblical literacy and lack clear theological understanding. And many of us have voices of influence in our lives that are functionally more authoritative than Scripture. Many of us are not students of God's word. Many of us are only fed from it for one hour each week as we gather together for worship. No wonder it doesn't influence:

our sense of identity;
the way we make decisions;
the shape of our friendships;
the way we approach our education;
the way we pursue our jobs and careers;
the way we approach romance and marriage;
the way we parent our children;
how we deal with conflict;
how we handle success and failure;
the things we do with our money;
where we look for fulfillment;
how we deal with difficulty;
the way we deal with media and entertainment;
our relationship to the body of Christ.

It's no wonder that the church of Jesus Christ is a dysfunctional army in many ways and in too many places, spending more time dealing with its weak, sick, and wounded than it does taking the next hill for the sake of

God's kingdom and the work of his glorious gospel of grace. If I could listen in on and watch a month of your life, what would I conclude about the place of God's word in your life? Other than our salvation and his presence now living inside us as his children, our Bible is God's most precious and valuable gift to us. The question is, In our everyday lives, do we act like it is?

Let us consider what God provides for us in and through his word, so that we may live as he has designed for us to live in the place where he has put us.

God's Word Saves

The apostle Paul tells Timothy, "From childhood you have been acquainted with the sacred writings [God's word], which are able to make you wise for salvation through faith in Christ Jesus" (2 Tim. 3:15). Without the Bible there would be no narrative of redemption, no clear gospel message, no knowledge of the attributes and plan of God, and no knowledge of sin and God's offer of forgiveness. No other tool is more central to God's work of redemptive rescue than the word of God, empowered by the Spirit of God. Without the Bible we would be hopelessly lost, without God and without hope in this terribly fallen world.

But there is so much more. God's work of salvation is not done. He is still at work in your heart, exposing remaining sin, convicting you of what is wrong, and enabling you by grace to live in brand-new ways. The word of God is essential not only for justifying grace but for sanctifying grace as well (John 17:16–17). If you are serious about growing in grace as a single person, as a student, as a professional, as a mom or dad, as a husband or wife, in your job, as a friend or a neighbor or a member of the body of Christ, then you should be committed to regular study of God's word. If you are concerned about a life of thought and desire that is pleasing to your Lord, then you should live in God's word.

If you are feeling defeated by secret sins, you should run to God in confession, but you should also run to his word. If you struggle with anger as a parent or too much conflict in your marriage, you should run to God for help, but as you do, run also to his primary tool of help, his word. If fear oppresses and discouragement overwhelms, you may need to seek help from others, but you also need the counsel and encouragement of God's word. If you seem to lack meaning and purpose, it is the word of God that will again and again give you reason to get up in the morning and a purpose worth living for.

God used his word to save you, he is now using his word to continue to rescue you and grow you, and he will continue to save you through his word until that work is complete and you are on the other side.

God's Word Points

Second Corinthians 5:15 contains a tiny phrase that is not only explosive in its implications, but also points us to one of the most important functions of the word of God in each of our lives: "And he died for all, *that those who live might no longer live for themselves*." Paul is saying that the DNA of sin is selfishness. Sin puts us in the center of our world and makes life all about us. Sin is about self-focus and self-glory. It is motivated by what we want, when we want it, and how we want it. Sin turns every human being into a glory thief, taking for ourselves what belongs to God alone. Sin is self-congratulatory and self-aggrandizing. Sin causes us to think that we are righteous, wise, and strong, when we are not. Sin makes us rebels, wanting to submit to no one's law but our own. Sin causes us to write our stories with us at center stage, commanding the attention and credit we think we deserve.

But one of the most important things God's word does is to confront us with another story. In this story we are not at center stage. In this story we were given life and breath to serve the purposes of another, and for the sake of the glory of another. The biblical story starts with God at the center. It chronicles the great glory war, with the great captain, Christ, gaining victory through his death. The war begins in Genesis 3 and will continue until the war is finally won and everything that exists serves God's glory in the new heavens and new earth.

This story reminds us again and again that self-glory is the ultimate human dysfunction and is always self-destructive. It teaches us that self-worship is bondage and true freedom is found only when you surrender your heart to the worship of God. The Bible reminds us that coming to Christ in repentance and faith is not just about forsaking your sin and receiving his forgiveness by faith, but it is also about forsaking your glory for his.

But here's what each of us needs to understand. As long as sin still lives inside of us, there will be a glory war in our hearts. So every day we need to see again that the life we have been welcomed to has God at the center, not us. Every day we need a message that points us to God. Every day we need to be reminded that life is not about our comfort or the success of our plans. It's not about how many people look up to us and want us in their lives. It's not about the size of our houses or the quality of our cuisine. It's not about whether we're fit and free of disease. Life is about God, his glory, and the success of his purposes in and through us. The Bible points us to this from cover to cover.

Self-glory will make you an easily irritated, critical, and judgmental parent. Self-glory will turn a marriage into a war of who gets what they want first. Self-glory will make you an exhausting, entitled friend. Self-glory will keep you from being satisfied and make it more natural for you to complain than to be thankful. Self-glory will make you more known for your demands than for your service. Self-glory will cause you again and again to take credit for what you could have never earned or produced on your own. Self-glory will make you threatened by and envious of the success of others. Self-glory will turn you into a church consumer instead of a committed participant in its work. Self-glory deceives us, distracts us, and entraps us, and it can ultimately destroy us. Self-glory leaves behind a mountain of broken people and things. It never produces good fruit.

Self-glory itself is an argument for how much we need the word of God in our hearts and in our thoughts every single day of our lives. We need the word to point us once more to a glory greater than our own, the only glory that will ever satisfy our hearts. We need our personal stories progressively embedded in the story of the one who made us and designed us to live for his glory. We need to be reminded that the gospel of the grace of Jesus has his lordship at the center. We need to hear again and again that living as his disciples means being willing to forsake everything to follow him. We need to be humbled again and again, to be called back again and again from our self-focus. And we need excitement ignited in us again as we acknowledge that there is nothing more freeing, satisfying, and healing than living for the glory of God. This means we need his word pointing us again and again to the centrality of his existence and his glory.

God's Word Teaches

I remember my days as a seminary student with fondness and thankfulness. By God's grace I was able to focus three years of my life on one solitary thing, the study of God's word. This was a singular blessing. I don't know when I have been more thankful and motivated by anything in all of my life. I soaked it all in, and to the suffering of my wife, at the end of each day I repeated, in great detail and length, each lecture I had heard. I read long portions to her from dense biblical theology books. I was obsessed, thrilled at what I was learning. It got me up early in the morning and kept me up late at night. It was just about all I thought about and talked about. My mind was blown away by the word of God in a way that it had never been before.

One day after classes, I ran up the steps to our third-floor apartment and said to Luella, "It's not just that I'm learning the content of the Bible and learning theology, but for the first time, I'm learning to think—really, truly think!" Not only was the Bible opening up to me; the whole world was opening up to me, with levels of meaning and understanding I had never known before. As I sat day after day studying the word, I was, in fact, sitting at the feet of the Creator of the world and everything in it. Yes, the word was the tool, but it was held in the hands of the ultimate teacher, my Lord. I was being taught as I had never been taught before, not just by wise and seasoned professors, but also by my Master through the majestic wisdom of his word.

God's word teaches in ways unlike anything else. It teaches you things that you will learn nowhere else. It doesn't just impart knowledge to you, but it also forms wisdom in you. It reveals to you the deepest, most profound spiritual mysteries that could ever be considered. Like a good teacher, God's word undoes you and then rebuilds you again. It deconstructs the thoughts and motives of your heart and then reconstructs them.

You cannot sit under the teaching of the word of God with an open and willing heart and remain the same. In teaching you, it recreates you in the likeness of the one who made you and gifted you. The Bible has been my best professor by far. Do you attend its class every day with heart and mind ready? Do you live your life as its student? The Bible is God's constant curriculum, and it has no graduation ceremony. No matter how long you have been a Christian, you will need its instruction today as much as you needed it on your first day as an infant Christian. You will find yourself going back again and again to passages that had previously taught you, only to realize that they are so deep that they have many more fresh and new things to teach you.

I love how David expresses the teaching power of Scripture in Psalm 119:97–100.

> Oh how I love your law!
> It is my meditation all the day.
> Your commandment makes me wiser than my enemies,
> for it is ever with me.
> I have more understanding than all my teachers,
> for your testimonies are my meditation.
> I understand more than the aged,
> for I keep your precepts.

We all have artifacts of old and unbiblical ways of thinking hanging around in our minds. We all have gaps in our theological understanding. We all need a deeper and more practical understanding of the plans, purposes, and call of God. We all need a fuller and richer understanding of the gospel of Jesus Christ. We all need to learn more about the dark tragedy of sin. We all need to understand more deeply what it looks like to grow in grace. And we all need to learn more about how these things apply to the situations, relationships, and locations we live in every day. None of us knows everything that the Bible has to teach us. If you think you have mastered this book, it probably means you haven't been mastered *by* it.

Has biblical literacy changed the way you approach your friendships, the way you parent your children, your conduct in your marriage, the way you use your money? Has theological understanding caused you to live with greater hope, courage, love, and joy in those places where you live and relate? Where, right now, are you struggling to apply your biblical and theological understanding to your everyday life? Is your biblical knowledge producing street-level, practical, agenda-setting wisdom? Do you still find the joy in the study of God's word that you once had? Is the Bible your most esteemed, sought-after, and influential teacher?

God's Word Rescues

God has designed the Bible to function as your spiritual first responder. If you are regularly reading, studying, and meditating on its content, you will be rescued again and again. The concept of rescue is both evocative and humbling. Rescue always implies that there is some danger near; that is, something that threatens your health and safety. In a fallen world, where evil still exists and the enemy moves about as a roaring lion, we are always near clear and present danger. But there is more.

Because sin still resides in our hearts, we are tempted to move toward danger rather than away from it. The fact is that sin doesn't always seem sinful or dangerous to us. The reason sin is able to lure, seduce, and entrap us is because it is so good at presenting itself to be beautiful and harmless, when it is neither. When a man is lusting after a woman, he isn't overcome with a sense of danger. No, what he sees is beauty, and what he experiences is pleasure. If you are gossiping about someone on your cell phone, you aren't feeling fear of the danger of what you are doing but rather the scintillating thrill of carrying a story about someone to someone else. If you are committing the sin of gluttony, you are so busy enjoying the pleasures of what you are consuming that you have little spiritual awareness of the danger of what you are doing. We need the rescuing function of the word of God not only because sin is dangerous but also because it masquerades as anything but dangerous.

The concept of rescue also connotes the need for help outside of what you are able to provide for yourself. If a person requiring the help of a first responder were able to rescue himself, he wouldn't need the first responder. The humbling truth is that on this side of eternity, somehow, someway, we will all need the rescue of the word of God. It provides power, wisdom, direction, and insight that we would never have on our own. One of the primary ways that the Bible rescues us is by contrast. Again and again, in a variety of ways, it contrasts the destructive danger of sin with the beauty and blessing of following our Savior. By story, Wisdom Literature, command, principle, and gospel encouragement it helps us to see the dark sinfulness of sin and the shining beauty of a life lived under the lordship of Jesus Christ.

Since we are not spiritually self-rescuing beings, we should constantly place ourselves under the rescuing mercy of the word of God.

God's Word Warns

Let's be honest here: there are some very threatening passages in the Bible. The Bible is marked throughout with God's clear and often stern warnings. God warned Adam and Eve of the cost of eating the fruit of the forbidden tree. He warned his children as they entered into a new set of temptations in the Promised Land. The theme of the Prophets is warning, whether it's directed to the idolatry of his people or to the injustices of wicked leaders. God sends Jonah to preach a message of warning to evil Nineveh. Christ sternly warns the self-righteous Pharisees. Jesus warns the disciples as he leaves his mission to them. And there are stark and scary warnings to believers; some of the strongest are found in a stream of passages in Hebrews (2:1–4; 3:7–4:13; 5:11–6:12; 10:19–39; 12:14–29).

Why are there so many warnings in Scripture? They are there because God loves us. You see, a warning isn't judgment. If all God intended to do was to judge you, he wouldn't first warn you. Parents constantly warn their children. They first warn to not touch the hot stove, the lit candle, or the electrical outlet. Later they warn what is safe to eat and what is dangerous, and down the road they warn about the dangers of the internet and social media. Then come the warnings about the dangers of driving a car or of sexual temptation. Later parents warn about the unique dangers of being at a residential university, the temptations of money, or the challenges of a serious romantic relationship. Every one of these warnings is motivated by tenderhearted parental love.

One of the ways we experience the fatherhood of God is in his unrelenting commitment to warn us of the various dangers of life in this fallen world. In each warning we are being loved by our Father in heaven. Each warning exhibits his patience, faithfulness, wisdom, and grace. Each warning reminds us of his care. Each warning teaches us again that he is ready and willing to forgive and restore. Each warning is a call to trust him and to follow him by faith. Each warning reminds us that our Father is infinitely smarter than us. He really does know better, and we should listen and obey.

Parents, what are you doing with God's warning to not provoke your children to anger? Husbands, what are you doing with God's warnings of the dangers of unfaithfulness to your marriage commitments? In your career, what are you doing with God's warnings about not loving the world? In every area of our lives, God blesses us with protective and preventative warnings. He does this because he loves us and he knows the susceptibility of our hearts.

You don't want to be like the toddler who refuses to listen to Mommy's warnings and burns his finger on the oven door. You don't want to be like the teenager who blows off his dad's warnings and makes decisions that alter the rest of his life. God loves us, so he has dotted his word with warnings. With fatherly care he says, "Don't look there, don't say that, don't desire this, don't do that, don't choose that, don't love that, watch out for this."

Taking the Bible seriously in your daily life means living a life that is shaped by the protection of the warnings of your heavenly Father. He warns you, and you are blessed. As a student, a boss, a mom or dad, a married person, a worker, a neighbor, a citizen, a man or a woman, a young person or an old person, a professional person or a laborer, in ministry or in everyday life, in private or in public, where have you failed to submit your heart and life to God's loving warnings? You and I would do well to resist thinking that in some areas of our lives, we are smarter than God and there will be no cost for ignoring his wise and loving warnings. Every sin, and the personal, relational, and situational dysfunction that follows, is a result of a failure to humbly heed God's warnings. And remember, he not only warns you, but he also empowers you with the grace you need to live inside of his warnings.

God's Word Protects

Human beings need boundaries. This was true even before sin entered the world and did its destructive work. Adam and Eve needed boundaries even though they were living as perfect people in a perfect world and in a perfect relationship with God. No human being has a wide enough base of experience and knowledge or is prophetically wise enough to be able to set his or her own boundaries. Only the Creator, who knows his creatures, the world he created them to live in, and the life that they were designed to live, can lay down the right set of protective and preventative boundaries. God's boundaries, that is, his laws, are an expression of his love for us. They protect us from danger and draw us toward a deeper dependency and communion with him. God graces us with his law.

Think about when God first gave his law on Mount Sinai. God, in a show of incredible divine power and authority, had just redeemed Israel out of their four-hundred-year travail in Egypt and delivered them into the wilderness to journey to the land he had promised them. But his children had a huge and potentially destructive problem. Because they had been in slavery for so many generations, they had no idea how to live. So God gave them his civil, ceremonial, and moral law. These laws were given to his children as a sign of his love and grace. The law organized their lives, shaped their worship, protected their hearts, structured their relationships with their neighbors, and provided a legal system. But most of all, it protected the Israelites from themselves. God's law was one of the primary ways God protected and preserved his people.

The same is true for us. God has retained and restated his law for us in the Bible. There is not a day in any of our lives when we are free from the need of the protection of God's rules as revealed in his word. If you're a mom, you need God's law to restrain you and direct you as you give yourself to the arduous and long-term task of parenting your children. As a husband, you need God's law so that you will treat your wife as God designed and remain faithful to your covenantal vows. As a worker, you need God's law to shape the way you do your work, relate to your boss, and cooperate with your fellow workers. In your university, you need God's law to shape your life there and the way you fulfill your responsibilities as a student. In your private life, you need God's law to set boundaries of thought, desire, and behavior.

As any loving parent would, God the Father, in his word, sets boundaries of protection for us. He does not do that to rob us of our freedom and joy, but so that we would be freed from the bondage and sadness that always result when sinners choose their own way. Although Jesus Christ fulfilled the law and bore the full penalty for our breaking of the law, he restated and reinstituted the moral law for us, because he knew we would need this protection until we are on the other side and free from our sinful susceptibility to go our own way.

God's Word Encourages

We all need encouragement. You and I can't live without hope. What is hope? It is both an expectation and an object. There is something that you set your heart on (expectation) and there is someone or something that you look to to deliver it (object). God knew that in this broken and groaning world, no longer functioning as God intended, we would need daily encouragement, that is, constant hope. God knew that this fallen world, populated by less-than-perfect people, would never be able to provide sturdy, reliable, faithful, and trustworthy hope. Horizontal, earthbound hope always disappoints.

So God gave us his word, and in giving us his word, he gave us himself. What do I mean by this? One of the greatest gifts of the word of God is that the glory of the God behind the word splashes across every page. God knew that in this world we would be desperate for hope, so he pulls back the curtain of separation and shows us himself in stunning glory. Consider Isaiah 40, where human language is stretched to its furthest elasticity to capture the majesty of God.

But he doesn't reveal just his power and glory; he also wants us to know he is sovereign (Dan. 4:34–35). But there is more. He wants us to know he is near: "I will never leave you nor forsake you" (Heb. 13:5). He also wants us to know he is a God of forgiveness and grace: "To the Lord our God belong mercy and forgiveness" (Dan. 9:9). These are just a few examples of themes of God's self-revelation in his word. He knows that we need hope, and he works through his word to focus our hope on him and assure us that hope in him will never, ever disappoint us.

How does God's word encourage us? It reminds us that vertical hope is not some dreamy, iffy wish, but rather a confident expectation of a guaranteed result. How can this be? Because the object of our hope is the Lord of heaven and earth, the Creator, the Savior, who bids us to rest our hope on him.

God's Word Motivates

Though I love what I have been called to do, I don't always wake up every day feeling motivated. Sometimes I feel unable. Sometimes the task seems too great. Sometimes I'm exhausted. Sometimes I doubt the outcome of my work. Sometimes laziness is more of a struggle than it was the previous day. Sometimes troubles distract me. Let's be honest:

faith isn't natural for us. Doubt is natural, worry is natural, denial is natural, fear is natural, but the courage of faith is not natural for us. Here again is one of the ways the word of God is a huge blessing. God stoops to meet me in my struggle and motivates me through the great and precious promises of his word.

We find literally thousands of promises in Scripture. God's promises mark every kind of biblical literature and litter every period of biblical history. Wherever his people are, whatever they are facing, God greets them with his promises. He does this to motivate their faith and to cause them to act with courage. His promises encourage, strengthen, and instill hope, and because they do, they motivate us to resist giving up and to continue to do what he has called us to do.

Because of God's promises to us, we don't gauge our ability or potential for success or victory based on our righteousness, wisdom, or strength, but on the magnitude and surety of what he has promised us. So even when we know we are weak and are aware of our failures, we continue, because of all of the good things that he has promised to be for us, do for us, and deliver to us.

You don't need me to tell you that life in this fallen world can be heartbreakingly discouraging. Everything from mechanical failures to the failures of family and friends can make life complicated and difficult. And because we're not able to see what is coming around the corner, we don't know when life will get tough again. We also have to deal with our own weakness and proneness to wander. But we see God's tender heart as he rains his promises down on us so that we would be soaked with his motivating grace. Hard, dry seasons will come, but we are invited to step into the rain of the promises of God's word to drink in new hope and strength, to rise up again with renewed motivation to do what God has called us to do in the places where he has positioned us.

You don't need to run to the current popular motivational speaker to boost your hope and courage. No, you just need to daily run to the word of God. God's promises not only motivate you; they also build confidence and trust in God into your heart and guide you according to how God has called you to live.

God's Word Confronts

We should give thanks every day that the word of God functions in the life of God's people as a mirror (James 1:22–25). When we look with ready minds and open hearts into the mirror of the word of God, we see ourselves as we actually are. This word picture is really quite helpful. When you stumble to the bathroom in the morning to take your first look in the mirror, to see the damage that the night has done to your physical appearance, the one thing you can count on is that your mirror will never lie to you. It will always confront you with what you actually look like. You probably have never been tempted to doubt or debate the accuracy of what your mirror reveals to you about you.

The same is true of the mirror that is your Bible. What it reveals to you about you is always accurate and always trustworthy. But the mirror that is your Bible doesn't have the limits of your bathroom mirror; that mirror can show you only your physical self. But the protective and restorative power and beauty of the mirror that is your Bible exposes to you your spiritual self, that is, your heart. Consider the words of Hebrews 4:12: "For the word of God is living and active, sharper than any two-edged sword, piercing to the division of soul and of spirit, of joints and of marrow, and discerning the thoughts and intentions of the heart." The Bible has a power that no other book has. God's word has the ability to discern and expose the true thoughts and purposes of your heart.

Why is this so important? Why is it so essential? Why should we celebrate the mirroring function of the word of God every day and its picture of God's rescuing, protecting, and redeeming love? Because sin blinds (Heb. 3:12–13). I have no problem seeing the sin of friends and members of my family, but I am often surprised when mine is revealed. We must give up the thought that no one knows us better than we know ourselves. This thought will tend to cause you to resist anything that the mirror of the word reveals that you haven't already seen, because in your confidence in your own self-knowledge, you will think its judgment is inaccurate. The truth is that as long as sin still lives inside of us, there will be inaccuracies in the way we see ourselves because there will still be pockets of spiritual blindness in us.

We all desperately need something that can cut through our blindness and confront us with who we are at the deeply formative level of the thoughts and desires of our hearts. The word of God has been given to us to do this very thing.

But our spiritual blindness is even more pervasive than I have just described. If you are physically blind, you know you are blind and you begin to develop a set of life skills to cope with this significant physical deficit. Not so with spiritual blindness. Perhaps the scariest and most spiritually debilitating aspect of our spiritual blindness is that unlike the physically blind person, the spiritually blind person is not only blind, but he is blind to his blindness. We tend to think we have accurate spiritual self-sightedness, when actually we are suffering from pockets of spiritual self-blindness and we don't know it. When you think you see, you don't reach for things that can help you to see. So we all need to do with Scripture what we do with the mirrors in our houses every day. We know that we don't see our physical selves accurately, so a day doesn't go by without us standing before a mirror, receiving its confrontation, and then making physical adjustments to our appearance. We need to place ourselves before the mirror of God's word every day, humbly submit to its heart-revealing confrontation, and run to God for his rescuing, forgiving, empowering, and transforming grace.

No matter what your place in life is, no matter what opportunities and responsibilities are yours every day, no matter what temptations regularly haunt you, no matter how long you have walked with your Lord, be thankful that your Bible is the world's most powerful, penetrating, and accurate mirror. The constant confrontation of this mirror is one of God's most loving and gracious gifts to you.

God's Word Convicts

Sadly, we all have a perverse ability to justify ourselves, that is, to argue that the wrong we have done is not that wrong after all. We are all too skilled at working to make ourselves feel good about what God says is not good. We need more than the confronting power of the word of God. It is wonderful that God has designed Scripture to expose and confront us at even the deepest level of the thoughts and desires of our hearts. It is a grace to us that when we look into the pages of the word, we not only see God in all of his glory, but we see ourselves with accuracy. But as long as sin still exists inside of us, we will still deflect Scripture's confrontation, calling to mind people who we think fit these confronting truths more than we ourselves do, and walking away unchanged.

So we all need the convicting power of the word of God. Yes, it is the Holy Spirit who convicts, but his primary tool is Scripture. Without grief over your sin, there will be no confession or repentance. Here's how conviction works. *You cannot grieve what you have not seen, you cannot confess what you have not grieved, and you cannot repent of what you have not confessed.* Our ongoing deliverance from sin and growth in Christian maturity depends on the Holy Spirit giving sight to our eyes and working grief in our hearts. First Thessalonians 1:5 captures this for us: "Because our gospel came to you not only in word, but also in power and in the Holy Spirit and with full conviction. You know what kind of men we proved to be among you for your sake." There is not a day in any of our lives that we don't need the ministry of the Holy Spirit to bring God's word to us in convicting, grief-producing, and confession-resulting power. Dads doing the hard work of parenting, you need the word's convicting power. Boss, you need the heart-exposing power of the word of God daily. Pastor, you need the word of God to convict you as much as you need it to prepare you for ministry. Student, as you face all the responsibilities and temptations of your university life, you need this heart-changing power. In the way we all handle our money, steward our time, care for our bodies, use our minds, live in our relationships, and do our daily work, we need that convicting combination of the word and the Spirit. The Holy Spirit will continue to convict us of sin until sin is no more, and the tool that he uses is your Bible.

God's Word Guides

When was the last time you needed to use your cell phone as a flashlight, perhaps to look for something in the garage, read a menu at a darkly lit restaurant, or find something in the backyard at night?[1] Why did you need it? Your answer probably includes some expression of *dark* or *darkness*. As a sinner living with other sinners in a fallen world, you encounter darkness every day. While you may experience Instagram-worthy, sunny-day picnic lunches, the reality is that life is more of a midnight walk through the woods. On any given day, you probably encounter more darkness than you do truth—both internally and externally. So to move forward without danger and get to where you are meant to go, you need something to light your way.

No passage gets at this need and God's provision better than Psalm 119:105: "Your word is a lamp to my feet / and a light to my path." You need light for your marriage and your parenting. You need light for your job and your relationships with your neighbors. You need light for your struggles with desires and temptations. You need light to help you deal with the unexpected. You need light to cope with new difficulties that emerge. You need light for when you have been sinned against. You need light to deal with weaknesses of the body and hardships of the heart. You need light for those moments when you're alone and overwhelmed. You need light for all the unknowns that will show up on your doorstep tomorrow, the day after tomorrow, and for the rest of your life.

It's hard to find a better description of Psalm 119:105 than what the great nineteenth-century preacher Charles Spurgeon wrote:

> "Thy word is a lamp unto my feet." We are walkers through the city of this world, and we are often called to go out into its darkness; let

1 Much of this section first appeared in my article "A Lamp and a Light," Paul Tripp website, April 11, 2018, www.paultripp.com.

> us never venture there without the light-giving word, lest we slip with our feet. Each man should use the word of God personally, practically, and habitually, that he may see his way and see what lies in it. When darkness settles down upon all around me, the word of the Lord, like a flaming torch, reveals my way. Having no fixed lamps in eastern towns, in old time each passenger carried a lantern with him that he might not fall into the open sewer, or stumble over the heaps of ordure which defiled the road. This is a true picture of our path through this dark world: we should not know the way, or how to walk in it, if the Scripture, like a blazing flambeau, did not reveal it. One of the most practical benefits of Holy Writ is guidance in the acts of daily life: it is not sent to astound us with its brilliance, but to guide us by its instruction. It is true the head needs illumination, but even more the feet need direction, else head and feet may both fall into a ditch. Happy is the man who personally appropriates God's word, and practically uses it as his comfort and counsellor,—a lamp to his own feet.[2]

You don't need to bloody your nose and bruise your toes by bumping into trees and tripping over roots. You don't have to grope around fearfully in the darkness. The light of the world has graced you with the light of his word! It will shine around your feet in the midst of the darkness so you don't stumble and fall.

• • •

How should we all think about and approach God's loving and essential gift of his word? We should first approach Scripture with a deep and abiding sense of need. This means that every time we open the book, we pray that God would grant us open eyes and a tender, humble, open, and ready heart. It also means that we don't read God's word in a quasi-guilty, sense-of-duty, this-is-what-good-Christians-do sort of way.

2 Charles Haddon Spurgeon, *Treasury of David*, vol. 5, *Psalms 111–119* (London: Marshall Brothers, n.d.), 342, *Christian Classics Ethereal Library*, www.ccel.org.

No, we approach our Bible reading and study with heartfelt joy. What is the DNA of joy? The answer is important: *gratitude*. You never hear much joy coming out of complaining people. We are grateful for God's word because we find him there, we find his saving grace there, we find astounding wisdom there, we find guidance for our daily living there, and there we find hope to do it all again tomorrow. We must also approach God's word with commitment. We must commit to study it, but even more to submit our hearts and minds to what we encounter there. We must determine to fight, in the power of God's grace, any resistance we have to its message and its call. Finally, every time we encounter God's word, we covenant with God that we will seek to apply it faithfully and specifically to our own lives. This means we carry it out of devotions and into those places where we live, decide, speak, act, and react. We do all of this with hearts that are amazed that God loves us enough to gift us with such a life-giving, life-changing book.

But you should also know that your Bible doesn't give you a manual for handling everything. It doesn't give you a script for handling every situation. It doesn't tell you what exactly to say to your argumentative teenager at 9:35 on a Tuesday night, or exactly how to have the gospel conversation with your coworker, or what exactly to say to your discouraged husband. But here is a word picture for what Scripture gives you.

I love the spontaneous journey of jazz, where a group of musicians start with a song but then play off-chart riffs and turns on the theme. Jazz is a form of planned spontaneity. The reason these riffs don't descend into a chaotic disharmony is the planned part of what makes jazz work. The players are able to take off in their individual directions harmoniously because they have all agreed on and submitted their playing to two foundational things. These two things give their individuality and creativity tracks to run on. The song that they started with was written in a certain key and had a certain time signature, or rhythmic structure. As long as they play within that planned structure, they are free to improvise and be creative, and yet be in harmony with one another.

Your Bible isn't exhaustive in that it speaks about everything and gives you sheet music for every action, reaction, or response. But the biblical narrative, with its law and gospel, gives you a key and a rhythmic structure for your heart and life. As long as you stay inside God's wise and lovingly revealed structure, when you improvise—and you will need to—you will do so in beautiful harmony with him. He hasn't given you sheet music for every situation, but he has given you his law, his wisdom, his revelation of himself, his plan for the world, and his gospel, to shape how you should think and what you should desire in the situations and relationships of your daily life. For example, he's told you to bring your children up in the "discipline and instruction of the Lord" (Eph. 6:4), but he hasn't told you exactly what to say to your argumentative seven-year-old on Friday morning. He's told you to love your neighbor as yourself, but hasn't given you sheet music for getting along with that supercompetitive coworker. He's told you to steward your resources well, but hasn't told you whether you should make a particular investment or not.

The Bible doesn't give you every note you will ever have to play throughout your life, but it does give you everything you need in order to play in every area of your life in harmony with your Savior, and the fact that it does is a wonderful gift of divine grace.

As I was writing this chapter, my wife, Luella, came to me with a devotional, written by Charles Spurgeon, that she had read that morning, and told me I should read it. Immediately after reading it, I knew that it should be the way this chapter ends. May God's wonderful word work in you as Spurgeon describes.

> "Great peace have they which love thy Law: and nothing shall offend them" (Psalm 119:165).
>
> Yes, a true love for the great Book will bring us great peace from the great God and be a great protection to us. Let us live constantly in the society of the law of the Lord, and it will breed in our hearts a restfulness such as nothing else can. The Holy Spirit acts as a Comforter

through the Word and sheds abroad those benign influences which calm the tempests of the soul.

Nothing is a stumbling block to the man who has the Word of God dwelling in him richly. He takes up his daily cross, and it becomes a delight. For the fiery trial he is prepared and counts it not strange, so as to be utterly cast down by it. He is neither stumbled by prosperity—as so many are—nor crushed by adversity—as others have been—for he lives beyond the changing circumstances of external life. When his Lord puts before him some great mystery of the faith which makes others cry, "This is an hard saying; who can hear it?" the believer accepts it without question; for his intellectual difficulties are overcome by his reverent awe of the law of the Lord, which is to him the supreme authority to which he joyfully bows. Lord, work in us this love, this peace, this rest, this day.[3]

3 Charles Haddon Spurgeon, *Faith's Checklist*, April 9 reading, *Spurgeon Archive*, archive.spurgeon.org/fcb/fcb-bod.htm.

3

The Doctrine of God

THERE IS ONLY ONE TRUE GOD. He is infinite in his being and perfection. He is invisible, without body, parts, or passions. He is unchanging, immense, eternal, and beyond human comprehension. He is almighty, most wise, and most holy. He is completely free and absolute, working everything according to the counsel of his own unchanging and righteous will and for his own glory. He is most loving, gracious, merciful, and longsuffering. He is abundant in goodness and truth, forgiving iniquity, transgression, and sin. He rewards those who diligently seek him. He is just and fearsome in his judgments. He hates sin and will not clear the guilty.

God is the source of all life, glory, goodness, and blessedness, in and of himself. He alone is all-sufficient in and unto himself. He does not stand in need of any of the creatures that he made, nor does he acquire any glory from them. Rather, he reveals his glory in, by, to, and on them. He alone is the fountain of all being. All things are from him, through him, and to him. He is sovereign over all things, to do by, for, and on them whatever he pleases. He sees all things, and nothing is ever hidden from him. God's knowledge is infinite, without error, and without dependence on anything he created. For God there is no chance or uncertainty. All his purposes, works, and commands are holy. He is due whatever worship, service, and obedience he is pleased to require from angels, people, and every other creature.

In the unity of the Godhead there are three persons of one substance, power, and eternity: God the Father, God the Son, and God the Holy Spirit. The Father is neither begotten nor proceeds from anyone. The Son is eternally begotten of the Father. The Holy Spirit proceeds eternally from the Father and the Son. See Gen. 17:1; Ex. 3:14; 34:6, 7; Deut. 4:15–16; 6:4; 1 Kings 8:27; Neh. 9:23, 33; Job 22:2–3; Pss. 5:5–6; 90:2; 115:3; 119; 145:17; 148:13; Prov. 16:4; Isa. 6:3; 46:10; 48:12; Jer. 10:10; 23:23; Ezek. 11:5; Dan. 4:25, 34–35; Nah. 1:2–3; Mal. 3:6; Matt. 28:19; John 1:14, 18; 4:24; 5:26; 14:11; 15:26; Acts 15:17–18; Rom. 11:34–36; 1 Cor. 8:4, 6; 2 Cor. 13:14; Gal. 4:6; 1 Tim. 1:17; Heb. 4:13; 11:6; 1 John 5:7; Rev. 5:12–14.[1]

Understanding the Doctrine of God

How could anyone read the above attempt to describe God, in his incalculable glory, and not be filled with a sense of awe?

This is your God. He is holy in every way possible, in all he is and all he does. He is the source of everything that exists, and he does not need anything that exists. His knowledge of everything is always accurate, and he is forever without the need of being taught anything. He is never surprised, never unaware, never unprepared, never confused, and never distraught. He never needs to discover, and he never needs to unlearn or relearn anything. What he thinks, purposes, declares, and does is always right and true. His judgments are never mistaken, biased, or wrong.

Everything that exists depends on him for its existence. He alone sits on the throne of the universe, and he rules it according to his all-wise and holy will. His perfect rule is not dependent on the instruction or

1 Author's paraphrase of the doctrine of God as found in parts of the Westminster Confession of Faith, chap. 2.

counsel of anyone. He does what he pleases, and what he pleases is always right and best.

He is the source and definition of goodness, love, grace, mercy, and forgiveness. He is holy and righteous, while at the same time being patient and tender. All good gifts, physical and spiritual, come from him. He hates sin, but forgives all who come to him in heartfelt confession.

God is a Trinity of three persons, but all of one substance: God the Father, God the Son, and God the Holy Spirit. These are not the delineation of three functions, but are three distinct persons. The Trinity is the ultimate community, functioning in perfect unity and love, without argument, debate, or disagreement.

I am now sitting silently before the light of my screen, amazed at what I have just written. The words are accurate, and they expand your mind and excite your imagination, but they still fall short of doing justice to the immensity of the being and glory of God. In my heart I am saying with the psalmist, "Who is like the LORD our God?" (Ps. 113:5). It's the ultimate rhetorical question that expects the resounding answer, "No one!" Nothing has ever existed or will ever exist that is remotely like him. There is a huge dividing line of holiness, power, glory, knowledge, wisdom, love, grace, justice, sovereignty, and sufficiency between the Creator and the creature. This line cannot and will not ever be crossed. So we bow in amazement, in submission, in dependency, in worship, and in love before his awesome majesty.

I was raised in a Christian home, but in my youth the God in my thinking was a shrunken pseudo-deity, far from the God of the Bible. My brother Tedd came home from college and began to talk to me about the total control of God over all things. It was a piece of the doctrine of God I had never heard or understood in the way he was communicating it. Our conversations flooded me with questions, hurt my pride, and made me angry. During one of our debates I got so mad that I took off my shoe and threw it at Tedd. A day or so later he brought me a paperback copy of the Bible and a yellow marker and said, "This summer read through the Bible and mark every instance of the sovereign rule of God over all things." I took the challenge, and it not only corrected my poor theology, it also changed the trajectory of my life. I was not only moved by the picture of God's complete rule, but I was also blown away by his inestimable glory.

Few believers suffer from a God who is too big, but many suffer from a God who is sadly too small. We all have to take care that our limited ability to conceive or imagine doesn't restrict our theology of God and his glory. We cannot allow ourselves to hold a theology that shrinks God down to a manageable size. The problem is that when you are working to understand any concept or term, you always begin your process of understanding from the vantage point of your own experience. If I use the term *father*, you will define that term based on your own experience of your own father, until I define more specifically what I mean by that term. When it comes to God, no experience in my life is comparable to who and what he is in the purity of his holiness and the expansiveness of his glory. So here are some thoughts about the glory of God's glory.

The Glory of God's Glory

I will never forget that evening. My ticket put me in the first row, and it was worth it. I was never more blown away by a musical composition than the night I attended the Chicago Symphony Orchestra. The music was powerful, foreboding, haunting, compelling, and glorious all at the same time. There were moments when I wished the night would never end and moments when I wanted to get up and run out of the concert hall. There were moments when the music caused your chest to rattle and moments when it lured you with a whisper. There were moments when musical joy collided with musical fear in a beautiful disharmony of sound. When the music was over, I felt both sad and exhausted. I both wanted more and felt like I had had enough. I didn't know why this particular performance had affected me so until I looked at the program and read the line under the name of the composition. It said, "God, the most formidable word ever spoken."[2]

I had experienced the wonderful attempt of a very gifted composer (whose name I cannot recall) to capture God, in all his amazing and variegated glory, in a single piece of music. It was in some ways a triumphant effort and in others ways a dismal and embarrassing failure. For any human being to think that he could capture the glory of God in a single artistic statement is delusional at best and vain at worst. To squeeze what is infinite into what is finite is vastly more impossible to do than trying to insert the full body of an elephant into a thimble so that no part of it sticks out. It won't happen, no matter how gifted you are and no matter how hard you try.

The composer had done marvelously well, but with his grandest piece he had captured less than a drop of the never-ending ocean that is the glory of God. It would be impossible for me to list all the verses that tout the glory of God, because glory doesn't work that way. Glory is not a thing like a shoe, a steak, a candle, or a cottage. Those are particular physical things that can be carefully described by words so that you would immediately have an accurate picture in your mind of what is being talked about. One could draw a picture or take a photograph of a shoe, and you could see it and know what it was, but glory is not like that. No single picture could ever capture glory. Glory simply cannot be photographed. Glory is not so much a thing as it is a description of a thing. Glory is not a part of God; it is all that God is. Every aspect of who God is and every part of what God does is glorious. But that's not even enough of a description of God's glory. Not only is he glorious in every way, but his glory is glorious.

Scripture does, however, put the hugeness of the glory of God into the smallness of human language so that we can at least get some sense of what it's like. For example, the prophet Isaiah, under the inspiration of the Holy Spirit in Isaiah 40, stretches human language in order to give

2 This section is adapted from my article "Why the Doctrine of Glory Matters," *Church Leaders*, September 6, 2018, www.churchleaders.com.

us a little glimpse of God's glory. "Who has measured the water in the hollow of his hand?" Imagine how much water you could hold in the palm of your hand, then consider that God could hold all of the liquid in the universe in his hand and not spill a drop! "Who has . . . weighed the mountains in scales? . . . Behold, the nations are like a drop from a bucket [to God]. . . . He spreads [the heavens] like a tent to dwell in" (Isa. 40:12, 15, 22). Isaiah is employing incalculably huge word pictures to help us to have even a twinge of understanding of how glorious God is. Yet even these very picturesque and helpful descriptions fall miserably short of capturing the awesome glory of God.

We cannot gain a full understanding of the glory of God from a few passages, because the reason glory is glory is because it lives above and beyond that kind of description and definition. You can say for sure that God is glorious, because your Bible declares he is, but you cannot accurately and fully describe in words the glory that Scripture declares. Perhaps the only workable path into some understanding of the grandeur of the glory of God is to read the entire word of God again and again, looking for divine glory. Why? Because the glory of God isn't hidden in his word; no, his glory is so grand that it splashes across every page of his book.

When the Bible speaks of God's glory, what is it talking about? *God's glory is the greatness, beauty, and perfection of all that he is.* In everything that he is, God is great beyond human description. Every attribute and action of God is completely beautiful in every way. God is totally perfect in all that he is and all that he does. This is what we mean when we talk of the glory of God. It is the stunning reality that there exists one in the universe who is the greatest, the most beautiful, and the most perfect in every way. He is gloriously great, he is gloriously beautiful, and he is gloriously perfect. There is no one like him, there is no one that rivals him, and there are no valid comparisons to be made to him. He is the great Other, in a category of his own beyond our ability to estimate, understand, or describe. Every part of God is glorious in every way possible. He is glorious; there is nothing more to be said. And because God is glorious in every possible way, he alone stands in this vast universe as the only one who is worth the worship, surrender, and love of every human heart.

The Glory War

We must understand that because God is glorious, life is one big glory war.

Each of us is hardwired by God for glory. We are glory-oriented human beings. We are attracted to glorious things, whether it's an exciting drama, an enthralling piece of music, or the best meal ever. God built this glory-orientation into us so that it would drive us to him. Because we're glory-oriented, our lives will always be shaped by the pursuit of some kind of glory. What glory right here, right now, has captured your heart, and how is it shaping the way you respond to the situations, locations, and relationships in your life?

Sin makes us all glory thieves. Though God created us to live lives propelled by the glory of God, sin causes us to live for ourselves (2 Cor. 5:14–15). Sin turns us all into glory thieves. We demand to be in the center of our world, the one place that should be for God and God alone. We take credit for what only God could produce. We want to be sovereign, and we want to be worshiped. We set up our own law and punish people who get in our way and break our rules. We tell ourselves that we're entitled to what we really don't deserve. We complain when we don't get whatever it is that we want. In living for our own glory, we steal glory that belongs to God.

Only God's glory can satisfy the glory hunger in our hearts. Inside every one of us is a glory hunger . There is a way in which everything we think, desire, choose, do, and say is done in the quest for glory. We all want what is glorious in our lives, but this hunger will never be satisfied by created things. If you could experience the most glorious situations, locations, relationships, experiences, achievements, or possessions in life, your heart still would not be satisfied. Creation has no capacity whatsoever to bring contentment to our hearts. The purpose of creation is not to satisfy our hearts but to point us to the glory of the one who can satiate our hunger, and in satiating our hunger, give peace and rest to our hearts.

God's grace alone has the power to defeat the glory war in our hearts. This glory war doesn't rage outside of us, no, it rages inside of us. Deep and abiding glory disloyalty resides in the heart of every sinner. We all tend to continually revert back to self-glory. We do this because living for the glory of self is more natural to a sinner than acknowledging and living for the glory of God. We buy into the lie that imperfect created things can do in our hearts what the perfection of God's glory can do. In our self-deception we tell ourselves that we really can satisfy our thirst by drinking from dry wells. So the only hope for us is that this God of glory would invade our lives and rescue us from our own glory thievery. This is why Jesus had to come to earth, to live righteously on our behalf, to die for our thievery, and to rise again, conquering sin and death. In amazing grace, Jesus willingly came on a glory rescue mission, and because he did, there is hope for us that we will finally be free from self-glory and live forever in the light of the satisfying glory of God.

There is only one who exists in the universe who is ultimate in glory, ultimate in greatness, ultimate in beauty, and ultimate in perfection, and he is all of these things in everything he is and everything he does. God has no glory inconsistency and he has no glory rival. Everything comes from him, everything that is continues to exist through him, and everything is made for him (Rom. 11:36). He is the bright and stunning star in the center of eternity, history, what is physical, what is spiritual, what is now, and what is to come. All life is found in him. To live in light of God's glory is not just about being spiritual. It is about recapturing your humanity, because this is how every human being was designed to live. Perhaps the vision of God in 1 Chronicles 29 is what should capture the thoughts of our minds and the imagination of our hearts every day, no matter if we are a man or a woman, a child or an adult, young or old, single or married, rich or poor, no matter our race or ethnicity, and no matter where we live and work. Put this passage on a card and tape it to the mirror you look in every morning.

> Therefore David blessed the LORD in the presence of all the assembly. And David said: "Blessed are you, O LORD, the God of Israel our father, forever and ever. Yours, O LORD, is the greatness and the power and the glory and the victory and the majesty, for all that is in the heavens and in the earth is yours. Yours is the kingdom, O LORD, and you are exalted as head above all. Both riches and honor come from you, and you rule over all. In your hand are power and might, and in your hand it is to make great and to give strength to all. And now we thank you, our God, and praise your glorious name." (1 Chron. 29:10–13)

Now, go back to the beginning of this chapter and read again the description of God's majesty. Take time to let awe of him capture the thoughts, desires, and emotions of your heart one more time. And then jump for joy that you are connected to this awesome one by grace.

4

God in Everyday Life

MUCH CAN AND NEEDS TO BE SAID about what it means to live in light of the existence and glory of God. The most important thing for your mind to contemplate is his existence. Perhaps, therefore, the first four words of the Bible, "in the beginning, God," are not only the four most important words of the Bible but also the four most important words ever written, examined, studied, unpacked, and explained. Because the existence of God is so foundational, everyone has a position on it and everyone lives in the context of how he or she thinks about it. There is no place where the existence of God doesn't press upon and shape how you live. There is no philosophical, scientific, psychological, political, sociological, educational, or entertainment system that is not shaped by whether you think God exists or who you think he is. The way you approach your children, your spouse, your neighbor, your fellow workers, your boss, your parents, your daily tasks, the joys and disappointments of life, your finances, your body, your sexuality, your education, your identity, meaning and purpose, and life and death will all somehow be shaped by your view of God. It is impossible for any human being anywhere to not live a God-referenced life. This orientation is wired into our humanity, so it is important to take time to think about what it means to live out a belief that God really does exist and that he is who he declares himself to be in his word. So let me trace a few of the practical implications of this foundational truth. I haven't arranged the following items in an order of importance, because they are all equally important.

We Can Respond to God's Existence in Four Ways

When we talk about how people respond to the question of the existence of God, we usually put people in one of two categories. Either they believe in God or they don't. But the closer you get to ground level, where all of us live, relate, and work, these categories seem woefully inadequate. I want to broaden the categories for you.

First are the people who deny God's existence. Psalm 14 says that anyone who says in his heart that there is no God is a fool. And Romans 1 explains why. God has made his existence so obvious in creation that you have to deny the evidence that you are confronted with every day in order to fight for your denial. As I will note in the next point, the revelation of God in creation is open for all to see, no matter who they are or where they live. Yet, because of the power of spiritual blindness and the self-deception of sin, people will not only argue against the existence of God, they will also disrespect and mock those who believe it.

We need to be aware that those of us who believe in God's existence and strive to live in light of it are generally no longer in center-culture positions of influence, but now live on the fringes. We should not live in discouragement or defeat, because God's holy plan still marches on, but we should be aware of the distorted story of reality that is told to us over and over again by people who have closed their minds to the primary fact of human existence, the existence of God. This does not mean that we should separate ourselves into a monastic echo chamber. Because of God's common grace, people who deny his existence still make wonderful contributions to our lives. And we have been called by God to live "in" the world but not be "of" the world. We're supposed to be like a city on a hill that at night is impossible not to see. So this means we must live with minds that are biblically and theologically informed and engaged. We cannot be the light that we are called to be if we are not only "in" the culture around us but have progressively become "of" it as well.

Parents, this is an important point for you. Your children in the public school system and at the university will be educated by brilliant and gifted teachers who know their subjects well, but who largely think we have evolved beyond any need to hold on to the unprovable tenets of ancient religion. This means these experts cannot give your child an accurate view of the universe or an accurate sense of who they are and what they should be doing, no matter how well these teachers communicate the facts of their subjects. Your children will also be entertained by systems that tend to have no time for the existence of God and few places of influence for those who do. You have a heightened position of responsibility for interacting from a biblical perspective with what your children are learning at school and viewing on all the popular media platforms.

A second category of people respond to the existence of God by saying they believe in the concept of god but seem to have little desire to know him, and it appears that their "belief" makes no difference in the way they live. Sadly, there are millions of people in this category. They do not actually believe in God; what they believe in is the "god-concept." These people tend not to have any semblance of a spiritual life or any kind of love for or worship of God. Their god is distant, impersonal, unattached, uninvolved, uncaring, inactive, powerless, and without authority. Whatever concept they have of God is distant from anything Scripture describes God to be.

It's important to understand that many people who say they believe in "god" are not, by any biblical description, people of faith. Their belief in god is at best a function of their minds, but it is not a life-transforming transaction of their hearts. These people will show up in national surveys as part of the percentage of people who believe in God, but they will not show up for a worship service on Sunday, let alone offer their lives in joyful, obedient service to God.

The third group of people believe in the God of the Bible and, because they do, have come to God in confession, surrender, and worship. They study Scripture so that they can know God better and serve him with greater depth and consistency. They don't think of God as an abstract philosophical concept but as a divine being with whom they have a relationship, because of the righteous life and acceptable sacrifice of Jesus.

If you are exercising biblical faith in the God revealed in Scripture, you seek to apply God's truth to every arena of your life. You seek to live in pursuit of God, live for the glory of God, and live dependent on his rescuing, forgiving, transforming, and delivering grace. You find joy in pleasing the Lord and grieve when you have broken his commands. You love to live in community with other believers and look for ways to be a tool of God's grace in the lives of others.

If I could sit with you and view the video of your last six weeks—at home, at school, at work, with friends and neighbors, and during times of leisure—would I conclude that you fit well within this third group?

There is a final category of response to the existence of God. I confess that this category includes me and, I would think, everyone reading this book. There is nothing more important, more central, more heart engaging, and more formative than my belief in and my relationship with my Savior and Lord. It is not only the center of my worldview, but he is the source of all of my hope in this life and in the life to come. If you would watch my video, you would see how my belief in and relationship with God motivates and directs me every day. I love him with all my heart, and everything I do is shaped by the worship of him . . . but not always.

That "but not always" depicts a category that, somehow, someway, as long as sin still lives inside of us, every true believer fits into. It is the category of practical atheism. No, I'm not talking about a philosophical/theological rejection of the existence of God. What I am pointing to here are those moments when we think, desire, speak, or act as if God doesn't exist. Perhaps it's a moment when we cheat on an exam or give way to gossip. Maybe it's a moment when we give way to lust or make ourselves the center of attention by taking too much credit. Maybe it's buying something that we do not need, and because we have, we then have nothing left to contribute to the work of God's kingdom. Maybe it's being nasty to your wife or selfishly demanding with your husband. Perhaps it's a moment when you decide the acceptance of your friends is more important than obeying your parents. Maybe it's permitting angry outbursts against the children you were called to patiently and faithfully nurture. Or it could be a moment of road rage or anger with a fellow worker. Perhaps it's a circumstance where you functionally worship a created thing more than you do the Creator. You may not have any inconsistencies in your theology of God, yet we all have functional inconsistencies in the way we live out that theology in the places, situations, and relationships of our daily lives.

Practical atheism is not first a function of the mind; at root it is a struggle of the heart. This is captured by one verse of that wonderful old hymn "Come Thou Fount of Every Blessing."

> O to grace how great a debtor daily I'm constrained to be;
> let that grace now, like a fetter, bind my wandering heart to thee.
> Prone to wander—Lord, I feel it—prone to leave the God I love:
> here's my heart, O take and seal it, seal it for thy courts above.[1]

We all need to confess this struggle and to cry out for protecting, rescuing, and enabling grace, so that we who profess to have given our lives over to belief in the existence, glory, power, and grace of the God of the Bible would have fewer and fewer moments in our lives where we insert ourselves in the center and act as if he doesn't exist. It is also important that we have hearts ready to confess our moments of practical atheism as God, in his convicting grace, reveals them to us. Where are you susceptible to act, reacting or responding as if God didn't exist?

1 Robert Robinson, "Come Thou Fount of Every Blessing," 1758, in *Trinity Hymnal* (Suwanee, GA: Great Commissions Publications,1990), no. 457.

We See the Beauty of God's Grace in His Revelation of Himself in Creation

> The heavens declare the glory of God,
> and the sky above proclaims his handiwork.
> Day to day pours out speech,
> and night to night reveals knowledge.
> There is no speech, nor are there words,
> whose voice is not heard.
> Their voice goes out through all the earth,
> and their words to the end of the world. (Ps. 19:1–4)

It is an amazing thing to consider that our Lord, who is boundless in love and generous in grace, would intentionally design the physical created world not only to point to him but also to reveal his character. It is no accident that all creation together is one big finger pointing to God. This message of God's existence and glory is so ever present and inescapable that it is not an overstatement to say that God is literally the environment that everyone on earth wakes up to and lives in every day. This message spans every period of human history, every location on the globe, every racial and ethnic group. It is seen by the young and old, by men and women, and by the rich and poor. It is visible to everyone's eyes and speaks everyone's language. The revelation of God in creation discriminates against no one. Moral and immoral people see it. Rebels and the obedient see it. The proud and the humble awake to its message each morning.

It should be lost on no one that God, who created us in his image and designed us for a relationship of love and worship with him, would design the environment in which we live to constantly point to him. The created world is jam-packed with glory. Luella and I once watched an elephant documentary and were amazed by the elephant culture we were coming to understand for the first time. That mind-blowing display is just one window revealing the glory of God. So much created glory is to be seen that it is impossible to take it all in.

You see it in the sand dunes in Dubai and in the lush green valleys of New Zealand. You see his glory in the frozen tundra of the polar ice caps and the dense jungles of the Amazon. You see it in the inexhaustible wings of a hummingbird and the lumbering gate of an elephant. You see his glory in the bright heat of the sun and in the twinkling starry night. You see it in the multitude of faces on the streets of New York and in the pride of lions in the bush of Africa. You hear it in the rhythm of ocean waves and in the whisper of the wind through the trees. You see his glory when water boils and smell it in well-roasted beef. You see it in the passing of the seasons and in the regularity of morning and night. Fish, fowl, and flowers constantly point to him. Your local park, your favorite pet, and the garden out back are all fingers pointing to him. It is a 24/7 glory display for everyone to see, no ticket needed.

Why would God do this? He did this because he is not only a glorious Creator but he is also glorious in grace. He designed us to know him, to serve him, to love him, and to worship him in everything we do. He knew that sin would divert the gaze of our eyes and the allegiance of our heart, so he made his presence inescapably visible. He hasn't required that we would deserve this message. He reveals himself freely so that we would acknowledge him, seek him, trust him, and live in service to him. It is not only a mission of revelation; it is a mission of rescue. The message of creation leaves no one out and it leaves no one without excuse.

You see, this powerful message of creation means, by God's plan, that it is more natural to acknowledge him than to deny him. It means worship is not a response by a spiritual few, but should be everyone's natural response to the glory display that greets them every day, everywhere they look. The fact that this is not true of most people reminds us once again of the blinding power of sin. If you can look at creation, with all of its glory displays, and not see God, you are a profoundly blind and disadvantaged human being.

There is a calling for all of us in this. It's a call to parents, to husbands and wives, to friends and neighbors, to workers and bosses, and to students and teachers to look for ways to function as an instrument of seeing in the lives of others. Parents, one of the scariest things that you're dealing with in your children is that they have the perverse ability to look at the world around them and not see God. If they don't see God, they will anoint themselves as God and make life all about them. Because they do this, they will resist your parenting and will not allow you to prepare them to live in God's world God's way. Talk with your neighbor about the God behind the roses and the sunset. Tell your friends that every time you go to the park and walk through the woods, you think about the one who created it all. Do everything you can to give blind people eyes to see, and pray that as they begin to see God, they will seek him.

Finally, humbly remember that you need this glory display every day too, because you have a heart that is still prone to wander. You can go through days when God is not in your thoughts and, because he's not, you are susceptible to taking life into your own hands, doing your will and not his. Thank him for the grace of this daily display and pray for eyes that are open and a heart that remembers. Determine you won't pick a flower, boil an egg, look out the window, pet the dog, or mash some potatoes without a moment of worship, and then ask for grace to follow through.

Nothing Is More Humbling Than Acknowledging God's Existence

The first four words of the Bible, "In the beginning, God," put us in our place. We didn't start things, we don't control them, the world doesn't function according to our plans, we don't know what's coming next, and we wouldn't know who we are and what we're supposed to be doing if it were not for the Creator. We will never be in the center of it all, and it is the height of spiritual delusion to act as if we are. Every part of our creaturehood is defined by limits. We have limits of wisdom and understanding, limits of strength and ability, and physical and spiritual limits of every kind.

Only God is above all and knows all. Only God plans and controls everything. Only God has no limits to his wisdom, righteousness, and strength. Only God is able to assure us that his will is always done.

Only God has the right and understanding to set the rules by which his creatures will live. Though made in his image, we are small, weak, and needy. So we all need good, biblical, and God-centered theology to humble us, to put us in our place. Bow before the throne of Almighty God and allow yourself to be in heart-trembling awe of his glory. Pride crumbles before the throne of Almighty God (see Isa. 6:1–6).

The holiness of God exposes how unholy we are.
The almighty power of God shines a light on our weaknesses.
The sovereignty of God shows how little control we actually have.
The omniscience of God causes us to face the limits of our knowledge and understanding.
The love of God exposes how unloving we can be.
The faithfulness of God confronts our wandering hearts.
The grace of God reveals how critical and unforgiving we often are.
The patience of God confronts our irritability and impatience.
The righteousness of God exposes our sin.

Humility is not about putting on some artificial self-deprecating front. No, humility is being willing to admit who you are. You will only ever get a true picture of who you are when you stand in the light of the holiness and glory of God.

Here's the problem: as long as sin is still an issue for us, pride will be as well. At the root of every sin is pride. Pride is not only wanting your way, but convincing yourself that your way is better than God's way. It is thinking, if even for a moment, that you're smarter than God. Pride is taking credit for what you could never achieve or produce on your own. It is naming yourself as more righteous than you are, and therefore you don't seek the help and protection of God's grace. Pride causes you to be critical and impatient with those whom you think are less righteous than you. Pride is putting your pleasure before the pleasures of God. It is being so assured of your biblical literacy and theological knowledge that you become resistant to instruction and counsel.

Pride is expecting and demanding of others things you are not committed to yourself. Pride consistently exchanges God's call and commands for what is expedient, comfortable, and pleasurable for you. The proud person craves to be recognized, to be seen, to be given credit, and to get attention. Pride causes us to use people whom we have been called to serve. A proud person holds on to offenses and finds reasons not to forgive. Because a proud person assesses that he is okay, it is not his habit to daily cry out for the rescuing grace of God. Pride will never produce a good harvest.

The sad brokenness, disharmony, and dysfunction of the human community is the dark harvest of proud hearts. It is humility that draws us to God. It is humility that causes us to own and confess our sins. It is humility that causes us to love God's law. It is humility that makes us patient and forgiving. It is humility that nails communion with God into our daily schedules. It is humility that sends us out as representatives of God's holy mission of redemption. It is humility that makes us agents of God's justice and mercy. Only in the shining light of God's existence and glory can you see yourself as you actually are. Acknowledging God's existence and his inestimable glory humbles us and causes us to plead for his forgiving, transforming, and delivering grace.

It Is Important to Understand What It Means to Believe in God

I wrote earlier that many people who say they believe in God don't believe in him in the biblical sense of what *believe* means. Hebrews 11:6 defines the two essential aspects of true faith: "And without faith it is impossible to please him, for whoever would draw near to God must believe that he exists and that he rewards those who seek him."

First, faith submits to and agrees with God's revelation of his existence and character. Acts 17:22–31 explains what it means to believe in God's existence. Paul is addressing Athenian philosophers who think that God is unknowable. Paul's answer to this contention is to declare who God is as Creator, Sovereign, and Savior. To believe that God exists means acknowledging and worshiping God as your Creator, your Sovereign, and your Savior. I will unpack the implications of these faith commitments later. But I must say here that you cannot claim to believe in God unless you acknowledge these three aspects of his revelation of himself.

But there is a second aspect of true biblical faith that the second half of the Hebrews passage captures: "and that he rewards those who seek him." Faith is never just a matter of what you do with your mind. It is always a transaction of a willing and submissive heart that alters the way you approach every area of your life. The heart of faith really does believe that God's way is the right and best way. It believes that there is blessing in following God no matter what the costs. Faith believes that obedience is its own reward, because it shelters me from the bitter harvest of sin. Faith produces a need for God that means I really do pray without ceasing. So if faith in God doesn't live where I live every day, if it doesn't alter the way I live at my university dorm, my home, my job, my neighborhood, my church, the mall, when I am all alone and no one sees, and all the other locations of my life, then it is not the kind of faith in God that is described in his word.

No matter who you are, where you are, or whom you live near or with, whether you're young or old, what you truly believe is depicted by how you live. This truth drives me to cry out for the help and rescue of the grace of God. What about you? May every area of our lives be a beautiful portrait of what it means to believe in God.

We Find Comfort in the Fact That God Hates Sin

What is your response when, in your Bible reading, you come across passages like the following? "The way of the wicked is an abomination to the Lord, / but he loves him who pursues righteousness" (Prov. 15:9). How do you respond to the many warnings of God's judgment against those who sin against him? What does it mean to you that God hates sin?

I want to point out one beautiful comfort in what could seem to be terrifying to those who are willing to admit that they are less than righteous. There is sweet, lasting, and hope-giving comfort in the fact that sin offends God all of the time and in every way. You would not want to live in a world where the one ruling the world had no hatred for sin. If God did not hate sin, we would have no hope of justice and mercy and no standard of right and wrong to guide and protect us. If God didn't hate sin, evil would reign unchallenged. It is God's hatred of sin that causes him to restrain evil at the personal and community levels. Without this restraint, it would not be safe to leave your house, to drive your car, to have relationships, or to do business. The fact that thievery and violence are not the constant experience of each of our daily lives is evidence that the one who sits on the throne of the universe hates sin. God's hatred of sin makes our lives livable.

But there is more. It is God's hatred of sin that drove Jesus to the cross. On the cross, God's anger with sin intersected with his grace. In his hatred of sin, God was unwilling to leave his image bearers and his world in their sin-marred state. So in holy justice, he moved to right the wrongs that sin had done. But instead of wholesale condemnation and judgment, he poured out his grace by sending his Son to be the atoning sacrifice for our sins. If God did not hate sin, there would be no cross, and if there were no cross, there would be no forgiveness, no restored relationship with him, and no hope of transforming grace. If there is no transforming grace, there is no hope of personal heart and life change. All of the blessings of grace come to us because God hates sin and loves righteousness. Because he hates sin, he sent his Son to take on our sin so that we could be called the righteousness of God (2 Cor. 5:21).

The hope of the final restoration of all things and our place in the new heavens and earth, where righteousness will dwell forever, is one of the most precious results of God's hatred of sin. Because God's hatred of sin is complete and unrelenting, he will not be satisfied until it is finally and completely eradicated in every way and in every place, along with all of its corollary damage. Because God hates sin, as his child you will be welcome to the funeral of sin and invited to live forever in a world unlike anything we have yet known or have the ability to conceive; that is, a world where sin is no more.

Since there is sweet comfort in knowing that God hates sin, wouldn't it then be good for you, wherever you are, whatever your daily relationships and responsibilities are, to hate sin too?

It Is Important to Understand That God Does Not Change

You and I literally have no constants in our lives. We, and everything around us, are in a constant state of change. Nothing stays the same. For us change is unchanging. It is a significant part of our daily experience. Much of the unpredictability of our lives, and the anxiety that results, comes from the fact that we live in a world of constant change. Our bodies are in a constant state of change. Our emotions swing widely and change constantly. The physical things around us are changing all the time. Things age, wear out, and break. The fact that people change all the time often makes our relationships confusing and difficult.

As parents, Luella and I dealt with a frustration that all parents have to deal with. Just about when we felt comfortable parenting our children through a particular stage of development, they would move on to another stage. The churches we attend change, though perhaps not theologically, but leaders change, locations change, and the congregation is always changing. The government and economy exist in a constant state of change. The values of a culture change and with it personal lifestyles, public morals, education, and entertainment. The technologies around us are changing so rapidly it is nearly impossible to keep up. And as we go through the stages of life, our daily opportunities, responsibilities, and temptations morph and change.

Because we are constantly changing and everything around us is changing too, we all seek for some rock of constancy or stability in life. We all would love to hook ourselves to something that we could be sure would stay the same no matter what. Human beings are in a constant search for what is changeless whether they know it or not.

Because unchanging change is the reality in which all of us live, it is hard for us to grasp that God never changes and to understand the glorious implications of this truth. Let me start this way. God is not like us: he has no past, present, or future. He exists in an eternal now. He is always what he is. He is what he has always been and will be what he forever has been. So God never becomes something, never needs anything, and never learns anything. God has no hopes and dreams, disappointments and regrets. He has no what-ifs or if-onlys. His character and purposes are without change. He will never grow into something different than he once was. God will only ever be what he eternally is.

Why is this important? It's important because the reliability of everything we believe rests on that fact that our God does not change. There is no better to-the-point summary of this than Malachi 3:6: "For I the LORD do not change; therefore you, O children of Jacob, are not consumed." You, see, like the children of Jacob, if our relationship with God, and our continued inclusion in his great redemptive plan, rested on whether or not *we* were unchangingly faithful, we would be doomed. Our fickle hearts don't alter his loving purpose. Our unchanging Lord is hard to grasp, because in our experience change is a normal, expected part of life. But the truth of God's unchangeability is glorious glory for all who have put their trust in him.

The fact that he has said to you "I the LORD do not change" is the reason you can get up in the morning and once again look for opportunities to be his tool of grace in the life of your children, even though that work is demanding and often discouraging. It is why you can be patient and forgiving toward your spouse, even though there are moments when you're tempted to give up and walk away. This is what gives you the courage to stand for Christ at your university, even in moments when you're misunderstood or mocked. It is why you dig into his word even on the mornings when you're tired and facing a full schedule.

"I the LORD do not change" is what propels you to love that neighbor who seems to be looking for a fight. It is what causes you to run to God and not away from him when faced with sex or money temptations. And it is what gives you a reason to come to him in humble confession when you have wandered away from his will. "I the LORD do not change" is the rock upon which every comfort and every call of your life as a Christian rests.

Let me give you one final example of how mind-blowing and unshakably encouraging this aspect of a biblical doctrine of God is. Geerhardus Vos vividly pictures the imagination-expanding wonder of this truth. Commenting on God's words in Jeremiah 31:3, "I have loved you with an everlasting love," Vos wrote, "The best proof that He will never cease to love us lies in that He never began."[2] If God loves you eternally, there was never a time when that love began, so there will never be a time when that love ends. It is an eternal, everlasting love. There was never a moment in time when God didn't love us. He has loved us eternally. He has forever loved us and will forever love us.

Whether on a given day you believe it or it feels like it,
you are eternally loved by God.
When you are plagued by doubt,
you are eternally loved by God.
When his promises seem absent and he seems distant,
you are eternally loved by God.
When his word seems dry and you find it hard to apply it to your life,
you are eternally loved by God.
When you feel alone and misunderstood,
you are eternally loved by God.
On your best day and during your worst, darkest moment,
you are eternally loved by God.
When pride crushes gratitude,
you are eternally loved by God.
When you follow him with a heart filled with the courage of faith,
you are eternally loved by God.

Your love is never your foundation; his eternal love is. Live in this hope.

• • •

2 Geerhardus Vos, *Redemptive History and Biblical Interpretation*, ed. Richard B. Gaffin (Phillipsburg, NJ: P&R, 2001), 298.

I feel a bit frustrated at the limits of a single chapter to capture the implications of the glorious glory of the existence and nature of God. I have shared with you a short list of some of the implications of the ultimate fact of facts of the human existence: the existence of God. But it would take volumes to exhaust what it means to believe in God. There is nothing you could ever exercise your mind to consider that would even come close to the importance of giving your mental capacities to meditate on the doctrine of God. This doctrine is the ultimate interpreter of everything that is. It is the only valid way of understanding your identity. It provides the only reliable way of answering questions of meaning and purpose. It is the only thing that can give you moral surety. And this doctrine is the only way to live with unbroken joy and peace of heart.

So I want to end this chapter by thinking about what it means to live a Godward life. Volumes could be written about Godward living and what that would look like in all of the situations, relationships, and locations of our daily lives. Because this is true, I want to focus on one essential aspect of a Godward life. You can begin each day in a way that has the power to launch you on a Godward trajectory.

Tune Your Heart Daily

I encourage you to tune your heart every morning to the existence and stunning glory of God. A world-class orchestra doesn't begin a concert by launching into the symphony that is on the music stands before them. No, they begin by tuning the various instrument groups until each player is ready to perform in harmony with every other player. If you want to live a life in harmonious worship, submission, obedience, celebration, dependency, rest, and service with the God of glory who sits on the throne of the universe, it is vital to tune your heart every morning.

Tuning your heart to live in harmony with your Maker is more than doing your obligatory Bible reading, coupled with a bit of prayer. Tuning your heart begins with admitting how God-disharmonious your living can be. It begins with recognizing that in a situation of high emotion, schedule pressure, fear, or temptation, you can lose your gospel mind. If even for a moment you lose your gospel mind, you will then take your life into your own hands and act as if God did not exist. Remember, an orchestra doesn't tune once every three months, but before each and every concert. Because of the distractibility and fickle nature of my heart, if I am going to live in harmony with the Lord of glory, it is important that I start every day by tuning my heart to him. I need to invest the time necessary to do this.

I am afraid that many of us simply don't give ourselves enough time to do anything more than a brief devotional reading and a prayer that scans the needs of the day. This means that for many of us, the tuning of our heats will require getting up earlier than we are used to. I know if you're a mom or dad, working a demanding job, or doing both, or if you're living alone with no one to assist you with all the necessary tasks of life, you go to bed exhausted and want to sleep as long as possible. I know what it's like to wake up already tired. But I think you will find that what I am counseling you to do will not only be spiritually rewarding but energizing as well. There is nothing like approaching your day with a heart filled with a sense of the presence and glory of the Lord and with all of the joy and courage that result. Let me suggest what it looks like to tune your heart to live in harmony with the God who is described by your theology.

Gaze. Follow David's example in Psalm 27. Run to the "temple" and gaze upon the beauty of the Lord. Take a few moments each morning to go to one of those wonderful passages in Scripture that displays for you the glory of God's glory. You do this to fight familiarity that would cause you to take for granted what once amazed you. Let your heart see again and be amazed again, morning after morning. It's like a good painting; each time you look, you see something more fully, you see something different, or you see the whole as you never have seen it before.

Search. You need time not just to read your Bible, but also to study it. You need to unpack it, tear it apart, reflect over and over on what you've read, and meditate on its implications. You need Bible study tools that help you to understand and apply what you have read. But here is my counsel to you as you study: search for your Lord of Glory in the pages of his word. What are you learning about his character, his purposes, and his glory? It is not enough to come to know the word of God; the goal of all Bible study is to come to know, love, worship, and serve the God of the word. Your Bible is a narrative of his glory. The story is about him. Start every day finding him in his story.

Worship. Fight letting your study of God in his word be an intellectual, academic exercise alone. Remember that biblical literacy and sound theological understanding are never ends in themselves, but are means to an end, and the end is the transformation of your heart. The whole purpose of God's revelation in his word is that idolatrous hearts would be rescued by saving and transforming grace and become hearts given over to the worship of God. Begin every day by bowing in adoration and awe before the great "I AM." Speak to him in praise for who he is and in gratitude for what he has done. Defeat the idols of your heart every morning with adoration of the one who alone is worthy of your worship.

Surrender. Each morning consciously surrender your heart and everything in your life to him. Give back to him the ownership of your personality, your mentality, your emotionality, your spirituality, your physicality, and your sexuality. Place your relationships, your money, your time and energy, and your hopes and dreams on his altar for his using. Open your hands and give him your house, your car, your wardrobe, and your collection of possessions for the use of his kingdom and his glory. Confess that the day before you took things back that you had previously offered to him. Remember that surrender that is not specific in time, person, place, and thing ceases to be true surrender.

Examine. In the light of God's holy glory, examine yourself once again. You will only see your heart and life with accuracy when you examine them in the searching light of his holiness. Where have you wandered away from his glory toward the temporary pleasure of the glories of self? Where have you permitted, into your thoughts, desires, words, and actions, things that pull you away from a life lived for his glory and in service of his call?

Confess. As you examine your heart in the light of God's glory, speak humble, specific, and heartfelt words of confession. Bring humble words before the Lord, free of excuse, free from shifting the blame, and free from self-atoning argument. Morning after morning, couple your sacrifice of praise with the sacrifice of confession. It's impossible to imagine, as people living in a fallen world and who are not yet fully free from sin, that you would have a morning with nothing whatsoever to confess. Start every morning by coming out of hiding, lifting off your shoulders the burden of sin that you carry, casting your burden on the Lord, and then basking in his forgiving and restoring grace.

Cry out. Admit that the greatest spiritual dangers are not outside of you but rather inside of you. Cry out to your glorious Lord for the one thing, no matter how spiritually mature you are, that you cannot provide for yourself, that is, that he would rescue you from *you*. Cry out for sight-giving, convicting, grief-inducing, confession-producing, rescuing grace. Start your day with a confession of spiritual poverty and neediness to the one who is rich in grace.

Celebrate. We who have come to know the Lord of glory and who have experienced the expanse of his grace should be the most celebratory people on earth. Celebrate not because you are healthy, successful, likeable, and financially secure, but because the Lord of glory exists and has become your Father by grace. Rather than starting your day by grumbling about what the day may bring, start your day by jumping for joy because the King of kings has welcomed you into his family forever.

Repeat. I am afraid many of us make spiritual commitments that end up not having a long shelf life. Determine to nail the tuning of your heart into your morning schedule and then pray for the enabling grace to follow through for the long run. Don't allow yourself to have a basement full of long-ago-discarded spiritual commitments, like the unused exercise equipment that gathers the dust of abandoned intentions. Pray for divine help to make the tuning of your heart to God's glory a long-term habit of your life.

• • •

The doctrine we have considered in this chapter takes you not only to the core of your spirituality but also to the essence of your humanity. The one that this doctrine considers is the one you were created by and created for. There is nothing you could give your mind to that is more important than the theology of God as unfolded in his word. May this theology live in every room of your house and in the places where you work and play. May it shape your friendships, your marriage, and your parenting. May it shape how you live in your classroom, boardroom, or warehouse. May it direct what you do with your TV, your cell phone, your tablet, and your computer. May it provide tracks for your thoughts to run on and a fence to protect your desires. May the doctrine of God shape your most public and most private moments. May it produce in you the deepest remorse and the highest joys. May it satisfy your longing heart and give you a rest that nothing else can provide. And may you glory in the glorious glory of God not just today or tomorrow, but for all the tomorrows that will ultimately lead you to your final address in the new heavens and new earth to commune with Glory forever.

5

The Doctrine of the Holiness of God

THERE IS ONLY ONE living and true God. He is infinite in being and perfection, a most pure spirit. God is holy in all his purposes, in all his works, and in all his commands. He is due whatever worship, service, and obedience he is pleased to require from angels, people, and every other creature. See Ex. 15:11; Lev. 19:2; 1 Sam. 2:2; Job 6:10; Pss. 22:3; 71:22; 77:13; 89:35; 99:5; Isa. 5:16; 6:3; 40:25; 43:15; 57:15; Amos 4:2; Hab. 1:13; Luke 1:49; John 17:11; 1 Pet. 1:15–16; Rev. 4:8; 15:4.[1]

Understanding the Doctrine of the Holiness of God

All children have a powerful capacity to imagine. It's the thing that makes the world of a child surprising, delightful, captivating, and wonderful. My granddaughter demonstrates this ability every time we are together. She carefully makes me tea and a sandwich, but the cup is actually empty and the plate has no sandwich on it. Yet she has the ability to see both,

1 Author's paraphrase of the doctrine of God as found in parts of the Westminster Confession of Faith, chap. 2.

and she's delighted when I tell her what a wonderful cook she is. This is what makes the life of a child so interesting. Sadly, as we grow into adulthood and the real concerns of relationships, employment, finances, diet, and more fill and control our minds, our ability to imagine dims.[2]

In matters of faith, imagination is important. When it comes to faith, *imagination is not the ability to conjure up what is unreal, but the capacity to perceive what is real but unseen.* When the center of your religious system is surrendering your life to a God whom you cannot see, touch, or hear, imagination is very important. Now, to enable you to do this, God has done two things for you. First, he has given you a dual sight system. You not only see physical things with your physical eyes, but you have another set of eyes: the eyes of the heart. God has given you this set of eyes so you can "see" the unseen world of spiritual reality. The problem is that the sin that infects all of us renders us all spiritually blind. What the eyes of our hearts need to see they cannot see. So God blesses us with the light-shining, sight-giving, eye-opening ministry of the Holy Spirit so we can "see" what cannot be seen with the physical eye but is every bit as real.

All of this is critical to understand before we begin to unpack the doctrine of holiness. Why? Because what we're about to consider is dependent upon the illumining ministry of the Spirit of God to open the eyes of our hearts to see. This is so far beyond anything in our normal experience that we have no comparisons or categories to help us understand it.

If you are a believer and at all biblically literate, then you know that the Bible, without equivocation, declares that God is holy. The prophet Isaiah, at the moment of his calling, receives a vision of the Lord sitting on his throne with seraphim on either side, and he hears one seraph make this declaration to another seraph: "Holy, holy, holy is the Lord of hosts; / the whole earth is full of his glory!" (Isa. 6:3). Take note of the emphasis made in this declaration. It wasn't enough to say "God is holy." No, the seraph had to say *holy* three times to capture the depth and breadth of God's holiness. It's as if I were to say you, "I saw this guy

2 Much of this chapter first appeared in my article "The Doctrine of Holiness," Paul Tripp website, Sept. 10, 2018, www.paultripp.com.

at the ballgame who was huge, huge, huge!" You would know right away that this was not an average big guy. You would know that this guy was the biggest guy I had ever seen. "Holy, holy, holy" is meant to stretch the boundaries of your imagination. Whatever it means to say that God is holy, you need to know that he is in an entirely different category of holiness; he is much holier than you ever thought holiness could be.

But even the thrice "holy, holy, holy" was not enough for the seraph as he tried to capture God's holiness. He adds, "The whole earth is filled with his glory." How great is the holiness of this God? Great enough to fill the whole earth. These words are crafted under the inspiration of the Holy Spirit to take your imagination where it has never gone before. They are meant to blow your mind with the thought that God is not like anything you have ever encountered before. They are to humble you with the realization that God is foundationally unlike you. They are intended to help you to understand that you are now dealing with someone different from everyone you have ever dealt with before. He is holy, holy, holy, earth-filling and gloriously holy. He is holy unlike anyone or anything that has ever been called holy. He is the sum and definition of what it means to be holy. When compared to God, nothing that exists is holy. He is holy, holy, holy.

Stop and pray that the eyes of your heart would open and that somehow, someway, you would get even a little glimpse of the mind-blowing grandeur of his holiness. Why? Because seeing his holiness will change you and the way you live forever. I'll explain how in a minute.

What does it mean to declare, as the seraph did, that God is holy? Our word for holiness comes from the Hebrew word, *qadowsh*, which means "to cut." First, to be holy means to be cut off, or separate, from everything else. It is to be in a class of your own, distinct from anything else that has ever existed or will ever exist. God is uniquely separate and different. There is no comparing to God. We can't say God is like *x*, because there is nothing in all the universe that he is like. We also understand things by comparing them to a standard. In sports, for instance, there are standards by which we evaluate an athlete's potential. But there is no standard by which we can measure God. He is above all, the one who creates the standards by which his creatures are measured. His holiness leaves us searching for descriptive words, but the words seem inadequate. God is the great Other, separated, unique, and different from any other thing that exists.

Second, to be holy means to be completely pure, all the time and in every way possible. God is so completely pure that he is distinct and unlike everything and everyone that exists. God is in a moral category that we have never encountered before. He occupies a moral space that no one has ever occupied before. God is in his essence something that we have never seen or experienced before. He is holy. We have no experience or frame of reference to understand what he is like because there is nothing like him.

But there's even more to be said. God's holiness is not an *aspect* of what he is. No, God's holiness is the *essence* of what he is. If you were to ask, "How is the holiness of God revealed?" the only right answer is, "In everything he does." Everything God thinks, desires, speaks, and does is utterly holy in every way. He is holy in every attribute and every action. He is holy in justice. He is holy in love. He is holy in mercy. He is holy in power. He is holy in sovereignty. He is holy in wisdom. He is holy in patience. He is holy in anger. He is holy in grace. He is holy in faithfulness. He is holy in compassion. He is even holy in his holiness; it is what he is. Exodus 15:11 asks,

> Who is like you, O Lord, among the gods?
>   Who is like you, majestic in holiness,
>   awesome in glorious deeds, doing wonders?

And 1 Samuel 2:2 declares,

> There is none holy like the Lord;
>   for there is none besides you;
>   there is no rock like our God.

But why is this doctrine so foundationally important? The holiness of God sits at the center of the grand narrative of the gospel of Jesus Christ. Without the holiness of God, there would be no moral law to which every human being is responsible. Without the holiness of God, there would be no divine anger with sin. Without the holiness of God, there would be no perfect Son sent as an acceptable sacrifice for sin. Without the holiness of God, there would have been no vindication of the resurrection. Without the holiness of God, there would be no final defeat of sin and Satan. Without the holiness of God, there would be no hope of a new heaven and earth where holiness will reign over us and in us forever. The biblical story would not be the biblical story if it were not written and controlled at every point by one who is holy all the time and in every way.

Any explanation of the holiness of God must lead us to seek and celebrate his grace. It is because of his grace that we know that our Lord is holy. It is because of his grace that we are accepted and not rejected by him. It is by grace that we are comforted by his holy rule, because by grace, it is not just for his glory but also for our good. It is because of his grace that we become aware of the gravity of the sin that infects us all. It is because of grace that we run to God for help and not away from him in fear. It is because of grace that God appointed his perfect Son to be the perfect sacrifice for imperfect people. It is because of grace operating within us that we experience both the conviction of sin and a desire to live holy lives. And it is because of grace that we have been invited to live in God's holy presence forever and ever. R. C. Sproul said it this way:

> When we understand the character of God, when we grasp something of His holiness, then we begin to understand the radical character of our sin and helplessness. Helpless sinners can survive only by grace. Our strength is futile in itself; we are spiritually impotent without the assistance of a merciful God. We may dislike giving our attention to God's wrath and justice, but until we incline ourselves to these aspects of God's nature, we will never appreciate what has been wrought for

> us by grace. Even Edwards's sermon on sinners in God's hands was not designed to stress the flames of hell. The resounding accent falls not on the fiery pit but on the hands of the God who holds us and rescues us from it. The hands of God are gracious hands. They alone have the power to rescue us from certain destruction.[3]

The holiness of God decimates our autonomy and self-sufficiency and drives us to the Savior, who alone is able, by his life and death, to unite unholy people to a holy God. God reveals his holiness to us not as a warning that we should run from him in eternal terror, but as a welcome to us so that we would run to him, where weak and failing sinners always find grace that lasts forever.

As I neared the end of writing this section, grief began to seep into my heart. It is impossible to do justice to the majesty of God's glory within the limited boundaries of human language. My writing caused me to reflect on the sad fact that this most stunning reality of life, one that should shape how I think about everything, not only doesn't always fill me with awe but sometimes doesn't even get my attention. Perhaps an illustration might help explain my sadness.

Everywhere you go in Dubai, you are confronted with the Burj Khalifa, the world's tallest building. Impressive skyscrapers are all around Dubai, but the Burj Khalifa looms over them all with majestic glory. It dwarfs buildings that would otherwise leave you in mouth-gaping awe. As you move around Dubai, you see all of these buildings and you say to yourself again and again, "How in the world did they build that?" But the Burj Khalifa is on an entirely other scale.

On a swelteringly hot Dubai morning, I got out of the car and began to walk toward this magnificent feat of architecture. Even from far away, it was hard to crank my head back far enough to see all the way to the top. The closer I got, the more imposing and amazing this structure became. As I walked, there was no thought of the other buildings in

3 R. C. Sproul, *The Holiness of God*, 25th ann. ed. (Sanford, FL: Ligonier Ministries, 2010), 221.

Dubai that had previously impressed me. As amazing as those buildings were, they were simply not comparable in stunning architectural grandeur and perfection to this one. Even though it was hot, I would stop every few minutes to take it in, snap a few pictures, and comment on what I was seeing.

When I finally got to the base of the Burj Khalifa, I felt incredibly small, like an ant at the base of a light pole. I entered a futuristic looking elevator and, in what seemed like seconds, was on the 125th floor. This was not the top of the building, because that was closed to visitors. As I stepped to the windows to get a feel for how high I was and to scan the city of Dubai, I immediately commented on how small the rest of the buildings looked. Those "small" buildings were skyscrapers that, in any other city, would have been the buildings that you wanted to visit. They looked small, unimpressive, and not worthy of attention, let alone awe. I had experienced the greatest, which put what had impressed me before into proper perspective.

This story illustrates the grief I felt after writing about God's holiness. By means of God's revelation of himself in Scripture, I have been able to experience the heights of his glorious perfection. I have been able to consider what the true perfection of holiness looks like. I have been able to see that there is no perfection like God's perfection. There is no holiness as holy as God's holiness. If you allow yourself to gaze upon his holiness, you will feel incredibly small, and what has previously impressed you and commanded your awe will do so no more. It is a good thing spiritually to have the assessments of your own grandeur decimated by divine glory. But here is what makes me sad: I don't always live with God's holiness skyscraper in view. I don't always look at everything else in life from the height of that perspective. And when I don't, not only do other things seem bigger and more impressive than they are but even unholy things can get my attention.

My prayer for me and for you is that when it comes to God's holiness, our perspective will be like mine was that morning in Dubai, standing at the base of the Burj Khalifa, and then looking down from its heights at everything else. I was thankful that I was privileged to experience the Burj Khalifa; how much more privileged should I feel that by grace I have not only seen God's holy glory, but have been eternally connected to this Holy One by grace. My prayer is that our awe in the face of the heights of God's holiness would not be a momentary or occasional thing, followed by wandering-hearted forgetfulness. My prayer for me and for you is that this truth would take hold of us and not let go, giving us proper perspective on everything else and putting what once commanded our attention in its proper place. May God in mercy do that for you and for me.

6

God's Holiness in Everyday Life

WHAT DOES IT MEAN to live every day, in the situations and locations of your life, in a constant recognition of the holiness of God? What does it look like to let this doctrine form the important places in your life such as friendships, career, marriage, parenting, sexuality, finances, civic life, education, leisure, entertainment, and church life? What does it mean to let this truth capture your heart and in so doing, shape your deepest longings, your most influential motivations, the way you make decisions, the things you say, and the actions you take? What does it look like to carry this truth out of the halls of formal theology and into the private places where the drama of your life unfolds? What follows is a beginning list. My prayer is that it would ignite in you a desire to practically understand what it would mean to carry this awesome truth to every domain of your life.

1. The holiness of God is to be at the center of how you make sense of life. Whether you are a homemaker, executive, pastor, plumber, farmer, designer, or professor, you are a theologian. You are constantly having conversations with yourself about what is true and what is false. You carry around theological assumptions and conclusions that, whether you are aware of them or not, become the basis of decisions you make and actions you take. All the time everyone everywhere lives theologically. I am not talking here about your more formal religious life. I am talking about the reality that the way you live your life is formed by what you have concluded is true. The holiness of God must be at the center of what you have concluded to be true, or you will not understand the universe properly, you won't understand your own life, and you won't live the way you were designed to live.

What captured the prophet Isaiah must capture you as well:

> In the year that King Uzziah died I saw the Lord sitting upon a throne, high and lifted up; and the train of his robe filled the temple. Above him stood the seraphim. Each had six wings: with two he covered his face, and with two he covered his feet, and with two he flew. And one called to another and said:
>
> > "Holy, holy, holy is the Lord of hosts;
> > the whole earth is full of his glory!" (Isa. 6:1–3)

This amazing scene, with its incalculable glory, must be at the epicenter of how you understand everything. Without this, it is impossible to understand anything in your life correctly. Every good thing ever created has existed because on the throne of the universe sits one who is holy in every way, all of the time. Your sense of identity, meaning and purpose, your goals for your life, what you long for your loved ones, how you use your energy, time, and money, your sense of right and wrong, your means of making decisions, how you use your gifts and abilities, and where you look for peace and rest must be connected to this declaration: "Holy, holy, holy is the Lord of hosts; the whole earth is full of his glory!"

The holiness of God should frighten you, while at the same time it should give you rest. It should both blow your mind and form the basis of how you make sense of everything. It should expose the darkest parts of you while leading you into the light and hope of life. It should stop you in your tracks with awe and wonder and provide the tracks for your life to run on. It should confront you with the distance between what you are and what God is, while making you want to draw near to him. While God's holiness exposes your moral weakness, it should also make you run toward his grace. The holiness of God should expose all the pseudoglories that fight for your heart while revealing to you the only glory that is truly glorious enough to hook your life to. God's holiness is your light in darkness, your GPS when you feel lost, your comfort in the face of the evils of this fallen world, the constant reminder of who you are and what you need, and the place you run when everywhere else has proven inadequate. It is impossible to overstate the significance of the fact that God is holy, holy, holy. He is so holy that the entire earth is filled to the brim with the incomparable glory of his holiness.

Here is the problem, though, that you and I face all day, every day. The culture around us, along with the systems and institutions of that culture, has abandoned the category of holiness. You see, when you deny that this God, the Holy One, exists, then you do not sense a need for holiness of any kind. You never hear politicians, educators, social media influencers, cultural critics, or entertainment icons use this category. It has no purpose or meaning to them. The people who write the dramas we stream don't have this category influencing what they write, how they think about right and wrong, or the way they present the moral character of a character. As a culture, we have philosophically walked away from *holy*. *Holy* is not in our definition of meaning and purpose. *Holy* doesn't enter into our concept of success. *Holy* is not seen as something to shape your marriage and guide your parenting. *Holy* never is discussed when people are talking about plans for their careers. *Holy* is viewed as a dusty religious concept with little practical meaning, held on to by a shrinking minority. Almost everyone wants justice, mercy, peace, forgiveness, and love, but they can exist in our lives only if the one in control is holy. Why? Because even though we have abandoned this truth, God has hardwired in all of us a hunger for what holiness alone can produce. But if you look around and listen, you will discover that in the practical scheme of things *holy* simply doesn't matter, and for many, it doesn't exist.

Much of what you read, hear, watch, and interact with as a citizen in this present world will not reinforce for you the essentiality of this doctrine. And the more your culture influences the way you think, the less *holy* will have any practical, functional purpose in your life as well. It is possible to believe in the holiness of God and yet in your daily life practice "holyless" living. This truth might not become a way of thinking that then becomes a shaping influence on everything in your life. It is possible, for instance, to include the holiness of God in your theological outline while forgetting that it's the reason why God's instructions for your marriage are paramount. It's possible to say you believe this truth while forgetting that parenting is primarily about representing this Holy One in the lives of your children. You can mentally assent to this truth while functionally ignoring that holiness is what keeps your sexuality safe and pure. You can embrace this truth intellectually and still not be brokenhearted that most of the people you encounter know nothing about the glory of this Holy One and live as rebels against his will and glory. You can sing of God's holiness in a worship service while not connecting it to the way you treat your children in the car on the way home. You can study God's holiness and then succumb to anxiety that forgets that the Lord of lords, who is in control, is good in every way.

Although it is impossible to capture the glory of God's holiness within the limits of human language, this doctrine is anything but esoteric and otherworldly. It is intensely and expansively practical. God's holiness changes the way you understand everything, and because it does, it changes the way you live with and relate to everything. Here is the most important thing you could ever think about: *the Lord is, and he is holy.*

What does it look like to live in light of this reality in every area of my life? The rest of this chapter will begin to address this vital question.

2. The holiness of God provides the only reliable means of knowing ourselves. Let's go back to Isaiah 6 and take note of Isaiah's response to the amazing vision of the glorious glory of God.

> And the foundations of the thresholds shook at the voice of him who called, and the house was filled with smoke. And I said: "Woe is me! For I am lost; for I am a man of unclean lips, and I dwell in the midst of a people of unclean lips; for my eyes have seen the King, the LORD of hosts!" (Isa. 6:4–5)

Isaiah's response is striking. He is immediately filled with a sense of doom. He doesn't editorialize about how incredible this scene is or talk about how wonderful it is that he gets to see it. No, his immediate reaction is overwhelming fear. This isn't overstated emotional catastrophizing. It is an accurate view of who he is and what he needs. Isaiah's confession has its roots in both Genesis 1 and Genesis 3. An accurate view of self must begin with Genesis 1. God created us to live in a relationship with him of unceasing submission, obedience, and worship. We understand we were made to live for a glory greater than our own. Our relationship to God, that we carry his image and are called to live for his glory, separates us from every other thing God created.

But an accurate view of self must also include the Genesis 3 tragedy. Instead of choosing to live with God and for God, Adam and Eve opted for the seductive delusion of autonomy and self-sufficiency that the deceiver sold them, and they disobeyed God's command. When you see Adam and Eve feeling shame toward one another and hiding in fear from God, you know something cosmically horrible has taken place. Sin exploded into the world God had created, blew up the beautiful shalom of the garden, and not only separated people from their Creator but left them, because of their disobedience, under his condemnation.

Only when you stand before the majestic grandeur of the holiness of God will you ever know who you are. Divine holiness and human identity are inextricably tied together. If you do not place yourself before the glorious glory of God's holiness, you will see yourself as more righteous, wiser, and stronger than you are, ever were, or ever will be. You will live as if there is no God, and if there were, you wouldn't really need him anyway. Only God's earth-filling holiness can fill your heart and capture the imagination of your mind so that you can grasp the extent of your unholiness and cry out with a sense of the extent of your own need.

"A man of unclean lips" is an interesting way of summarizing the depravity of sin. You could stand holy before God only if you were able to say, "I have never said anything to anyone, anywhere, at anytime that was in any way wrong in the eyes of God" (see James 3). You and I don't need any greater evidence of the depth of our sin than what comes out of our mouths. Our speech is constant evidence of why we deserve God's wrath and are saved from it only by the atoning grace of Jesus.

Most people have turned their backs on the ultimate moral fact of the universe, the holiness of God, and are content to live with a personal assessment of "okayness." They carry with them no sense of personal moral brokenness, they have no fear of God, and they feel no sense of need for the rescue of his grace. They eat the forbidden fruit again and again, and they possess little shame and fear. They believe that they are able to be what they're supposed to be and do what they're supposed to do in life without any divine rescue, forgiveness, or assistance. Although they are spiritual beings, there is no intentional spirituality in the way they live. God is not in their thoughts, and his holiness not only has no shaping influence in their lives but it doesn't receive the slightest recognition.

This is where we would all be if it were not for God's eye-opening, heart-exposing, conscience-inflicting, forgiving, and empowering grace. By grace we have seen his holiness; it has exposed to us who we are and what we need. But we have not been left to our doom. We have been greeted in our doom with the justifying mercies of the Savior. Parents, don't just talk to your children about God's grace; open their blind eyes to his holiness as well. If they do not understand the bad news of their doom, then the good news of God's grace won't mean anything to them.

Husbands and wives, if you want to evaluate the true health of your marriage, hold your marriage before the holiness of God. If you want to evaluate the moral condition of your sexuality, your finances, your thoughts, desires, and motivations, hold them before the searching light of the holiness of God. You will never stand in front of the expansive glory of the holiness of God and walk away with an assessment of "okayness" in any area of your life.

It really is true that you and I will know ourselves most fully and accurately when we place ourselves under the light of the glory of the one who is completely holy in every way all of the time.

3. The holiness of God confronts us with the sinfulness of sin. Sin is deceitful. This means that sin not only blinds you, but it also presents itself as something less than sinful. Sin doesn't always seem sinful to us. It often looks more beautiful and pleasurable than dangerous and destructive. If you're eating your third piece of chocolate cake in a moment of gluttony, at the moment you are experiencing not destruction and danger but the taste of deep, rich chocolate wrapped in silky buttercream. The pleasure of the moment overwhelms your sense of the sinfulness of the moment. When you're on your cell phone trashing someone's reputation, you don't think about moral transgression at that moment, but rather you are carried along by the scintillating buzz of carrying the sordid tale. When you are lusting after a woman in the line at Starbucks, you are taken up with fantasies of possessing her physical beauty for your own pleasure; you're not thinking about the horribly immoral violation of that moment. Temptation's seductive power is that it distracts us with pleasure so that we'll fail to see sin's moral danger.

Also, sin doesn't always seem so sinful to us after the fact. Even when our consciences are a bit bothered by transgressing God's moral boundaries, we quiet our consciences with self-atoning arguments. We participate in our own deceit by working to convince ourselves that the wrong we did wasn't so wrong after all. We go back and rewrite the narrative of the moment to make ourselves look more righteous than we were. So we walk away feeling okay about what God says is not only not okay, but is a repudiation of his holiness. We recast the gossip on the phone as a prayer request, the lust as an appreciation of God's creative artistry, and the extra dessert as a silly little thing.

We are in moral danger when we are able to minimize or deny the inexcusable sinfulness of sin. I want to say something here that bears consideration and explanation. The sinfulness of sin is its *verticality*. What is most sinful about sin is not that it has a host of negative horizontal effects. Yes, sin will hurt you and those around you. It harms government and the institutions that we live with and depend on. Sin leaves its mark and a trail of destruction wherever it goes. But you and I will only understand the heinous sinfulness of sin when we understand that every sin is a sin against a holy God. In his heart-wrenching confession of adultery, David gets it right when he says, "Against you, you only, have I sinned / and done what is evil in your sight, / so that you may be justified in your words / and blameless in your judgment" (Ps. 51:4). Every time I sin, I take my life into my own hands, ignore the existence of God, and turn my back on his holy rule. Every sin ignores the holiness of God and his command to be like him. Every sin repudiates his authority, his holiness, and his moral call. It is morally impossible for any sin to be only horizontal.

Every sin is a sin against God himself. Each act of unholiness is a rebellion against his holiness, and anytime I work to make my sin seem less than sinful, I betray him. The disobedience of a child is more than an act of disrespect of God; it is a rebellion against God and his holy standard. But parents, your children don't know this. A lack of marital love is not just a relational violation between a husband and a wife, but it dishonors a holy God. You and I will only ever have hearts that are broken by our sin when we acknowledge its verticality. Only when we stand with Isaiah before the Holy One on the throne and are in awe of his holiness will we see our sin for what it is. Before the holiness of God, sin is never seen as less than sinful.

So what do we do with this? I suggest you find a place where you can be alone, turn off your screens, cut out all noise and distraction, get down on your knees, and open your heart to the sinfulness of your sin. Do it right now if you're able. Confess that you minimize sin, learn to live with it, and even make friends with it. Confess that you hide it, deny it, and explain it away. Confess that much of the grief you feel over your sin is because of its bad horizontal fruit and not because it violates the existence and character of your Creator. Let the sinfulness of sin grip you, and weep. Weep for your casual response to it, weep because of its blinding power, weep for the hold it has on those around you, but most of all weep because every time you sin, you betray your holy Lord.

I am afraid that in our obsession with the distraction of distraction, where anything is better than quiet mediation and where self-reflection finds no welcome, we have forgotten how to mourn. We love the clock-free passivity of the mindless drone of incessant entertainment. We seem afraid to be left alone with our souls exposed to our God. We can't even wait at a stoplight without yanking out our little pocket screens to have the light of distraction shine on our faces once again. We love spending our time seeing what will keep us from seeing what we need so desperately to see. Meanwhile we are being more than distracted; we are being numbed, dulled, and deceived into believing we are okay. In light of the holiness of God, "okay" is not a category of human evaluation that we should be comfortable with. We need seasons where we unplug, shut down, turn off, and sit in the presence of our holy God with eyes open and hearts ready to bow before him and mourn. It is when you weep your way into the presence of a holy God that you've gotten it right. Only then, in the face of the vertical heinousness of your sin, will you cry out for the grace that is your only hope in this life and the one to come.

Let me say it again: our problem, whether we know it or not, is that sin doesn't always seem sinful to us. Our ability to minimize or deny the gravity of our iniquity and the vertical awfulness of our transgressions is a personal moral disaster. Our willingness to be blind never leads us anywhere good. Holiness begins with the desire to see ourselves with heart-convicting clarity and accuracy, and that clarity comes only when we stand before the throne of our holy God. Remember, you cannot confess what you do not grieve, you cannot grieve what you have not seen, and you cannot repent of what you have not confessed. Cry out for eyes to see and a heart to weep, and in weeping, may you find the joy of discovering mercies that are new once again.

4. The holiness of God is meant to be the ultimate quest of our lives. What are you living for? What do you want in life? Hunger for what drives you? What gives you an unshakable sense of purpose? What keeps you working, pressing on, and continuing? What thing do you value more than anything else? What is the big reason behind everything you do? Why do you do what you do in the way that you do it? Why do you do what you do as a friend, student, worker, boss, parent, spouse, neighbor, citizen, or member of the body of Christ? What in the world are you running after?

Another passage points us to the significance of the truth of the holiness of God. The context of this passage frames its practical importance.

The apostle Peter is addressing people who were suffering for their faith. But surprisingly, Peter's letter is not first a letter of comfort but rather one filled with marching orders to scattered believers. Peter is laying out what it means to live as a believer in the gospel of the Lord Jesus Christ, no matter what you're facing and what human powers are in control. Early in his letter Peter delineates the core of what it means to live in light of the gospel in this fallen world between the "already" and the "not yet."

> Therefore, preparing your minds for action, and being sober-minded, set your hope fully on the grace that will be brought to you at the revelation of Jesus Christ. As obedient children, do not be conformed to the passions of your former ignorance, but as he who called you is holy, you also be holy in all your conduct, since it is written, "You shall be holy, for I am holy." And if you call on him as Father who judges impartially according to each one's deeds, conduct yourselves with fear throughout the time of your exile, knowing that you were ransomed from the futile ways inherited from your forefathers, not with

> perishable things such as silver or gold, but with the precious blood of Christ, like that of a lamb without blemish or spot. (1 Pet. 1:13–19)

Rather than living as one controlled by the self-oriented passions of your former life, Peter says you are called not only to obey the Lord but to quest to be holy as he is holy. This call is to be your highest value, your constant commitment, the ultimate long-term quest of your life. Peter is so bold as to call people to what is impossible apart from their being rescued and empowered by the grace of the Holy One they are called to imitate. Between your conversion and your homegoing, the focus of God's redeeming work is on radical personal transformation. Therefore, when you quest to be holy as God is holy, you are committing yourself to make *God's* purpose for you *your* purpose.

It is important to understand that we have been saved not just for heaven, but for holiness as well. We cannot ignore God's call or allow ourselves to lower his standard. In the glory of his holiness, he is the standard for everything we think, desire, say, and do. My fear is that in our pleasure-obsessed world, where comfort is king and temporary personal happiness is the definition of the good life, this quest of quests will get lost in the endless din of our cravings for the next amusement. The highest human joys are found when we take seriously God's call to a life committed to holiness and when the commitment is applied to the situations and relationships of our daily lives. But this trust gets lost. For example, the best biblical definition of a good marriage is when a husband and a wife are committed to responding to one another, in words and actions, in a way that is holy in the sight of God. If the goal of marriage were comfort, it would make no sense to put a flawed person next to a flawed person in such a comprehensive relationship. Rather, the struggle of marriage is one of God's most efficient tools in forming us into a holy people; that is his call, and it is possible only by the power of his grace.

Good grades, athletic skill, acceptance into a prestigious university, and a successful career are not high enough goals for your parenting. Raising mannerly children who don't embarrass you in public is not a sufficient purpose for your parental labors. Here is your parenting goal: that you would be a tool in God's hands in producing children who have surrendered their lives to him, rest in his grace, and are committed to live in ways defined by him as holy.

Likewise, your sexual life has a goal that is deeper than that you would achieve mutual satisfaction. Here, too, the highest goal of sexuality is not human pleasure, but that our holy God would be pleased by every sexual thing we give our thoughts, desires, and bodies to. God also has a purpose for your money beyond daily provision. Your money is one of the principal ways you surrender your life to his holy call.

Now, all the practical implications of this call to holiness are impossible for every one of us. I have no ability to transform my heart. I have no independent ability to escape the sin that still lives in me. I have no autonomous power to harness my thoughts and desires. I have just as much ability to be holy as God is holy as I have to jump high enough to touch the top of the Empire State Building. So, this high and holy calling is an argument not only for our desperate need for right-here, right-now grace, but also for the humbling fact that we will never be grace graduates. Till our final day we will be reaching out for holiness and crying out for the grace that alone has the power to produce holiness in us. May we love being holy in God's eyes more than we love all the self-oriented pleasures that tempt us to give our love elsewhere. May we bask in the blessings that result when we make God's purpose for us the purpose of our hearts.

5. The glory of God's holiness propels us to give ourselves to his mission of redeeming grace. When faced with the glory of God's holiness and the disaster of his own sin, Isaiah responds not only with confession but also with willingness to give himself to God's mission. "And I heard the voice of the Lord saying, 'Whom shall I send, and who will go for us?' Then I said, 'Here I am! Send me.' And he said, 'Go'" (Isa. 6:8–9). Isaiah does not hesitate. His response has no ifs, ands, or buts. He offers no excuses or negotiations. The holiness of God and the tragedy of sin should form one thing in us: willingness.

Here is another area of your life that should be marked by weeping and rejoicing. How is it possible to read the biblical narrative of the destructive power of sin, to understand how it has separated us from God and that it ends in death, and not weep. Consider how sin bends, twists, and complicates everything in your life and everything around you. Consider its constant trail of destruction. Consider its evil seduction. Consider that sin is the ultimate liar, promising over and over again what it has no power to deliver. Consider and mourn.

But you also have reason to rejoice. Because God loves the glory of his own holiness and has a tender heart toward those he made in his own image, he would not let sin win. He would not let sin have its horrible way. So, in justice coupled with mercy, he made a way for forgiveness to be granted, for sinners to live in relationship with him, and for sin to ultimately be defeated. His holy zeal to pour out his redeeming grace is the most beautiful thing in the universe. Nothing should produce greater joy in us. Rejoice that there is a God of holiness on the throne of the universe and he has made a way for us to be holy in his sight too.

This combination of weeping and rejoicing causes us to give our lives to his service. This means wherever we are, whatever is going on, and whomever we're with, we look for ways to be ambassadors of his mission of grace. In many ways, sadly, the church is a sleeping giant. Imagine the results if every believer were committed to being on God's mission of redeeming grace. But the church is often populated more by consumers than participants, those whose commitment to the church is restricted to a formal worship service on Sunday morning, a little money dropped as the plate passes by, and episodic moments of short-term ministry. Many of us don't share Isaiah's willingness. We view our lives as belonging to us, and we're willing to give God occasional portions. I'm not talking here about vocational ministry, but rather each of us is called to be on God's mission, no matter what he has gifted and called us to do.

May we be ambassadors of this Holy One, we sad celebrants who give ourselves to his mission of redeeming grace. May mourning mix with joy in a way that propels us to carry the message of the tragedy of sin and the triumph of grace wherever we go. May the response of each of our hearts be "Here am I! Send me."

6. *The holiness of God is the reason we'll never outgrow God's grace.* The scene in the throne room, where the glory of God's earth-filling holiness meets the ugliness of sin, argues that you and I will never outgrow God's grace. The scene confronts us with the huge moral distance between God and Isaiah. If it were not for God's forgiveness, the scene would be hopelessly depressing. But it is not hopeless, because we know that the grace that forgives also empowers. The grace that justifies also sanctifies. The grace that convicts also rescues. The grace that delivers us from the power of sin will not relent till we have been delivered from its presence as well.

But the task is immense, and the closer you get to your Lord, the more you are aware of how unholy you are. The grace of this Holy One doesn't take dependent people and make them independent, but rather it takes independent people and produces in them a deeper and more willing dependency. If we are called to be holy as God is holy, our need for grace will never end. Remember, the glory of God's holiness is that he is holy in all that he is; he is holy in every way and all of the time. I am thankful that I have grown in grace. I am thankful that areas of sin have been defeated in my life. I am grateful every day that because of the zeal of God's grace, I am not the man I once was. But I am miles and miles away from being holy in every way all of the time. Today I am more deeply aware of my sin than I was when I confessed it for the first time. I take comfort that there is biblical evidence that I am not alone. Consider these words from the apostle Paul: "The saying is trustworthy and deserving of full acceptance, that Christ Jesus came into the world to save sinners, of whom I am the foremost. But I received mercy for this reason, that in me, as the foremost, Jesus Christ might display his perfect patience as an example to those who were to believe in him for eternal life" (1 Tim. 1:15–16).

It's important to understand what Paul is saying with these humble words of self-evaluation. Don't misunderstand; Paul is not mourning just his past life here. He is speaking in the present tense, which is why he talks about being an example of the wonder of the ongoing patience of God's redeeming grace. You see, the longer you live in the presence of God's holiness, the more you become aware of the depth and extent of your sin, the more you are dependent on God's grace, and the more you are amazed by his patience.

When we first come to Christ, of course we are aware of our sin. If we weren't, we wouldn't have run to him. But the sins we tend to confess in the early days are the more overt sins of our unconverted state. The longer we live in the light of God's holiness, however, the more we become aware of the more subtle deceptive sins of the heart, the nagging idolatries and places where we lack godly character. As we walk with the Lord, we become more and more aware of the labyrinthine pathways of sin that course their way through every area of our lives. You simply cannot stand before the searching light of the glory of God's holiness with an open heart and walk away proud of yourself. The longer this light shines on you, the louder your cry for grace grows. You cannot stand before his holy throne and think that you have arrived spiritually. And that is a good thing.

7. Everyone longs for a world ruled by a holy God. Everyone in some way wants things to be better than they are. We all want to live in a world where justice is a real thing and is dispensed with equity. We would all love for violence to end in our streets and in our homes. We all would love to live in a world where no human being was ever taken and used for another human being's selfish pleasure. We all think it would be wonderful if governmental corruption would end forever. We all mourn the abuse of children, the denigration of women, and racism of any kind. We all wish that no one would starve and that war's endless presence would end. We wish disease would claim no more lives. The specifics of our longings differ, but we all long for something better. In some way we all long for a world that is just, peaceful, loving, safe, and righteously ruled. We all long for shalom, that is, everything in its right place, doing what the Creator designed it to do.

This longing is in everybody's heart because we were designed to live in a world that was put together and ruled by one who is holy in every way all of the time. Because he is always holy and good, we would be assured that we would live in a world that was peaceful and safe. Sin shattered the glass of shalom, but our longing is still there, and what we long for is possible only if the one in control of it all is holy and good.

It seems contradictory, but it is true: the most unholy people have places in their life where they cry out for holy rule. Human beings were created to find their everyday safety in the existence and rule of one who is gloriously holy in every way. People may deny God's existence, they may desecrate what he designed to be holy, they may repudiate his holy commands, but they still long for things that only his holy will and his holy rule can deliver.

If one day a thousand people scrolled down their news feeds and came across the death of a defenseless child at the hands of an abusive parent, every one of them would be disgusted, every one of them would be angry, and every one of them would wish it would never happen again. In so doing, every one of them would long for God's holy rule to intervene. A cry for justice is a cry for a holy God. A cry for peace is a cry for a holy God. A cry for safety is a cry for a holy God. A cry that every human being would be treated with value and dignity is a cry for a holy God. You may deny him, but in tearful moments of pain, you will cry out for what his holy presence and rule alone could ever produce. It is vital for us to remember that God's holiness is essential to every human being's emotional, physical, and spiritual well-being, whether we realize it or not.

8. True meaning and purpose are found in the holiness of God. We must consider the conflict between our purpose for our lives and God's holy purpose for us. Think for a moment about the story that God has written for you and me. By grace God called us and drew us to himself. We are united to him forever, his adopted children and the objects of his unshakable love and grace. He lovingly provides for our needs, controls what we can't control, and guides us with divine wisdom and power. He gifts us with his church, the body of Christ, where true community is found, discipleship can thrive, and where we can be about his mission. He gives us his Spirit to counsel and convict and empower us. He gifts us with his word so that we can know him, know ourselves, know sin, know grace, and know his design for how we are to live.

These are all wonderful and beautiful, but there is one thing that our Lord has chosen not to do. When we come to him in confession and faith, he doesn't give us an immediate ticket out of this terribly fallen, broken, and dysfunctional world that fails to operate as he intended. No, between our conversion and our homegoing, our address remains the same as it was before we came to know him. Now, pause and think about this. If God's intention were to exercise his power so that your life would be predictable, comfortable, and easy, it would make no sense to leave you in this flawed world as a flawed person in constant relationship with flawed people. Rather than a recipe for comfort, this is a recipe for disappointment, hurt, pain, anger, weakness, bewilderment, and longing. Why would God plan this for us?

The answer is that this present address was not intended to be our final destination. This will never be the paradise our hearts long for. No area of your life will turn out to be paradise for you, no matter how hard you try to make that happen. This time and place is intended to be a preparation for our final destination. This means that everything in your life serves a higher purpose than your momentary pleasure and enjoyment.

God has planned to use your marriage for more than your mutual definition of marital bliss. He means to use your job for more than financial provision and success. He has a greater purpose for your friendships than for you to have people in your life with whom you feel comfortable. He wants more out of your educational endeavors than academic achievement and degrees. Each of these is messy and hard because God has left you in a messy place. But the mess is meant to call you out of your self-reliance, your self-focus, and your love for the world to a greater dependency on him. But it is meant to do more.

God intends the messiness of this time and place to be transformative. Each area is meant to prepare you for what is to come; that is, to be a tool of an increasing spiritual hunger and growth. God uses all of the difficulties of life in this fallen world to accomplish the most important thing that could ever be accomplished for you and in you; that is, that you would progressively become holy as he is holy. As this happens, you become more and more ready for your final address, where holiness is the eternal norm. Here is where ultimate meaning and purpose are found. God uses even the hardest things to produce the most wonderful of things. I don't live in an impersonal, irrational world where bad things happen for no reason and with little good resulting. I don't have to live with the hopelessness of what seems to be a constant dimming of meaning and purpose as I face the unexpected and seemingly unproductive failures of people and things around me. No, this world is under the rule of one who is not only almighty in power but is also holy in every way, all of the time. And this Holy One wants better for me than I would ever want for myself, and he uses my present address to accomplish that purpose.

So everything in my life is blessed with holy meaning and purpose. Everything becomes more than it would have been without his holy rule, his holy grace, and his holy purpose for me as his child. No situation is meaningless, no circumstance is without purpose, and no trial is useless. Now, at street level, life won't always seem that way, and God's divine purpose doesn't mean that my life will be free of pain and suffering. But I can be assured that I am being prepared, and at the heart of that preparation is this purpose: that I would progressively become holy as he is holy. Ultimate meaning is found in God's holiness. Human meaning is rooted in the existence and plan of a God who is gloriously holy in every way. Your Lord would never plan, rule, and direct your life in a way that is anything less than perfectly holy. Now, that should give you reason for rest and celebration.

9. Holiness is the purpose of all biblical and theological study. The ultimate reason humans have rational and communicative abilities is so that we can know God and commune with him. This, however, has a distinct direction when it comes to exercising your mind to explore and understand the expansive theology of Scripture. Let's examine what I think is a "says it all" passage when it comes to understanding the purpose for the study of the word of God, the doctrines that it reveals, and the knowledge that results.

For as the rain and the snow come down from heaven
and do not return there but water the earth,
making it bring forth and sprout,
giving seed to the sower and bread to the eater,
so shall my word be that goes out from my mouth;
it shall not return to me empty,
but it shall accomplish that which I purpose,
and shall succeed in the thing for which I sent it. . . .
Instead of the thorn shall come up the cypress;
instead of the brier shall come up the myrtle;
and it shall make a name for the LORD,
an everlasting sign that shall not be cut off. (Isa. 55:10–11, 13)

This promise in Isaiah has been held dear by theologians, preachers, students of the Bible, and people in the pew for generations. And what is the promise? It is that the word of God, empowered by the Spirit of God and received by the people of God, will always accomplish its purpose. This gets us to the heart of what this chapter is about. Imagine that I approached you and said, "I will always accomplish my purpose in my relationship with you." What would your immediate response be? You would want to know exactly what my purpose for my relationship to you was. When God says to you, "My word will always accomplish its purpose," your question should immediately be, "What is the purpose of God's word?" This question gets at the heart of God's purpose for all biblical and theological study, whether at the highest level of scholarship in an academic setting or in the average person's daily Bible study. Why study God's word? Why study theology? What should result from our study?

Isaiah's word picture is incredibly helpful. He pictures plants being nourished by snow and rain. As we considered in chapter 1, if I have a little thornbush and it is nourished by the snow and the rain, what do I expect to get? I expect to get a bigger thornbush. You won't find me saying to my wife, "Honey, if it continues to rain, I think our thornbush is going to become a cypress tree." I don't expect the briar out back, after it has been nourished by the rain, to turn into a myrtle tree. But this is what Isaiah's word picture is proposing.

The prophet is pushing his illustration beyond what would naturally happen in the physical world to make a profound point. The purpose of the word of God is something deeper than the dissemination of biblical and theological information. The goal is radical heart and life transformation. God intends the information to be transformative. Biblical literacy and theological knowledge were never meant to be ends in themselves, but rather means to an end. The end is personal holiness. A perfectly holy God gifts us his holy word so we would be rescued from the sin we could not escape on our own and be progressively transformed into his likeness. "Be holy as I am holy" is God's call, and his word is his principal tool in creating in us what he has called us to be. A holy God gifts us with his word so that through it we would become like him: holy. Progressive growth in godliness (holiness) is God's goal for biblical and theological study, no matter who is doing it or where it is being done.

• • •

This brief study of the holiness of God should leave us *weeping* and *rejoicing* at the same time. If you stand before the throne of our perfectly holy God, you will have reason for both. I am persuaded this is why we are called to both of these responses in Scripture and why they are both important pieces of a spiritually healthy life. God's word calls us to mourn, actually pronouncing blessing on those who do (Matt. 5:4). How could you stand before the holiness of God and not weep at the condition of your own heart and the sin everywhere in your world? God's word also calls us to rejoice (1 Thess. 5:16–18). When we gaze upon the holiness of God, we have reason to rejoice. How unshakable is your joy, when you wake up each day knowing that your world is under the rule of one who is perfectly holy in every way, all of the time, and that this Holy One is your Father by grace?

So, weep! Your Lord is holy. Don't stop rejoicing! Your Lord is holy. Live the life of a sad celebrant. Mourn the ways that you are far from the holy goal God has set for you, while you rejoice in the potential you now have to be what you could have never dreamed of being if this Holy One had not met you with his heart- and life-transforming grace. May your tears mix with joy until you are on the other side with him and like him forever and ever.

7

The Doctrine of God's Sovereignty

FROM ALL ETERNITY GOD, by the wise and holy counsel of his own will, freely and unchangeably ordained all that comes to pass. Yet God is neither the author of sin, nor does he violate the will of his creatures, nor is the liberty of second causes removed, but rather established. Although God knows whatever may or can come to pass, he has not decreed anything because he foresaw it as that which would come to pass.

God, the Creator of all things, upholds, directs, and governs all creatures, actions, and things, from the greatest to the least, by his wise and holy providence, according to his infallible foreknowledge and the free and unchangeable counsel of his own will, to the praise of the glory of his wisdom, power, justice, goodness, and mercy. In his ordinary providence, God makes use of means, yet is free to work without, above, and against them at his pleasure. See Gen. 8:22; Num. 23:19; Job 38:11; Ps. 135:6; Prov. 16:33; Isa. 46:10–11; 55:10–11; Dan. 3:27; 4:34–35; Hos. 1:7; Matt. 10:29–31; John 19:11; Acts 2:23; 4:27–28; 13:48; 15:18;

27:31, 44; Rom. 4:19–21; 9:11–18; Eph. 1:3–14; Heb. 1:3; 6:17; James 1:13, 1 John 1:5.[1]

Understanding the Doctrine of the Sovereignty of God

It is a question first asked by toddlers as they learn to form language and try to understand the world around them, and it is a question asked again in old age: *Why?* Why are things the way they are? Why did this happen? Why can't I . . . ? Why this family? Why this sickness? Why this location? Why this situation? Why would God allow . . . ? How could a good God let this happen? Is God really in charge? Why didn't God stop me? Why? It is one of the most profound and practical questions a person can consider. Are we and our world under control? Is God sovereign?

I could not begin to number the volumes written on this topic, and there surely will be more to come, precisely because the way you answer this question shapes the way you interpret your world, directs the way you live, and determines the nature of your hope and peace of heart: What does it mean that the Bible teaches that God is sovereign? It means that God is in absolute control of his world and everything that happens, without any gaps, limits, interference, or thwarting of his rule. It means that God alone determines all that will happen and rules the means by which everything will happen. This means that God never has questions, never is surprised, never is frustrated, never wonders, never is greeted with mystery, never wishes he could have, never looks back with regret, never is hoping, never is waiting, never feels helpless, has nothing he can't figure out, and never finds himself at a loss. No one can back God into a corner. He is never pressed to do something. There is no authority over him that he has to answer to. He does what he pleases, decides whatever he wants, and acts as he wants. To say God is sovereign is simply to say that God is God and there is no one like him.

Everything in the world that is ordered and regular, like the passing of the seasons, day and night, the rise and fall of the tides, and infancy

1 Author's paraphrase of the doctrine of the sovereignty of God as found in the Westminster Confession of Faith, chap. 3.

to old age, are all the result of God's sovereign rule over his world. He decides how his world will operate and then rules over the operations he has decided upon. Everything in the world that seems disordered and chaotic to us is also the result of God's sovereign rule over his world. His wisdom doesn't always seem wise to us. What would seem best to us is not the "best" that he has ordained for us. What seems tragically out of control is under his careful and constant control. Understanding that we live in a world under God's unshakable and unchangeable rule changes everything we think about ourselves, our world, and life itself.

There are two aspects of God's sovereignty: his *decrees* and his *providence*. A decree is a decision or order made by an authority. God's decrees are his eternal plan. God has decided what will come to pass. According to his own will and for his own glory, he has ordained everything that will come to pass. Because God is infinite in power and wisdom, his decrees are eternal and unchangeable. What God decrees will happen, will happen.

The second aspect of God's sovereignty is his providence. God doesn't just decree what will happen and then sit passively above his world. God is an active participant in his world. He governs, sustains, effects, and controls. God not only decrees what will be but actively rules over the processes by which it will be. God is in constant contact with the universe that he has made. He has not set the world in motion and walked away; no, the motion of the universe is the result of his active sustaining and governing control. He governs the most momentous things in the universe all the way down to the smallest and largely unnoticed things. God is the ultimate actor on the stage of the universe, ruling all that he has made. God is sovereign; that is, he decrees what will be. God is sovereign; he rules what he has made.

Six Biblical Windows on the Sovereignty of God

Scripture shows us the sovereignty of God in action. We see it in living color in the situations, locations, and relationships in his word. We're going to briefly look at six passages that each gives us a different window on God's sovereign rule. My prayer is that this would ignite in you an awe that produces worship of heart and surrender of your life.

1. The liberation of the Israelites from Egypt (Exodus 7–12). If you had any doubt about God's rule over his world and his willingness to unleash his power and authority for the good of his people, this passage will dispel it. For four hundred years God's chosen people had been enslaved in Egypt. God, in the tenderness of his heart, heard the cries of his people and was going to move to deliver them. The beginning of Exodus 7 gives us a window on the absolute sovereignty of God. God announces that he will do three things: he will deliver his people out of their bondage, he will do this by bringing great judgments down on Egypt, and in so doing he will demonstrate that he alone is Lord.

Notice that there is nothing tentative about God's declaration. He needs to ask no one's permission. There is no wondering as to whether he has the right to make such a declaration or whether he will be able to accomplish what he has declared. He is the Lord. He can do what he wishes, when he wishes, and with whom he wishes, and no one can stop him.

When God declared that he was going to demonstrate to the Egyptians that he alone was the sovereign one, he meant it. He will parade before the eyes of the Egyptians and his own children his complete control over the physical elements of creation and the way they function. He will make them do what they were not designed to do. In so doing, he will demonstrate that the physical world operates under his sovereign command. Every plague was a direct assault on the "gods" of Egypt. God used the liberation of his people out of slavery to display the grand, expansive glory of his sovereignty, not just for the Egyptians and the Israelites, but for every generation to follow who would read the history of this moment in his word.

He is the Lord, the sovereign one. The world he created, with its vast array of elements, does his bidding. He answers to no one and has no weaknesses. There are no limits to his authority and power. He uses his power and authority when he wishes and with whom he wishes. He displays the glory of his sovereignty for his own glory. He is the Lord. So the hope of his people is always him. It is his rule over all things and his rule on their behalf that give his people rest and courage. What he chooses to do no one can question and no one can stop. The liberation from Egypt is an "I am the LORD" moment, his sovereignty on full display. Be in awe. Worship. This is your Lord.

2. Daniel and Nebuchadnezzar (Daniel 4–5). Whatever you think about politics and elections, you need this window on God's sovereignty to make sense out of what seems at times to make no sense at all. Proverbs 21:1 says, "The king's heart is a stream of water in the hand of the LORD; / he turns it wherever he will." Psalm 22:28 says, "For kingship belongs to the LORD, / and he rules over the nations." Daniel 2:21 says, "He changes times and seasons; / he removes kings and sets up kings."

Beneath what appears to be the chaos of human government, the rise and fall of leaders, and the frustrations and fears that these can produce in us, stands a sovereign Lord who rules the times and seasons of history, who puts "kings" in place and brings them down. No human authority has ultimate authority. Every human leader has limited sovereignty for a limited time. Every human authority exists and continues under the authority of God. A street-level case study of this is the historical account of Nebuchadnezzar. King Nebuchadnezzar had declared himself the ultimate authority, was obsessed with his own glory, and demanded worship and service rightly due only to God himself. So the King of kings and Lord of lords rose to demonstrate to Nebuchadnezzar, and generations to follow, who was truly sovereign. Nebuchadnezzar would soon learn that he had power only by the Lord's will and under his command. He would soon learn that at God's command he could be powerless and humiliated in a moment. He would learn that there is one who governs the affairs of heaven and earth, who charts the course of history, and by whose will the kingdoms of earth rise and fall.

The picture of God taking Nebuchadnezzar from palace to pasture should come to mind when you're tempted to give up hope, quit praying, and give way to compromise when it comes to elections and the rule of presidents, congressmen, governors, and mayors. As Nebuchadnezzar learned, no human leader has autonomous power. No human leader is the final authority. No human leader has independent rule. There is one who is the King over kings; he rules the leaders, and in so doing charts the course of history. The Lord alone is sovereign.

3. Jonah. You may wonder why a rather strange story of a running prophet and a fish is in the Bible. It's placed among the Prophets, but there's almost no prophecy in Jonah. Why is this forty-eight-verse story in the Bible? I am persuaded that it's because Jonah gives us an entire biblical worldview in a Facebook-like post. In this narrative you are presented with a God of awesome power and glory, who rules his world; a world that is terribly broken by sin; the reality that we were made to live for something bigger than ourselves; and the presence and power of God's unrelenting grace.

One of the glorious things about the glory of God, as it is presented to us through the vehicle of the Jonah story, is the specificity of God's sovereign rule over his creation. When Jonah runs from God, God "hurled a great wind upon the sea, and there was a mighty tempest" (Jon. 1:4). Pay attention to the word picture here. God picks up a gob of wind and hurls it into the exact location of the boat Jonah was using for his escape. God causes the sea to get so rough that it scares seasoned sailors. God did this. Don't let modern scientific cynicism close your mind here. It is true that God is sovereign over the wind and the waves. Do you want to understand the extent of his active rulership over everything that is? The winds and the waves obey his command. He can throw the forces of nature at whomever he wills, wherever he wills, and whenever he wills. He is the Lord.

But his rule over his creation is even more specific than what the story has so far unfolded. Jonah 1:17 says, "And the Lord *appointed a great fish* to swallow up Jonah." Let your mind grasp and your imagination envision what is being said here. Animals, in this case fish, live under and are responsive to God's sovereign rule. Fish obey his command. I must note here that this story is never presented as an allegory or a parable, but rather as history. If what the book of Jonah presents as history did not actually happen, then how could we rely on any of the history of God's word?

There really was a fish who really did obey God's command and really did swallow Jonah and really did vomit him up on the beach. God appoints animals to do his bidding. He is the Lord. But the narrative of the specificity of God's sovereignty over his creation gets even more specific in Jonah. After preaching in Nineveh, Jonah sits outside the city pouting, so God decides to expose his heart through a physical object lesson: "God appointed a worm that attacked the plant [which was providing shade for Jonah]" (Jon. 4:7). Even worms obey God's commands! Worms! He is Lord of everything, including creepy, crawly subterranean creatures. He is Lord over every single thing he created. He commands, and nature obeys.

In the Jonah story, God is not simply pumping out his chest and showing us what he can do. Yes, he is revealing to us the awesome glory of his sovereign rule, but there is something we need to see. There is something incredibly encouraging and hope-giving about the way God employs his rule. He unleashes his power and rule as a tool of his grace. The storm is a tool of his grace, the fish is a tool of his grace, and the worm is a tool of his grace. God is after Jonah, and even after all of the running and pouting, at the end of the story, he is still after this prophet's heart. God employs his sovereign rule over creation to rescue and redeem his own, and that's good news.

4. The sparrows (Matt. 10:29–30). "Are not two sparrows sold for a penny? And not one of them will fall to the ground without your Father. But even the hairs of your head are all numbered." Is anything more normal and incidental than the death of little birds? On the surface, birds dying seems like the regular cycle of nature. In fact, because I was intrigued by this passage, I googled how many birds die each day in America and was astounded at the number: thirteen million, seven hundred thousand! That is five billion per year. Now, prepare to have your mind blown. Jesus declares that not one of them falls, not a single bird, without God's involvement. It's important to note that Jesus doesn't say "without your Father's *knowledge*." What he says is much stronger than that. He says, "without your Father," which means his rule, his causal authority. What a picture of the detailed intensity of God's sovereign governance over his creation.

But there is something more that you just can't miss in this passage. Jesus identifies this sovereign one as "your Father." So much for a distant, impersonal view of God's authority over and rulership of his world. It is our *Father* who rules this world. He does so with the wisdom and protective care of a father for his children. He does it with love and grace in his heart. He will always do what is best, even if his children lack the capacity to see it as best. He is the Father, and for the sake of his children, he will not abandon his authority or surrender his control to another, and he will take no rest.

As if you aren't encouraged enough already, Jesus states one more amazing aspect of the Father's rule. He says, "Even the hairs of your head are all numbered." God has such an intimate involvement with everything that happens in the lives of his children that he keeps an accurate accounting of the number of hairs on their heads. Open your mind, let your imagination expand, and fight against discounting the impossibility of this. Say to your heart, "This is my God, and he is my Father by grace."

5. The Conversion of the Gentiles (Acts 13:13–52). Paul and Barnabas are in Antioch in Pisidia. After preaching in the synagogue on the Sabbath, the crowd spills into the streets and the people beg them to preach again the next Sabbath. Word of the power and uniqueness of their message must have spread, because the whole city gathers to hear them the next Sabbath. The Jews are threatened by the size and receptivity of the crowd, so they do their best to contradict these gospel preachers. Paul and Barnabas are not intimidated and continue to preach with clarity and boldness.

After recounting the history of this situation, Luke interjects his summary of what happened. His summary is a brilliant, brief, and theologically rich explanation of how God's rule over his creatures operates. "And when the Gentiles heard this, they began rejoicing and glorifying the word of the Lord, and as many as were appointed to eternal life believed" (Acts 13:48). It is not enough to say that these people were chosen by God to believe, because Luke says more than that. God also ordained that Paul and Barnabas would be there, that they would publicly preach a clear gospel message, that it would be heard by these Gentiles, and that they would gladly receive it with joy. God was not just sovereign over the results, but also over every aspect of the process that produced the results.

God rules his world in a way that does not violate the true significance and validity of secondary agents. What does this mean? It means God establishes what he has ordained without ever reducing us to robots. What we *think* is real and important. What we *say* has meaning and purpose. Our choices are valid. Our thoughts, desires, actions, choices, experiences, relationships, and locations are all the means by which God accomplishes what he has ordained. So we can never say that since God has ordained everything that happens and rules everything all the time, then what we do and say doesn't make a difference. He rules his world in such a way that our choices are valid and our actions are important. He is sovereign over the ends and the means.

6. Paul in Athens (Acts 16:16–33). Paul is at the Areopagus, preaching. He is confronting philosophers who were "religious" but who were convinced that God was unknowable. Paul presents to them, powerfully and clearly, who God is: "He made from one man every nation of mankind to live on all the face of the earth, having determined allotted periods and the boundaries of their dwelling place, that they should seek God, and perhaps feel their way toward him and find him. Yet he is actually not far from each one of us" (Acts 17:26–27). Let me put what Paul says in my own words. Not only did God create each one of us, but he also determined the exact length of our lives and the particular places where we would live. Paul says that God did this so he would not be far from us, so that at any moment we could reach out and touch him.

I find such comfort and joy in Paul's description of God's sovereignty. There is condescending love and tender grace in the way God rules his world. We often think of God's sovereignty as one of his transcendent qualities, but Paul preaches the theology of immanent sovereignty, that God is sovereignly near to each and every one of us all the time. He is not separate from your world. He is not far off and hidden. His rule guarantees he is near, and that is some of the best news you and I could ever have.

• • •

The theology of God's sovereignty always leads you to Jesus. God exercised his sovereign rule to author the most wonderful story ever written. He has ruled every situation, every location, every person, and every family that was necessary for human history to march toward the coming of Jesus. He ordained patriarchal covenants, the liberation of his people from slavery, the giving of his law and its sacrificial system, the occupation of the Promised Land, the rise and fall of kings and kingdoms, the preservation of the line of Judah, and the preparation of all things necessary for the coming of Jesus.

He ruled the birth in Bethlehem, the collection and commissioning of the disciples, the opposition of the Pharisees, and the compromise of Pilate, all so the Son would be the final sacrifice on the cross. He chose that borrowed tomb and that it would be soon empty. God ordained the postresurrection appearances of Jesus and his ascension to the right hand of the Father. He ruled over the birth and spread of his church and the proclamation of the gospel to the world. He ordained and ruled over the writing and preservation of his word. He ordained the continued preaching of the gospel until it came to your ears and created belief in your heart. He ordained that your story would be embedded into the glorious story of Jesus, and he ruled over every individual and circumstance that made it happen. His sovereignty gave the world Jesus, and his rule led you to his Son. He is Lord over the story that has given you Jesus, and that not only assured your destiny, but also guaranteed life in him and with him until then.

8

God's Sovereignty in Everyday Life

IN A WORLD THAT SEEMS out of control, where difficult things happen to you, to those you love, and to people you've never met, it is hard to hold on to the reality that one who is perfect in every way is in absolute control of the world. God's sovereignty in many ways appears counter-intuitive. It doesn't seem like we are being ruled; we make seemingly free choices a thousand times a day. It seems like some things just happen outside of any control. And it seems like bad things happen without interruption or restraint. So what does it look like to believe and live in light of the truth of God's sovereign control over everything, all of the time and everywhere? Here is a look at the sovereignty of God in everyday life.

Be Careful How You Interpret Your World

Theology is more than an organized way to understand the truths un-folded in the pages of Scripture. Theology is something that you live. The truths of Scripture are meant to be the means by which you make sense out of your life, your relationships, and your world. They guide the choices you make and the actions you take. You cannot make proper sense of your life and your world, of the things you face every day, if you do not include the sovereignty of God in the way you understand what is.

As a being made in the image of God, you are a meaning maker. You are rational, which means you have a built-in desire to know, to understand, and to be free of things that don't make any sense to you. This means that you live life based not on the facts of your experience, but rather on your particular interpretation of the facts. It also means that you are the most influential person in your life because you talk to yourself more than anyone else does. The things you say to yourself every day are profoundly important because they structure the way you live.

If you really do believe that your world is not out of control or driven by fate or change, but rather that it is under the careful control of one who is the definition of power, wisdom, and love, then you will live with a peace of heart, a confidence, and a hope that you could find no better way. Think of how different life looks when you really do believe that there is no situation, location, or relationship that you could ever be in that isn't ruled by King Christ. Think of how different your attitude and emotions are when you believe that we are not caught in an endless cycle of history repeating itself, but that we are in a world where God is progressively working out his prefect, preordained plan.

Much of our regular anxiety, worry, fear, and discouragement is the result of thinking that when things are out of *our* control, then they are out *of* control. But the Bible tells us that if you want to properly understand what is happening horizontally, you first need to look vertically. Allow me to suggest a life tool that results when you carry the theology of the sovereignty of God into your daily life. I developed this tool to help people understand and live in light of the practical implications of the sovereignty of God for everyday life.

Imagine I have placed a sheet of paper in front of you with a small circle inside of a much larger circle. We'll call the inner circle *the circle of responsibility* and the outer circle *the circle of concern.* The circle of responsibility represents things that God has called you to do that you cannot give to anyone else. These are your daily, God-ordained duties, your calling, if you will. The only proper response to this inner circle is to carefully and faithfully obey, trusting God for the empowering grace to do so.

But many things in life grab your attention, capture your mind, and weigh heavy on your heart, but are not your responsibility or within your ability to do or produce. These things fit in the outer circle, the circle of concern. The only proper way to respond to these concerns is to entrust them to your Lord, who governs them all for his glory and your ultimate good. You can do this because the Bible teaches you that things out of *your* control are not out *of* control because of God's ordained plan for all things and his active rule over all things.

Living as God has called you to live requires knowing which things in your life fit into which circle. For example, if you are a parent, you are called to bring your children up in the nurture and admonition of the Lord, but you have no power whatsoever to produce faith in the hearts of your children. Of course, this would be a concern, a heavy burden on your heart; but you must understand that you cannot produce faith. If you misunderstand this, then you will do things that you should not do as a parent. One mother once said to me, "If it's the last thing I do, I'll get my children to believe!" I immediately thought to myself, "I'm glad I'm not one of your children." When parents try to force faith on a child, they crush the spirit of the child and drive them further away.

If you load things into the inner circle that actually belong to God, you will be domineering and controlling, and your life will be marked by anxiety and fear. God hasn't given us just a set of responsibilities, but he has also pulled back the curtain of the heavens to reveal to us his sovereign throne. He has done this so we would be good stewards of the few things he has placed under our control, while resting in knowing that the things that are out of our control, but that still concern us, are under his sovereign control. The question for you is, "Do you have a clear understanding in your life of the things that God has called you to do and the things that he welcomes you to entrust to him?"

Belief in God's Sovereignty Results in Humility and Joy

It is humbling to stop and consider the limits of our sovereignty. We must be willing to admit that there are very few things we can control. I have a hard time controlling my car keys, my cell phone, and my ear buds. The theology of the sovereignty of God should humble us. Consider what James says about this.

> Come now, you who say, "Today or tomorrow we will go into such and such a town and spend a year there and trade and make a profit"—yet you do not know what tomorrow will bring. What is your life? For you are a mist that appears for a little time and then vanishes. Instead you ought to say, "If the Lord wills, we will live and do this or that." (James 4:13–15)

It is tempting to act as if we are in more control then we actually are. It is tempting to take credit for things we could have never produced on our own. It is tempting to think that we can make life work according to our plan. It is tempting to be proud of ourselves in places where we should instead be praising God. The fact is, we have no idea what tomorrow will bring, because we don't plan or control tomorrow; God alone does. Scripture's teaching on the sovereignty of God should humble us. You see, good scriptural theology doesn't just define who God is, but it also redefines who we are as the children of God. The sovereignty of God teaches us that we are not independent actors on the stage of life, but rather we are constantly dependent on the one who has planned and daily orders everything in our lives.

Consider a lucrative career as an example. No matter how hard you have worked or how well you have stewarded your gifts, there is no way you could have controlled all the things in the economy or all the people and things in your company that had to work together to make you successful. I think of my decades-long marriage to Luella. How could a girl from Cuba and a boy from Ohio ever end up in the same place at the same time, unless our story was woven together by someone of awesome sovereignty? Yes, we have worked hard on our marriage, but there has been a seemingly endless catalog of things that have needed to be in place for us to have experienced our journey together and the health of our marriage. If you forget the sovereignty of God, you will tend to take credit for things you never could have accomplished, produced, or controlled on your own. And when you take credit for what you couldn't have done on your own, you fail to give praise to the one who deserves credit.

Here is the point. The sovereignty of God is deeply humbling. A humble heart is a worshiping heart. A humble heart is a grateful heart. A humble heart is an obedient heart. A humble heart is a loving, serving heart. The sovereignty of God, carried in your heart, will produce a harvest of good fruit in your life.

The truth of the sovereignty of God should also produce in us a joy that simply cannot be shaken. Few things produce greater comfort and joy than knowing that your world is not a place of impersonal chance and chaos but is under careful rule, and the one that rules is your Father by grace. Wherever you go, your Father rules. Whatever you face in your life, your Father rules. When you pray, your Father who rules also hears. In amazing grace, he unleashes his power and authority for your good. If this doesn't produce joy in you, it's hard to imagine what would.

I have endured much physical sickness and suffering in the last several years. Though I am doing well now, I will deal with sickness and a weakened body until I die. The most severe moments of my suffering were marked with a deep and untouchable joy. No, I wasn't celebrating my pain, but I knew that in those moments, I was crying out to one who was sovereign over every element of what I was experiencing. I knew when I cried, "Lord help me, Lord help me," that my sovereign Father heard me and had both the willingness and the power to answer. I can't imagine going through these moments having no one to cry out to who had the power to answer.

I trust I will not have to endure that pain again, but I am thankful that those moments were infused with the joy of knowing that my Father is King of kings and Lord of lords.

The Only Proper Response to God's Sovereignty Is Surrender

Let's visit one of the most remarkable moments in the narrative of redemption. It is the stuff of intense cinematic drama. The spiritual lives of God's people had been polluted by the worship of Baal. The culture had spiritual schizophrenia; the people would do homage to Baal and "worship" God at the same time. God raises up Elijah to confront this moral outrage. Elijah's challenge to Israel is preserved for and applicable to each one of us: "How long will you go limping between two different opinions? If the LORD is God, follow him" (1 Kings 18:21). Then Elijah challenged the prophets of Baal to a contest that would prove who the true God was. Mount Carmel was the scene of this spiritual drama. The four hundred and fifty prophets of Baal built their altar, placed the sacrifice on it, screamed, danced, and cut themselves for hours—and nothing happened. Nothing. Silence.

Elijah built an altar, placed the sacrifice on it, doused it with gallons of water, and then prayed a simple prayer. That prayer ended with these words: "Answer me, O LORD, answer me, that this people may know that you, O LORD, are God, and that you have turned their hearts back" (1 Kings 18:37). Immediately fire came down from heaven and consumed not only the sacrifice, but the stones of the altar and all of the water as well. This happened because the one to whom Elijah prayed is the sovereign Lord over heaven and earth. He rules the elements of the world that he made and exercises his power for the good of his people. He alone is Lord over all. Case settled. Debate ended.

Elijah's response to the sovereign rule of the Lord is "If the LORD is God, follow him" (1 Kings 18:21). The only appropriate response to the truth of the sovereignty of God is surrender, that is, offering everything that you are and have to him. Surrender is the epicenter of the spiritual war that rages in and around us. It is possible to be subtly duplicitous in the same way the Israelites were openly duplicitous.

You can say you believe in the sovereignty of God, and have various forms of idolatry shape your marriage, your work, your parenting, your identity, and your spiritual life. Where are you tempted to exchange worship and service of the Creator for the creation? What person, place, or thing exercises the kind of control over your heart that only your Lord should have? Does the Lord rule your thoughts, desires, choices, words, and actions? If the Lord is God, follow him. Belief in the sovereignty of God that doesn't produce willing surrender isn't biblical belief.

Mystery and Confusion Will Remain

Since you and I aren't privy to God's secret counsel or informed by him as to what is coming next, we will always face confusion, mystery, and surprise. Belief in the sovereignty of God will not remove these things from your life. Here is the rub. Because we've been given intellectual and conceptual abilities by God, we will hunger to know, hunger for life to make sense, and hunger to understand. We don't like to be confused, we don't like to be surprised, and we don't like to live with unsolved mystery.

But we must all be willing to accept that there is a creature/Creator line that we are unable to cross. Some things God has not told us and never will. This means there are things that we will never fully understand. Mysteries will enter our lives and trouble our minds that we will not be able to solve. The fact that God has not told us all that we would like to know is a sign of his understanding, fatherly love.

When our children were young, with little understanding of life and its dangers, I would at times have to say no to them when I knew they wouldn't have the capacity to understand why. They would be upset and ask, "Daddy, why? Why?" and I would say, "Daddy would love to help you to understand why, but if he told you why, you still wouldn't understand. Does your daddy love you? Does he want good things for you? Does he want to keep you safe? Then trust your daddy. Walk down the hall and say to yourself, 'I don't know why my daddy said no to me, but I know my daddy loves me.'"

Think about this for a moment. Rest for children is not found in figuring everything out, but in trusting their parents, who have it figured out. Rest is not first found in understanding things, but in trusting the existence, power, authority, wisdom, and love of the one who rules all the things you wish you could figure out. Rest of heart is always personal. Peace of soul is always relational. The fact that God hasn't opened the door to the details of his sovereign plan to us indicates that he loves us. He protects us from what we would not be able to handle with our feeble minds and weak hearts. Every loving parent does this with his or her children. If you are struggling with your finances, you protect your children from that scary burden, because you love them. If you are going through a tough patch in your marriage, you don't lay that in your children's laps, because you love them. Loving parents keep many things from their children, precisely because they wouldn't be able to bear the weight of knowing.

God answers our desire to know and understand not by giving answers, but by giving us himself. He reveals to us his existence, his rule, his wisdom, his faithfulness, and his love so that we can experience peace and rest of heart even as we are faced with painful mysteries. And the more you come to know him and understand the character of his loving care, the deeper your rest becomes. So walk down the hallway of your life today and say, "There are many things I don't understand, but I know my Father is in control. I know he is wise and good, and I know he loves me." You'll need to say that to yourself again and again, because there will be other mysteries, other things that seem to make no sense and bring pain to your heart, because God is God and you are not. Ultimately, rest is not in knowing but trusting. Asking yourself why something happened won't always give you rest, but reminding yourself who is in charge of what happens will.

God's Control Is Not Always Obvious

Here is the practical problem everyone who takes the theology of God's word seriously will face. What is true will not always be obvious. This is why it is important to base the way you live not on your interpretation of what is going on around you or in the wider world, but on what God has revealed to you about his character and plan. The Bible declares to us that God is in constant and active control over the world he made, the march of history, and the people he made in his image. But your world often does not seem like it is under any kind of righteous and wise control. You awaken to experience relative chaos in your home, and your iPad exposes you to what is wrong and out of control all over the world. It doesn't seem like anyone is in control, that is, anyone you would care to worship.

This has been the problem of believers of every generation. Did the world of Egypt seem under God's control to the Israelite slaves? Did it seem under God's control when Israel was ruled by wicked kings, or when Jerusalem and the temple were destroyed? Did it look like God was in control when Rome ruled with a heavy hand? Does it look like God is in control when the forces of nature run wild, killing thousands, when political corruption crushes liberty, or when disease snuffs out millions of lives? Does it seem like God is in control when you seek to follow him and you experience suffering, while your unbelieving neighbor seems to have the good life? When racism, violence, and war seem unending, it's hard to put these things in the context of God's rule in a way that makes sense. What God declares to be true is often far from being experientially obvious.

This is the tension we all live with. The writer of Hebrews, discussing the lordship of Jesus Christ, hints at this tension: "Now in putting everything in subjection to him, he left nothing outside of his control. At present, we do not yet see everything in subjection to him" (Heb. 2:8). You develop your theology of God's sovereignty not by horizontal observation but by vertical faith. Between the "already" and the "not yet" the world doesn't seem to operate under the kind of complete divine control that will be obvious in the new heavens and the new earth. This means that right here, right now, trust in God's self-revelation in his word is infinitely more reliable than your ability to observe, interpret, and conclude. You cannot base your confidence in the accuracy, reliability, and trustworthiness of what God has said about who he is and what he is doing on what you have observed about the world around you. Here is the bottom line: you can rest with confidence in God's sovereignty precisely because God, in his word, has clearly and repeatedly said he is sovereign. This requires a willingness to live with the tension of not always being able to see with your eyes and understand with your mind what God has declared to be true about himself.

We have been given the ability to observe and interpret; but if those abilities were all we needed as a parent, spouse, student, neighbor, worker, citizen, or member of the body of Christ, God would not have guided, preserved, and delivered his self-revealing word to us. What God declares about himself is true even in those moments when his sovereign control seems far from obvious.

The Truth of God's Sovereignty (Rom. 8:28–29)

I could not discuss what it means to practically live in light of the truth of God's sovereignty over everything without looking at one of the most misinterpreted passages in the New Testament. The misinterpretation of this passage has caused many sincere believers to have unrealistic expectations of God and then to struggle with the disappointment and doubt that results. In the passage Paul is making an important application of the sovereignty of God to the life and hope of every believer. The problem is that it's not the application many *think* he is making. Too often I have heard people point someone who is suffering or experiencing a time of difficulty to this passage, meaning to give hope but creating the opposite.

The passage is Romans 8:28: "And we know that for those who love God all things work together for good, for those who are called according to his purpose." When this passage is lifted out of its context, it appears to say that if you are a child of God, all things in your life will turn out well. Many Christians take this passage to mean that hard things in their life will eventually have a happy ending. Well-meaning Christians often say to someone struggling, "Don't give up, all things work together for good."

I call this a *happy endings theology*. It is the belief that God has promised his children a good ending to bad things that they are going through, and it has infected the church.

Let's look at the context of the passage. Beginning with Romans 8:18, Paul addresses the topic of the suffering that all of us will face because we live in a sin-broken world that is groaning, waiting for redemption. What follows is a treatise on God's grace between the "already" and the "not yet." What Paul wants his readers to understand is that nothing they are facing has the ability to stop the march of God's redemptive plan or can separate them from his love.

Notice how the verses that follow Romans 8:28 are meant to reinforce this theme. "For those whom he foreknew he also predestined to be conformed to the image of his Son, in order that he might be the firstborn among many brothers. And those whom he predestined he also called, and those whom he called he also justified, and those whom he justified he also glorified" (Rom. 8:29–30). These verses explain the "good" that is being promised in verse 28. It is not situational good. It is not relational good. It is not financial good. It is not locational good. This is not a promise of a happy family, a good marriage, a successful career, a wonderful church, physical health, or a comfortable retirement.

The "good" that is promised here is the most wonderful kind of good that anyone could ever be blessed with. It is better than anything we could ever earn, deserve, or hope for. It is the good of God's rescuing, forgiving, transforming, and delivering grace. Nothing can stop his work of grace in the lives of those he has chosen. He will complete what he has begun. His grace will win, no matter what. Paul's encouragement is that what God will give you is way better than the happy ending you are hoping for. What he gives you in your pain and struggle is himself. He is in you, with you, and for you, and continues to deliver the gift of gifts to you: his redeeming grace.

Yes, God does promise to exercise his sovereign authority and power for your good. He does bring good things out of bad things, but not happy circumstantial endings; he promises the good of his unrelenting, unstoppable grace. You can celebrate God's sovereignty not because it guarantees you a happy and comfortable life, but because it connects you to him and the wonder of his inseparable love and unstoppable grace. The problem with misunderstanding Romans 8:28 is not that it offers you more than God has promised. No, the sad thing about this misinterpretation is that it tragically offers you much less. As we continue to live in the uncomfortability of this groaning world, may we reclaim the true glory of the promise of Romans 8:28.

The Sovereignty of God Gives You Reason to Get Up in the Morning

Many of us experience times when it's hard to get out of bed in the morning. You wake up with your mind flooded with the concerns that you carried the night before. You worry over the horrible conversation you had with your husband, your teenage son who seems to be losing his way, the job you lost and your upcoming rent payment, or the medical test that came back positive. Maybe you wake up and you're weary of both heart and body. Perhaps you awake with regret over choices you made that you can't undo. Maybe you're a pastor and you are awaking to the reality that ministry is much harder than you ever thought it would be. Perhaps waking reminds you that you are old and not the person you once were.

Many of us struggle to awake with anticipation and joy, because the hardships of life have entered our door and don't seem to be going away. Pulling the covers over your head to escape reality is a vain attempt. Short-fused grumbling isn't good for you and surely isn't helpful for those near you. But it is precisely in these moments that the theology of God's sovereignty is so helpful, encouraging, and restorative.

This truth reminds you that no matter what trials you might face on any particular day, you wake up to a world that is under wise and righteous control. This doctrine reminds you that the one who is in control is your Father. He rules your life with a father's loving care. And because he is sovereign over the details of your life, he is near—so near that he is reachable. The Bible tells us that this one who is in control is tenderhearted: "The Lord is near to the brokenhearted / and saves the crushed in spirit" (Ps. 34:18). God's sovereignty means that you never awake to a world where you are alone in your circumstances and left to your own wisdom and power.

But as you awake for another day, the truth of God's sovereignty offers you something more. You have the peace and security of knowing that what you're dealing with won't last forever. You have a destiny that is secure. God will not abandon you, he will not get weary, he will not get mad at you and walk away. He will carry you by his grace until you are in your final home, where sin, sickness, and suffering are no more. And when you look back from the forever and ever, what seemed to be so unlivable and unrelenting will look to you like a flash of a moment.

The sovereignty of God gives you a reason to get up in the morning and be a loving parent again, be a faithful spouse again, work with joy again, reconcile that relationship again, suffer with courage and hope again, reach out to someone in generosity again, and do it all over again the next day. You are not alone. Your world is ruled by your Father, and you are on your way to a place more wonderful than you could ever imagine. And until you get there, your Father walks with you, giving you the grace you need to face this day and all the days that follow.

We All Want to Be Sovereign

We get easily frustrated because we lack the power to make things work the way we wish they would work. This is the cause of much of our internal, relational, and situational distress. It's why we get angry at other drivers or at the person in front us in the line at the grocery store with a cart full of items. It's why vacations often disappoint or we have less than patient responses to our loved ones or friends. Deep in our hearts is a desire for the world to follow our sovereign plan and for the people around us to do our bidding.

When we go back to Genesis 3 and examine the account of the temptation and disobedience of Adam and Eve, we see that what hooked them was not the beautiful, succulent, and pleasurable fruit. No, the fruit was a means to a more attractive end: "You will be like God." What they were after was independent, self-sufficient, autonomous self-sovereignty. They wanted a life that did not call them to depend upon and submit to the rule of their Creator. The horrible lie of the serpent was that human sovereignty was possible. At the root of all sin is a desire to be like God, to have what God has, and to be able to do what God alone can do. We want rule over things that we have no ability to rule. We get mad as God's will is being done in the relationships and situations where we live, because we would rather have our will be done.

Husband, you get mad because your wife is not doing your will. Wife, you wish you had greater control over your husband. Parents, often you are frustrated with your children, saying and doing things no parent should, because you are tasked to nurture them but you have no control over their responses. We grow impatient with our churches, wondering if we should go shopping again for an alternative, because church isn't what it would be if we were in control. We get discouraged with our jobs, because God places us in situations that we would not be in if we ruled our workplaces.

One of the themes of this book is that sound biblical doctrine doesn't just define who God is, but it also redefines who we are as his children. Sometimes the way good theology defines us is encouraging and hope giving. But sometimes good theology exposes the darker things in our hearts. Good theology always comforts and confronts. Good theology should produce celebration and grief in us. Good theology will expose those places where we are susceptible to being at odds with our Lord and, therefore, where we are less than loving to those we live and work with. If you deny your desire to be sovereign, letting it live in your heart, you will find it difficult to entrust yourself to the one who alone is sovereign.

It is vital that we own not only the places where we want the rule that God has, but also the harvest of bad fruit that results. Where does the desire to be sovereign rear its ugly head in your life? What sin reveals itself in your words and actions when you give way to that desire? Every one of us would benefit from making this a daily item for personal prayer, saying, "Father, I confess that I often desire to have the rule over people and things that you have. May you give me the grace today to resist those desires and to entrust my life and the people and things around me to you. I confess my sin against you and others and rest in your forgiveness." Then leave your time of prayer thankful that you are free of the burden of sovereignty and that the one who sits on that throne is your Father.

The Sovereignty of God Guarantees the Reliability of God's Promises

If you are thankful for the promises of God, and if you are thankful for the rich rescuing, protecting, providing, and transforming grace that they offer you, then you should celebrate the sovereignty of God every day of your life. If God's promises motivate you, give you courage, and fill you with hope, then you should find joy in God's eternal and unshakable rule. If in moments of weakness, discouragement, anxiety, or fear you reach out for and hold on to God's promises with both hands, then you should be grateful that God sits on the throne of the universe and controls everything with incalculable power and authority.

You cannot depend on God's promises, as a mom or a dad, a husband or a wife, a worker or a student, young or old, rich or poor, in good circumstances or bad, without at the same time finding joy in his rule. Here is why. The reliability of God's promises is only as good as the extent of his rule. You can only guarantee the delivery of what you have promised in situations and locations over which you have control. I can assure you that I will do what I promised in my home because I have some control there, but I cannot give you the same assurance in my neighbor's home, where I have no control.

You never have to question God's ability to deliver what he has promised you, because he has unstoppable control over every situation, location, and relationship where those promises will need to be fulfilled. Since you are never in a place that lives outside of his control, you are never in a place where what he has promised can't reach you. He rules every situation where his promises need to meet us. He rules. His promises are reliable and secure.

The Sovereignty of God Gives You Real Hope When You Pray

Some people say that if God is in complete control of everything, then there is no reason to pray. He controls the beginning, the middle, and the end of everything. What he wills will happen. It seems like I'm praying to someone who has already decided what he will do, so what's the point? But the Bible never encourages you to think this way. The Bible commands you to pray. The Bible welcomes you to pray. Jesus gives you a model for how to pray. The Bible records stories for you of how God answered the prayers of his people. James says that the prayer of a righteous person "has great power" (James 5:16). You simply cannot read your Bible and conclude that prayer is an empty, meaningless religious activity.

So how can the Bible present to us a God who is in complete control of everything while at the same time calling us to be faithful in prayer? Remember what we have already said about our initiative and God's sovereignty. God doesn't just determine the end (final results), but he also determines the means (all the actions, reactions, and responses that produce the final result) to the end. And one of the ways God has chosen to work out what he has planned is through the faithful prayers of his children. Your prayers are not outside of his sovereign plan, but rather a crucial part of the working out of his sovereign plan for his world. Your prayers are an essential part of God's sovereign rule.

Rather than God's unchallenged rule over everything being a discouragement to prayer, it is your hope and encouragement as you pray. You are not praying to someone who lacks power and authority. You don't pray to someone who has limits to what he is able to do. We have all been frustrated in moments when we have shared a need with someone who cares for us, but who lacks the authority or ability to do anything to help us. It's nice when people care, but that does not change the situation we are caught up in. This is never your situation when you bring your needs to your heavenly Father. Not only does he love you with an everlasting love, greet you with new mercies, and lavish his grace on you, but he also controls everything that would concern you, press in on you, and potentially defeat you. There is nothing you could ever face that is outside of the span of his authority or power. And he has promised to unleash his power for your good. Rather than discouraging prayer, the sovereignty of God gives us reason to pray and reason for hope as we do so.

I have been writing this chapter with a weary and shattered heart. The world has been in the grip of a global pandemic that has shut down the world economy, caused untold suffering, and has already claimed 106,000 lives in the United States alone. American cities have become hollow, boarded-up caverns. Churches have not been able to gather for over two months, and it remains unclear when they will be able safely to meet again. To add to this sad drama, we were greeted in the last several days with a cell phone recording of a black man, George Floyd, who died as a policeman sat for more than eight minutes with his knee on his neck. The horror of this killing has been followed by protests in every major city in America. Peaceful protests have turned violent, destroying commercial districts all over the country. The violence was very close to where we live in Center City, Philadelphia. We have spent fearful nights, praying for our own safety and for our city. Meanwhile we were watching a pandemic, a massive economic downturn, and racial unrest develop and converge into the perfect storm of social chaos. If there has ever been a time in my life when the world seemed like it was out of control, it is this moment as I am writing.

If you had any tenderness in your heart and commitment to love your neighbor as yourself, you couldn't watch the video of the murder of George Floyd without a brokenhearted righteous indignation. How could you consider the toll this pandemic has taken on the world and not want to weep? My heart has been heavy, broken, and weary. The big issue in these moments is what you do when you are weary and distraught. What do you do when your heart seems like it can't carry any more? In these moments, where do you run? Like David, I run to the "temple" to gaze upon the beauty of my Lord once more. And as I look on him, I am reminded of what this chapter is about: no matter how things look at street level, he is Lord over every situation and location that confuses and distresses me. I rest in knowing that what I don't understand, he perfectly plans and understands. I find peace in knowing that what I could never rule, he rules.

No, the pain of life in this sin-shattered world won't fade away, and I will face dark moments again, but I can be free from panic because there is one who is in control, and he is perfectly wise and good.

In both hard times and easy times, it is glorious to know that God rules and we don't. It is encouraging to know that our world is not out of control, no matter how chaotic and confusing it may seem, but under the wise and careful control of the Lord Almighty. It is sweet to know that the one who rules everything all of the time is our Father by grace. It is comforting to know that, because he rules, nothing can stop the march of his life-producing, sin-defeating grace. It is good to know that there is a greater King who sits above the less-than-perfect kings of this earth. It lifts burdens off your shoulders to know that you can entrust to his wise rulership things that concern you deeply but which you have no ability to change. It's good to remember that your sanity is not found in figuring everything out, but in trusting the one who has it all figured out from before origins to beyond destiny. It's spiritually healthy to wake up every morning and worship God as sovereign.

I can think of no better way to end this chapter than with the updated words of an ancient hymn. As you read these words, hear the chorus of saints who for ages have sung these words and then gone out to live with hope and courage renewed.

Whatever my God ordains is right
In His love I am abiding
I will be still in all He does
And follow where He is guiding

He is my God, though dark my road
He holds me that I shall not fall
And so to Him I leave it all

Whatever my God ordains is right
He never will deceive me
He leads me by the proper path
I know He will not leave me
I take content, what He has sent
His hand can turn my griefs away
And patiently I wait His day

Whatever my God ordains is right
Here shall my stand be taken
Though sorrow, or need, or death be mine
Yet I am not forsaken
My Father's care circles me there
He holds me that I shall not fall
And so to Him I leave it all

Whatever my God ordains is right
Though now this cup in drinking
Bitter it seems to my faint heart
I take it all unshrinking
My God is true, each morn anew
Sweet comfort yet shall fill my heart
And pain and sorrow shall depart[1]

1 "Whatever My God Ordains Is Right," orig. words by Samuel Rodigast 1676, trans. Catherine Winkworth 1863. Music and alt. words by Mark Altrogge copyright © 2007 Sovereign Grace Praise (BMI) (adm. at CapitolCMGPublishing.com).

9

The Doctrine of God's Omnipotence

GOD IS OMNIPOTENT, almighty in power. He can do, without effort, whatever he wills at any time and in any place he chooses to exercise his power. This is the highest possible definition of power. This means God is utterly and completely unique in power. There is nothing in heaven or on earth that is comparable in power to God. God's power has no limits. There is nothing that God cannot do, according to his holy will and pleasure, and nothing that can inhibit or stop God's exercise of his power. See Gen. 17:1; 18:14; Num. 11:23; Job 24:22; 41–42; Pss. 24:8; 115:3; 145:1–3; Isa. 14:24–27; 44:6–8; 45:5–18; Jer. 32:17; Zech. 8:6; Matt. 19:6; Mark 14:36; Luke 1:37; Eph. 3:20–21; Rev. 1:8.

Understanding the Doctrine of the Omnipotence of God

As a writer, my life is about the power of words. Words can expand your vision. Words can stimulate and strengthen your imagination. Words can give you sight in places where you have been blind. Words can help you understand things that are beyond the boundaries of your own experience. Words warn, confront, and comfort. Words can diminish fear and ignite hope. Words can humble you or make you proud. Words have power. I love words. I work with them every day. I am surely guilty of thinking too much and saying too much. People who know me don't think of me as a man who suffers from a loss of words. But as I write this chapter, I am confronted with the limits of my vocabulary and my ability as a writer.

What I must write about here is something of such gargantuan glory that it defies description and comparison. What we are now considering is a galaxy away from anything we have ever normally considered or experienced.

I have a son who is a sports broadcaster, and he texted me one Saturday afternoon telling me to turn on one of the sports channels because something amazing was happening. What I witnessed in the next hour was astounding. I had never seen anything like it. In fact, I didn't know anything like it existed. Even after watching it take place, I wondered if I had actually seen it. As I tuned in, a reporter said a contestant was about to lift 501 kilograms. I knew that was incredibly heavy, but I didn't know precisely how heavy. So I quickly googled 501 kilograms and was amazed that it is 1,104 pounds. Now, that just seemed impossible to me. Even though the weightlifter was a huge human being, I could imagine that amount of weight blowing one of his knees apart, tearing off an arm, or exploding a vein in his head.

I have to admit, I was a bit nervous as he stepped up to the platform and stood before the bar. Suddenly he began to pound on his chest and scream and then, as he summoned his strength, he bent down and lifted that enormous weight for the regulated time. Screams and cheers of celebration followed in recognition of this athlete accomplishing what had never been done before. I just sat there thankful that both of his knees were intact and neither of his arms was lying on the floor. My son and I texted back and forth about how crazy this was.

What I saw that afternoon was amazing. I don't know if I'll ever see anything like it again. It was more human strength than I knew existed.

This man had power, and he knew it. The 501 kilograms hanging on the bar didn't frighten or intimidate him whatsoever. He knew that he was of a different category than the rest of us. He wanted the cameras there because he knew he was going to lift that weight and walk away the victor, uninjured. It was the intersection of power and confidence, and it was quite amazing. But it also took effort, unrelenting effort, to lift that weight.

As I thought about this chapter, which is a meditation on the omnipotence of God, I thought of that afternoon, watching that weightlifter. But this time the amazement had drained out of me. What I had watched was not the world's strongest man, but a man limited by human weakness. He had great power, but he would never be almighty. He could train more and lift a greater weight, but he would never be omnipotent. He didn't do what he did simply because he chose to do it. He had trained hour after hour, day after day, month after month for year upon year. He had to train in order to defeat his own weakness and build strength. He had to research and study. He had to learn from other athletes. He had to listen to the advice of sports physiologists. He had to submit to the rigors assigned to him by sports dieticians. Sports psychologists had to teach him how to defeat his fear. He had to learn the physics of weightlifting. He had to spend years building his muscle mass. For years he had worked his way up, lifting heavier and heavier weights until he was finally able to stand before 1,104 pounds with the confidence that he could lift it. He had to do all of this because, although he might not look or act like it, he is like you and me, a weak and limited human being.

When it comes to considering the limitless power of God, we are hampered by the fact that everything in our field of experience has limits. The most powerful thing we know has limits to its power. Even when you are impressed with the power of something, you are impressed with it because it has pushed the boundaries of expected limits. When we think of power, it is normal for us to think of limited power. We would immediately think that someone who thought he could do absolutely anything was ridiculously proud, sadly delusional, or tragically insane.

Here's that creature-Creator line again. Everything on the creature side of the line is limited in power. No person has the power to do anything he or she wants to do. No animal has unlimited power. Everything on this side of the creature-Creator line suffers from weakness, inability, and limits. God is utterly unique in power. There are no comparisons to be made. There are no categories to put him in. There are no workable analogies to be made. To say that God is omnipotent is to say that God is God. The consideration of the power of God will always lead us to that age-old rhetorical question, "Who is a God like our God?"

But there is value in considering what it means to believe that there is one who sits on the throne of the universe who has the power to do whatever he chooses to do, without question of ability or effort. I want to consider two things in Scripture that define and explain for us the kind of power that is the power of God: the *power of creation* and the *power of resurrection.*

Chapter 12 will consider the doctrine of creation in detail, but for our purposes here, I want to look at creation as a public display of the almighty power of God. If you are a Bible believer, you already know and believe that God made this world out of nothing. It was spoken into existence by the power of his will and word. What concerns me are two things. First, we often don't take the time to unpack that which we say we believe, so we therefore are unmoved by the full extent of its glory. Second, I am afraid that amazing truths like the omnipotence of God become familiar items in our theological outline, and because they do, they fail to move us as they once did. Our lives are shaped and directed by what has us in awe. Since we have been hardwired for awe, something will always capture the awe capacity of our hearts, and what has captured our hearts functionally has control over us. If for no other reason, studying the theology of the word of God is important because it is one of God's primary tools he uses in the recapturing and realigning of our hearts.

It is stunning to read through Genesis 1 and to watch God speak the various elements and creatures of our world into existence. "Let there be light," and there was light. What? "Let the earth sprout vegetation," and it was so. Are you paying attention? "Let the waters swarm with swarms of living creatures, and let birds fly above the earth across the expanse of the heavens," and God saw that it was good. Amazing! May wonder fill our hearts.

Think with me for a moment. You have never spoken anything into existence in your entire life, and you never will. Bouquets, bread, and furniture don't burst into existence at our command. What kind of power is it to speak, and things physically generate with their distinct beauty and the perfect design to do what they were intended to do in their place in the creation order?

Let your imagination loose, and look in on that moment when God took a handful of dust from the ground, breathed life into that dust, and created a living, breathing, thinking, relating adult human being, Adam. We see dust become a fully functioning human being, with all that this physically and spiritually means, with one divine breath! It is the impossible made possible. There are no analogies to this moment. It stands alone as one of the singular wonders of the awesome power of God. He breathes life into dust; there is no one like him. Here is one of power's highest definitions: the power to breathe life into what had no life.

As wonder fills your heart, let me make an important distinction. Human beings are creative, but we do not have the power to create. Everything we "create" begins with raw material. Even the microbiologists, who claim that they can generate life in a petri dish, always begin the process with the mixing of chemical substances. They haven't actually created anything; they have simply manipulated created substances to generate something new. They are very skilled and creative scientifically, but it would be disingenuous for them to claim they have the power to create. There are few better definitions of almighty power than the power to create a world using no raw material whatsoever.

Bad things happen when we lose sight of how creation defines for us the almighty power of God. This is why God lovingly takes time to unpack for Job the difference between what it means to be the Creator and what it means to be a creature. As God does this, we get to see the process of God exercising his power as Creator. The descriptions are meant to blow our minds and humble our hearts; that's why they've been preserved for us.

In the final chapters of Job, God is yanking Job out of his grief, the kind of grief that makes Job all too self-focused and self-absorbed, by taking Job on a mind-bending, heart-changing tour of the cosmos. But the focus of this tour is not the glory of the cosmos, but the God of awesome power who created it and makes it do his bidding. In Job 38–39 we find some of the wildest, most beautiful and imagination-expanding descriptive word pictures that have ever been written. It takes this kind of writing to even come close to capturing the creation power of the Lord Almighty in a way that would allow us to grasp even a bit of its glory.

> Where were you when I laid the foundation of the earth?
> Tell me, if you have understanding.
> Who determined its measurements—surely you know!
> Or who stretched the line upon it?
> On what were its bases sunk,
> or who laid its cornerstone,
> when the morning stars sang together
> and all the sons of God shouted for joy?
> Or who shut in the sea with doors
> when it burst out from the womb,
> when I made clouds its garment
> and thick darkness its swaddling band,
> and prescribed limits for it
> and set bars and doors,
> and said, "Thus far shall you come, and no farther,
> and here shall your proud waves be stayed"? (Job 38:4–11)

The "Where were you?" question is meant to humble Job. It's meant to confront him with the vast difference between him and God. It is meant to confront him with his weakness. God is enabling Job to see that everything in the universe exists and is held together by one thing, the power of God. It is power that never wonders about capability. It is power that never requires the exercise of effort. It is power with no lack of knowledge or understanding. It is power that never needs instruction or to ask permission. It is power that is without challenge or rival. It is power that is gloriously autonomous and self-sufficient.

> Can you lift up your voice to the clouds,
> that a flood of waters may cover you?
> Can you send forth lightnings, that they may go
> and say to you, "Here we are"?
> Who has put wisdom in the inward parts
> or given understanding to the mind?
> Who can number the clouds by wisdom?
> Or who can tilt the waterskins of the heavens,
> when the dust runs into a mass
> and the clods stick fast together?
> Can you hunt the prey for the lion,
> or satisfy the appetite of the young lions,
> when they crouch in their dens
> or lie in wait in their thicket?
> Who provides for the raven its prey,
> when its young ones cry to God for help,
> and wander about for lack of food? (Job 38:34–41)

The "Can you?" question of this passage is the ultimate rhetorical question. It is meant to lay that creature-Creator line down in broad fluorescent-red ink for us. "Job, can you do what I do? Job, do you have the power over everything that exists that I have?" The only rational answer is, "No, my most powerful moment is a universe away from the power that you have. You alone, Lord, have the power to create everything that exists, to put it in its appropriate place, to make it work in coordination with other created things, and to hold them all together, so that the cosmos doesn't descend into irreparable chaos. You alone are almighty."

The argument from creation is clear and unassailable: there is no power like the omnipotent power of God. To say that God has the power to create and control his universe and everything in it is simply to say that God is God. There exists no one like him. The power to speak creation into existence is the highest form of power.

But there is a second way the Bible describes God's almighty power. The Bible tells us that God's power is not just creation power but also resurrection power. And the closer you get to examining and understanding resurrection power, the more you are left in the humbling silence of awe and wonder.

We are all used to the finality of death. We learn early that when something or someone dies, it is the end, and there is nothing whatsoever that we can do about it. You are crazy or delusional if you deny that what's dead is dead or if you try to defeat death after it has happened. We have all learned that we must accept death because we have a complete lack of power over it. In this way, death really is the ultimate enemy. Not only can we not defeat death, but we can't seem to escape it either. We live in a world where every living thing is in the process of dying, and we can't do a single thing to stop it.

So death makes us feel weak and unable. Death confronts us with how small our power is. Death seems to be the enemy that wins every time. We walk away defeated once again because, for all of our power, we have no power over death. None.

My two oldest sons were confronted with this reality when they were just three and five years old. We lived in Scranton, Pennsylvania, in a neighborhood with lots of trees and lots of birds. Wandering around the yard one day, my sons found a bird that was either sick or injured, and they asked me if we could help it. I got a box, put tissue in it, and laid the bird in the box. While they were sitting watching the bird and I was thinking about what I would do next, the bird died. My sons saw that it wasn't moving and asked me what was wrong. I had the regrettable job of telling them that the bird had died. They looked at me frustrated and sad, but they knew. Death is final. Even at this young age, they instinctively knew that there was nothing I could do. Death had taken the bird and had defeated me.

We don't have to fantasize about what it would be like to conquer death, because the Bible shows us what it's like and tells us how important it is. The apostle Paul argues that this resurrection power, the power to cause the dead to live again, is at the heart of biblical faith (see 1 Cor. 15). If there is no resurrection, then Jesus did not rise again from the dead, and if Jesus did not rise again from the dead, then our sin has not been defeated and our faith is worthless. God's unique resurrection power is not just another item in our theological outline, but it is the heart of what gives us new life and future hope. Christianity is a resurrection religion. God's grace is resurrection power.

Consider with me the magnificence of the resurrection of Jesus. He was in the tomb long enough to be certifiably dead. Dead. Rising again after death meant that the synapses in his brain suddenly began to fire; electric charges fired through his nervous system; the muscles in his heart started to pump; fresh blood coursed through his veins; his muscles suddenly became soft and flexible; his organs turned on and functioned in symmetry with one another; his eyes became moist and able to focus; he suddenly could breathe, smell, taste, and feel. His balance and orientation returned. His ability to relate and communicate instantly turned on. Thoughts and desires, plans and purposes suddenly rushed in. This is but a limited summary of everything that had to happen all at once for Jesus to be able to get up, fold his grave cloths, and walk alive out of that tomb.

Here's what it means to be almighty: no effort was required for Christ to rise again. There was no consideration of whether or not it was possible. There was never a flash of doubt at any point in God's mind. There was no consideration of a plan B. Resurrection was the plan, and God had the power because God is God. Almighty means that not even death has the power to defeat you. Omnipotent means that raising the dead is within the scope of what you are able to do. Resurrection power means your power is unique and unparalleled. The power to resurrect is the highest form of power. Resurrection power means that the most powerful created thing is very, very small and very, very weak when compared to you. Omnipotent means that there is nothing and no one like you. The resurrection is a finger that points to the omnipotence of God. The power to resurrect separates God from us and everything else. Only Almighty God has the power to bring life out of what was once dead.

We find many demonstrations of the power of God in Scripture, but so often they fall short of displaying for us the full extent of the power of God's power. The closest we have to being confronted with and comforted by the power of God's power is the ability to create and the ability to resurrect. Creation and the resurrection both draw the uncrossable line between the creature and the Creator. He creates, he resurrects, he is omnipotent—behold your God! You are his child by grace. He unleashes his power for your good. Yes, you will hit the wall of your own powerlessness, but your Lord has no such wall. There is hope for the powerless, because, in tenderness, God meets your weakness with his strength.

10

God's Omnipotence in Everyday Life

DEBBIE NEVER THOUGHT parenting would be this hard. It was exhausting and discouraging. It seemed like somehow every day she was confronted with her inability to get her children to desire to do what was right. She had read all the best Christian parenting books, but she still struggled with her powerlessness. At times it was a burden that was almost too hard for her to bear.

Tim was a business wiz; he was successful and accomplished, but he was frustrated. The more he developed his businesses, the more he felt like his work was negatively affected by forces over which he had no control. Whether it was the decisions of politicians, a downturn in the economy, or a weather event, Tim was always dealing with messes he didn't make. With all his success, Tim still had moments when he felt powerless.

Ron accepted the call to be the pastor of a church that had existed for over a hundred years. The glory days were over and revitalization was needed. Ron was excited at the thought of this church being a bright gospel light in its community once again. But it didn't take long for him to hit the wall of people's deeply held thoughts and attitudes about their church. Never in his ministry had Ron felt such resistance. He had never seen so many people walk away from a ministry he led. He knew the vision he was holding out was right, and he knew he had communicated it well, but he had no ability to reach inside of people and change their hearts and minds. As a pastor, Ron felt more powerless than he ever had before.

Between the "already" and the "not yet," in this sin-marred world, powerlessness is a universal human experience. Some experience it as physical weakness, others as relational dysfunction. Some are keenly aware of cultural chaos, while others feel most powerless in parenting or marriage. We feel powerless in the workplace, in church life, or with friends and extended family. Some experience it when attempting to deal with the past, while others fear the future. Somehow all of us long for change we can't create or for control that we will never have. All of us have things that make us sad and that we cannot alter, and all of us feel called to do things that seem beyond our individual ability to do.

It is therefore vital for all of us to understand the comfort and calling that is to be found when we apply the truth of God's boundless power to the situations, relationships, and locations of our daily lives. What follows is not an exhaustive list, but these seven truths will help you begin to understand the helpfulness of living in light of God's omnipotence.

1. We are all tempted to doubt the power of God. Whether it's supplying our material needs, working in the hearts of our children, rescuing our marriages, protecting us from temptation's seduction, keeping church leaders spiritually healthy, or providing opportunities to have hard but much-needed conversations, we all struggle at times to entrust our needs to the care of our Almighty Lord. Now, let me make it clear here that trust in the power of God is not passive. We do not sit around waiting for God to intervene. Believing that God is always active, unleashing his omnipotent power for the sake and good of his children, results in stepping out in courage and hope into situations you would otherwise have been paralyzed by or avoided. You are not alone in this struggle.

Sarah and Abraham had staked their entire life on one single promise of God: they would have a son, and through him all the nations of the earth would be blessed. But now they were both old, and Sarah was decades beyond her childbearing years. The thought of God's promise still coming true made her laugh. So God said to Abraham, "Why did Sarah laugh and say, 'Shall I indeed bear a child, now that I am old?' Is anything too hard for the LORD?" (Gen. 18:13–14). Sarah's problem was not what she thought about her own power, but what she failed to believe about the power of God and how he exerted it for his covenant children.

After generation upon generation of slavery, God heard the cries of his children in Egypt and was coming to deliver. He sent Moses to communicate God's promise of freedom from captivity to the Israelites. You would think they would have been filled with joy, but they weren't. "Moses spoke thus to the people of Israel, but they did not listen to Moses, because of their broken spirit and harsh slavery" (Ex. 6:9). Two things were in the way of Israel having hope in the power of God. First was their situation. They had been in slavery so long and it had been so hard; they had given up hope that things could ever be different for them. Second was their hearts. When Scripture says that their spirits were broken, it means that they were so deeply discouraged that they were unable to muster up even the faintest of hopes. Some of you have been in difficult situations for so long that you've let go of any hope that things can or will change. Some of you have broken spirits. You're so discouraged that you can't even muster up the words to pray anymore. I plead with you to keep reading. Resist letting your theology become a meaningless abstraction. Fight letting the hardships of life in this fallen world crush your heart and its ability to have hope. God hears your cries. He knew what your address would be, and he has made the most amazing provision for you. Keep reading.

It is one thing to believe in the almighty power of God, but it is another thing to live out your belief in the situations, relationships, and locations of your daily life. If you fail to trust in the exercise of God's almighty power on your behalf, you will avoid dealing with things that you assess are outside of the range of your personal power. Or you will try to do things that you do not have the power to do. When it comes to the power of God, Scripture has wonderfully encouraging things to say to all of God's children. Being a child of God means you are no longer left to the limited resources of your own power. No matter what you're facing, here is what you need to remember: God acts in power on your behalf and gifts you with power that is divine. Consider these encouraging words from the apostle Paul:

> . . . and what is the immeasurable greatness of his power toward us who believe, according to the working of his great might that he worked in Christ when he raised him from the dead and seated him at his right hand in the heavenly places, far above all rule and authority and power and dominion, and above every name that is named, not only in this age but also in the one to come. And he put all things under his feet and gave him as head over all things to the church, which is his body, the fullness of him who fills all in all. (Eph. 1:19–23)

Ephesians 1:15–23 is a prayer that believers would know the hope into which they have been saved. We all hook ourselves to some kind of hope. Some of us are struggling because we've hoped in the wrong things and some of us have practically given up hope altogether. Paul knows that the people to whom he is writing would struggle as we do. So Paul prays that the believers in the Ephesian church would understand the tremendous hope that is now theirs as the children of God. I too think so many of us live in the throes of discouragement and anxiety. If you look around and listen carefully, you will see that many of us have a hope problem.

So what is this hope for which Paul prays, and does it have any practical application to the hard and discouraging things we face in our daily lives? *The hope of every believer is resurrection power right here, right now.* The same power by which life was breathed into Christ's dead body is now yours as his child. Paul wants you to know that God's power is not some abstract theological thing; it is your hope right now, no matter who you are and what you are facing. Yes, you, the one reading right now, have been blessed right here, right now with the same power that raised Christ from the dead. It is ultimate power, bigger than anything you face inside or outside of you.

You don't have the power to make your children want to do what is right, but God does. You don't have the power to change your boss, but God does. You don't have the power to work up courage in your defeated heart, but God does. You don't have the power to bring sweet peace into your marriage, but God does. You don't have the power to reconcile that relationship, but God does. And if you believe he is with you, for you, and in you in power, then you will live with hope and act with courage in those places where you have tended to give up hope and where you've quit trying.

Paul also wants you to know that God not only gifts you with his power, but he also rules in power on your behalf. He exercises his almighty power to rule what you cannot rule, so that you would have everything that you need. When you lack power, it does not mean that you are powerless, because God never lacks power and he never forsakes his commitment to unleash the power of his presence and rule on your behalf. You may feel weak, but God's resolve to exercise his power so that you have what you need in the situations of your daily life never weakens.

Where have you been tempted to give up? Where have you quit doing the good things that God calls you to do because they just don't seem to make a difference? Where have you let your weakness shape your responses to life more than the resurrection power that is yours right now as a child of God?

2. It is vital that the power of God become a key way you interpret your world and your identity as his child. We are all under an influence that is virtually impossible to escape. This influence is present in everything you binge-watch on your favorite streaming service. It is at your children's public school or the secular university you attend. It is present in the back-and-forth on Twitter. It is behind the worldview of hundreds and hundreds of the politicians who make decisions that shape our lives. This influence is the view of life held by most of the leaders of the industrial and corporate worlds. If you have a cell phone, iPad, or laptop, it is pumped at you multiple times every day. And this influence is an absolute denial of everything this book and this chapter are about.

What is this inescapably influential thing I am talking about? The answer is *scientific naturalism*. Remember, one of the themes of this book is that you are always interpreting, always making sense of what has happened and is happening all around you. The sense that you make then shapes your decisions and actions. You are also assigning to yourself some kind of identity. Your sense of identity then shapes the way you act, react, and respond. This is why it is so important to be aware that a biblical worldview, which has an omnipotent God at the center of all things, ruling in power and glory, is absent in the conversation of the culture that beams into your home and into your heart every day.

We must also realize that the biblical worldview is not just absent, but it has been replaced by a polar opposite way of making sense out of life. The view of life that dominates today says that everything in life has a scientific or natural explanation. This is the view of life that public schools teach our children from the earliest grades. Scientific naturalism underlies what students at secular or state universities are taught, no matter what one's major is. If you take a couple hours each night to relax and watch the latest popular comedy, drama, documentary, or reality series, scientific naturalism is the life view of the vast majority of people who write, direct, and produce what you are consuming.

According to Psalm 14, this view is not just an alternative; it is utter and complete foolishness. A fool sees the world upside down and inside out. A fool prides himself in what he understands, while he fails to recognize that he has ignored the most important thing to understand. A fool claims to be rational, while he denies reality. Foolishness will never lead you anywhere good. Foolishness will never produce good things in your life. Foolishness is not only destructive, but it ultimately leads to death. We should fear listening to the voices of fools. Note what the apostle Paul says in 1 Corinthians 1:

> For the word of the cross is folly to those who are perishing, but to us who are being saved it is the power of God. For it is written,
>
> "I will destroy the wisdom of the wise,
> and the discernment of the discerning I will thwart."
>
> Where is the one who is wise? Where is the scribe? Where is the debater of this age? Has not God made foolish the wisdom of the world? For since, in the wisdom of God, the world did not know God through wisdom, it pleased God through the folly of what we preach to save those who believe. For Jews demand signs and Greeks seek wisdom, but we preach Christ crucified, a stumbling block to Jews and folly to Gentiles, but to those who are called, both Jews and Greeks, Christ the power of God and the wisdom of God. For the foolishness of God is wiser than men, and the weakness of God is stronger than men. (1 Cor. 1:18–25)

This passage warns us to constantly ask, "Whose 'wisdom' am I listening to?" At street level, who or what shapes the way you think about life? The Bible declares that your hope in life and death is the power of God. He rules in power on your behalf, and he gifts you with power as his child. Any other way of making sense out of your world and who you are is not only wrong, but it is foolish. All of us should be concerned about the profound influence of scientific naturalism on us, but we should particularly be concerned for our children. We need to raise little theological thinkers, who learn early to interpret who they are and where they live from the perspective of a world ruled by an omnipotent God. Few gifts we could give our children are more important than this. Wouldn't it be sad for our children to be raised in Christian homes, but to grow up to think and live as fools, denying the ultimate fact of facts, the power and glory of God?

3. We all need to understand the power of God for our everyday living. I will keep saying this throughout this book: theology is not just something you think, but it is more importantly a way that you live. Belief and disbelief always become a lifestyle, a result that occurs either self-consciously and intentionally or unwittingly and unawares. Your life is always a portrait of some kind of faith. The way you live is always an expression of some kind of hope. You and I are always hooking our lives to some kind of redeemer. So it is with the power of God. This truth not only defines the expansive glory of God, but it also redefines both your identity and potential as a child of God.

To be a Christian means you are the child of this omnipotent one. It means his power is not just an expression of who he is, but now, by grace, is a gift to you as his child. In your job, you probably noticed that it is nearly impossible for you to love each and every one of your coworkers. For some reason, someone at your job irritates you and pulls out of you more disrespect than love. If you have an extended family, you know that it is hard to have long-term family peace. Often holidays or reunions result in more hurt and divisions than deeper unity and love. If you're elderly, you know it is hard to be happy, thankful, and content as you deal with the loneliness, physical weakness, and hardships of old age.

If you are a mom or dad, you know it is hard to be consistently patient, kind, gentle, sympathetic, loving, and gracious as you exercise your God-given authority in the lives of your children. If you're married, you know there are days when it is hard to love your spouse with self-sacrificing, forgiving, and patient love. If you are in college, it is hard and costly to stand for your faith in a place where it is not esteemed. It is hard to steward your money well. It is hard to keep your heart sexually pure in a culture that is growingly pornographized. In the busyness and tiredness of modern life, it's hard to be faithful in personal Bible reading, prayer, and worship.

It is not enough to say that life between the "already" of your conversion and the "not yet" of your homegoing is hard. Here's what we need to understand and be willing to confess: the Christian life is impossible. It is impossible for me, left to myself, to live as God has called me to live. It is impossible to love as I have been called to love. It is impossible to forgive as I have been called to forgive. It is impossible to serve as I have been called to serve. It is impossible for me to guard my mind and rein in my desires. It is impossible for me to control my tongue or harness my wandering eyes. If left to myself, all of these things are impossible for me, but the glorious message of the gospel is that I haven't been left to myself.

Read the next sentence carefully; it is a picture of how amazing God's grace really is. *God meets our weakness with his power.* If you really believe that, not only will you have hope but you will also change the way you think about and deal with the hard places in your life. God doesn't save us, accept us into his family, and then leave us to our own resources to be "holy as he is holy" on our own. In fact, because of his grace, our weakness isn't a curse, but it becomes the doorway to greater power and potential than we have ever known. This is why Paul says, "For God gave us a spirit not of fear but of power and love and self-control" (2 Tim. 1:7) and, "Now to him who is able to do far more abundantly than all we ask or think, according to the power at work within us" (Eph. 3:20). The exact words here are very important. The power of this omnipotent one, power that is unique and unlimited, is now *at work* within the heart of every single one of his children.

Here is a definition of right-here, right-now grace. Your Almighty Father's power is at work even when you are tired, discouraged, hopeless, and about to give in or give up. The rescuing, protecting, and providing power of your Savior is never passive or idle and it never sleeps on the job. It never gives up.

Now, if you really do believe this, you quit being ruled by anxiety and worry, you quit living in fear, and you refuse to give up hope. If you really do believe that the omnipotent power of your Lord is at work in you, then you step into those hard places that you would have once avoided, you determine to love, you commit yourself to forgive, and you get up and do it all again the next day. You do this not because you think you have power, but because your Redeemer has power beyond your ability to calculate. You will no longer be imprisoned by your weakness but freed by it to tap into the greatest resource of power the universe has ever known.

When you step out in weakness and trust God's power, you unite with generations of God's children. The characters in your Bible are not a hall of fame of the strong. No, every man and woman in Scripture, even those who accomplished great things, was like you, a package of weaknesses, held together and enabled by the grace of the gift of God's power. Where in your life do you need to confess weakness and believe in the power of God that is at work in you? Where do you need to step out with renewed commitment, courage, and hope?

4. We all need to abandon our delusions of autonomy and self-sufficiency. Let's return to the garden of Eden and that world-changing conversation Adam and Eve had with the serpent. We tend to miss something as we think about this horrible moment of deception and temptation. Embedded in the serpent's seduction are two lies that everyone tends to believe at some time, in some place, and in some way. Note the essential piece of the serpent's temptation and Eve's response:

> But the serpent said to the woman, "You will not surely die. For God knows that when you eat of it your eyes will be opened, and *you will be like God*, knowing good and evil." So when the woman saw that the tree was good for food, and that it was a delight to the eyes, and that *the tree was to be desired to make one wise*. . . . (Gen. 3:4–6)

Do you see the bait the serpent holds out before Adam and Eve? "You will be like God" and "the tree was desired to make one wise." These two lies still seduce us today. Embedded in the temptation of the serpent were the lies of *autonomy* and *self-sufficiency*. God is the only autonomous and self-sufficient being in the universe. Autonomy says that you are an independent being with the right to do with your life whatever you want to do.

The lie of autonomy is what makes parenting hard. This lie is what causes your children to fight your authority; they do not want someone else telling them what to do. The lie of autonomy is also what makes you think you can exercise your parental authority however you want. The lie of autonomy makes it hard for you to be thankful at work for a boss that tells you what to do and how to do it. All struggles with authority are rooted in this lie and, as long as sin still lives in us, there will be moments when we are tempted to give in to it.

The lie of self-sufficiency says that you have everything in yourself to be what you are supposed to be and to do what you have been designed to do. Eve ate the fruit that was "desirable to make her wise." She was after independent wisdom, that is, wisdom that doesn't need to rely on God. This lie is at the root of our struggle to ask for directions, to esteem guidance, to seek counsel, and to submit to instruction. The theology of the omnipotence of God is so helpful here.

God over and over again reveals to us that he is almighty in power precisely because we are not. We were never created to be independent. Even in a perfect world and in a perfect relationship with God, Adam and Eve were dependent on him. They did not have either the power of independent wisdom or of independent strength. Sin added a whole catalog of weaknesses of heart, mind, and body to the natural dependence of human beings. The limits of those made in God's image were designed to drive them to him in thankful dependency and joyful submission.

Adam and Eve did not have the independent power to know how to live nor did they have the power to live as God revealed that they should, apart from God's help.

No one but God is autonomous and self-sufficient. To think and act otherwise never results in good in your life. This means that the move of God's grace in your life is not from dependence to independence, but from independence to dependence. As you grow in grace, becoming more spiritually mature, your eyes open to more of your weaknesses and you become more and more thankful for and reliant upon the grace of God's power that is at work within you. Because you are more willingly and self-consciously dependent on God, you then quit taking credit for things you could never have done or produced on your own. The gospel of human weakness and divine power doesn't produce achievement-proud Christians. It produces people who are not only humble themselves, but who are also gentle and patient with the people around them who share their weaknesses.

Acknowledgement of weakness will produce in you a greater reliance on God; a greater reliance on God will produce an enhanced awareness of his help; and a greater awareness of his help will produce a lifestyle of humble gratitude. Boisterous, proud, self-congratulatory, overly self-confident Christianity is simply not what the gospel of human weakness and divine power produces. It is a false gospel that deceives those who preach it and discourages those who listen. A mature Christian is confident in weakness.

Here is the hope of a mature believer: "He gives power to the faint / and to him who has no might he increases strength" (Isa. 40:29). No matter what mask it wears, the gospel of self-reliance is not the gospel of the grace of the Lord Jesus Christ.

5. Our problem is with the limits of our faith, not with God's power. Our problem is never the extent of the power of God or the willingness of God to exercise that power for our good. Our problem is that we experience moments in life when we seem to lose our theological minds; we seem to forget who God is and then lose sight of who we are as his children. When we do this, the problems of life loom even larger and our estimation of our potential to deal with them shrinks. You are never in a situation that is bigger than the extent of God's power, and there is never a moment when his power for you and within you is inactive. Yet, we do fall into moments of amnesia. We forget who God is, we forget what it means to rest in him by faith, and we lose motivation, hope, and courage. In these moments when we are discouraged and feel small and unable, the power of God and his willingness to exert his power on our behalf is not our problem. Our problem is the limits of *our* ability or willingness to rest in that power in a way that transforms the way we live.

The Old Testament provides a provocative example of what we're talking about. In 1 Samuel 17 we find the army of Israel in the valley of Elah, facing the Philistine army. The Israelite army is the army of Almighty God. No human army has the power to defeat God. He had promised that he would deliver these pagan nations into the hands of his children so they could take possession of the land he had promised to them. They have every reason for hope and courage as they prepare for battle.

On the first day of battle the giant warrior Goliath taunts the Israelite soldiers. They see the size of this Philistine soldier and his weapons, hear the thunder of his voice, and immediately retreat in fear to their tents. They do this for forty days. Forty days! There is something dramatically wrong with their reaction. The drama of the moment is not a drama of normal human power against giant human power. No, the drama is about this weak and limited giant against the omnipotent power of God. There is no question as to who will win. You simply can't know who God is and who you are as his child and retreat into your tent in fear for forty days. Faith in the power of God, who is with and for Israel, won't produce that response.

David shows up on the scene to deliver provisions to his brothers. He assesses the scene and essentially says, "I'll go fight that giant warrior." Is he crazy? Is he delusionally arrogant? Does he not fully understand the threat? No, David tells us what motivates his courage and willingness. He says, "The Lord who delivered me from the paw of the lion and from the paw of the bear will deliver me from the hand of this Philistine" (1 Sam. 17:37). David is saying that, as a shepherd, he saw the power of God in action. He had experienced being able to do what he normally would not have had the power to do because the Lord Almighty was with him and for him.

So David walks into that valley with no armor and only a slingshot and a few stones. He does what he would never have had the courage to do were it not for his faith that God will unleash his power for the protection and provision of his people. He knows that the equation is not the puny, untrained shepherd, who lacks the weapons of warfare, against the mighty weapons of this huge and mighty warrior. David knows his God of omnipotent power will go with him into that valley. So he walks forward with confidence and courage and, in the power of God, defeats the giant and routs the Philistine army.

Any soldier in the army of Israel could have done what David did. He had no greater power, skill, or weaponry than the other soldiers. What separated David was his faith in God, the one whom all of the soldiers, hiding in the tents, would have said they believed in too.

Life in this fallen world is hard. Unexpected, unwanted, difficult, and painful things will enter your door. You will find yourself caught up and concerned about things that are far beyond your power, authority, and control. In these moments it is vital to hear the welcome of your theology. These occasions are invitations to look at your life and the difficult things you face not through the lens of your power and ability but through the lens of the presence and omnipotence of your Lord. His power is at work for you and in you, and he will not forsake that work until you are in that place where these trials are no more.

We need to look at our jobs through the lens of the power of God. We need to look at our marriages, families, and friendships through the lens of the power of God. We need to look at every aspect of our life—the difficulties, responsibilities, and opportunities—through the lens of the power of God. While we work to make good choices, we need to entrust our spiritual, physical, and mental health to the power of God. God has promised to exert his power so that we have everything we need. When it comes to the power of God, do we live like we believe what we say we believe?

6. You and I will not always be happy with the way God exercises his power. Our problem is not just whether we will believe that God will exercise his power for our good, but whether we will like it when he does. One of the struggles of God's people has always been doubting God's goodness because of the way that he chooses to exercise his power. This is a struggle for me, and I'm sure it is for you too. God is always exercising his power, yet we are often discontent with what he does or does not do. There are times when God's exercise of his power for our good doesn't look good to us at all. In power, God will lead us down hard pathways, not because he is angry with us but because he loves us and the hard pathway is a tool of his redeeming grace. I think that often when we feel disappointed and overwhelmed it is not because God isn't working, but rather because he isn't exerting his power toward us in the way we wish he would.

Numbers 11 chronicles for us a pointed illustration of how we may struggle with the way God exercises the power he has promised to unleash for our benefit. The children of Israel are on their forty-year journey from Egypt to the Promised Land. Because they are nomads, they can't plant crops and raise cattle like they would if they stayed in one place. So God, because he loves them and has taken them to be his children, exerts his power to feed them. This situation is one of the most beautiful pictures of God's unleashing his almighty power to provide for the needs of his children in all of Scripture. He literally causes edible material to fall like dew every morning, so the Israelites could collect it, bake it into cakes, and have their hunger satisfied. This is such a wonderful picture of God's covenant love that Jesus takes "manna" as his name. He is the bread, come down from heaven, to give life to his people.

But here is how God's children respond to this loving exercise of God's omnipotent power:

> Now the rabble that was among them had a strong craving. And the people of Israel also wept again and said, "Oh that we had meat to eat! We remember the fish we ate in Egypt that cost nothing, the cucumbers, the melons, the leeks, the onions, and the garlic. But now our strength is dried up, and there is nothing at all but this manna to look at."
>
> Now the manna was like coriander seed, and its appearance like that of bdellium. The people went about and gathered it and ground it in handmills or beat it in mortars and boiled it in pots and made cakes of it. And the taste of it was like the taste of cakes baked with oil. When the dew fell upon the camp in the night, the manna fell with it. (Num. 11:4–9)

Manna didn't provide the most exciting cuisine. It obviously didn't have much taste, because we're told that when the cakes were baked, they tasted like the oil they were baked with. But this boring food was the result of a magnificent exercise of God's limitless power for the purpose of providing for the physical needs of his children. But the people of Israel weren't thankful. They didn't like the menu that God in his power had provided, so they cried and complained. But they did something else that you need to notice.

Because they were dissatisfied with how God exercised his power to provide, they began to dream of being back in Egypt, where they had fruit, vegetables, and spices. In our dissatisfaction with God, our memory can be scarily selective. If you listen to the description of the complaining rabble, Egypt sounds more like a great grocery store than it does a place of toil, suffering, slavery, and death. Discontent distorts your vision, causes you to question how God has exercised his power on your behalf, and tempts you to crave what you should not crave, while rejecting what should cause you to be grateful.

I wish I could say that I am always happy with the way God exercises his power in my life. I wish I could say that I speak only words of gratitude and never words of complaint. I wish I could say that I have never questioned the wisdom or the love behind God's exercise of his power in my life. I, too, go through moments of discontent, and when I do, I am tempted to look elsewhere for satisfaction. The drama of our lives is not about the power of God or his willingness to exert it for our rescue, provision, protection, and transformation. No, the daily spiritual drama is about whether we will respond with gratitude or complaint when we experience what his power provides for us and where his power leads us. God's people have not always been content with how he chooses to exert his power. What about you?

7. God's power is essential to his fathering care for us. The minute our children came into the world and into our family, I lived with a new sense of purpose. Parenting didn't seem burdensome to me. Suddenly there was something high on my list of values that motivated me more than most of the things in my life. It kept me working hard. It shaped the way I invested my money, my energy, my gifts, and my time. It was in the back of my mind from the moment I awoke until I went to sleep. Not infrequently, it was the thing that interrupted my sleep. My children knew I loved them, but they didn't understand how much. They surely didn't know how much this one thing occupied my heart and motivated me.

The moment my children entered our family, I determined to exert whatever power I had as their father to protect and provide for them. My power was not unique as a dad and it surely wasn't unlimited, but whatever I had, I was committed to use for their present benefit and their lasting good. Yes, I looked for every way to communicate to them that I loved them each with all of my heart, but one of the ways I lived out that love was to use whatever power I had to keep them safe and provide for their everyday needs.

One of the most encouraging ways God identifies himself in his word and defines our relationship to him is by saying this amazing thing: "I am your Father." The Lord of heaven and earth is my Father by grace. The one who sits on the throne of the universe with almighty power is my Father, and I am his child. It seems impossible, too good to be true. Grace birthed me into his family and, because it did, it unleashed his fatherly care. Here's what I want you to understand. One of the best ways to understand the glory of God's fatherly care for his children is seeing that he exerts his power to protect us and to provide for us. Listen to the words of Psalm 103:13. If you believe them, if you embrace them, and if you live inside of them, they will change you and the way you think about everything in your life.

> As a father shows compassion to his children,
> so the LORD shows compassion to those who fear him.
> (Ps. 103:13)

The Hebrew word for compassion here is specific and evocative. *Racham* is a tender, intimate, and loving familial term. The psalmist could have used a variety of other words for compassion, but he chose this one for a reason. *Racham* is related to the Hebrew word for *womb*. It is the unique kind of compassion a mother would have for a child she carried in her own womb. It is used to capture the kind of intimate, sturdy, active love parents have for their children that they have for no one else. It is why a mom or dad gets up early in the morning and stays up late at night, day after day, for the welfare of their children. It is what motivates all of a parent's care, from changing diapers to difficult talks with a teenager and all the self-sacrificing things they do in between. We see *racham* in the unique expression on a mother's face as she looks at her nursing child or in the tenderness of a father as he comforts and defends his son who has been bullied at school. The word *racham* captures the love that motivates every act of parental provision, sympathy, and protection.

It is this lovely word that the psalmist uses to say to you, "This is how your heavenly Father loves you." As God's child, by grace, *racham* is behind God's exercise of his power toward you, for you, and within you. You are precious to him. He is committed to meeting every one of your needs. He exercises his power with parental sympathy, tenderness, and forgiveness. His power is exercised toward you with inexhaustible parental affection. Your heavenly Father loves you, and his power is an instrument of that love.

So whether you are a parent, student, worker, boss, pastor, politician, educator, man, or woman—elderly, young, single, or married—no matter what you are facing or how you are feeling, no matter where you are, if you are God's child, you are never powerless or unloved. *The fatherhood of God is where boundless love meets unlimited power.* The result is never-ending provision, care, and protection. Now, that is a reason to have hope, to refuse to give up, and to continue to do those good things God has called you to do. Your heavenly Father loves you and unleashes his power for your good. The hymn "Children of the Heavenly Father" says it best:

Children of the heav'nly Father
safely in his bosom gather;
nestling bird nor star in heaven
such a refuge e'er was given.

God his own doth tend and nourish,
in his holy courts they flourish;

from all evil things he spares them,
in his mighty arms he bears them.

Neither life nor death shall ever
from the Lord his children sever;
unto them his grace he showeth,
and their sorrows all he knoweth.

Though he giveth or he taketh,
God his children ne'er forsaketh;
his the loving purpose solely
to preserve them pure and holy.[1]

I find the following words by the apostle Paul comforting and hope giving. They remind me that I am not alone in my struggle, but I am met there and loved there by an omnipotent Redeemer.

> So to keep me from becoming conceited because of the surpassing greatness of the revelations, a thorn was given me in the flesh, a messenger of Satan to harass me, to keep me from becoming conceited. Three times I pleaded with the Lord about this, that it should leave me. But he said to me, "My grace is sufficient for you, for my power is made perfect in weakness." Therefore I will boast all the more gladly about my weaknesses, so that the power of Christ may rest upon me. For the sake of Christ, then, I am content with weaknesses, insults, hardships, persecutions, and calamities. For when I am weak, then I am strong. (2 Cor. 12:7–10)

It is a sweet thing to be liberated from the fear of weakness. It is wonderful to be freed from the burden of acting strong. It is a gift to be freed from being overwhelmed each time you face something bigger than your ability or stronger than your strength. It's freeing to know that

1 Carolina V. Sandell Berg, "Children of the Heavenly Father," 1858, trans. Ernst W. Olson 1925 in *Trinity Hymnal* (Suwanee, GA: Great Commission Publications, 1990), no. 131.

weakness is not a curse, but rather the very thing God uses to produce true strength in us. True strength does not come from building bigger muscles and exerting more effort. True strength comes when you are no longer afraid of confessing your inability. True strength does not feign power and hide weakness. The admission of weakness is the doorway to true strength. It is when I quit denying weakness that I begin relying on one of the sweetest gifts of God's grace, his power at work within me.

Here's where the theology of the omnipotence of God should lead you. In response to the weakness, which none of us can honestly deny, what God gives us is *himself*. He is what we need. He comes to us to dwell inside of us and to unleash his power in the places where we are weak and unable. The truth of God's creation/resurrection power is not an abstract impersonal thing. It is your daily hope. Resurrection power is yours right now.

Your potential is not restricted by your weakness, because it's no longer you (alone) who lives, but Christ lives (in almighty power) in you (Gal. 2:20).

Your salvation is not just about past forgiveness and future hope, but it's also about a new identity and new potential right now. Every piece of the theology we are considering not only helps you to know and understand God, but it also defines who you are and what is yours as a child of God. Here's who you are: you are the son or daughter of the most powerful being in the universe. He is your Father, and he exercises his power with fatherly affection and care. Here is your potential: the power of your omnipotent Father is now at work within you. You are not left alone on the stage of your own little drama. You are not left to your little bag of resources. The omnipotent one has come near, he has adopted you as his own, he exerts his power for your good, and he blesses you with power from within. Like every other piece of divine theology, the doctrine of the omnipotence of God preaches amazing grace to us.

God is omnipotent.
He is our Father.
His power is ours by grace.
We have hope.

11

The Doctrine of Creation

IT PLEASED GOD the Father, Son, and Holy Spirit, in the beginning to make from nothing every visible or invisible thing that exists and to declare that all he had made was very good. He did this so his eternal power, wisdom, and goodness would be on constant display for all to see.[1]

Understanding the Doctrine of Creation

It is impossible, in a sentence, paragraph, chapter, or even a whole book, to do justice to the once-in-the-history-of-the-universe wonder of the creation of the world and everything in it. You and I have to work hard to make anything. Even when you buy a piece of furniture from Ikea, with all the pieces properly designed and a booklet of instructions, you are driven to the edge of your sanity trying to follow the instructions and assemble something that represents what you thought you bought. All of our DIY projects require mental focus, physical dexterity, and perseverance. We struggle to make things, even though we always start with raw materials, are following instructions, and have collected the

1 Author's paraphrase of the doctrine of creation as found in the Westminster Confession of Faith, chap. 4.1.

appropriate tools. But you and I have never *created* anything; we do not make something out of nothing. C. S. Lewis said it this way: "This act [creation], as it is for God, must always remain totally inconceivable to man. For we—even our poets and musicians and inventors—never, in the ultimate sense make. We only build. We always have materials to build from."[2]

The truth of creation should stop us in our tracks, fill us with awe and wonder, humble us, and drop us to our knees. God, with nothing more than his will and his word—literally, no exaggeration here—spoke the universe into existence. Think of huge galaxies and little ants. Think of flowing bodies of water and hardened shafts of granite. Think of the body of an elephant and the translucent creatures that swim in the deepest trenches of the sea. Think of huge towering trees and microscopic organisms. Think of the technology of the human eye and the intricate design of your hand. Think of sound waves and chemical reactions. Don't read Genesis 1 and 2 in some kind of mental monotone. Don't let the astonishing glory of what is being described elude you. Genesis 1 and 2 are meant to take your breath away, and if they don't, you haven't handled them properly. Genesis 1 and 2 are meant to put you in your place and insert God in his proper place in your heart and life. There is nothing abstract, impersonal, or distant from your life in the words "In the beginning, God created the heavens and the earth." These words define and explain everything. They give you identity and dignity. These words define the meaning and purpose of life. Here in Genesis 1 and 2 is your introduction to everything. The biblical narrative begins with God on center stage doing something that is so mind-bending, we will spend the rest of eternity unpacking it and trying to fully absorb its expansive glory.

To say that God created this universe and everything in it is simply to say that God is God. He has no rivals. No one and nothing compares to him. No one can lay claim to his power and authority. No one has a mind

2 C. S. Lewis, *Letters to Malcolm: Chiefly on Prayer* (1963; New York: HarperOne, 2017), 97.

that can contain this kind of wisdom and knowledge. And if someone were able to think up creating a world, he would completely lack the power to do what he conceived. Genesis 1 and 2 is the game changer. If God created the world, then everything is defined by that reality and he is worthy of our constant awe, submission, and obedience.

But most of us have a problem. I am afraid the doctrine of creation has become so familiar to us that it no longer moves us in the way it should and once did. Familiarity with any aspect of God's truth is a wonderful thing. It means that grace has met us and opened our hearts and minds to truths that God uses to rescue, redeem, and transform us. But it's important to understand that familiarity with biblical truth can also be a dangerous thing. When we bump across something with which we are familiar, our minds tend to quit thinking, our eyes tend to quit looking, and our hearts stop responding. It is sad when considering something like the doctrine of creation becomes just an intellectual exercise and no longer fills our minds with wonder and our hearts with worship. How is it possible to watch the hands of God at work, forming the world and putting things in place, yet pass on by unnoticing and unmoved? Here is the center of your reality, the focus of your spirituality, and the essence of your humanity. There could be nothing more important than what is written in Genesis 1 and 2. Minimizing its significance and wonder is the seedbed of all kinds of idolatries. Properly understood, what is written in these two chapters will lead you to God, to yourself, and ultimately to the cross of the Son.

Open your eyes and your heart to the glory that is everywhere around you. Every glorious created thing is designed by God to be a finger that points to his glory. We need to pray for grace that we would always see the glorious one who is behind the glorious physical thing we are seeing, hearing, tasting, or touching. How can we boil water, mash potatoes, or scramble eggs without seeing the glory of God? How can we hold an infant in our hands without being in awe of her Creator? How can the ever-changing variegated hues of a sunset not produce awe of God in us? How can tadpoles in a stream not make us smile in worship? How can the whistle of wind through the trees not become a hymn of praise in our hearts to God? If we can look around at the glory display that is available to us every day yet not see God, we are profoundly disadvantaged human beings in desperate need of the eye-opening, heart-enlivening rescue of God's grace.

If you are a Christian, this is the epicenter of everything you say you believe. If God did not create this world and everything in it, then every piece of biblical theology and history comes crashing down. Then God is not God, the world is not what he has said it is, you are not who he has said you were, and everything you thought was true is now something else. If God is not what he has said he is, then what about his law, what about his promises, what about his gospel, what about the hope of eternity, and what about the trustworthiness of his grace? The doctrine of creation is foundational; remove it, and the whole house of the Bible's theology comes crashing down. And if it does, you don't know who God is, who you are, what the world is, or what life is about. You are lost in a universe that has no center. Irrational, impersonal forces interact with one another and with you. There is no such thing as meaning and purpose, good or bad, moral or immoral.

Good biblical theology is creational theology. It's a theology that puts God at the beginning and in the center. It's a theology that is driven more by awe and worship than it is by the organizing of truths. "In the beginning, God created the heavens and the earth" shapes our posture as we handle all of the other truths that unfold in the biblical narrative. Creational theology is humble theology; we are handling God's things, and we do it in worship, amazed at the grace that allows us to handle what is sacred.

Genesis 1 and 2 are not intended to be a scientific description of the process of creation. It is clear that we do not have a detailed description of everything that happened as God was creating his world and putting everything in its place. Genesis 1 and 2 do record for us foundational historical facts, but in a way that is selective and poetic. Consider that there isn't just one record of creation; there are two. Genesis 1 puts God at the center of the creation of this huge cosmos. Genesis 2 presents God as the Creator of Adam and Eve, unique in all of creation because these two beings bear God's image. Rather than being a piece of detailed scientific literature, Genesis 1 and 2 contain brief and fuzzy details. Genesis 1 and 2 are more theological in style than scientific. They introduce you to the centrality, power, and authority of God over creation, and they introduce you to the nature and purpose of human beings made in his image. God designed Genesis 1 and 2 to put the reader's focus not on the process, but rather on him. Both chapters are meant to ignite Godwardness in everything we think about life, our world, and ourselves. In Genesis 1 and 2, God defines reality this way: he puts himself in the center of everything, and he places us in a unique connection to him. Everything we understand about life is meant to begin here.

So what are we meant to take away from the doctrine of creation? What is the deeper meaning of this breathtaking piece of Christian theology?

Purpose

I am a painter by avocation. I have painted for decades. I have an art studio a few blocks from my house, and I labor there on a body of work until it's ready for a gallery exhibition. I paint in a certain style and always with a purpose. I never begin a painting and say to myself, "I sure hope this turns into something beautiful." Before I start, I have a vision in mind of what I want the final product to be. So with that in mind, I lay out the steps of the process and gather the paints, chemicals, and tools that I will need to realize my vision. I want to create something beautiful that helps you to see something in a new way and that you would want to purchase and display where you live or work. Making always includes purpose.

God, the ultimate artist, designed everything he made with a purpose in mind. Each thing is carefully designed for the purpose for which God intended. So God designed human beings with a purpose in mind. He knew what he wanted us to be, he knew how he wanted us to live, he knew what he wanted us to do, he knew how he wanted us to relate to one another and to him, and he knew how he wanted us to interact with the rest of creation. This means that the ultimate goal of our lives is not working so that we will one day finally experience our definition of happiness. The goal isn't making sure everyone loves us. The purpose of your life is not material achievement, success, and affluence. The ultimate purpose is not acquiring power and control. It's not being fit and beautiful. It's not public acclaim. It's not finally loving yourself, no matter what. The ultimate goal is not a happy marriage and responsible and successful children.

No, if there is a Creator, then it's not my place to choose how I want to invest my life or to decide what I want my purpose to be. As Creator, God alone has the ability and the right to tell me how to live and what the driving purpose should be for everything in my life. He designed me in a certain way for a certain purpose. This means that making *God's* purpose for me the driving purpose of my life should be my deepest motivation and my constant commitment, no matter who I am or where I am living. The doctrine of creation teaches us that we do not look to ourselves for purpose, but we look to our Creator. And the Creator has sent us into the world with an "owner's manual," just like the one that comes with a new car. God's manual, the Bible, not only lays out God's purpose for us; it also shows us what happens when we forsake God's purpose for our own as well as how he rescues and restores us through the gift of and grace of his Son.

Ownership

When I am done with a painting, it belongs to me. Nobody questions that. I own every painting in my studio. Every one of my paintings hanging in an exhibit is owned by me until purchased by someone else. It is the logic of creation: you make it, you own it. So it is with God's creation of the world and everything in it. The physical universe belongs to the Lord. It was created by him and for him. Romans 11:36 says, "For from him and through him and to him are all things. To him be glory forever. Amen." God is the rightful owner of all things. Treating the physical world as if it belongs to you, to do with it whatever you want, never goes anywhere good. Trees, flowers, streams, birds, animals of all kinds, the sky, the air, the wind and the rains, the sand and the sea, mountains and valleys, the cows in the field, and the dog under your table all belong to the Lord. It's humbling to understand that you are not the owner; you are simply the resident manager.

My mom and dad moved to Southern California and became the resident mangers of a large apartment complex. They owned nothing there, not even the apartment where they lived. But they had been tasked with the job of caring for the property and overseeing how the renters cared for the property. All this was done with respect for the expressed desires of the owners. My mom and dad couldn't treat the place like it belonged to them; they couldn't do whatever they wanted with the grounds; and they surely couldn't treat the renters however they wanted. They were employed to steward the complex according to the plans, purposes, and rules of the owners.

We must interact with and steward the physical environment—plants and animals, land, air, and water—with a humble recognition that it doesn't belong to us. This means we are the resident mangers of a place made by the Lord for his glory and held together by his power. So, with humility, thankfulness, and commitment, we give ourselves to care for what belongs to another, so he will be pleased and get the credit that is due him and him alone. This stewardship doesn't extend just to our physical environment, but to each other as well. We are called to represent God's love and care for all those made in his image. As his resident managers, we must take seriously our calling to represent to one another God's love, justice, compassion, mercy, protection, and provision. In recognition of his ownership, we commit ourselves to a stewardship lifestyle toward our neighbor, never turning our back on suffering of any kind until we are in that place where suffering is no more.

God's Creator ownership calls us to one more thing. It's important every morning of your life to remind yourself that you don't belong to you either. All kinds of dark and unholy things, all kinds of selfish and abusive actions, so much hurt and destruction, so much idolatry and addiction, and so many sad endings result when human beings live like they own their lives and can do whatever they want. Sexual abuse is an ownership problem. Emotional abuse of your spouse is an ownership problem. Racial hatred is an ownership problem. Corrupt politics is an ownership problem. Materialistic greed is an ownership problem. Eating yourself into ill health is an ownership problem. Adultery is an ownership problem. Thievery and violence are ownership problems. Selfish use of your resources is an ownership problem. Misogyny, whether subtle or overt, is an ownership problem. Failure to care for the disadvantaged and oppressed is an ownership problem. Anytime you take your life into your own hands and do with it, even for a moment, only what you want to do, you have an ownership problem.

Here is what the doctrine of creation tells me. I don't own my rationality, spirituality, personality, emotionality, physicality, psychology, gifts, or volition. Everything I am, that is, all that works together to make me *me* belongs to the Lord. I am to steward the various aspects of my body and personhood, recognizing that it all belongs to him and exists for his purpose. A life well lived is lived with the understanding that you don't belong to you.

I have to pause for a moment and reflect with you on the reality that living with God's purpose and ownership in mind is not natural for us. It's not natural to approach every thought, desire, choice, word, and action remembering that you don't belong to you. It's not natural to approach your responsibilities and relationships in light of God's purpose. It's natural to be moved by your own desires and to define a good day as a day when you got what makes you happy.

The doctrine of creation leads us to the grace of Jesus. The doctrine of creation, properly understood, leads us the cross. It is there where I find forgiveness for every Creator-forgetful moment and every act of selfish ownership. It is there I can cry out for the help to do what does not come naturally. It is there that I am rescued from myself and employed to live for something and someone vastly bigger than me. It is there where I am liberated from the burden of living for my own glory and find the freedom of living for the glory of another. It is there where I am reminded of this reality: "For it is God who works in you, both to will and to work for his good pleasure" (Phil. 2:13). The doctrine of creation drives me to Jesus. It is only because he is with me, for me, and in me that I will ever submit to God's ownership and live according to his purpose. He will not leave me to struggle on my own, but fights for me, even when I myself am too exhausted and discouraged to fight.

Authority

My mom and dad had authority, and the renters knew it. They exercised their authority in various ways every day. Sometimes their authority was welcomed and other times it was resisted, but they were faithful in using their authority as needed. The thing they didn't have was autonomous authority. They did not have the right to exercise their authority however they wished, because they didn't own the complex.

This is where the doctrine of creation leads us when it comes to authority. Since God made the world and owns it, he is the ultimate authority over everything. This means that there is no such thing as independent human authority. Anyone who has a position of authority as a human being has representative authority. All human authority is ambassadorial; that is, it is designed to be a visible representation of the authority of God. Paul says it this way: "Let every person be subject to the governing authorities. For there is no authority except from God, and those that exist have been instituted by God" (Rom. 13:1).

Whether you are a parent, spouse, teacher, boss, politician, manager, judge, pastor, or some other authority figure, you have been placed there by God to be a representative of his authority. You do not have the right to wield your power and position however you want. Every expression of human authority should be a representation of God's values, purposes, and character. Wouldn't the home be a safer and more loving place if parents were like this? Wouldn't the classroom work better if teachers understood that? Wouldn't the workplace be more peaceful and productive if bosses led this way? Wouldn't government work better for the good of its citizens if every elected official saw him- or herself as a representative, not just of their constituents, but more importantly of God? God is the ultimate authority. All other authority looks to him for its character and purpose.

It is vital to remember that the most powerful human leader, the one whose rule is the largest and who possesses the highest of human authority, is at the same time a person living under authority. Even the greatest of leaders is called to bow before the ultimate King and willingly submit to his authority. There is no such thing as human authority that is not answerable to God. So we can rest, not because the human authorities over us are good, loving, and wise, but because our Creator Lord is the final authority and he is holy in every way and boundless in love.

Worship

The stunning, shocking, gripping account of creation, which is the first thing you encounter when you open your Bible, is there for a reason. Your Bible is written in such a way that you encounter God, in all the hugeness of his glory, right away. From the beginning you witness God doing something that you will never see rivaled or repeated. This one who existed before time, before the physical universe existed, speaks everything that is into existence. With words he calls things into being. His glorious power, wisdom, and authority are not hidden for a moment. From the very first words of Scripture they are spotlighted for every reader to see. God, big, glorious, and powerfully active, dominates reality. When faced with this incredible display of all-surpassing greatness, you can't help but feel small and weak.

This original sight-and-sound, multisensory, Technicolor glory display was meant to astound you, to overwhelm you, and to change you. It has been retained to stimulate in you the most significant, intimate, profound, and formative of all human functions: worship. This account is meant to drive you to what you were created for. It is written to take you to the core of your humanity and to there discover your true identity. It is meant to chase into the background of your heart all the other things that would woo you, seduce you, and capture you. It is meant to give you back your sanity again, to take you to the only place where real life will ever be found. It is meant to put you in your place to understand exactly who you are and what it is you were meant to do all of the time. The words are written to make God loom so large that you drop to your knees in awe and worship. But these words are also meant to help you begin to understand your identity and place in this cosmos that this amazing one has put together. Here is more than a call to a certain activity. No, it is profoundly more than that. This glory display is retained for you so that you would own your identity.

Worship is more than a spiritual, religious activity. Worship is our identity. It's what we were made for. Genesis 1 and 2 present to us, in incredible glory, the only one who is worthy of the worship drive and the worship capacity of our hearts. The worship of something will shape everything we say and do. Worship sculpts our deepest desires and directs our most powerful motivations.

So, in the only-once-in-the-world display of incredible divine ability at creation, you and I are meant not only to find God, but also to finally find ourselves. We are required to deal with him. There is no escaping the light of his majesty. There is no avoiding the shadow of his power. The passage leaves us nowhere to run or hide. He is too overwhelmingly huge to avoid. The glory of his majesty completely fills the stage that we may have thought was ours. From the beginning he invites us to know him, experience his grandeur, and give ourselves to the only thing that makes sense, worship. This is not worship as a religious part of our lives, but rather worship that is the offer of our lives to this one who alone has ushered us into the place where we are witnesses to the glorious glory of his glory.

Humility

The doctrine of creation is meant to release us from our bondage to us. It is meant to welcome us out of the prison of our own self-centeredness.

Genesis 1 and 2 remind us that we are but witnesses to something we had no part in. The world didn't begin with and wasn't started by us. The great narrative of the cosmos didn't begin with us. The most amazing thing that ever happened, happened without us. If called upon, there is no way that we could have done even the most miniscule piece of what the great Creator did when he spoke existence into existence. He was there in awesome grandeur and glory before the first human breath was taken.

The doctrine of creation reminds me that I am not at the center of what is. God is not only the great author of the story of life, he is also the principal actor, the great star that dominates the stage and compels our attention. Everything comes from him, everything points to him, and everything continues to him. He gets the spotlight, he gets the accolades, and he is the one who takes home the honors. He humbles all who stand in the light of his glory. There is no greatness debate to be had. There is no one who could seriously claim to be his equal. All creation bows to his majesty.

Here is where the humbling process of grace begins. As you begin to bow to his centrality and confess your smallness and dependency, you begin to be free from the dangerous delusions of your own majesty. Here's where you begin to forsake your reliance on your own wisdom and power. Here's where you quit trying to write your own story. Here's where you start to be free from your obsession with your own glory and your constant need to be right, to be in control, and to be acclaimed. Here's where you give up writing your own rules and let go of thinking that you're smart enough to plan your own life. Here is where God, in love and mercy, invites you to confess and to surrender.

The great and wonderful gospel narrative, which is the hope of all who believe, doesn't begin with the arrival of Jesus on the human stage. Redeeming grace flows at Genesis 1. The display of God's glory is at the same time the pouring out of his mercy. It beckons you away from the dysfunction and disaster of self-glory to find your life in surrender to him. Divine love welcomes you in to see the most glorious display of majesty ever, even though you could have never afforded the ticket. It is love that confronts you with God: big, dominant, and all-surpassing. In humbling you, he extends you his grace. What is written in the creation accounts is not just for his glory; it is for your eternal good. Creation is on display because redeeming grace is God's plan.

12

Creation in Everyday Life

IF FAITH IS NOT JUST something you believe with your mind but also something that shapes the way you live, then it is important to consider what it means to live in light of the truth of the doctrine of creation. Living in light of this foundational truth is much more than rejecting evolution. This truth doesn't only require us to have a position on the origin of our world. It also reaches, in some way, into every dimension of our daily lives.

The Doctrine of Creation Calls Us to Live Like We Own Nothing

Let's take a closer look at the issue of ownership.

Our first home was a little cottage that Luella and I rented on the secluded grounds of a colonial manor home in South Carolina. For a newly married couple, it was a great place to live. In exchange for a drastically reduced rent, I did gardening on the property. Gorgeous old trees, lush bushes, and flowers grew everywhere. When the sun would shine through the trees, the property would be painted with light and shadows. The quiet of that serene place was broken only by the singing of birds. The owners of the property had other homes, so they were seldom there. Although we had this beautiful place to ourselves, I was very aware that nothing there belonged to me. I was invited to enjoy it and to take care of it, but it all belonged to someone else.

When God says to us, "The earth is the LORD's and the fullness thereof, / the world and those who dwell therein" (Ps. 24:1), he means it. The doctrine of creation is not just about origins, but it's also about how you think about and approach everything in your life. We live in God's world, as God's possessions, handling God's things. This is a radically different way of living from the way most people live. Instinctively people think that their life is theirs for the living and the things in their life have no greater purpose than to bring them happiness. But God says, "No, not only does the whole world belong to me, but you do too."

Believing in the doctrine of creation is much more than having the right view of the origin of the universe. This truth calls you to surrender everything you are and everything you have to the ownership of your Lord. When you do this, everything changes. When Luella and I lived in that little cottage, virtually everything we did was shaped by our recognition that the house and everything in it belonged to someone else.

Consider how something like marriage changes when you believe that you don't own yourself, your spouse, or your marriage. Sadly, ownership drives most marriages and creates most marriage problems. Most young men or young women who desire to get married begin to shop for a life partner who fits well with them and makes them happy. They get married and begin to build a life together. The problem is that two owners will inevitably get in one another's way. The man wants the woman to do something because it makes him happy, but it doesn't make her happy. Or the woman wants the man to be something that isn't natural nor what he wants to be. Skirmishes break out over money, decision-making, sex, schedules, church, and more. The problem is that no matter what they believed about the origin of the world, they both went into marriage viewing their lives as belonging to them, with little consideration of a greater purpose.

The Bible is very clear that marriage, instituted at creation, belongs to the Lord. It is his for his purpose and for our good. By God's plan, marriage is the foundational building block of human culture. It is the place where human beings express most fully the communal nature of their personhood. It is the only relationship in life, other than our relationship to him, where God uses covenantal language. Marriage is also designed by God to picture the relationship between Christ and his bride, the church. It is meant to be a physical portrait of gorgeous spiritual realities. Further, marriage is a primary tool that God uses to advance his ongoing work of forming us into the likeness of his Son.

The meaning and purpose of marriage, by God's creation design, is not first human happiness. Marriage is a foundational community, it's a picture of redeeming love, and it's an instrument of sanctifying grace. When you submit to God's design, you have a completely different attitude toward and way of dealing with the ups and downs that every married couple faces. Marriage is about learning how to deal with God's thing (marriage) God's way. And when you do this, you are on your way to marriage longevity and fulfillment, because the Creator of marriage really does know what is best. *Where are you experiencing trouble in your marriage because you're living like it belongs to you?*

Think about your money. God created money, and he made a world where money is a significant part of daily life. Money is so significant that the Bible discusses it frequently. I am sure that most believers think that the money they earn belongs to them, with the exception of the small percentage of money God asks them to return to him. But consider how Paul talks about the money we earn: "Let the thief no longer steal, but rather let him labor, doing honest work with his own hands, so that he may have something to share with anyone in need" (Eph. 4:28). Now, you would expect Paul to say, "Quit providing for yourself by stealing, but rather get a job, so you can pay for what you need by the labor of your own hands." But it is very important to notice that this is not what Paul says.

Paul has a very different view of money. He understands that our money belongs to the Lord and is stewarded by us. So the important question is, "What does the Creator want to do with his money that I am holding?" Paul's answer to the question is surprising. The primary purpose for your money is not providing for your needs. Your Creator has committed himself to that. The primary purpose of your money is generosity. Your money allows you to be part of God's generosity mission on earth. The biblical story is a generosity story, captured by these words: "For God so loved the world that he gave. . . ." Yes, God will use your work to provide for you, but he wants the driving purpose of his money, entrusted to your care, to be used for the greater purpose of his kingdom. That's why Proverb 3:9 says, "Honor the Lord with your wealth / and with the firstfruits of all your produce." Your financial life takes a radically different shape when you really do believe that your money doesn't belong to you. *Where is the doctrine of creation calling you to change the way you think about and handle your money?*

Sex is for many of us a place of unfulfilled expectations, hurt, disappointment, temptation, and trouble. I am persuaded that sexual dysfunction, temptation, hurt, and difficulty begin with the belief that our bodies belong to us. This leads us to believe that sex belongs to us for our happiness. Yet if it is true that sex belongs to the one who made it, then the highest goal for my sexuality is not my pleasure, but the pleasure of the Creator. This isn't some weird theological view of sex; no, it is intensely practical.

If I think that my body and sex belong to me, then when I am naked with another person, in the most intimate and vulnerable of human connections, I will use that person's body as a tool for my satisfaction. But if I believe that sex belongs to the Creator of sex, then who I have sex with and how I respond to my partner become of highest importance. If sex belongs to the Lord, then I don't just want sexual excitement and fulfillment, but I want God to be pleased by everything I think, desire, say, and do in my sexual life, and I want my partner to feel loved and cared for in the same way my Creator loves and cares for me. Thinking your body belongs to you starts you down the road to all kinds of sexual dysfunction and sin.

We could carry this conversation to every area of our lives, because everything becomes different when you really believe that "the earth is the LORD's and the fullness thereof." The doctrine of creation calls you to live like nothing belongs to you—even you. Living this way is where the highest joys of life are to be found because you are living as the Creator designed for you to live. *Where has thinking your body belongs to you set you up for sexual temptation and trouble?*

The Doctrine of Creation Reminds Us That Life Is a Glory War

Driving home from the beach at sunset, I was blown away by how the sky was painted at dusk. The pink, yellow, orange, and blue hues were beautifully brushed across the sky by the world's best painter. I whipped out my phone and began taking pictures to post on Instagram. We had just left the veranda of a great old hotel, where we savored wonderful morsels as we took in the beauty of the gardens that surrounded us. The ocean, with the endless rhythms of the waves, was steps away. It was a great day, and we headed home full and happy.

God did make his world a pleasurable place and he did design us with the ability to take in and enjoy those pleasures. Enjoying the pleasurable glories of creation is not sin. Being ruled by that pleasure or by the thing that gives you pleasure is. Because creation has been made glorious by our Creator Lord and because, in our sin, we have wandering hearts, life is a glory war. This inescapable war is fought in our hearts every day. All of us are tempted somehow, someway, to worship and serve something in the physical creation rather than the one who created it. Our lives are always shaped by what glory is in functional control of the thoughts and desires of our hearts.

I find the way John talks about this struggle to be very helpful. You remember the story of Jesus feeding that large crowd of people with a little boy's lunch. After the miracle, the people were so impressed that they wanted to make Jesus their king. It seems like they got it right, because this is what Jesus came to be. But rather than stepping forward into this amazing moment, Jesus hides from the crowd, leaving them confused.

When they finally find Jesus, they ask him when he had gotten there, wondering why he had run away. Jesus's answer is very important: "Truly, truly, I say to you, you are seeking me, not because you saw signs, but because you ate your fill of the loaves" (John 6:26). Jesus is essentially saying that you ate the bread, but you didn't see the sign. The bread you ate was pointing you to something much more necessary and satisfying. So it is with this incredibly beautiful world that God created. The world is a sign pointing to something more glorious and more satisfying than the Creator ever intended his created world to be.

If you were taking a vacation with your family, it would be insane and delusional to stop at the sign that pointed you to the destination miles away, unpack your car, and hope the sign would live up to what the destination could deliver. Your family would think that you had lost your mind, and they would have no hope that a good time would be had by all. Now, the sign has a very important purpose. It is meant to point you in the direction that you want to go. A sign is an important thing, but it is not the thing, so it must not be your destination.

Perhaps this silly illustration isn't so silly after all. In our daily lives I think we stop at the sign again and again, asking it to do for us what it was never intended to do. The result is all kinds of disappointment, addiction, and brokenness inside of us and around us. We are tempted to look to the creation to deliver to us what only the Creator can. We walk away disappointed only to camp out at another sign down the road.

A sign points you to a thing, but it is not that thing. Scripture after Scripture tells us that one of the primary roles of the created world is to point us to the Creator. Every glory of the physical world is meant to point you to the glory of the one who made it. We were made by the Lord and for the Lord, so nothing in the created world will ever satisfy the deepest hunger in our hearts. Asking food to satisfy your heart will result in you being obese and in ill health. Asking sex to satisfy your longing heart will end up in obsession and deviance. Asking your husband or wife to satisfy your heart reduces you to being endlessly demanding, critical, and discontent. Asking material things to satisfy your heart will cause you to never stop shopping and possessing, while you sink deeper in debt. Asking physical health to satisfy your heart will surely disappoint you as sickness and old age get in the way. Asking your job to satisfy your heart will turn you into a workaholic, with all of the relational dysfunction that results. Here is the point: earth will never be your Savior.

You and I were created by God for God. In love he placed us in a beautiful world, so that everywhere we look we would see his glory and be reminded that life can only ever be found in him. But in the idolatry of sin, we look for life elsewhere, hoping that some created thing will do for us what only the Creator can ever do. Nothing good ever happens when, in our hearts, we put the creation where only the Creator should be. Nothing good results when created glory replaces God's glory in our hearts. Know that on this side of eternity there is a glory war that still rages in your heart. It is a war for what will control your thoughts, desires, words, and actions. This glory war will determine how you invest your time, energy, and money. It will shape how you relate to the people in your life. It will sculpt the way you think about and pursue your work. It will shape your attitude toward your possessions. Everything in your life is shaped by some kind of glory. Will your life be ruled by God's glory or by creation's glory? There are few more important questions in all of life than this.

God knew that this glory war would be won in only one way. So he set a rescue plan in place. This plan is captured by these beautiful words.

> And the Word became flesh and dwelt among us, and we have seen his glory, glory as of the only Son from the Father, full of grace and truth. (John bore witness about him, and cried out, "This was he of whom I said, 'He who comes after me ranks before me, because he was before me.'") For from his fullness we have all received, grace upon grace. For the law was given through Moses; grace and truth came through Jesus Christ." (John 1:14–17)

What an amazing plan. Jesus took on created glory so that he could reveal to us divine glory in a way we had never seen before. He did this so that we would see and cry out for his fullness, the grace upon grace that we all need and that the created world could never, ever give us. Run to this one; he not only holds satisfying life in his hands, but he also has the power and willingness to protect you from the rule of other glories in your heart.

Keep Asking the Best, Most Practical Question Ever

Recognizing God as the Creator of heaven and earth and everything in them presses us with a question. It may be the best, most practical question you could ask yourself right here, right now, between your conversion and your entrance into the presence of Jesus. Here it is: *What is God's purpose for ______?* Asking this question reminds you of your place in the world. You are not the designer or the ultimate craftsman. You are the product of God's craftsmanship. So you should always be asking, What was I made for and what is the reason for these things in my life? Because God is gracious, kind, and wise, he answers this question again and again in his Word, addressing particular things with divine wisdom and clarity. Earlier we looked briefly at this issue of purpose, but I want to unpack it more specifically and practically. Let me give you an example of the formative importance of asking this purpose question.

Pain is one of the most difficult things we all face. It often seems random and unexpected. Because pain is always transformative in some way, either for good or bad, and because your experience of pain is never neutral, it is important to ask, "What is God's purpose for my sufferings?" Now, this question that everyone asks at some time in their life doesn't have to be a disheartening mystery because the Bible addresses it with clear and direct answers.

God created our bodies with the capacity to initiate and communicate pain. God created our emotions to experience and evaluate pain as well. The capacity to suffer pain (touch, nervous system, rationality, emotions, etc.) was hardwired into human beings before suffering existed. There is purpose in God's equipping us with the capacity to experience pain.

First, pain is *protective*. In your body, pain alerts you that something is wrong. Pain tells me something is broken or diseased and needs attention. Emotional pain is an alert too; it tells me that something in me or around me is broken or dysfunctional and needs help. The pain of a guilty conscience is a good thing too, because it causes me to face my sin and seek God's forgiving and empowering grace.

Pain is also *transformative*. Scripture is clear that God employs the difficult and painful things in life to expose, mature, and transform our hearts (Rom. 5:1–5; James 1:2–4; 1 Pet. 1:3–9). God takes what seems to be a bad thing and makes it a redemptive thing. God has chosen to leave us, for this moment, in this world where pain will enter our door, not because he's forgotten us or is lacking in care for us, but because he is still working on us.

Pain is also *qualifying*. Second Corinthians 1:4 says that God uses our suffering to equip us to bring others the same gospel comfort we received in our moment of suffering. We suffer not only for our own redemptive growth and good, but also so that we would be qualified to bring gospel comfort to those near us who are enduring painful experiences in this fallen world.

God knew where the story of the world he made was headed, so he built within us the capacity to recognize and feel pain. As hard as pain is, the capacity to feel pain has been created by God with good purposes in mind. This does not mean it is wrong to cry out for healing from physical pain or deliverance from situational pain. It does mean we should resist thinking that pain is a sign that God has forgotten us or turned his back on us. We should not think that pain is a random impersonal thing, detached completely from God's wise and loving purpose. God created my capacity to experience pain with a purpose in mind.

God created *everything* with a purpose in mind. If I go into a workshop armed with planks of wood, carpentry tools, hardware, glue, and finishing compounds, I don't start sawing and hammering and say to myself, "I hope this turns into something." No, I enter my workshop with a purpose in mind. Everything I do in my workshop is done in order to make something that will be able to do what I purposed it should do when I began the project.

Because God really did make this world and everything in it, I should continually be asking myself what God's purpose is for everything in my life. Can you answer the following questions in a way that will guide your choices, decisions, words, and actions?

What is God's purpose for:
My husband or wife?
My material possessions?
My children?
My ability to think?
My emotions?
My physical body?
My ability to communicate?
My relationships?
My natural gifts?
My ethnicity?
My gender?
My home?
My church?
My financial resources?
My sexuality?
My spirituality?
The physical world around me?
My ________ (fill in the blank)?

If God created everything in my life for a purpose, then living in light of the doctrine of creation means making God's purpose *my* purpose in every area of my life. This means surrendering my will to God's will, my plan to God's plan, and my purpose to his purpose. Now, this isn't natural for you and me, so for this there is rescuing and empowering grace.

We commit to respond to things, to use things, and to interact with things in a way that is in tune with the Creator's original purpose for those things, seeking always to bring our street-level purposes in line with the purposes of our Creator Lord.

We Are Created to Care for the World That God Made

God used a particular word after he created Adam and Eve that should jump off the page as we read it. This word seems foundational, not something you quickly pass over and then move on. This word is a commissioning word, a job description given to two people who don't fully understand yet who they are and what their role is in this newly created cosmos. Genesis 1:28 says, "And God blessed them. And God said to them, 'Be fruitful and multiply and fill the earth and subdue it, and have dominion over the fish of the sea and over the birds of the air and over every living thing that moves on the earth.'"

The word that should stop and get our attention is *dominion*. Adam and Eve were not just more of the many creatures that God made. No, they were in a unique place in all of creation with a significant role to play. They were to exercise dominion over the rest of creation. To have dominion means to have control, that is, a position of leadership and authority over something. Consider Genesis 2:15: "The LORD God took the man and put him in the garden of Eden to work it and to keep it." Here we get a more specific picture of what Adam and Eve's dominion responsibilities would look like. Psalm 115:16 says, "The heavens are the LORD's heavens, / but the earth he has given to the children of man." These passages form a picture of the unique calling human beings have to care for the physical world that God created. God says, "I am putting you in a managerial position over the world I have just created, to control it, to fill it, to work it, and to keep it."

You and I simply can't take the doctrine of creation seriously and have a passive or uncaring attitude toward the physical well-being of this amazing world that God made and entrusted to our care. Environmentalism is not some weird, left-wing, pseudopantheist obsession; no, it is your and my calling. No one should care more about the state of the physical environment, its health and flourishing, than those of us who believe in the doctrine of creation. Given God's immediate commission at creation, the church's passivity regarding the care of the world the Creator entrusted to us is scandalous.

Here's what has happened to us in our sin. Rather than working to care and to keep the creation, as per God's dominion command, our response to the physical world has been to conquer and use. We have looked at the world as ours to consume, for our satisfaction and pleasure. So the waters God created have become polluted, the soil sucked of its natural nutrients, huge forests dewooded, and toxins pumped into the air. Sprawling developments are built without care for their impact on plants, animals, water tables, wetlands, and farmlands. Big factories pump waste into bodies of water until the life-forms that are dependent on those bodies of water become diseased and die.

And the world around us is breaking under the weight of our hunger for more.

The doctrine of creation doesn't allow us to be passive or uncaring when it comes to the state of the physical world. It doesn't leave room for us to use and consume and then walk away unconcerned. Our Creator has commissioned us to care for the physical environment that is our address. He has commanded us to control it, to fill it, to work it, and to keep it. Look around, and you will see that we are experiencing the sad results of our failure to do this. How has environmentalism become the work of those who do not know God or recognize him as the Creator of all that is? Why are the people of God not on the forefront of these concerns? How is it that we have almost universally turned our back on God's clear dominion command? Why is this message of responsibility seldom preached or taught? What changes will need to take place in order for us to live out our calling as God's appointed creation caregivers?

The Doctrine of Creation Reminds Us That Independence Is Not Our Goal

You see it in toddlers who resist when their parents tell them what they have to eat. You see it in the rebellion of a teenager. You see it in the resistance of a husband when he is being lovingly confronted by his wife. You see it in an old man who pushes away loved ones who try to convince him that he needs help. In some way all of us buy into the delusion of our ability to live independently. But the doctrine of creation exposes our quest for independence to be the delusion that it is.

When you take a closer look at the creation of Adam and Eve, one thing is clear. Adam and Eve are far from independent. Notice what God immediately does after creating them. He talks to them. Here they are, perfect people, living in a perfect world and in a perfect relationship with God, yet they have no clue who they are and how they are meant to live. So God begins to download his wisdom to them. Embedded in God's wise counsel are meaning and purpose, structure for their relationship to one another, the nature of their relationship with him, a moral structure for their living, and a description of the daily work they are to give themselves to. Adam and Eve are utterly dependent on profound and practical wisdom outside of themselves in order to live life. Our need for the theological, structural, and practical content of God's truth isn't the result of sin, but is the product of being human. Adam and Eve were created with a need for God and for things that only God would be able to supply. And their continued ability to live as they were designed to live would be determined by their willingness to continue to live in a dependent relationship to their Creator.

Adam and Eve were also designed to live in dependent community with one another. When God said that it was not good for Adam to live alone, his statement was not a response to Adam's complaint that he was lonely. Rather, God's statement revealed his understanding of the person he had created. He hadn't created a man who was designed to live independently, supplying within himself everything that he needed. No, he would be fully completed and fully functional only when he lived in community with another image bearer. Adam and Eve were created to live in interdependent community with one another. Outside of that community, Adam and Eve would not be able to be what they were designed to be and would not do well what they were commissioned to do.

Human independence is a dangerous delusion, but sin makes attractive what God says is dangerous. So we all are tempted to buy into our own independent wisdom, strength, and righteousness. We are all tempted to tell ourselves that we can do what we have no independent ability to do, and we all are tempted to take credit for things we could have never accomplished or produced on our own.

Note how Paul talks about redeeming grace in 2 Corinthians. He first reminds us that selfism is the DNA sin: "He died . . . that those who live might no longer live for themselves" (2 Cor. 5:15). Sin deceives us into thinking independent, self-oriented living will actually work. Then Paul reminds us that the clear call of the gospel of Jesus Christ is, "Be reconciled to God" (2 Cor. 5:20). The gospel calls us away from our self-focused, self-deluding independence to be drawn into a willing, joyful, and worshipful dependence on God, the kind that Adam and Eve were created for in the beginning.

Paul is reminding us that the move of God's grace is not from dependence to independence, but just the opposite. The more time grace has to work in your heart, the more afraid you are of independent isolation and the more willing you are to live a life of vertical and horizontal dependence. How about you? At your university, at your job, in your marriage, with your children, with your neighbors, in your church, with your friends, in your finances, in your sexual life, in times of leisure and entertainment, or in private moments, do you take your life into your own hands, acting independently of your need for God's wisdom and his protective and empowering grace? Are you humbly approachable when your spouse, your children, your friends, or a brother or sister in the Lord seeks to lovingly point out a wrong attitude or action? Do you act as if you don't need help?

Genesis 1 and 2 contain the seeds of the two Great Commands. These life-shaping commands were not newly created by Jesus in Palestine, but were woven into the very fabric of humanity in the garden of Eden. People were made to live in a vertical and a horizontal community of love. If someone were to ask you what the deep desire in the heart of every human being is, you wouldn't have to think much, because the answer is obvious. Everyone desires to be loved. What makes any human community work? Again, the answer is obvious. Communities work when the people in that community are committed to love one another as they would desire to be loved. But only people who love God above all else will ever love their neighbor as they would desire to be loved. Love God, love neighbor; it's how God's prized creatures are designed to live.

The doctrine of creation confronts our independence and calls us back to the dependent living that is God's norm for those made in his image. Again, God's grace provides the rescue, protection, resources, and power we need to fight the temptation to try to do on our own what we will only ever be able to do in willing community with God and others.

The Doctrine of Creation Requires Us to Admit and Accept Our Limits

Everything God created was created with limits. Fish don't do well in a pasture and sheep can't live in a lake. Elephants are mighty animals, but you'll never see one fly. The winds, water, and ground are all designed with different physical properties that set limits on their function. Even a day has a limited amount of hours and a week has a limited number of days. There will never be thirty-seven hours in a day and fifteen days in a week.

In the garden of Eden the only unlimited being was the Creator Lord Almighty. Adam and Eve were designed with limits of gender, strength, wisdom, and talent. Every human being has physical and spiritual limits. An important part of applying the doctrine of creation to your everyday life is recognizing and living with the limits the Creator has chosen for you. Let's consider the example of time.

The Creator-ordained limits of time are clear in Genesis 1 and 2. You see the creation of the structure of a day, evening and morning. You see the creation of the shape of a week, six days and a Sabbath. This is the structure of time that every human being who ever lived has been limited to by God. All of our commitments, all of our values, all of our responsibilities, and all of our opportunities must be lived out inside of the constraints of time that our wise Creator has set for us. There is no time available outside of the time structure that God has created.

This means it is not always the best, most godly choice to say yes to the next opportunity, no matter how spiritual it may seem. You have to be faithful to family, work, and church within the limits of time that God has set for you. You might allow one area to grow and grow because you keeping saying yes to commitments, but it can't grow outside of the 24/7 that God designed, because there is no more time out there. So overcommitment to one area will restrict your commitment to another area of responsibility.

You should be committed to the ministry of the body of Christ, but you cannot do so without remembering your limits of time. Many ministry people continue to say yes to ministry opportunities and become absentee parents or spouses. Sometimes saying yes to work opportunities restricts your commitment to your own spiritual health and participation in the body of Christ. It is often spiritually wise to say no to something of importance and value, because you can't keep adding things to the limited time you have without damaging other things of value in your life. Genesis 1 and 2 call us to live out the values of our Creator with a humble recognition of the limits of time the Creator knew were best for us.

The institution of the Sabbath in Genesis 2 reminds us of both our physical and spiritual limits. We need to stop our normal daily labor to rejuvenate both our physical and spiritual health because neither are unlimited. God has no limits to his strength, but we do. God has no limits of time, but we do. God has no limits to his wisdom, but we do. God has no limits to his control, but we do. God does not age, but we do. God has no limits to his knowledge, but we do. God has no limits to his holiness, but we do. God has no physical limits, but we do. God has no limits, but we have many.

The doctrine of creation calls us away from our delusions of grandeur to accept, with joy and discipline, the limits that the Creator, in the foresight of his wisdom and the protection of his love, has set for us. All of our limits are designed by him to draw us to come and lean on him with humility, dependence, gratitude, obedience, and worship. Our limits shrink our glory while they preach to us the unlimited glory of the majesty of the one who made us.

The Doctrine of Creation Rightly Understood Leads Us to the Cross

When you read and meditate on the majesty of the Creator and the beauty of the world he created, you are seeing shalom in action. The word *shalom* means much more than peace. It is a word for an overarching, universal order. Shalom means everything is in its right place, doing exactly what it was meant to do. Shalom is everything working in harmony with everything else. Shalom is every instrument in the orchestra perfectly in tune and playing in a collective harmony that makes every instrument sound better together with the other instruments than it would sound alone. Shalom is every system and organ of the human body, free from disease or dysfunction, working in perfect synchronicity with every other system and organ. It is a state of perfect health and function. Shalom is a beautifully glorious thing. God created a shalomic universe, one that could only be created by one of such majestic perfection, power, and wisdom.

But you don't have to look very far, you don't have to live very long, and you don't have to have much insight to see that the shalom God created has been shattered by sin. As we look back on the gorgeous world God made, untainted by sin, we should weep at the brokenness that is everywhere around us. Yes, there are still beauties to be seen, but this world is a broken world that simply no longer functions as its Creator intended. In Romans 8, Paul says that the world we live in is groaning. It groans under the weight of its own brokenness. Even the physical world around us is crying for redemption (Rom. 8:18–25).

Yes, there really is a direct line from the beautiful shalom of the garden to that cruel cross on the hill outside the city. This line is carefully painted through history by a Redeemer who intends to restore shalom again. He will make all things new again. And the way he will do that is by sending his Son on our behalf to live the perfectly righteous life that we would never be able to live; to die, paying the penalty for sins we committed; and to rise again, conquering sin and death. His life, death, and resurrection secure for us the return of shalom. They guarantee that there will be a day when we are perfected people, living in a perfect relationship with God in a place where everything is in its proper place and working in perfect union with everything else. May we live with the hope of that day in view.

• • •

The doctrine of creation is not about just origins, but also who we are and how we are designed to live right here, right now. The doctrine of creation invites us to be reconciled to the God we were made for and to look forward to the restoration of all that was lost when sin shattered the gorgeous shalom that he created. I want to end this chapter with words from Psalm 65, written in praise of our Creator Lord.

> By awesome deeds you answer us with righteousness,
> O God of our salvation,
> the hope of all the ends of the earth
> and of the farthest seas;
> the one who by his strength established the mountains,
> being girded with might;
> who stills the roaring of the seas,
> the roaring of their waves,
> the tumult of the peoples,
> so that those who dwell at the ends of the earth are in awe at your signs.
> You make the going out of the morning and the evening to shout for joy.

You visit the earth and water it;
  you greatly enrich it;
the river of God is full of water;
  you provide their grain,
  for so you have prepared it.
You water its furrows abundantly,
  settling its ridges,
softening it with showers,
  and blessing its growth.
You crown the year with your bounty;
  your wagon tracks overflow with abundance.
The pastures of the wilderness overflow,
  the hills gird themselves with joy,
the meadows clothe themselves with flocks,
  the valleys deck themselves with grain,
  they shout and sing together for joy. (Ps. 65:5–13)

13

The Doctrine of the Image of God in Man

AFTER GOD HAD MADE all other creatures, he created people, male and female. He designed them with reasonable and mortal souls, and he endowed them with knowledge, righteousness, and true holiness, after his own image. Adam and Eve had the law of God written in their hearts and were created with the power to fulfill it, but also with the possibility of transgressing. They had the liberty of their own will, which was subject to change. Besides the law that was written in their hearts, God commanded them not to eat of the tree of the knowledge of good and evil. While they obeyed this command, they were happy in their communion with God. See Gen. 1:26–27; 2:7; 3:6; 5:3; 9:6; Eccles. 7:29; Acts 17:26–28; Rom. 2:14–15; 8:29; 1 Cor. 11:7; 2 Cor. 3:18; Eph. 4:23–34; Col. 3:10; James 3:9.[1]

Understanding the Doctrine of the Image of God in Man

Luella and I had been waiting for the day when we would receive our little girl. She had been assigned to us at birth, but we had to wait four

1 Author's paraphrase of the doctrine of the image of God in man as found in the Westminster Confession of Faith, chap. 4.2.

long months to finally hold her in our arms. A gate area at the airport had been reserved for us. I will never forget the sight of our caseworker walking down the concourse carrying our new little one, face forward, so we could see her and she could see us. The caseworker walked over to me, placed this tiny little human being in my arms, and then stepped away. It was a thunderous moment. I had been handed a real, living human being. The image of God had been placed in my hands for me to love, nurture, instruct, guide, provide for, and protect. I told her how much I loved her as tears streamed down my face. I was bowled over with the realization of the uniqueness of this little person in contrast to all of the rest of creation. I stood in that holy moment holding this little dependent and defenseless baby girl, brimming with dignity, significance, and value because stamped on her was the image of God himself. My hands trembled as my heart worked to take it all in.

Now, what I am about to write may seem ridiculous to you, but the point is important. We had a lot of pets in our house, from tokay geckos to Jack Russell terriers. It was always a bit amazing when we would bring a new animal home. It was fun to bond with new pets and watch them develop, but those experiences were wholly unlike that incredible moment in the airport. No one needed to tell us that this moment was unprecedented, mysterious, glorious, and holy. The uniqueness of this little female person, made in the image of God, flooded our minds and captured our emotions.

"Like God" is an amazing thing to declare. "Made in his image" is a profound announcement. But these are the things God immediately declares upon creating Adam and Eve. In those words he is defining their identity and the utter uniqueness of their relationship to him. Adam and Eve are not just part of the catalog of creatures that God made. They are above, they are special, and they are christened with a dignity that separates them from everything else. We must not ever forget this foundational definition of who human beings are. With these words God names the intrinsic worth of people. This worth is never earned and cannot be taken away. To be human is to have dignity and worth because you carry the image of God himself.

Human value is not achieved by success or accomplishment. It is not the product of your race. Human value is not the result of the building of financial wealth, power, authority, or control. It's not a matter of how fit and attractive you are. Human value is not about intellectual, athletic, or artistic ability. It is not a matter of personality or giftedness. When we think that human worth is earned by one of these things, bad things happen. When we forget the image-bearer dignity of every human being, we end up doing things to one another that we should never do. And we must always remember that hatred of an image bearer is hatred of God, violence against an image bearer is violence against God, and dishonor of anyone made in the image of God dishonors the Maker.

The most powerful leader in the world and the lowliest person in the world are both made in God's image. Men and women, boys and girls equally share his image. The hyperfit athlete and the frail elderly woman are alike in that they are made in God's image. The lost rebellious teenager, the college overachiever, and the self-conscious middle schooler are all image bearers. Racists and civil rights activists share this same foundational identity. The doctor and the patient, the worker and the boss, the homeless man and the rich man, the pastor and his people, the government official and the ordinary citizen, and the person who lives in Paris and the child born in the Andes all carry God's image forever stamped on them. Look into the face of any person, anywhere at any time, and remember that the one thing you know for sure is that he or she bears the stamp of God's image. Everything you think about people and all the ways that you would relate to them should be shaped by God's declaration, *made in my image*.

These words, "made in the image of God," form the fundamental definition of who we are. The story of humanity and all it was meant to be and do begins with these words. Captured in these words are human identity, human meaning and purpose, the definition of how humans are to function, and a finger pointing to human destiny. The narrative of humanity is captured by these words. Here is the all-encompassing and inescapable human identity. It is stamped by the Creator on everyone.

By his good and wise will, this is who God has chosen us to be. All other identity markers are subservient to this one. "Like God." There is no more basic thing that you could say about every human being that has ever lived.

But here's the problem. When it comes to the image of God, we have a divine declaration without a clear definition. After this amazing identity declaration, God doesn't turn and say, "And this is exactly what it means when I said that you are made in my image." So we have to look at the other places where this term comes up; we need to unpack the places where Scripture talks about who we are and what we are meant to do, so we can piece together some sense of what this incredible identity statement means. Below are six words that help develop a portrait of what it means to be made in God's image.

Relationship

Most people who know me only as a writer or as a speaker on a platform would not know that I'm naturally shy. When Luella and I attend a party, in ten minutes Luella is best friends with everyone and I'm off in a corner hoping no one talks to me. That might be bit of an exaggeration, but it does speak to how different we are when it comes to relationships. But I have been confronted with the fact that God did not design me to live an independent, isolated life. You don't have to go very far to see that relationships are an essential part of the way the Creator perfectly designed people. We see it in the very beginning, when God declared that he made Adam and Eve in his image, in his likeness. God is the ultimate relational being. No, I don't mean that God needs relationship with us, because he is self-sufficient, needing nothing outside of himself. What I mean is that God *is* a community. Father, Son, and Holy Spirit dwell in a relationship of perfect communion with one another. In his prayer for his followers in John 17:20–23, Jesus lets us know that the unity and the communion of the Trinity is the bright and shining standard for the oneness he wants for his people. He prays, "That they [his followers] may be one even as we are one" (John 17:22).

So to be made in the image of God surely means that we are made for community. We are made to dwell in willingly dependent relationship to God and others. In the words "made in the image of God," we have the seeds of the two Great Commands. I will fully live out of the image, which the Creator has stamped on me, only when I love God above all else and love my neighbor as myself.

Let's be honest here: sin makes this unnatural for all of us. We *are* relational, but we make life all about us. Rather than worshiping God, we insert ourselves into God's position, and rather than loving people, we use people to get the things that we love. We all do this in some way. It's the upside-down, inside-out life that is the definition of the foolishness of sin.

The relational nature of the image of God preaches to us our need for the gospel of the grace of Jesus. If we are ever going to dwell in harmonious, worshipful community with God *and* in loving, self-sacrificing community with our neighbor, we need to be rescued and empowered by God's grace again and again, until we are in the place where sin and division are no more.

The doctrine of the image of God in man places relationship as one of God's highest design values for us. This means that success in life is not measured by the size of your accomplishments, your power, your acclaim, your money, or your possessions. Success is not about a great education, a great job, a great house, great vacations, and a great retirement. I think many of us who say we are followers of Jesus have bought the world's definition of success. We chase those same dreams ourselves, and we pass those hopes and dreams down to our children. Meanwhile, our families are broken, many of us feel terribly alone, we are more consumers of what our churches have to offer than participants, and we live with constant anxiety that these right-here, right-now material success dreams will elude us.

At the heart of living like you really do believe that you were made in the image of God is living a life of vertical and horizontal love. That is why Paul wrote these words:

> If I speak in the tongues of men and of angels, but have not love, I am a noisy gong or a clanging cymbal. And if I have prophetic powers, and understand all mysteries and all knowledge, and if I have all faith, so as to remove mountains, but have not love, I am nothing. If I give away all I have, and if I deliver up my body to be burned, but have not love, I gain nothing.
>
> Love is patient and kind; love does not envy or boast; it is not arrogant or rude. It does not insist on its own way; it is not irritable or resentful; it does not rejoice at wrongdoing, but rejoices with the truth. Love bears all things, believes all things, hopes all things, endures all things.
>
> Love never ends. As for prophecies, they will pass away; as for tongues, they will cease; as for knowledge, it will pass away. For we know in part and we prophesy in part, but when the perfect comes, the partial will pass away. When I was a child, I spoke like a child, I thought like a child, I reasoned like a child. When I became a man, I gave up childish ways. For now we see in a mirror dimly, but then face to face. Now I know in part; then I shall know fully, even as I have been fully known.
>
> So now faith, hope, and love abide, these three; but the greatest of these is love. (1 Cor. 13)

Would your husband or wife say that loving relationships are of highest value to you?

Would your children?

Would your friends?

Would the staff you minister with?

Your neighbors?

Your boss?

Your coworkers?

Your fellow students?

Your colleagues?

Your parents?

Your extended family?

The people who serve you at the local store or restaurant?

Every aspect of God's design is also a calling. God purposed to make us relational, so taking his design seriously means we make his purpose for us the purpose of our lives. We were designed to be like God; that is, to live in communities of unity and love. May we humbly confess our selfishness and seek the grace we need to do so.

Morality

Adam and Eve were also made like God in true (perfect) righteousness and holiness. It is a stunning thing to consider. This is so far from our field of experience that it is difficult for us to extend our imagination far enough to envision what this means. We are flawed people, not perfect in any way, and we live with and near flawed people. We live with conflicting thoughts, fluctuating desires, changing opinions, and mixed motives. We don't always think, desire, or choose the right thing. What is right isn't always attractive to us, and what is wrong sometimes looks beautiful to us. Sin still resides in our hearts and is the seedbed of a catalog of destructive idolatries. We may look at someone and say, "That is a really good woman," or, "That is a fine man," but we say of no one, "He or she is perfect."

Until they rebelled against God's wise and loving command, Adam and Eve were like God, perfect in righteousness and holiness. Embedded in this is the fact that human beings were created by God as moral beings, the law of God written on their hearts. It means they were instinctively oriented to standards of right and wrong. They operated with moral consciousness. Human perfection was shattered in that moment of rebellion in the garden, but moral hardwiring still exists. You may be thinking, "Paul, where? It seems like everywhere you look, morality is dead."

Let me give you an example. Say you were shopping in a busy mall and in front of you was an elderly lady, leaning on a cane and walking with difficulty. Imagine that all of a sudden a kid tore through the crowd, knocked the elderly lady down, took her purse, and ran away. Everyone in that crowd would be thinking the same thing: "What that kid did to that lady was wrong." Some would run after the kid while others would seek to give the lady aid and comfort. What is operating in that moment is God-designed moral consciousness. No, it's not perfect, but it is still there.

Everyone thinks about right and wrong and carries around with them some kind of moral code. Every person submits to some kind of moral law. Everyone has a set of rules they live by, and everyone carries around a set of rules for others. Every human being functions morally; the place we differ is where we get the moral standard that we submit our lives to. No one thinks everything is right and nothing is wrong. Few people live without regret and few people refuse to ever admit failure. We are moral beings.

Here's where the moral nature of the image of God in man takes us. It is sad to live in a world where moral perfection has been shattered but where moral inclination still exists. It means we will submit our lives and our judgment of others to rules of our own making. It means that the rules by which most people live have been divorced from the perfectly holy wisdom of the Creator. Yes, there will be moments in the mall when moral consciousness will operate well, but we won't do well if we repudiate God's law, remove the concept of sin from our vocabulary, and write laws of our own making. Here we are again, seeing how the doctrine of the image of God in man, like all the other doctrines we have been considering, points us to the cross of Jesus. Jesus perfectly obeyed the law on our behalf, he took on the penalty for our sin, and on the cross he purchased a new heart and a renewed mind for us. His grace empowers us to obey and his work guarantees that we will one day be like him and live with him in perfect righteousness and holiness forever and ever. What is now broken in us will, by grace, be fully restored.

Spirituality

That morning when our daughter, at just four months old, was placed in our hands, we were overwhelmed with wonder, with the depth of our responsibility, and with all the emotions that resulted. But our wonder and weeping were not because just a body had been placed in our hands, although it was unique and beautiful, as if our job were to care just for this physical entity. Surely, physical care was important to us, but what really blew us away was that God had called us to care for the soul of this little one. Made in the image of God, she was a spiritual being. No, not in a self-conscious, religious way, but rather, in her essence she was like God, a spiritual being.

God designed this little one to be able to know him, relate to him, love him, talk to him, and worship him. These capacities separated Adam and Eve from the rest of creation as they did this little one that I held in my hands. She was made for God, she was made to live with God, she was made to listen to God, she was made to obey God, and she was made to offer her heart to God in awe, wonder, and worship. Human spirituality is at the core of who human beings are, why they were made, and what should motivate how they live. Humans were designed with a catalog of spiritual capacities. The ability to think, the capacity to give and receive communication in language, the ability to feel a range of emotions—from love to hate and everything in between—and the motivation to worship were all designed by God because human beings were made to "live and move and have our being" in him (Acts 17:28).

In this way every human being is religious, because we all are made in God's image and wired with Godward capacities, and we will either give ourselves in worship to God or we will worship something that God has made. Every human being is searching for God, though most don't know it. Much of human disappointment, despondency, anger, and hopelessness exist because we ask something to do for us what only God can do. Because we are spiritual beings, we name things as "god" that are not God. Because we are worshipers, we will always hook our hopes and dreams to something. Wired with imaginations, we envision what life will be like, calculating if this "god" will come through for us. Children do it, husbands and wives do it, students do it, the hourly worker does it, career people do it, pastors do it, and so does everyone they pastor. Everyone is on a great life-shaping spiritual search. No one is excluded.

Detached from God, our spirituality drives us into various forms of functional insanity. Careening from god to god and from disappointment to disappointment, we attach ourselves to yet another created thing and hope once again it will do for us what it can never do. We put godlike expectations on one another, and we break under the burden. We keep hoping creation will do what it simply has no capacity to do for us, and that it will offer what God alone can.

The deepest, most beautiful and mysterious human abilities were given so that we would be able to commune with and worship God. We were designed to communicate so we could talk to God. We were given rational and interpretive abilities so we could think about what God has said to us and apply it to our daily lives. We have been given emotions so we would be able to experience the joy of loving God and being loved by him and so we could hate what God hates. We were built with the capacity to worship so our hearts would be drawn to the Lord in gratitude, wonder, and praise. All of these abilities are ours because we, made in the image of God, are spiritual beings, and we were made to be able to live Godward lives.

Divorced from God, these capacities can go dark and become dangerous. Sadly, in our sin, we often use these abilities to manipulate, seduce, and oppress others. We use them to plan how we will disobey God and cover when we have. We use them to diminish others and to aggrandize ourselves. The misuse of these spiritual capacities is itself an argument for the necessity of the incarnation, the cross, and the resurrection of Jesus Christ.

Husband, look at your wife and know that her communicative, interpretive, and emotional capacities weren't first made so that she could know and love you, but so that she could know and love God. You cannot act as if they belong to you. In fact, the highest, purest way to express the depth of your love for her is to work to deepen her acknowledgment of and affection for the one who made her. Yes, she should love you, but the end goal of marriage is not mutually satisfying human love. No, the goal of marriage is that it would stimulate an ever-deepening love for and worship of God. Wife, I would say the exact same thing to you. The same is true of friendship.

Parents, your children are not to be seen as potential trophies on the showcase of your success. Your children are the trophies of God. They do not exist to give you identity, to make you feel good about yourself, or to enhance your reputation before others. Your children are made for God to live Godward lives. Everything you do in parenting must have the goal of pointing your children to God as the focus of their greatest motivation and the object of their deepest love.

We cannot think of our emotional, rational, and communicative abilities as just the means to build satisfying human relationships. Good human relationships are made possible by these abilities and are a blessing, but God intends for these abilities to be means to an end. The end is joyful, grateful, and worshipful communion with him.

Representation

Read carefully the flow of the language in Genesis 1:26: "Then God said, 'Let us make man in our image, after our likeness. And let them have dominion. . . .'" The most immediate and clear definition of what it means to be made in the image of God is to "have dominion." To be made in God's image is to be made for rule. Since God is the designer and he is communicating the purpose for his design, we know that human beings were not made for independent rule. The scene here isn't Adam and Eve deciding that they would like to exercise a little power over the rest of creation. No, God says, "This is how I have designed you, this is what I have created you for, and this is what I want you to do."

Humanity's ability, desire, and calling to rule is inextricably tied to God. It is rule that has come from him, is designed to be done through him, and must be done in obedience to him. This means that to rule as God's image bearer is to represent the heart and will of God on earth. God's design is to make his invisible rule visible as his divine values form the way men and women relate to him, to one another, and toward the rest of creation. This means, then, that our ability to exercise dominion in a way that would please our Creator depends on a life of submission to and worship of him.

We are not just part of creation. We have been designed for a unique leadership role. In every area of human life, we are meant to rule in a way that represents the existence and values of the one who created and commissioned us. A book could be written on how this mandate at creation is meant to define and shape the way we relate to one another, build institutions, deal with problems, and steward the rest of creation. God did not design us to be in a consumeristic relationship with the rest of creation, but rather to live with a constant sense of our stewardship responsibilities. We are not meant to use up and walk away, but rather to rule over and care for what God has made.

Because we are all stamped with God's image, we are all commissioned. Now, I have a confession to make. I don't get up every morning and ask myself how I might represent the heart, story, and plan of God in the situations, locations, and relationships that occupy me throughout the day. I am, however, filled with the urgency of so many things that are important to me, whether tasks that I want to complete, plans that I would like to accomplish, or pleasures which I would love to enjoy. It is easy to forget that God has stamped "Agent" on me. This is who I am and it is how I am meant to live, and because it is, I am in constant need of his rescuing and empowering grace. I would suspect you are too.

Damage

Even with all the ravages of sin on the human community, even with the fact that every aspect of our humanity has been touched by evil, the image of his own likeness that God stamped on us has not been destroyed. There is no living, breathing human being, no matter how noble or how depraved, who does not carry that likeness. No aspect of our image bearing functions as God intended. It all has been bent and twisted by sin. People still have moral consciousness but do not love God's law, and each person lives as a law unto himself. We still have the amazing ability to think and interpret, but we have forsaken God's revelation as the standard by which we understand and judge everything in our lives. We still are spiritual beings who live out of the heart, but we no longer offer the worship of our heart to God. We still have representational capabilities, but we do not live as ambassadors of the King because we have set ourselves up as king. We still have the emotional capacity to love and to hate, but it has been divorced from its core, the love of God. You can see the stamp of the glory of God on us, but its reflection has been dimmed by the dirt and damage of sin.

When they placed our daughter in our arms at the airport, we were filled with the sense of the glory of this little one. There is no glory under heaven like the glory of a human being. Watch a child, observe her development over the years, and be blown away by the image of the glory of God stamped on her. Look at a couple in love, and see the depth of their connection to one another—and see the likeness of God. Look through the eyes of an artist as she begins to lay paint on the canvas, creating beauty with each stroke, and see God's image. See the homeless man reach out his hand for a few of your coins, and see God's glory imprinted on him. Look at the elderly lady, all dressed up, moving slowly with her walker down the street, and see an image bearer. Look into the eyes of the server at your favorite restaurant, and see the likeness of God. Watch the thief, handcuffed in the courtroom waiting for his sentence, and see a man who carries with him the image of his Creator.

The image may be marred, dinted, dirty, and damaged, but it is still there. That dignity, that value, that worth is carried by every person who has ever lived. It is not something earned; it is printed there by the Lord Creator. Sin does not have the power to wipe it away. It is the foundational identity of every human being, each one made in the image of God.

But we should weep at the damage that has been done to this glory, knowing that the glory of humanity is the glory of God. Every human being should be a clear, undistorted, and unspotted window to the stunning glory of the Creator. Every glorious aspect of humanity should point us to the Lord of perfect glory. But damage has been done. There are times when the damage seems so great that the likeness of God is barely visible. And so, like each doctrine, the doctrine of the image of God in man causes us to cry out for redeeming, restoring, healing, and delivering grace. We really do need to be recreated in Christ Jesus. We really do groan, waiting for the day when we will finally be made completely new again. And we should be quick to give thanks that, because of redeeming grace, we are being renewed day by day. Grace upon grace is progressively restoring the glory that once was. And while we wait for the final renewal, we commit ourselves to gospel work, longing that every damaged image bearer would receive that same grace that is now at work in us.

14

The Image of God in Man in Everyday Life

SO MANY OF OUR relational difficulties and so much of the sadness that results occur because we have lost sight of what it means to live with and relate to one another as persons made in the image of God. From bullying on the playground, to internet stalking, to violent acts of inhumanity, the human community will not operate as God intended unless we recognize who God designed human beings to be. When you look into another person's face and see the face of God, your behavior toward that person changes. Volumes of application could be written about this truth, but here are a few to consider.

Identity

We all assign some kind of identity to ourselves and to others. It helps us make sense out of life. Few questions influence life more than "Who am I?" and "Who are you?" The way you answer these questions will shape the way you think, act, and react to everything and everyone around you, wherever you are. I am afraid, however, that when it comes to identity, most of us get it wrong.

From early childhood, Josh was convinced he didn't matter, that he had no value. He was shuttled from foster home to foster home, never quite sure why he was leaving one and arriving at another. He had no idea who his natural mom was and there was never any thought of a father. In most of the foster homes, he was seen as different from the other children who lived there, and in many of the homes he suffered some kind of abuse. With learning difficulties, school reinforced his experience of being different, of being in the way and not mattering. Convinced he was an outcast, he lived like one. Josh's story is too complicated and too tragic to fully tell here, but everything about his life would have been different if he had learned the full meaning of the value imparted by the words "made in the image of God."

Sam was determined to make something of himself, no matter what. His parents had been poor, but Sam refused to be. He was athletic and was awarded a college scholarship. He studied hard, so he excelled both athletically and academically. Graduation didn't mean much to Sam apart from the fact that it was a necessary step to doing what he really wanted to do: make money. Material success was where Sam would find identity. He wanted it all: big house, flashy cars, country club membership, lavish vacations, and a beautiful wife. He was determined to let nothing get in his way.

Sam did get married and have children, but he never felt satisfied. No success was enough. Material success as an identity is a cruel master, never delivering what was promised. In business, Sam was highly successful, but he made a mess out of his personal life. His wife finally walked away, and as his children grew up, they had little time for him.

Looking at another pile of dirty clothes, Sarah wondered to herself, "Is this who I am?" She had done well in college and had a bright future. Tim seemed to complete the dream. Married right after college, Sarah worked for a while, but then the children came. One, two, three, and then four. Four children under the age of six, and the work was never done. She dragged herself out of bed every morning, exhausted from the day before, having no time to take care of herself because a child was always needing some kind of help. She hated looking into the mirror and didn't find much joy in the monotonous duties each day brought. She watched those beautiful ladies on TV and didn't feel like she had much worth.

Jodi doesn't remember the exact year, but she remembers being very young when she walked out of the pediatrician's office with her mom and announced that she wanted to be a doctor. "Doctor" was the identity that fueled Jodi's focus and dedication throughout her school years. It was the reason she chose the university she attended and why she decided on biology as her major. With her 4.0 grade point average, Jodi got into the medical school of her choice and eventually was able to do a residency in pediatric oncology. Each morning when Jodi put on her lab coat, with her name and her specialty inscribed on it, she welled up with pride. She was a doctor!

Five years into her practice, the buzz of that identity was gone. The long working hours and the exhaustion she experienced when she wasn't at the hospital left Jodi with few close friends outside of her medical colleagues. She had a distant relationship with her church, and the years of focus on her training had put distance between Jodi and her family. Jodi had been too focused to have any time for romantic involvements. She was tired of coming home exhausted and alone. She was a doctor, but that identity no longer fulfilled her as it once did. Medicine wasn't her problem, but what she had hoped it would do for her was.

Although their lives were very different, Josh, Sam, Sarah, and Jodi made the same mistake. They searched for their worth horizontally. Josh concluded from the way he was treated that he had no value. Sam was convinced that material success would give him value. Sarah thought that a life of domestic servitude had robbed her of her value. And the value that Jodi thought medicine would give her had faded away. They all had done the same thing. They looked for basic human worth, value, and dignity where it would never be found.

It is vital to understand that a stable sense of identity, and along with it basic human value and worth, can only ever be found vertically. You know who you are by looking first to creation and second to the cross. (I will discuss identity and the cross in a chapter to come.) So, parents, children, husbands and wives, students, business people, employees, neighbors, citizens, pastors, politicians, educators, and members of the body of Christ must have a robust theology of personhood. The foundation of a biblical theology of personhood is found in these words: "Let us make man in our image, after our likeness" (Gen. 1:26).

Forgetting the value and dignity imparted by these words will force us to look elsewhere, not only for an understanding of our identity, but for our sense of value and worth. Your relationships, the way people react to you and treat you, are never a stable place to find identity. The purpose of your job or career is not to give you identity and value. If you're a parent, looking to your children for identity never works. It is an unlivable burden to place on the shoulders of your children. Physical beauty and athletic prowess will not give you a lasting sense of who you are. Success as the source of your identity requires more and more success. You never get enough for your heart to rest. Material wealth and possessions don't work as identity markers. No matter how big your pile of stuff, if it's your source of identity, enough is never enough. None of these things will impart a rich sense of personhood.

The value, uniqueness, significance, and inviolability of every person who has ever lived is found only in the words "Let us make man in our image, after our likeness." This means that no human being, no matter who he or she is, should be devalued, desecrated, infringed upon, oppressed, dealt personal harm, neglected, rejected, or destroyed, because every person carries the image of the Creator.

If you're a business owner, you must not look at your employees as simply tools needed for your success. If you're an employee, you must not look at fellow employees as objects in the way of your advancement. If you're a politician, you cannot allow yourself to look at your constituents as little more than your means of acquiring political power. If you're a pastor, you should never think of the people under your care as your means to gain ministry prominence and success. If you're a mom or dad, you cannot reduce your children to problems in the way of an otherwise enjoyable week. If you're a coach, the athletes you lead must be viewed as more than the ingredients needed to put together a good season. No one should objectify anyone else. No one should question the value of another person just because he or she is different.

Look into the face of anyone, and see the face of God. Human dignity is a holy thing. Value as a person is not something that is achieved. Human significance is not something that is imparted by some to others, or denied by some to others. You don't buy your value by your achievements, relationships, or appearance. You have value because you are made in the image of God. A stable definition of and sense of identity is only ever found at the hands of the Creator as he picks up dust and breathes his image into Adam and Eve and into us as their children.

This means that any act of dishonor against another person is an act of dishonor against God. Violence against an image bearer is violence against God. Rejection of any human being is rejection of God. Abuse of another person is rebellion against God. Objectification of anyone at any time is a violation of the plan, pursuit, and character of God. This is why it was right for David to say his sexual possession of and aggression against Bathsheba was a sin against God (see Ps. 51). To take and misuse an image bearer is to act sinfully against the design and glory of God.

So many of the problems of human culture are the result of the depersonalization of the individual. Nothing good ever comes out of forgetting or denying the holy worth of every person, stamped on them by the Creator. He imparted dignity. He assigned worth. He created significance. He designed human uniqueness. It is our calling to understand ourselves and to treat others with the dignity and value that is already theirs by the mandate of their Creator. To do anything else dishonors him and carries with it an endless catalog of cultural chaos and human carnage.

We must remember that the story of every human being doesn't begin with his or her birth somewhere as the child of someone. No, the story of every human being begins in the holy and eternally important design of the Creator as he stamps his likeness on each and every one. If you try to understand people's stories without remembering their roots in the Creator's words in the garden, you will misunderstand who they are and what their life is about. Reading the narrative of any human being without the Genesis narrative is like reading a great novel and skipping the most important explanatory chapter. There is no way you will ever properly understand the book.

We all need to be careful about whom we allow to tell our story and the story of those around us. The first chapter of the human story is from dust to divine likeness. Missing this first chapter inevitably leads to devaluing people and rebelling against God's commands for how we are to see and treat others. We who take the Bible seriously can and must do better.

Justice

You cannot read your Bible without being confronted by God's heart for justice. In fact, you could say that the biblical narrative is a justice story. You'll find in the footnote below a small collection of passages about God's justice.[1] This is by no means an exhaustive list, but these verses represent a significant biblical theme. Not only is justice near to the heart of God, but God commands it to be near and dear to our hearts as well. It is important, then, to understand the root of this prominent biblical theme and the agenda that it sets for the way we regard and treat one another.

Justice doesn't have its roots in human law, although human law should faithfully regulate and adjudicate justice. Justice doesn't even have its roots in God's law, given at Mount Sinai. Justice for every human being is instituted in the garden of Eden as God dyes every human being with his likeness. We know this from Genesis 9:6: "Whoever sheds the blood

1 Pss. 9:7; 10:17–18; 25:8–10; 33:5; 36:5–6; 82:3–4; 89:14; 103:6; 146:5–9; Prov. 18:5; 21:3; 29:26; Isa. 1:16–17; 9:7; 56:1; 58:6–10; 61; Jer. 22:3; Ezek. 18:27; Hos. 12:6; Amos 5:24; Mic. 6:8; Zech. 7:9; Matt. 12:18; 23:23.

of man, / by man shall his blood be shed, / for God made man in his own image." Murder is the ultimate injustice because people are not animals; no, they are the image bearers of God himself. An attack of any kind against the dignity of any human being is an attack on God himself.

As you study the justice passages in Scripture, you are comforted with the promise that one day perfect justice will reign again. But those justice passages also confront us with God's plan for us. His plan is to make his invisible justice visible by sending people of justice to bring justice to people who are experiencing injustice. But there is more. Justice is not just biblical work; it is gospel work.

The gospel story is not only a grace story, but it is a justice story as well. On the cross of Jesus Christ, the grace of God and the justice of God kiss.

We see this in Micah 6:8:

> He has told you, O man, what is good;
> and what does the LORD require of you
> but to do justice, and to love kindness
> and to walk humbly with your God.

What does God require of all his children? Justice, kindness (mercy), and humility. Of all the character qualities in Scripture, why does God choose these three? The answer is that *justice*, *mercy*, and *humility* summarize the entire redemptive narrative. God looked at his sin-scarred world and the scourge of people's inhumanity toward one another and decided, in righteous anger, that he would deliver his *justice* and right the wrong that sin had done to those made in his image. He would do this not by unleashing his wrath on humanity, but by pouring out his *mercy*. In order for mercy not to violate his justice, there had to be a perfectly righteous substitute, one who would be the perfectly acceptable sacrifice for sin. So Jesus *humbled* himself and became obedient, even to death on the cross. The redeeming plan of God, captured in these three provocative words, is his mission for us between the "already" of the sin in the garden and the "not yet" of the new heavens and new earth.

We are called to be ambassadors not only of God's saving mercies but also of his wrong-righting, oppression-defeating justice. You cannot have grace without justice and you cannot have justice without grace; the redemptive narrative makes this very clear. Yet, many believers don't seem to understand this. We might be committed to being representatives of God's saving mercies, but we don't seem to have the same enthusiasm to carry his heart for justice wherever injustice is found.

Let me share my own experience. For many years now my personal mission statement has been "Connecting the transforming power of Jesus Christ to everyday life." My goal in my writing and teaching ministry is to look at everything through the lens of the Genesis-to-Revelation gospel narrative. When I do that with topics like sex, money, parenting, midlife, marriage, communication, counseling, leadership, and more, people respond with gratitude. But when I do the very same thing with the issue of racial injustice, people get mad at me. I have been called a socialist and a Marxist. I have been accused of forsaking the gospel. One person responded with, "Goodbye, Paul Tripp."

Often when I speak to the issue of racial injustice, I get what I call a "What about?" response. People will say, "What about abortion?" "What about sex trafficking?" "What about violent rioting?" Of course, all of these things are sin in the eyes of God, and the people of God should speak and act against them all. But this "What about?" reaction seems to be a defense mechanism to somehow weaken or negate the justice concern. If I posted a short video on the horrors of adultery, I don't think I would have people responding with "What about stealing?" or "What about bearing false witness?" What is it about the issue of racial injustice that draws out such defensive and often angry responses? If God is generous in both grace and justice, shouldn't we be also?

It does make me wonder if we have fallen into the same error as the Pharisees. Hear Christ's words: "Woe to you, scribes and Pharisees, hypocrites! For you tithe mint and dill and cumin, and have neglected the weightier matters of the law: justice and mercy and faithfulness. These you ought to have done, without neglecting the others" (Matt. 23:23).

It is not some social justice warrior who calls justice, mercy, and faithfulness "weightier matters of the law." No, it is our Savior King who makes this value judgment.

In God's value system justice is a high-value issue. Working for justice for anyone who is experiencing injustice of any kind (racial, political, sexual, etc.) is a part of our calling. Scripture doesn't call us to "just preach the gospel." No, it calls us to tirelessly preach the gospel while we tirelessly work as God's agents of mercy and justice. We cannot stand silent while any image bearer is denigrated, oppressed, devalued, or living with regular injustices. Because every human being is an image bearer, every act of injustice is sin against the honor and authority of God.

One day shalom will return to the earth and perfect justice will reign without end. There will be no more objectification, oppression, abuse, denigration, or racism ever again. Perfect righteousness will shape the lives and relationships of everyone. While we wait in expectation for that day, we do not wait passively. No, our waiting is a call to action. We wait as ambassadors, taking up the values of our King and representing his holy justice and his heart of mercy wherever they are needed. To do anything less is to forsake a significant aspect of our gospel calling.

Charles Spurgeon summarizes the church's call to justice:

> The church that does not exist to reclaim heathenism, to fight to destroy error, to put down falsehood, a church that does not exist to take the side of the poor, to denounce injustice and to hold up righteousness, is a church that has no right to be. Not for yourself, O church, do you exist, any more than Christ existed for himself.[2]

Women

You can barely open your computer, watch Netflix, go to a movie, or follow popular music without encountering our culture's objectification, negation, and sexual exploitation of women. Our society attaches

2 Charles Spurgeon, *Spurgeon's Sermons on the Death and Resurrection of Jesus* (Peabody, MA: Hendrickson, 2004), 294.

a woman's worth to her beauty or views them only as objects for sexual pleasure; the degrading of female image bearers is all around us. Why are female pop stars pressured to dress provocatively? Why are fashions designed not to cover the woman's body but to expose it? Why do countless women find the workplace to be sexually threatening? Why are a woman's breasts often more esteemed than her brain?

Popular media oppresses women with norms of beauty that literally take surgery to obtain. How far away have we fallen from the dignity of women as image bearers of God himself? When it comes to the value, dignity, significance, and uniqueness of the imprint of the image of God, men and women are equals. Hear these words again: "So God created man in his own image, / in the image of God he created him, / male and female he created them" (Gen. 1:27). To reduce a woman down to the shape of her body, to dishonor, denigrate, or objectify her, or to negate the value of her gifts and her God-given contribution as one of his image-bearing resident managers, dishonors not only her but God himself.

I wish I could say that the issue of devaluing the image-bearing giftedness of women is an issue only outside the church, but I cannot. Now, I do believe that God has designed different roles for men and women in his church. I think Scripture is quite clear that the role of pastor/elder is, by God's design, for men. But I also am convinced that we have undervalued and underutilized the God-given and essential gifts of women. The Bible does not teach that the primary role for women is in the home. The Bible does not teach that a woman's spirituality comes through her husband. The Bible does not teach that a woman's life will only be complete if she is married. The Bible does not forbid a woman from being highly educated and having a successful career. The Bible does not prohibit women from leading men in political, education, and business situations.

Let me give you two examples of how these truths connect to the life and health of the body of Christ. One woman in the church where we are members is a professor of black history at a local college. She is not only a historian, but she is a theologian whom God has used to help our church think through and navigate issues of race. Because her gifts are valued, she has been an essential contributor to the health of our church in tumultuous times. Her combination of historical expertise and gospel literacy is a gift of God to our church, but it is important to note that giftedness had to be recognized by leadership and given a voice in order for our congregation to be helped and blessed by it.

Years ago I was one of the pastor/elders of a church in the Philadelphia suburbs. Once a year we would go away for an elders' retreat with our wives. We would eat together and do activities together. But when it came time to discuss the church, the men would go into one room for those talks while the women went to another room to share parenting stories and recipes. Luella, my dear wife, found it both strange and uncomfortable. She reminded me that each of these wise and godly ladies had a different experience of the church than the elders did, and it might be helpful to hear from them. She wasn't asking for women elders but for the gifts and experiences of women to be valued and given expression.

So one Saturday morning after breakfast the women joined the men in a discussion about church. It was one of the most important and eye-opening conversations the elders had ever had. We learned things about ourselves and the life, culture, and ministry of our church that we would have never known any other way. As the women lovingly shared with us, some of our weaknesses and failures were exposed. We began to see these women as not only wives and mothers but also as God's gifted image bearers, built by him to be essential contributors to the life and health of his church. We scheduled a time for our wives to be part of the conversation at every retreat after that.

A woman who comes to her pastor with a concern about issues in the church, questions about a sermon, or concerns about leadership attitudes or decisions should not be brushed off, wrongly criticized, dismissed, or silenced. A woman who has not gotten married or who has pursued a career should not be judged. Married women should not be viewed as attachments to their husbands but rather as God-called and God-gifted contributing members of the body of Christ who happen to be married. Women do not experience the body of Christ as men do. Women see things that men don't see. Women communicate truth differently than men. A body of Christ is healthiest when women are esteemed and their gifts highly valued, not just in the home but also in the church. The church needs highly trained women theologians. The church needs to give voices to gifted gospel-communicating women. We need to encourage gospel-wise women to write. To do anything less fails to treat women with the honor that was stamped on them at creation.

One of the ways to build a culture that values the essentiality of the gifts of women in the body of Christ is to highlight the robust role that women had in God's unfolding plan of redemption in Scripture. As you walk your way through biblical history, it becomes clear that the work of God is not solely a man's domain; it is the ambassadorial calling of men and women alike. Sarah, Rebekah, Miriam, Rahab, Deborah, Ruth, Hannah, Esther, Anna, Mary, Elizabeth, Mary Magdalene, and Phoebe are just a few of the women God used to move along his plan of redemption. Men *and* women are called to be Christ's disciples, his instruments, his representatives, and his messengers.

We should teach this history to our boys and girls. We want boys to grow into men who value the presence and gifts of women in the body of Christ, and we want girls to be clear about their calling and the need to hone the gifts God has given them.

The theology of the image of God in all people should radically influence the way we view and respond to women, co-image bearers by God's design. This theology calls us away from denigrating and objectifying women and calls us to honor them as those who bear the very likeness of God himself. It calls us to honor their gifts, to give their unique experience a voice, and to train them for work as God's agents in the world and as essential members of his church. Hear Spurgeon:

> We cannot say to the women, "Go home, there is nothing for you to do in the service of the Lord." Far from it, we entreat Martha and

> Mary, Lydia and Dorcas and all the elect sisterhood, young and old, rich and poor, to instruct others as God instructs them. Young men and maidens, old men and matrons, yes—and boys and girls who love the Lord—should speak well of Jesus and make known His salvation from day to day.[3]

Respect

Understanding that the image of God has been imprinted on every one of us not only forms our foundational understanding of who we are, but it is meant to shape the way we view, live with, react toward, and respond to one another. The biblical commands to love one another, to treat everyone with honor, and to never do evil in the face of evil, grow out of the soil of the truth of the image of God in man. We are called to look in the face of our enemy—even in the face of someone who may otherwise disgust us—and see the image of God himself. Only when we do this will we treat one another with the love, respect, honor, and goodness to which we have been called.

We are in a cultural moment where respect has been replaced by outrage. Little cultural gentleness remains. We react toward those with whom we disagree with the harshest of responses and accusations. In many cases it seems like we are not content with disagreeing with people who we are convinced are wrong; we want to harm them or to erase them in some way. We seem to have lost our ability to have civil discourse, where ideas are discussed with dignity, restraint, and respect. We seem to think it's valid not only to critique people's words, but also to judge their motives. We are way too quick to speak and too quick to react in anger. It makes public, private, political, cultural, and church communication very difficult and, in some cases, impossible.

We are in trouble if we reduce people to a set of ideas, beliefs, philosophies, political positions, theologies, or social constructs. We are in trouble if we depersonalize those with whom we disagree, failing to

3 Charles Spurgeon, "All At It," sermon 2044, September 16, 1888, *Christian Classics Ethereal Library*, www.ccel.org/.

remember that behind the opinion is a person made in the holy image of God. We cannot allow ourselves to reduce people down to a set of sentences on a page which we might find distasteful, without regard for the harm our response may do—harm not to the position on the page, but to the person behind the position.

I wish I could say that this problem exists only in the culture and not in the church, but I cannot. Every day I am saddened as I read my Twitter feed and witness the harsh, unkind, judgmental, mocking, angry, and disrespectful responses of brothers and sisters in Christ toward one another. It often seems like responders enjoy the opportunity to join in and take someone down. Outrage like this is devoid of any functional recognition of God's call to be gentle, to love even your enemy, and to do good to everyone, especially those in God's family.

We are never forced to make a choice between theology and love. We are called to speak the truth in love (Eph. 4:15). Love that has forsaken truth ceases to be love, and truth not spoken in love loses its purity, because it gets bent and twisted by other agendas. Good theology never produces angry, arrogant, bullying, disrespectful, harm-producing outrage. Theology that does not produce gentle, patient, and respectful love falls short of God's standard for how his truth should be handled and what it should produce. Faithfully biblical theology and its good relational results are rooted in these words of God: "Let us make man in our image."

We cannot say we believe in the theology of the image of God in man without living out the mandate of the passages that follow in the way we live with and respond to one another.

> A soft answer turns away wrath,
> but a harsh word stirs up anger. (Prov. 15:1)

> Do not rejoice when your enemy falls,
> and let not your heart be glad when he stumbles. (Prov. 24:17)

You have heard that it was said, "You shall love your neighbor and hate your enemy." But I say to you, Love your enemies and pray for those who persecute you, so that you may be sons of your Father who is in heaven. For he makes his sun rise on the evil and on the good, and sends rain on the just and on the unjust. For if you love those who love you, what reward do you have? Do not even the tax collectors do the same? And if you greet only your brothers, what more are you doing than others? Do not even the Gentiles do the same? You therefore must be perfect, as your heavenly Father is perfect. (Matt. 5:43–48)

Bless those who persecute you; bless and do not curse them. Rejoice with those who rejoice, weep with those who weep. Live in harmony with one another. Do not be haughty, but associate with the lowly. Never be wise in your own sight. Repay no one evil for evil, but give thought to do what is honorable in the sight of all. If possible, so far as it depends on you, live peaceably with all. Beloved, never avenge yourselves, but leave it to the wrath of God, for it is written, "Vengeance is mine, I will repay, says the Lord." To the contrary, "if your enemy is hungry, feed him; if he is thirsty, give him something to drink; for by so doing you will heap burning coals on his head." Do not be overcome by evil, but overcome evil with good. (Rom. 12:14–21)

So then, as we have opportunity, let us do good to everyone, and especially to those who are of the household of faith. (Gal. 6:10)

Be angry and do not sin; do not let the sun go down on your anger. (Eph. 4:26)

Let no corrupting talk come out of your mouths, but only such as is good for building up, as fits the occasion, that it may give grace to those who hear. (Eph. 4:29)

> Let your reasonableness be known to everyone. The Lord is at hand. (Phil. 4:5)

> Remind them to be submissive to rulers and authorities, to be obedient, to be ready for every good work, to speak evil of no one, to avoid quarreling, to be gentle, and to show perfect courtesy toward all people. (Titus 3:1–2)

> Know this, my beloved brothers: let every person be quick to hear, slow to speak, slow to anger; for the anger of man does not produce the righteousness of God. (James 1:19–20)

> When [Jesus] was reviled, he did not revile in return; when he suffered, he did not threaten, but continued entrusting himself to him who judges justly. (1 Pet. 2:23)

> Do not repay evil for evil or reviling for reviling, but on the contrary, bless, for to this you were called, that you may obtain a blessing. (1 Pet. 3:9)

Parents, when you are teaching your children how to respond to you, to their siblings, to their friends, and to others in the culture, don't just tell them to do it because you said so. Start early, teaching them about the identity, dignity, and value that everyone carries because they are made in God's image. Theologize with your children. They won't understand at first, but they are putting together a view of everything that will shape how they interpret life, make decisions, and choose to live. Make sure good theology is the foundation of their view of life. The image of God in man is both a critical and practically helpful piece of that theology.

Students, the truth of the image of God in man shows you how to treat others in your school or university with whom you disagree. Employers, this truth tells you how to care for those under your employ.

Workers, here is direction for how to respond to your boss and treat your fellow workers. Civic leaders, there is direction here for how you are to respond to those on the other side of the aisle. Husbands and wives, there is direction here on how to handle conflict in your marriage. Pastors, here is a call for how to deal with theological and missional differences in your church. And for all of us, we would do well to remember that behind the social media post is someone who was formed by God to bear his likeness.

Jesus

Every point of the theology of Scripture, when rightly understood, leads us to the cross of Jesus Christ. Now, you may think, "Paul, how do you get from the words 'Let us make man in our image' to the hill of Calvary?" The answer is that the image of God is most powerfully expressed and most fully seen in the Son of God, the Son of Man, Jesus Christ. On earth, in the flesh, Jesus stands before us as the ultimate image bearer. In him the image is not dented or damaged in any way. In him we see God's image in perfect expression in every decision, every word, every thought, every desire, and every aspect of his character, all spotlessly righteous. It is an amazing, important, and life-changing thing to behold.

Excitement should build in us as we read the Gospels and see and hear Jesus, because in Jesus we see what we, by grace, will someday be. The very life character of Jesus is a prophecy of what is in store for us as his children. There is going to be a day when we will not only be with him forever, but will be made like him, God's image fully restored, living in us in perfect expression forever. Jesus, in the flesh, lives before us as our eternal hope. We have no better picture of the image of God as it was meant to be, before sin tragically entered the world, than the picture that has been retained for us in the Gospels.

We tend to emphasize that Jesus, being the Son of God, reveals who God is to us. Jesus said, "Whoever has seen me has seen the Father" (John 14:9). It is right to unpack the glory of God loving us enough to send the Son to make himself further known to us. But it is also important to recognize that he was not only God; Jesus was also fully man. And as a man, Jesus became the fullest expression of what the image of God in man looks like when it isn't damaged by sin. How stunning to be able to observe all the characteristics of an image bearer in someone with untainted perfection.

Observing the image of God in its ultimate expression in the Messiah man, Jesus, should fill us with enthusiasm and hope. He is a living representation of what we will one day be, when the burden of sin has been fully lifted and the image of God is given full expression in us in every way and all of the time. Observing the perfect expression of the image of God in man in Jesus should also break our hearts. It should cause us to weep at the damage sin has done. You are confronted with it in yourself and all around you every day: when it comes to the image of God imprinted upon us, things are not the way they were meant to be.

So how do we get from the sadness of the present moment to the celebration of what will be? Again, Jesus is the answer. He comes not only as the ultimate image bearer but also as our substitute. In his perfect righteousness, Jesus measures up to God's holy standard in ways we never could. In our place and on our behalf, Jesus perfectly meets the demands of God's law, and because he does, is able to be the perfect Lamb of sacrifice. In his death, Jesus paid the penalty for our sins so we could be forgiven by the Father, adopted into his family, indwelt by his Spirit, and progressively transformed into the image of the Son.

Through the life, death, and resurrection of Jesus, the ultimate image bearer, God begins the process of restoring his image in all who believe. The work of Jesus on our behalf is a promise and a guarantee that one day God's image in us will be fully restored. There is a day coming when, by the grace of Jesus, we will be more fully human than we have ever been.

Until that day we follow him by faith, we pray for grace to live as Jesus lived, we cry out for convicting, rescuing, and transforming grace, and we fix our eyes on the ultimate image bearer, deeply convinced that the image restoration work will be completed someday and we will be like him forever.

Yes, it is true that every point of the theology of the word of God leads you to Jesus, the life of Jesus leads you to his cross and resurrection, and his cross and resurrection lead you to hold on to hope in this life and to joy as you look to the life that is to come.

15

The Doctrine of Sin

OUR FIRST PARENTS, who were seduced by the subtle and tempting lies of Satan, sinned in eating the fruit that God had forbidden. Because of this sin, they fell from their original righteousness and communion with God and, as a result, became dead in sin and completely corrupt in every faculty and every part of their soul and body.

Since Adam is the root of mankind, the guilt of his sin was imputed, and the same death in sin and corrupted nature were conveyed, to all who descended from him by ordinary generation.

From this original corruption we are utterly disinclined, disabled, and antagonistic to all that is good, and we are wholly inclined to all that is evil. It is from this original corruption that all actual transgression proceeds.

During this life, this corruption of nature continues to remain in those who have been regenerated by God's grace. Though it has been pardoned and put to death through Jesus Christ, this corruption of nature and all the ways it is expressed are still, in fact, sin.

Every sin, both original and actual, is a transgression of the righteous law of God and contrary to it. Every sin in its own nature brings guilt on the sinner, leaving him bound over to the wrath of God and the curse of the law. He is therefore subject to death, with its miseries spiritual, temporal, and eternal. See Gen. 2:16–17; 3:12–13; 6:5; Job 14:4; Ps. 51:1–5; Eccles. 7:20; Jer. 13:23; 17:9; Ezek. 14:1–5; Matt. 5:28; 15:19; Luke 6:43–45; Rom. 1:28–32; 3:9, 23; 5:12–19; 6:20; 7:18–23; 8:7; 1 Cor. 6:9–10; 15:21–22, 45–49; 2 Cor. 11:3; Gal. 5:19–21; Eph. 2:1–3; Col. 1:21; 3:5; 1 Thess. 1:10; Titus 1:15; Heb. 2:14–15; James 1:14–15; 4:17; 1 John 1:8.[1]

Understanding the Doctrine of Sin

The biblical truth that we are considering here lies at the very epicenter of Christian doctrine. Along with the existence of God, it is a significant worldview watershed. If you believe there is no such thing as sin, in the way the Bible describes it, you then see no need for God's moral law, the wisdom of Scripture, dependency on God, the rescuing grace of the Redeemer, the ministry of the church, or the bright hope of eternity. There are really only two groups of people when it comes to the human drama: those who put their hopes in human systems of redemption and those who see that human hope requires a Redeemer.

One of the sad results of sin is that the average sinner on the street carries with him little, if any, awareness, understanding, or guilt of sin. Sin is no longer a category in people's minds or in our culture. Sin is not viewed as a tool that explains people's motivations or behavior. The concept of sin is not taught in philosophy or psychology classes at your local university. Sin is not a category that shapes our view of law enforcement. The truth of human sinfulness doesn't shape the way most people think about racial injustice, totalitarianism, or abuse. The doctrine of sin isn't typically used to help counselors understand the difficulties of marriage and parenting. Sin isn't understood to be the force behind the pornographication of popular media. Few people think that corruption of politics and government has anything to do with sin. When sin is

1 Author's paraphrase of the doctrine of sin as found in the Westminster Confession of Faith, chap. 6.

a category you've left behind, you have to explain human tragedies in some other way.

If you do not believe in the tragedy and universality of sin, then you will think that humans have the power to fix humans. So you put your hope in education, politics, philosophy, psychology, medicine, and so on. All of these things are beneficial, but they have no power whatsoever to rescue us from the darkness, deceit, destruction, and death that sin has rained down on us all. If, however, you believe that the deepest problem for every human being is sin and if you believe that no human being is able to escape it, then you know that together we cannot save ourselves. If there is such a thing as sin, living in the heart of everyone, then our only hope is divine intervention.

The cry of everyone in the face of the brokenness, danger, disappointments, difficulties, and injustices of life in this sin-scarred world is actually a cry for God and his redeeming, rescuing, and restoring grace, whether the person crying knows it or not. The doctrine of sin tells us that the hope of humanity will never be delivered by humanity, but will come only by means of God's intervening grace. This truth really is one of the great dividing lines. If you believe it, it will fundamentally change the way you view yourself and what you need, your thinking about the meaning and purpose for life, your view of right and wrong, your perspective on what is true and false, where you look for comfort and strength, what is important to you and what is not, and where true, sturdy, and lasting hope can be found. If sin is the ultimate cancer, then there is no cure to be found outside of the intervening mercies of redeeming grace. If sin is the problem, then God is our only hope.

So it is important for us to understand what we mean when we say we believe in the doctrine of sin. As I reread this chapter's opening statement defining the doctrine of sin, deep sadness washes over me. The incalculable horror of the tragedy of sin takes my breath away. I experience moments of spiritual depression when I consider the complete destruction of human righteousness and communion with God. It's as if I am watching the horrible video and hearing the awful sounds of the shattering of shalom. Sin is the ultimate bomb, leaving a trail of destruction in its path. Sin is the ultimate pandemic, infecting everyone, leaving everyone sick. Sin is the ultimate curse, sentencing everyone to death. Sin is the ultimate deceit, telling you endless lies and making promises it can't keep. Sin is the ultimate interruption, changing the human story forever.

It takes your breath away when you consider that Adam and Eve's selfish, idolatrous, and rebellious choice in the garden cursed every human being who would follow them—yes, even you and me. The disaster is not only that Adam and Eve were punished for their sin; it is also that, because of sin, they became completely different people. No longer perfectly righteous in word, thought, and action, they were now corrupt in every way. No longer lovers of God and his law, Adam and Eve were now alienated from God and attracted to what is evil in God's sight. And all of this is passed down to their children and their children's children and every generation that would follow. Sin is the heartbreaking, tragic drama of human history. Sin shattered shalom, and we are still dealing with the horrible results every day.

To fully understand the disaster of sin and its implications for all of us, it is important to unpack that first sin in the garden of Eden.

> Now the serpent was more crafty than any other beast of the field that the LORD God had made.
>
> He said to the woman, "Did God actually say, 'You shall not eat of any tree in the garden'?" And the woman said to the serpent, "We may eat of the fruit of the trees in the garden, but God said, 'You shall not eat of the fruit of the tree that is in the midst of the garden, neither shall you touch it, lest you die.'" But the serpent said to the woman, "You will not surely die. For God knows that when you eat of it your eyes will be opened, and you will be like God, knowing good and evil." So when the woman saw that the tree was good for food, and that it was a delight to the eyes, and that the tree was to be desired to make one wise, she took of its fruit and ate, and she also gave some to her

husband who was with her, and he ate. Then the eyes of both were opened, and they knew that they were naked. And they sewed fig leaves together and made themselves loincloths. (Gen. 3:1–7)

To understand Adam and Eve's disobedience in the garden and how it helps us to understand the nature of sin we will focus on two things. First, you have to understand Satan's deceitful pitch. "For God knows that when you eat of it your eyes will be opened, and you will be like God, knowing good and evil." Satan is not tempting Eve with a better menu than what God had provided. He is tempting her with *autonomy* and *self-sufficiency*. His pitch is "you can be like God." God is the only being who has ever existed that is truly autonomous and self-sufficient. His existence belongs to him to do with it whatever is his good pleasure. There is no law above God, and he is answerable to no one. He is also completely self-providing and self-sufficient. God needs nothing and requires the help and assistance of no one. He knows everything without ever having been taught, and he can do everything without training or help. The point is that Satan's pitch to Eve actually defines who God is and is impossible for a human being. The attraction is far more than succulent fruit; it is God-like autonomy and self-sufficiency.

It is also important to understand what hooked Eve. "So when the woman saw that the tree was good for food, and that it was a delight to the eyes, and that the tree was to be desired to make one wise, she took of its fruit and ate." The seductive hook that ensnared Eve wasn't that this was the most beautiful fruit she had ever seen, although it was attractive. No, the phrase "it was desirous to make one wise" is what magnetized Eve. This phrase should get your attention. Why would Eve be hungry for wisdom, when she was in a perfect relationship with the one who was and is the ultimate source of everything that is wise? Why wasn't God's wisdom enough for her?

What attracted Eve was not just wisdom but *autonomous wisdom*, that is, wisdom that did not require reliance on and submission to God. The only one who has ever existed who is independently wise is God.

He alone has never needed a teacher, counselor, mentor, or guide. He alone knows everything about everything. The Creator knows how his creation is meant to operate and how the creatures made in his image are designed to live. He is wisdom's ultimate source. Eve wants God's position. She does not want to be dependent on God; she wants to be him. In this moment, Eve inserts herself in the middle of her world and makes life all about her. When I read this account of the fall and what attracted Eve at this disastrous moment, I think about Paul's words in 2 Corinthians 5:15: "And he died for all, that those who live might no longer live for themselves." In that moment in the garden, Eve is living for herself, and because she is, she will disobey God and eat what he has forbidden.

What Paul tells us in 2 Corinthians 5:15 is that the DNA of sin is selfishness. Sin really does make life all about me. Sin causes me to shrink my world down to the size of my wants, my needs, and my feelings. Eugene Peterson says that sin causes us to replace the Holy Trinity with a new trinity: "But the three-personal Father, Son and Holy Spirit is replaced by a very individualized personal Trinity of my Holy Wants, my Holy Needs and my Holy Feelings."[2] Sin is self-absorbed, self-focused, self-aggrandizing, and selfish in the truest sense of what those words mean. Because of sin, we want our own way, we want to write our own rules, and we don't want anything in our way or anyone telling us what to do. Sin turns all of us into glory thieves, causing us to want what rightfully belongs to God alone.

The idol of self is the ultimate idolatry. It is the idol from which every other form of idolatry flows. If you worship yourself, you will then exchange worship and service of God for worship and service of created things. If you worship yourself, you will then bow before the idols of comfort and pleasure. If you worship yourself, your heart will be ruled by a desire for power and control. If you worship yourself, you will crave the praise of people. At the base of all forms of human dysfunction is the

2 Eugene Peterson, *Eat This Book: A Conversation in the Art of Spiritual Reading* (Grand Rapids, MI: Eerdmans, 2006), 31.

idol of self. Every sin is idolatrous; it puts us on God's throne, sovereign over our own lives and doing what is our good pleasure. So it is right for David to confess to God, "Against you, you only, have I sinned / and done what is evil in your sight" (Ps. 51:4).

In this moment in the garden, for the very first time Eve worships something other than God. No, the thing that replaces God as the focus of Eve's worship is not wisdom. The thing that replaces God in the worship of Eve's heart is Eve. Love of self replaces love for God, and the result is that Eve rebels against the clear, wise, and loving command of God—she eats what is forbidden. When love of self replaces love for God, there is no end to the evil that will result. So Paul says that Jesus came not so much to rescue us from the evil outside of us. No, he came to rescue us from us, that is, to deliver us from the evil inside of us. If I am the idol that has entrapped me, there is no escape for me. I can run from situations, locations, and relationships, but I cannot run from myself. If sin is idolatrous, then the only hope for me is a powerful Savior, who has the willingness and the might to free me from my bondage to me.

I want to return to David's confession in Psalm 51, because in his confession we find one of the Bible's best definitions of what sin is and what sin does. This foundational definition of sin is expressed in three provocative words.

> Have mercy on me, O God,
> according to your steadfast love;
> according to your abundant mercy
> blot out my transgressions.
> Wash me thoroughly from my iniquity,
> and cleanse me from my sin!
> For I know my transgressions,
> and my sin is ever before me. (Ps. 51:1–3)

In his expression of grief over his sin, David uses three words that capture the nature of this thing called sin: *transgression*, *iniquity*, and *sin*. Each word carries a unique nuance that is designed to flesh out our understanding of what sin is and what sin does. Let's begin with the word *iniquity*. Iniquity is moral impurity. This word alerts us to the fact that sin is deeper than just behavior. Yes, sin results in us doing what is wrong in God's eyes, but sin doesn't begin with behavior. Sin is a condition, an inescapable state of being that causes us to rebel against God's authority and to break his law.

Note David's words found later in his confession: "Behold, I was brought forth in iniquity, / and in sin did my mother conceive me" (Ps. 51:5). David is confessing that his problem is not only that he *did* what was sinful, but, even more significantly, that he *is* a sinner. Now, pay careful attention to what I am about to say next. David doesn't have a problem with sin only when he does something wrong, because sin is a part of his very nature. Sin was as much a part of David's nature when he came into this world as the fact that being a biological male is part of his nature. He is not a man because on occasion he does male things. No, he does things that only a man can do because he is, by nature, a man. David is confessing that sin is a condition he inherited at birth. It is as much a part of his spiritual constitution as the physical characteristics that he inherited from his parents are part of his physical constitution.

Consider the words of Jeremiah: "Can the Ethiopian change his skin / or the leopard his spots? / Then also you can do good / who are accustomed to do evil" (Jer. 13:23). This passage powerfully presents the implications of declaring that sin is not just wrong behavior, but wrong behavior that exists because sin is a matter of our nature as human beings. I cannot escape my sin, which is part of who I constitutionally am, any more than a black-skinned Ethiopian has any power to alter the beauty of God's design of his physical appearance. It is just as impossible for people, who are by nature sinners (iniquity), to become good in God's eyes (without divine intervention) as it is for a leopard to decide that he no longer wants to be spotted. You could shave that cat down to its skin, and it would grow a new pelt that is still spotted. Spottedness is wired into the nature of that animal, and so he is hopeless to relieve himself of his spots. So it is with the tragedy of sin. It is not just what we do; it is who we are.

I used the word *hopeless* above. This is where this biblical concept of sin as our nature should leave us. We have no power whatsoever to manage, control, minimize, or escape our sin, because it is not just what we occasionally do, but it is who we are. However, when it comes to the condition of sin, hopelessness is the only doorway to hope. If we are ever going to seek and celebrate the rescuing, forgiving, transforming, and delivering grace of God through his Son Jesus, we need to abandon any hope in our own ability to defeat sin. We may briefly harness a particular behavior, but we have no power to cleanse ourselves of the iniquity that is part of our nature. We are not those who occasionally do sin but who have the power of self-renewal and self-reformation. No, we *are* sinners, hopelessly trapped in our iniquity apart from the amazing grace of God's intervening redeeming love.

Transgression is another explanatory word for sin. To transgress is to knowingly and willingly cross boundaries that an authority has set. When we transgress, we trespass into a place God never designed for us to go. Imagine you are looking for a parking place on a busy city street and you see an open spot—but you also see a "No Parking" sign there. When you park there anyway, you have transgressed. The word *transgression* points us to the high-handed rebellion of sin. Sin is a rejection of God's authority and his law, setting yourself up as your authority and writing your own laws. Transgression is choosing to disobey God because there is something more important to me than loving, serving, and obeying God.

What this means is that sin is much more than breaking an abstract set of regulations that has been passed down to us from God. Sin is a breaking of relationship with God that then leads us to break his commands. Sin is a relational transgression that always produces a moral transgression. If you love God above all else, then you will keep his commands. Consider the Ten Commandments. The first three commands are about honor and worship of God. The point is, if you don't keep the first three commands, you won't have a prayer of keeping the next seven. The Bible speaks of transgression not just as a rebellion against a moral code, but as a rebellion against God himself. In fact, one of the ways that the Bible helps us to understand the seriousness of our rebellion is to characterize it as spiritual adultery. Consider the strong and stinging words of God through the prophet Jeremiah as he confronts Israel with her sins.

> The LORD said to me in the days of King Josiah: "Have you seen what she did, that faithless one, Israel, how she went up on every high hill and under every green tree, and there played the whore? And I thought, 'After she has done all this she will return to me,' but she did not return, and her treacherous sister Judah saw it. She saw that for all the adulteries of that faithless one, Israel, I had sent her away with a decree of divorce. Yet her treacherous sister Judah did not fear, but she too went and played the whore. Because she took her whoredom lightly, she polluted the land, committing adultery with stone and tree. Yet for all this her treacherous sister Judah did not return to me with her whole heart, but in pretense, declares the LORD." (Jer. 3:6–10)

This passage is raw and hard to read. Every sin is an act of vertical unfaithfulness. Sin is adultery at the most profound heart level. We were created to live in a lifelong, committed love relationship with our Creator that would then shape everything we think, desire, choose, say, and do. Sin is about forsaking our allegiance to God and offering the deepest allegiance of our hearts to other lovers. First John 2:15 captures this well: "Do not love the world or the things in the world. If anyone loves the world, the love of the Father is not in him." Our hearts are always ruled and our lives shaped by the love of something. And it needs to be said that spiritual adultery is not just about loving bad things. No, love of even a good thing becomes a bad thing when it becomes a heart-ruling thing.

Transgression is deeply immoral not just because we willingly step over the boundaries of God's law, but more importantly because we give the love of our hearts to things other than God, and because we do, we end up disobeying his commands. Transgression is not just legal rebellion, but also moral unfaithfulness at the deepest possible level. Jeremiah's raw description of Israel's unfaithfulness (spiritual adultery) to God makes that very clear. Sadly, this spirit of unfaithfulness lives in the heart of every sinner. All of us are guilty of moral transgression. All of us are spiritual adulterers. None of us has been perfectly faithful to God. All of us have run after other lovers. All of us have given our hearts away in some way. All of us have stepped over the boundaries of God's law, because there is something we love more than him.

God's charge against Israel falls on us as well and leaves us guilty before him. Maybe it's giving our eyes to pornography. Maybe it's cheating on our taxes. Maybe it's being bitter and unforgiving in our marriage. Maybe it's patterns of gluttony. Maybe it's subtle racial animosity. Maybe it's greed and materialism. Maybe it's patterns of gossip. Maybe it's worship of success that has left a legacy of damage behind us. None of us can say that we are not transgressors, that we have never been unfaithful to God or his moral law. So for all of us, hope will never be found in our track record but only in the grace of the one who, on our behalf, was perfectly faithful in every way. His righteousness and his forgiveness are our only hope.

The final word for sin that David uses in his Psalm 51 confession is the word *sin* itself. A popular definition of sin is "missing the mark." The picture is of an archer aiming at a target and missing it to the right or left every time. I think a better and more biblical way of defining sin is that every arrow of the archer falls short of the target. Lying in front of the target are hundreds of arrows, representing hundreds of attempts to reach the desired standard and every single one of them falling short. At some point it becomes clear that the archer, no matter how committed or skilled he is, will never pull back the string on his bow and hit the target. He is hopelessly unable to do what he's trying to do. The goal stands beyond his ability and desire. He has met a standard he cannot attain. He is simply unable.

The apostle Paul says it this way: "For all have sinned and fall short of the glory of God" (Rom. 3:23). The word *sin* gets at our moral weakness, our inability to live up to God's holy standard. The condition of sin renders us unable to love God in the way that we should and to live in the way that he has commanded us to live. When it comes to sin, it's not just that we *will not* do what is right (rebellion); we *cannot* do what is right (inability). Since the effect of sin on us is total, we have lost our ability to live as God has designed. The total effect of sin doesn't mean that we are as evil as we possibly could be, but rather that the damage of sin reaches to every aspect of our being and personhood. Sin has left us lame and limping. Sin has left us blind and deaf. Sin has left us irrational and foolish. Sin has left us sick and dying. We do not have the power to help ourselves. We cannot reverse sin's damage. We are as unable as the crippled man languishing by the pool of Bethsaida, who had been there thirty-eight years. He had no hope of getting up without divine intervention. If Jesus hadn't said, "Get up, take up your bed, and walk," he would have languished on his mat for many more years (John 5:1–15). Just as he desperately needed the grace of physical healing, we need the grace of spiritual healing. Because of sin, we are not well. It has left us morally weak, unable to be what we are supposed to be and do what we have been created to do.

• • •

I have just written about the saddest thing that could ever be put down on paper. My heart is heavy. Sin leaves us impure, condemned, and unable. We are not just found weak, but we are found guilty. We are not just unable, we are unwilling. We are not just frail, we are adulterers. Sin is the heart-wrenching drama of humanity. If the biblical story ended here, it would be the saddest story ever written. No curse has fallen on humanity that is worse than the curse of sin. What we have considered is the worst thing that could ever happen.

But this worst thing is not the final chapter of the biblical story. In the face of this worst thing that could ever happen, the Bible presents to us the best thing that could ever happen. Entering the scene is the God-man, Jesus Christ. He came as the second Adam to do, on our behalf, what the first Adam failed to do. He was perfectly faithful to God. He perfectly obeyed in every way. He took on our guilt and bore our penalty. He defeated sin and death. He breathes life into the dead. He is our righteousness and redemption. He empowers us by his grace. He is the only answer to the horror of sin. He is the only rock of hope for sinners. There is salvation for sinners. The worst thing that could ever happen is not the final chapter, and that is worth celebrating now and forever.

16

Sin in Everyday Life

SIN IS EVERYWHERE you look, twisting and distorting the good things God created. You don't have to do a deep-dive analysis to see its trouble in you and all around you. It gives us grave concern for the trouble we see in others, while causing us to minimize the trouble in ourselves. It produces a vile, self-interested anger in you, while at other times giving you reason for righteous indignation. Its presence means temptation is all around, leaving you susceptible to its draw. It causes young people to demand their own way and to lose their way. It corrupts our institutions, creates social unrest, prompts nations to war, and divides families and churches. It gives falsehood a platform and foolishness the power to seduce. It will be with us until the final trumpet sounds the note of our liberation. We will be battle-scarred and exhausted as we burst forth with a never-before-experienced joy. Yes, sin truly is humanity's ultimate disease, its dark dilemma, and its woeful curse.

Imagine how much easier marriage would be if there were no such thing as sin. Imagine the joy of untainted unity, understanding, and love. Imagine living in this lifelong union with no mixed motives, no susceptibility to unfaithfulness, and no selfish conflict. Imagine sex never being selfish or impure. Imagine money never seducing and never being a battleground. Imagine marriage never becoming dark and violent. Imagine extended family never igniting loyalty battles. Imagine love, uncorrupted by sin, for decade after decade.

Think what it would be like to guide your children to maturity with no sin in the way. Imagine no child ever being abused in any way. Imagine being patient and kind toward your children all the time. Imagine your children always having a heart to obey, desiring to do what is right, and living free of the temptation to go their own way. Imagine complete family cooperation, servanthood, and love. Imagine never being heartsick over your children or feeling guilt for how you have responded toward them. Imagine being at perfect peace with the choices your children make. Imagine never fearing what they are up to when they're out of the house. Imagine anger and rebellion never getting in the way of a loving relationship with your children.

Imagine friendship with no conflict whatsoever. Imagine never having petty disagreements, selfish jealousies, or entitled demands. Imagine always being willing to serve and to give. Imagine no one taking a quick offense and no misunderstanding getting in the way. Imagine never having to confess, forgive, restore, and reconcile.

Imagine your job or career unaffected by sin. Imagine every boss being motivated by love for each worker and a commitment to their welfare. Imagine the workplace free of selfish competition, back-stabbing, jealousy, deceit, and thievery. Imagine a work environment where people were more important than money, love was more highly valued than success, and decisions were made with pure motivations. Imagine never dreading going to work, your career not leaving you emotionally spent, and never wishing you could finally do something other than what you're being paid to do. Imagine work always being a place of peace and joy.

Imagine there being no such thing as corrupt government. Imagine that all politicians were upright, trustworthy, and altruistic. Imagine every civil servant loving people more than power. Imagine every citizen feeling cared for, feeling protected, and living unafraid. Imagine no national scandals, no citizens with nefarious intent, and no violence anywhere to be found. Imagine every level of government run by people who always do what is right and good all the time.

Imagine no global pandemics, no poverty anywhere, no disease, and no famine. Imagine no refugee camps, no war-torn cities, no parent-less children. Imagine no war, no nuclear stand-offs, and no terroristic threats. Imagine a world at peace everywhere and all the time. Imagine no ethnic animosity and no racial hatred and no systems of injustice. Imagine every person being respected as God's image bearer. Imagine no infant's life stolen from him before he is born. Imagine no dictators, no anarchist cells, and no international unrest. Imagine classrooms around the world only ever teaching what is true and imparting to students what is wise. Imagine everything that God created, every plant, animal, land mass, and body of water, stewarded with care and to the honor of the Creator. Imagine global cooperation for the good of creation and the welfare of everyone made in the image of God.

Imagine media always broadcasting what is true and beautiful all the time. Imagine every technology that is developed being used for the good of the earth and for the cause of human thriving. Imagine all people loving God above all else and loving their neighbors as themselves. Imagine peace and harmony everywhere all the time. Imagine no falsehood ever spoken or ever believed. Imagine unbroken, never-ending shalom. Imagine our world without sin.

Examine your own life, examine your own heart, and examine your own track record. What would your story be like, what would your life be like, and what would your relationships be like if they were not stained and twisted by sin? Imagine doing everything out of a pure heart of love for and worship of God. Imagine never being wrongfully angry. Imagine never saying a word that wasn't motivated by love and a desire to give grace to the hearer. Imagine never wanting to be the center of attention. Imagine never being attracted to what lies beyond God's boundaries. Imagine always loving what is true and always speaking the truth. Imagine living without fear, disappointment, and discouragement.

Imagine never having your heart broken. Imagine never doing anything to hurt or harm another. Imagine always being gentle, kind, and patient. Imagine always loving to spend time in God's word and adoring your communion with God in prayer. Imagine always being a joyful servant of God and others. Imagine your life being a chronicle of unbroken righteousness. Imagine a life without sin.

I am afraid we are so used to a sin-stained world, which is so much a part of our normal daily lives, that we lose sight of the fact that it has messed up everything in our lives. I am afraid we have gotten used to the horror that we live with every day. I am afraid we forget that sin makes everything in our lives more difficult and dangerous than God ever intended it to be. I am afraid that what should deeply disturb us doesn't disturb us at all. I am afraid that what was never meant to be has become what we now expect. I am afraid that things that should get our attention and break our hearts are so routine that they barely get our attention anymore. I am afraid that we learn to live alongside of what we should mourn and abhor. I am afraid that the presence of sin in us and around us is so familiar that it doesn't make us as afraid and sad as it should.

When we ignore or minimize the horrible results of sin, when they become just another part of life to us, then we devalue the rescue of God's reconciling grace and our hearts do not long for that place where sin is no more. When you are brokenhearted by the damage of sin, nothing is more beautiful to you than God's redeeming love. When you recognize and confess the damage that sin has done to your life, nothing is more wonderful to you than the rescuing power of divine grace. When you live with an awareness of the damage and danger of sin, you are deeply grateful for the presence, promises, and power of your Savior, Jesus. When you live with the destruction of sin in view, you want to be God's tool of justice, mercy, and compassion to those who are suffering sin's consequences. You simply cannot minimize sin without devaluing God's grace and your call to be a tool of that grace in the Redeemer's hands.

So it is important that we think about the biblical doctrine of sin in our daily lives. I cannot track all of the implications of this biblical truth here. That would be a lengthy book itself. But here are some truths that everyone who believes what the Bible says about sin should carry into everyday life.

Sin Is a Matter of the Heart

Hope for sinners is only ever found in the person and work of the Redeemer, Jesus Christ, because sin is not just a matter of behavior, but it is a matter of the heart. If our problem were simply that we do wrong things, then various systems of behavioral management, control, and reform could help us deal with the problem. But if sin is, in fact, a problem of the heart, then lasting change in a person's behavior will always travel through the pathway of the heart.

Sadly, many Christian parents lack a biblical theology of sin, so they reduce Christian parenting down to a careful system of managing and controlling the behavior of their children. Their parenting is a daily system of law, judgment, and punishment. Without knowing it, they have placed their hope in a system that contradicts the gospel that they say they hold dear. The gospel tells us that if the law had the power to rescue and transform our hearts, Jesus would not have had to come. The gospel tells us that if we had the power in ourselves to keep God's law, then the righteous life and substitutionary death of Jesus would not have been necessary. The law will expose the sin of your children, the law will give them a guide for their living, but it has no power to change the content and character of their hearts—only the grace of Jesus has the power to do that. Parents, if the right threat, an increased volume of your voice, and tight enforcement were all your children needed, the narrative of the gospel would not have been needed.

The same is true of marriage. Many Christian marriages are law bound. They are shaped by a cycle of rules, expectations, disappointment, and punishment. Husbands and wives place the hope of change for their marriage in rules and consequences. Wives assign to themselves the power to change their husbands and husbands do the same with their wives. But a biblical theology of sin and redemption tells us that no human being has the power to change another, and that change in the heart and life of a person is always the result of the intervention of divine grace. A grace-based marriage isn't about being permissive, because grace never calls wrong right. Rather, it is dealing with wrong in a marriage with the intention of being a tool of God's rescuing and transforming grace in the life of your spouse. You can't take the doctrine of sin seriously and think that all your marriage needs is the right set of rules.

So a theology of sin always requires a theology of the heart. Note again the confession of David in Psalm 51.

> Behold, you delight in truth in the inward being,
> and you teach me wisdom in the secret heart.
> Purge me with hyssop, and I shall be clean;
> wash me, and I shall be whiter than snow.
> Let me hear joy and gladness;
> let the bones that you have broken rejoice.
> Hide your face from my sins,
> and blot out all my iniquities.
> Create in me a clean heart, O God,
> and renew a right spirit within me. (Ps. 51:6–10)

It is impossible for David to confess his sin without talking about his heart, because he understands that this is where his problem with sin resides: in the thoughts and desires of his heart. So David cries out for heart cleansing because he knows that is where his problem lies. David understands that his behavior can only go where his heart has already gone. His struggle with sin is not because of his environment, or because Bathsheba was near, or because he had too much power as a king. No, this confession comes from a man who knows that he did the horrible things he did not because of what was outside him, but because of what was inside of him.

This is also why the bright, golden promise of the new covenant is a new heart, the heart of stone removed and replaced with a heart of flesh. The word picture here is very helpful. A new heart doesn't mean a perfected heart, but a *renewable* heart. If I have a stone in my hands and I squeeze it with all my might, nothing happens because it is hard and resistant to change. But a soft, fleshy object is malleable and can be molded into any shape I desire. The promise of the new covenant is heart change, without which there is no victory over sin.

Jesus pointed to the significance of sin in the heart in his lengthiest teaching, the Sermon on the Mount. "You have heard that it was said, 'You shall not commit adultery.' But I say to you that everyone who looks at a woman with lustful intent has already committed adultery with her in his heart" (Matt. 5:27–29). Notice that when it comes to the sin of adultery, Jesus erects the moral fence not at the borders of behavior, but in the heart. The physical act of adultery is always the result of adultery of the heart. Sins of behavior are always the fruit of sins of the heart. You cannot let your heart go beyond God's fences and expect your actions to stay inside of them.

Consider just a few of the many biblical passages that remind us of the centrality of the heart when it comes to our struggle with sin.

> The LORD saw that the wickedness of man was great in the earth, and that every intention of the thoughts of his heart was only evil continually. (Gen. 6:5)

> Who can say, "I have made my heart pure;
> I am clean from my sin"? (Prov. 20:9)

> But I say to you that everyone who looks at a woman with lustful intent has already committed adultery with her in his heart. (Matt. 5:28)

> But what comes out of the mouth proceeds from the heart, and this defiles a person. For out of the heart come evil thoughts, murder, adultery, sexual immorality, theft, false witness, slander. (Matt. 15:18–19)

> And he said, "What comes out of a person is what defiles him. For from within, out of the heart of man, come evil thoughts, sexual immorality, theft, murder, adultery, coveting, wickedness, deceit, sensuality, envy, slander, pride, foolishness. All these evil things come from within, and they defile a person." (Mark 7:20–23)

> For no good tree bears bad fruit, nor again does a bad tree bear good fruit, for each tree is known by its own fruit. For figs are not gathered from thornbushes, nor are grapes picked from a bramble bush. The good person out of the good treasure of his heart produces good, and the evil person out of his evil treasure produces evil, for out of the abundance of the heart his mouth speaks. (Luke 6:43–45)

> Let no one say when he is tempted, "I am being tempted by God," for God cannot be tempted with evil, and he himself tempts no one. But each person is tempted when he is lured and enticed by his own desire. Then desire when it has conceived gives birth to sin, and sin when it is fully grown brings forth death. (James 1:13–15)

The fact that sin always originates in the heart destroys our hope in systems of self-reformation.

"I will do better next time."
"It was just a weak moment."
"I'm smarter now than I was."
"I think I know what to do next time."
"I think I've learned what I need to know to avoid this in the future."

The fact that sin originates in the heart also destroys our ability to say that the big problem is something outside of us.

"You don't know what my boss is like."
"It has been a tough month."

"I wasn't feeling well."
"She came on to me."
"He pushes my buttons."
"You haven't met my children."

We must humbly confess that when it comes to sin, our biggest problem is us. We are led astray not primarily by things outside of us but by the thoughts, desires, motivations, cravings, and choices of our own hearts. It is humbling to confess that we have no power whatsoever to change our hearts or the hearts of anyone else. Lasting change is only ever an act of divine grace. So we run to our Savior for the rescue and transformation that only he can provide. And as husbands, wives, parents, children, friends, neighbors, members of the body of Christ, pastors, bosses, and workers it is important to understand that what sin has broken in the heart of the other person, we have no power to change. So we constantly ask, "How can I be God's tool of change in the life of this person?" Since sin is a matter of the heart, God is the only reliable change agent; we are only ever tools in his powerful, gracious, and redemptive hands.

Sin Blinds

One of the most devastatingly dangerous powers of sin is its power to deceive. I have no problem seeing the sin of the people around me, but I can be surprised when mine is exposed. There are so many layers to this spiritual dynamic. First, sin is a liar. It makes promises to us that it will never keep. It instills hopes in us that it cannot fulfill. It paints dreams for us that will quickly evaporate. It makes bargains with us that it will break.

Sin is also deceptive because it presents as beautiful what God says is ugly. When you are on your third burger, you are not seeing the danger of gluttony; you are experiencing the pleasure of succulent meat, dripping cheese, and that soft bun. When you are lusting after a woman, you are not seeing the destruction it is doing to your heart; you are enjoying the temporary pleasure of your fantasy. When materialism has you spending money that you don't have on things you don't need, you are not feeling the danger of your greed and thievery; you are taken up with the pleasure of your new possessions.

Sin is an evil monster masquerading as your best friend. Sin is a slave trader masquerading as your liberator. Sin is a grim reaper masquerading as a life-giver. Sin is destruction masquerading as fulfillment. Sin is darkness masquerading as light. Sin is foolishness masquerading as wisdom. Sin is disease masquerading as a cure. Sin is a trap masquerading as a gift. No matter how it presents itself to you, sin is never what it appears to be and will never deliver what it promises.

Sin is deceptive because it lulls us into minimizing our transgressions. We fall into thinking our anger is inconsequential, that the little lie doesn't make much of a difference, that our gossip won't hurt anyone, that our impatience isn't a big deal, or that everyone is envious once in a while. In that endless private conversation that we have with ourselves, we are either reminding ourselves of the seriousness of sin or we are working to convince ourselves that our sin isn't that sinful after all.

Because sin is deceptive and because it blinds, as long as sin still lives inside of us, spiritual blindness will also reside in all of us. The author of Hebrews addresses this sad reality: "Take care, brothers, lest there be in any of you an evil, unbelieving heart, leading you to fall away from the living God. But exhort one another every day, as long as it is called 'today,' that none of you may be hardened by the deceitfulness of sin" (Heb. 3:12–13). This passage begins with a warning, "Take care." When the Bible says "take care," whatever the situation or the context, that's exactly what we should do. And what is it that we should take care about? The answer is, the deceitfulness of sin.

The warning of the passage is followed by a description of how we are deceived by sin. Here is the process: evil→unbelieving→falling away→hardened heart. I open my heart to things that God would call *evil* (lust, anger, greed, envy, gossip, etc.). When I do this, my conscience bothers me, which leaves me with only two choices. I will either admit my guilt, run to God, and confess my wrong, or I will manufacture self-excusing arguments that make my sin look less than sinful. This is where the second step in the process comes in: *unbelief.* I back away from the clear indictment of God in his word, denying that what he says is true of me. I have responded to my troubled conscience with unbelief.

Backing away from the clear moral standards of the word of God, when it comes to sin, happens more often than we tend to think. To mollify our guilt, we convince ourselves that whatever the passage is talking about doesn't apply to us. This produces the third step in this process of deceit. Since God intends the Bible to be my moral anchor, when I become used to backing away from its judgment of my behavior, the result is always further *falling away.* I have cut my moral anchor rope, sending me morally adrift. The final result is a *hardened heart.* My heart is no longer sensitive and tender as it once was. It is no longer malleable as it once was. So what once bothered my conscience doesn't bother me anymore.

Now let's remember the opening phrase of this passage: "Take care, brothers." The word *brothers* alerts us to the fact that this passage is addressed to believers. This is written to people who really do know the Lord, who really have been rescued by his grace, redeemed by his blood, and filled with his Spirit. How can a believer end up with a hardened heart? The answer of the passage is clear: "the deceitfulness of sin." But examine the process again. The writer is warning us about participating in our own deception. Yes, sometimes we are *blindly willful*, but there are times when we are *willfully blind.* There are moments when we become participants in the deceiving of our own hearts. We participate in our own spiritual blindness when we commit the following.

We compare ourselves to others, rather than God's word.

We rewrite our history.

We minimize our wrongs.

We hide our sin by putting on a good public face.

We shift the blame to something or someone else.

We use participation in formal religion as our defense.

We tell ourselves we'll do better next time.

We mistake biblical and theological knowledge for spiritual maturity.

We fail to examine our hearts.
We resist the loving confrontation of others.

Now notice the call of the passage: "but exhort one another every day." This is very humbling. Our susceptibility to personal spiritual blindness is so great that we require daily intervention. We need instruments of seeing in our lives; we need others' eyes to help us see what we cannot. Unlike a physically blind person, who is profoundly aware of his physical deficit, spiritually blind people are blind to their blindness. When sin deceives, it deceives you about its deception. You may be convinced that no one knows you better than you know yourself, but that is not true. When you say this, you set yourself up for resisting anyone who comes to you with something about you that you haven't already seen yourself. The truth is that as long as sin still lives inside of me, there will be troublesome inaccuracies in my view of myself, and for this, God has graciously provided the intervening mercies of the body of Christ. "The heart is deceitful above all things, / and desperately sick; / who can understand it?" (Jer. 17:9).

Your biggest problem in life is not your spouse, neighbor, friend, parent, children, church, culture, government, physical disease, financial stress, boss, fellow workers, godless professor, or seductive media. Your biggest problem lives inside of you. It is remaining sin, with its power to deceive. But your Savior hasn't left you alone. He has given you his insight-giving word. He has given you his convicting and empowering Spirit. And he has surrounded you in his church with instruments of seeing. Open your heart to his gracious provisions so that you'll have a defense against the blinding power of sin.

Sin Turns All of Us into Addicts

It happened rather innocently the first afternoon. Sam was twenty-seven years old and had committed himself to living a sexually pure life. He was doing some internet research when he happened upon a website presenting nearly naked women using gym equipment. Sam immediately shut down the site and quit his search, but he couldn't get those women out of his mind. With heart pounding, the next night alone in his apartment he went searching for the site and spent an hour looking at images he had no business seeing. Before long he was looking every day and looking for sites that offered a bigger sexual buzz.

As months went by, Sam was hooked on deeper and darker forms of pornography, progressively needing more and more graphic material to satisfy his hunger. It became more and more impossible for Sam to be alone with his laptop without ending up on yet another pornographic site. Sam was no longer in control of his sexual desire; he was under control. He was an addict. He was hooked. He was enslaved. The guilt and shame kept Sam hiding his addiction and made him lie to himself about how enslaved he actually was. Sam had tried to control what he could not control, and his sin was eating up more of his heart and controlling more and more of his life.

Andrea was an accountant for a moderately sized family business. She loved her job, and her employers loved her. Andrea's bosses entrusted the financial books to her and didn't ask many questions. One week when Andrea was hit with unexpected bills and struggling to make it to the next paycheck, she thought of a way to get through. She decided to give herself a hundred dollars from petty cash, write her firm an IOU, and put it in her desk drawer. She knew that no one would know and that she would replace it when she got paid.

Andrea did replace that first "loan," but she realized how easy it had been. The next time it was five hundred dollars and there was no IOU. Andrea told herself she'd remember and pay it back, but she didn't. As the months when on, again and again when Andrea needed or wanted something out of the ordinary, she'd take some money out of petty cash or write a "reimbursement check" to herself. Andrea had not only become a thief, she was also addicted. When her boss finally examined the books, he discovered that Andrea, his trusted employee, had embezzled thousands of dollars from him. Sadly, throughout the process, Andrea never thought of herself as a thief, repeatedly told herself that she would pay her bosses back, always told herself this time would be the last time, and denied that she was addicted.

One aspect of our struggle with sin that we don't talk about enough is the power of sin to enslave. The enslaving power of sin is why we seek and celebrate the liberating power of divine grace. As we have seen already, sin is more than a bad thing you do; it is a master. And if you welcome it into your life, it has the dark power to enslave you. Somehow, someway, sin turns us all into addicts. The only difference between us is the object of our addiction.

Hear the words of Jesus: "Truly, truly I say to you, everyone who commits sin is a slave of sin" (John 8:34 NASB). Or hear the words of Paul: "Do you not know that if you present yourselves to anyone as obedient slaves, you are slaves of the one whom you obey, either of sin, which leads to death, or of obedience, which leads to righteousness?" (Rom. 6:16). Or consider these words from Proverbs: "The iniquities of the wicked ensnare him, / and he is held fast in the cords of his sin" (Prov. 5:22). Sin is not just attractive, presenting as beautiful what God says is ugly, but sin is also addictive. The pleasures of sin pass quickly, but its mastery over you remains.

Part of the addicting power of sin is its noetic effects. That is, sin distorts our thinking: "For although they knew God, they did not honor him as God or give thanks to him, but they became futile in their thinking, and their foolish hearts were darkened" (Rom. 1:21). Sin also distorts and redirects our desires: "The LORD saw that the wickedness of man was great in the earth, and that every intention of the thoughts of his heart was only evil continually" (Gen. 6:5). The result is that "people loved the darkness rather than the light because their works were evil" (John 3:19).

The ultimate foolishness of sin's distorted thinking is the denial of the existence of God. This may not be a philosophical or theological denial, but rather living as if God doesn't exist. If you live as if God doesn't exist, then you look for life in the people, places, things, and experiences of this right-here, right-now world. So you are susceptible to believing sin's lies and embracing its false promises. You buy into thinking that something outside of God will satisfy the longings of your heart. You are on your way to the addiction/enslavement of sin.

Because sin presents as beautiful that which God calls ugly and because it does give you momentary pleasure, you reach out for what God forbids. But the pleasure quickly fades. So you reach out again, hungry for more because created things have no ability to satisfy your heart. Each time you reach out for more, you need more to achieve the pleasure you are craving. Whether it's gluttony, pornography, materialism, gossip, thievery, the idols of power and control, or the lust for appreciation and success, what temporarily satisfied you yesterday doesn't do so today. So you have to have more and more. You want more, and you want it more quickly. Before long you can't stop thinking about the object of your sinful craving. It occupies much more of the thinking and desires of your heart than anything should. What you once were convinced was harmless and under your control, now controls you and is beginning to rob you of important things in your heart and life. You are addicted to what God has forbidden, but you will do your best to convince yourself that you're not. Sin is never harmless; it is a cruel slave master, out to kidnap your heart and control your life.

The addicting/enslaving power of sin should make each of us thankful for the power of the Messiah Jesus to "proclaim liberty to the captives, / and the opening of the prison to those who are bound" (Isa. 61:1). He is our only hope of escape from the bondage-inducing power of sin.

Stop right now and examine where you are experiencing the controlling power of sin in your life. Where are you finding it hard to say no? Where are there desires that are a bit out of control? Where are you minimizing sin's power over you? Is there any place where you have a secret life, behaviors that you hide and patterns that you deny to yourself and others? Do you need to run to your Savior for his bondage-breaking grace? He is able and he is willing and he will not turn you away.

Sin Is the Complicating Factor in All Our Relationships

Why is it that none of us has ever had a relationship that hasn't disappointed us in some way? Why is it that the places where we have experienced the deepest of human love are also the places where we experience the most stinging hurt? Why is it that there are so many misunderstandings and so much conflict in our relationships? Why do we get so impatient with or so irritated by the people we say we love? Why do human relationships become dark, violent, and abusive? Why do we have such a hard time getting along?

No passage more directly addresses these questions than James 4:1–4.

> What causes quarrels and what causes fights among you? Is it not this, that your passions are at war within you? You desire and do not have, so you murder. You covet and cannot obtain, so you fight and quarrel. You do not have, because you do not ask. You ask and do not receive, because you ask wrongly, to spend it on your passions. You adulterous people! Do you not know that friendship with the world is enmity with God?

Think about what James is telling us. Our relationships are made difficult and become conflictual because of our sinful passions (desires). And Paul argues in 2 Corinthians 5:15 that Jesus came so that "those who live might no longer live for themselves." The DNA of sin is selfishness. It causes us to make life all about our wants, our desires, and our feelings. These selfish desires battle with God for rulership of our hearts.

I want something, but you are in the way of it, so I am instantly angry with you. When selfish desires rule our hearts, conflicts always result. Those conflicts are deeper than poor communication, gender, differences in life experiences, race, unspoken expectations, age, or culture. It is sin that sets these relationship complicating factors on fire.

> Why do we get angry in traffic?
> Why do we get upset when someone disagrees with us?
> Why does it make us mad when someone makes us wait?
> Why do our children irritate us?
> Why does conflict mar our holidays and family gatherings?

Why do children fight on the playground?

Why do bosses speak disrespectfully to their workers, and workers get angry with one another?

Why do we fight over parking spaces?

Why do husbands and wives quarrel?

Why do neighbors find it hard to live at peace with one another?

All of these questions are answered by the brilliance of James's sin/heart analysis here, but he goes even deeper. He says, "You adulterous people!" Why does James begin to talk about adultery? Is he changing the subject? No, James is helping us to understand that sinful human conflict is rooted in spiritual adultery. Sin turns our hearts upside down. Instead of loving and serving God, sin causes us to love and serve created things. Instead of loving people and using the things in our lives as a means of expressing that love, sin causes us to love things and use people to get them.

If God is not in the rightful place in my heart, you won't be in the appropriate place in my life. If God is not in his rightful place, I will insert myself in his place, make life all about me, and end up in conflict with you. Only those people who keep the first Great Command will ever keep the second.

This is all very humbling, because it requires us to confess that the biggest conflict-producing problem in our marriage, at work, in the neighborhood, at church, in the mall, or with in-laws did not start with flaws in another person. Since the problem lives in our hearts, we brought it into each of these relationships. Each one of us drags the selfishness of sin, and the spiritual adultery that it causes, into every one of our relationships.

James is arguing if we're ever going to experience peace in our relationships, we must fix them vertically—or they'll never get fixed horizontally. Vertical confession has the power to produce horizontal peace, and for that we need help. Sin's relational havoc is another powerful argument for our constant need for the rescuing intervention of divine grace.

Because of Sin, Life Is War

I am afraid that many Christians have forgotten where they live. No, I don't mean that their cognitive abilities are failing, but that they live with a functional amnesia when it comes to what the Bible says about life between the "already" and the "not yet." Here is how Paul characterizes the address where we live.

> For the creation waits with eager longing for the revealing of the sons of God. For the creation was subjected to futility, not willingly, but because of him who subjected it, in hope that the creation itself will be set free from its bondage to corruption and obtain the freedom of the glory of the children of God. For we know that the whole creation has been groaning together in the pains of childbirth until now. And not only the creation, but we ourselves, who have the firstfruits of the Spirit, groan inwardly as we wait eagerly for adoption as sons, the redemption of our bodies. For in this hope we were saved. Now hope that is seen is not hope. For who hopes for what he sees? But if we hope for what we do not see, we wait for it with patience. (Rom. 8:19–25)

Because of the destructive power of sin, the world we live in is groaning, crying out for redemption. Notice the three descriptive phrases Paul uses to describe the present state of our world: "subjected to futility," in "bondage to corruption [decay]," and "in the pains of childbirth." Because of the widespread damage of sin at every level of human culture and every part of the physical creation, this world cannot operate as the Creator intended. Our environment is in the middle of a great spiritual struggle that only the Redeemer can solve. A great war rages that only the Savior can win. In the meantime the world, in pain, groans. Sometimes this spiritual war is a deeply personal battle.

> For we know that the law is spiritual, but I am of the flesh, sold under sin. For I do not understand my own actions. For I do not do what I

> want, but I do the very thing I hate. Now if I do what I do not want, I agree with the law, that it is good. So now it is no longer I who do it, but sin that dwells within me. For I know that nothing good dwells in me, that is, in my flesh. For I have the desire to do what is right, but not the ability to carry it out. For I do not do the good I want, but the evil I do not want is what I keep on doing. Now if I do what I do not want, it is no longer I who do it, but sin that dwells within me.
>
> So I find it to be a law that when I want to do right, evil lies close at hand. For I delight in the law of God, in my inner being, but I see in my members another law waging war against the law of my mind and making me captive to the law of sin that dwells in my members. Wretched man that I am! Who will deliver me from this body of death? Thanks be to God through Jesus Christ our Lord! So then, I myself serve the law of God with my mind, but with my flesh I serve the law of sin. (Rom. 7:14–25)

Paul's humble confession is an honest description of the war that often rages within us between our conversion and our homegoing. Notice that he uses war language to characterize the struggle between delighting in God's law and the evil that lies close at hand. This war will not completely cease until the King puts the last enemy under his feet (1 Cor. 15:24–26).

Sometimes this war is everywhere around you, in the relationships and institutions of your daily life. Ephesians is very helpful here. After Paul has done a wonderful examination and explanation of the gospel of Jesus Christ, he then turns to help the Ephesian believers to understand what it means to live in light of the gospel he has just laid out.

For Paul, the gospel reshapes the way you approach your church, your thinking, your desires, your communication, your anger, your work, your relationships, your sexuality, your marriage, your parenting, and more. He writes to help his readers to see the wide-ranging impact of the gospel on the situations, locations, relationships, and institutions of their daily lives. Then in chapter 6 he calls the Ephesian believers to be ready, armed for spiritual war.

> Finally, be strong in the Lord and in the strength of his might. Put on the whole armor of God, that you may be able to stand against the schemes of the devil. For we do not wrestle against flesh and blood, but against the rulers, against the authorities, against the cosmic powers over this present darkness, against the spiritual forces of evil in the heavenly places. Therefore take up the whole armor of God, that you may be able to withstand in the evil day, and having done all, to stand firm. Stand therefore, having fastened on the belt of truth, and having put on the breastplate of righteousness, and, as shoes for your feet, having put on the readiness given by the gospel of peace. In all circumstances take up the shield of faith, with which you can extinguish all the flaming darts of the evil one; and take the helmet of salvation, and the sword of the Spirit, which is the word of God, praying at all times in the Spirit, with all prayer and supplication. To that end, keep alert with all perseverance, making supplication for all the saints, and also for me, that words may be given me in opening my mouth boldly to proclaim the mystery of the gospel, for which I am an ambassador in chains, that I may declare it boldly, as I ought to speak. (Eph. 6:10–20)

After all of his practical gospel instruction, it seems as if Paul is changing the subject, but he isn't. Rather, he is helping his readers to understand that you cannot live in your marriage, your parenting, your work, your church, your neighborhood, your school, your extended family, or your country with the luxury of a peace-time mentality. Peace is coming—it has been guaranteed by grace—but right now we are living in a spiritual war zone.

This does not mean that you should have a negative relationship with the people in your life or an adversarial attitude toward the culture and institutions around you. The gospel calls you to loving, patient, gentle, kind, forgiving, joyful, and self-controlled living right here, right now, in the place where God has put you. Our battle is not with or against people, but against the devil and the spiritual forces of evil that wage war against God, his kingdom, his church, and his people.

Rather than changing the subject, Ephesians 6:10–20 is Paul's summary of all the practical applications of the gospel he has just made. He wants his readers to understand that what makes gospel living both important and a constant struggle is that every situation and relationship where the gospel needs to be lived out is also a location of a great spiritual conflict. The entrance of sin into the world did not ignite a legacy of peace and harmony, but rather the daily drama, deceit, and destruction of spiritual war. This war is splashed across the pages of Scripture from Genesis 3 through Revelation.

It is important to understand that you bring your children into a world that is a spiritual war zone. Your marriage is a spiritual battleground. Your church life is made messy because of this spiritual war. Spiritual wars take place at your work. Nothing escapes this great conflict between light and darkness, between good and evil, between God and the devil. This war explains why so many things in our lives are complicated and difficult, and it explains why we should live with eyes open and hearts engaged. Imagine how much easier our lives would be if this war were not raging in us and all around us. It's important to understand that sin is not just a matter of your heart and your behavior, but it is also a war, and therefore we must be ready, armed with the gospel and resting in the presence and power of our captain, Jesus.

Yes, in the midst of this great spiritual war we don't need to panic, because our Savior is a victor. He is now reigning, and as the reigning victor, he is putting enemies under his feet. This means we don't battle alone or in our own wisdom and strength. He battles on our behalf, and he will not stop until the last enemy is defeated. If you're married, your primary enemy is never your spouse. If you're a parent, your primary enemy is never your children. If you're a child, your primary enemy is never your parent. Your friends, fellow workers, or neighbors are not your primary enemy. Your culture or government is not your primary foe. Paul says it clearly: we don't battle against "flesh and blood" but against "evil forces in dark places." Whether it is the war within or the war raging around you, you can be thankful that your Savior King is up to the battle, and he will win. Until then, we put on gospel armor, we pray for guardian grace, and we celebrate the presence, power, and promises of Jesus.

We Cannot Solve the Great Problems of Humanity without a Theology of Sin

Brokenness is all around us. We see it in marriages lurching toward divorce, gender confusion, human trafficking, domestic violence, terrorism and war, political corruption, the unborn ripped from the womb, poverty, racial injustice, violence in the streets, rampant and all-too-available pornography, and a host of other global ills. We will never solve these problems without a deeply biblical and comprehensively applied theology of sin. It is true that the Bible teaches us about the essential role of government as a tool for good in God's hands; we know that good education is vital; it is right to peacefully protest in the face of injustice and inequality; social welfare and advocacy groups can do great good; and we should, as individual believers and as a church, give ourselves to missions of mercy. But a biblical theology of sin says that something more is needed.

If human institutions were capable of reversing the sad brokenness of our world, then the life, death, and resurrection of Jesus would not have been necessary. God sent his Son on his redemptive rescue mission because there was no other way to get at the deepest cause of the problems that press in on each one of us every day. When it comes to what will right the wrongs and restore the earth to the shalom that was God's original intention, our message is singularly radical. Because sin is at the heart of all of the evil, brokenness, and dysfunction of human culture, hope of rescue and restoration will not be found in a philosophy, theology, psychology, politics, education, or any other humanly built system or institution. If sin is the root of all of these ills, then hope will not be found in a thing, but in the intervention of a person, one who has not been infected by the disease and who is willing to invade our brokenness with the power to do what is necessary to rescue and restore. There has only ever been one such person, the Lord Jesus Christ, Son of Man, Son of God, the promised Messiah, Emmanuel.

Every cry of a forsaken wife is a cry for Jesus. Every oppressed person's longing for justice is a longing for him. The fear of an abused child cries out for the Messiah. The longing for safety of the person who has been mugged is a longing for him. The homeless person, ignored by the passersby who refuse to see, aches for Emmanuel's restoration. Each one of us, as the morning greets us with problems we would like to avoid, hungers for the rescue and restoration of the renewing and transforming grace of the Lord Jesus.

Any consistently biblical theology of sin is a long, twisted, rocky, and dark road that leads you to Jesus. If sin is the ultimate cause, and it is, then hope is a person and his name is Jesus. Yes, we will give ourselves to the institutions and actions that help make life in this groaning world better, but as we do, we must remember where our ultimate hope and rescue is to be found. He alone is able to rescue us from us, guard us by his grace, empower us to do what is good, employ us as tools in his hands, and finally deliver us to a place where all things are new and where peace and righteousness reign forever and ever.

Parents, start early to help your children acknowledge what is broken in them and around them, and help them to understand what life looks like when your hope is in Jesus. Husbands and wives, work to ignite a deeper hope in Jesus in one another. Look for opportunities to point your neighbors, friends, and fellow workers to the hope found only in the Messiah. It really is true that people who have centered their hope on Jesus, because of their gratitude, tend to reflect his tenderness, his mercy, and his generosity. We should work for good, we should be generous in mercy, we should make sacrifices of love. But we know what has caused the dysfunction in and around us, and because we do, we know where hope is ultimately to be found. As we wait for his kingdom to come, we become instruments of his kingdom work here on earth, always remembering that our work will not wipe out sin and all the ills that flow from it, and always remaining sure that sin, biblically understood, points you for help in one direction, Jesus.

> No more let sins and sorrows grow,
> nor thorns infest the ground;
> he comes to make his blessing flow
> far as the curse is found.[1]

1 Isaac Watts, "Joy to the World," 1719 in *Trinity Hymnal* (Suwanee, GA: Great Commissions Publications,1990), no. 195.

17

The Doctrine of Justification

THOSE WHOM GOD CALLS, he also freely justifies, by forgiving our sins, and by counting and accepting us as righteous. We are not justified because of anything done in us or done by us, but solely because of what Christ has done for us. God does not justify us by declaring that our faith or our obedience count as righteousness, but rather God justifies us by declaring that the obedience of Christ and his payment for our sin by grace count as ours. So we need to receive, accept, and rest in Christ and his righteousness as the sole means of our justification, always remembering that even our ability to believe is not from us, but is a gift of God to us.

Faith that receives and rests on Christ and his righteousness is the only means of justification, but is always accompanied by all the other saving graces. This faith is not a dead faith, but it works itself out in love.

By his obedience and death, Christ fully paid the debt of all who are justified. He made real and full satisfaction of the Father's justice on our behalf. Because he was given by the Father for us and his obedience and payment were freely accepted in our place, our justification is only by free grace. It is in the justification of sinners that both the exact justice and rich grace of God shine with glory.

From eternity, it has been God's good pleasure to justify those who are chosen. Christ, when the time was right, died for our sins and rose again for our justification, yet we are not justified until the Holy Spirit at a later time actually applies the work of Christ to us.

God continues to forgive the sins of all who are justified. Even though we can't fall out of our justification, we may fall under our Father's displeasure because of our sin. But if we humble ourselves, confess our sins, plead for forgiveness, renew our faith, and repent, the light of God's face will once again shine on us. Pss. 32:5; 51; 89:31–33; 110:1; Isa. 53:5–6; Matt. 6:12; 26; John 1:12; 6:37; 10:15–16, 28; 17:2, 6–9; Rom. 3:24–28; 4:5–8, 22–25; 5:10–19; 8:9, 14, 30–32; 1 Cor. 1:30–31; 15:25–26; 2 Cor. 5:21; Gal. 3:8–9; 5:6; Eph. 1:7–9; 2:8–10; Phil. 3:8, 9; Col. 1:21–22; 2:13–15; 1 Tim. 2:6; Titus 3:4–7; Heb. 9:14–15; 10:14; James 2:17, 22, 26; 1 Pet. 1:2, 18–19; 1 John 1:7–9; 5:20.[1]

Understanding the Doctrine of Justification

I spent one year in my personal devotions in the Pentateuch. It was a rich experience that deepened both my understanding and thankfulness for the justifying work of the Lord Jesus Christ. I am persuaded that you cannot see the multihued glory display of the doctrine of justification until you look at it through the lens of the Old Testament sacrificial system. In that system of repeated daily, monthly, Sabbath, and special-day sacrifices you begin to see how seriously God takes sin. Nothing gets the attention and the pages of instructions like the sacrificial requirements do. The sacrificial system is not only Israel's means of having ongoing fellowship with God, but it is the central institution of their entire culture. Nothing else rises to the level of the importance of this call to regular sacrifices,

1 Author's paraphrase of the doctrine of justification as found in the Westminster Confession of Faith, chap. 11.

because no other reality is more important in the life of Israel, with the exception of the existence of God, than acknowledging the presence of sin and the need for atonement.

At the center of the life and culture of Israel was a scene of daily violence and gore. This blood-spurting, animal-resisting, and wild-wails-of-death scene was a part of everyday life. The scene of priests, covered in blood as they struggled to slaughter a huge bull or cut up the lifeless corpse of a lamb, was a normal thing. The blood never stopped flowing and the animals never stopped dying day after day after day. It is brutal and stomach-churning to consider. I've butchered chickens on a farm, and I know how bloody, smelly, and disgusting it is, but that experience is nothing compared to the daily routine in Israel.

Every drop of animal blood was a reminder of the huge gap between a perfectly holy God and his consistently unholy people. Every bellow or bleat of an animal as it was being slaughtered was a cry for a better sacrifice, one that would finally satisfy the righteous requirements of a Holy God. Every step of the priest, as he trudged his way to the tabernacle to do his bloody, smelly job one more time, was a sign that something more was needed. Every time an Israelite family culled through their flock to find the appropriate lamb for sacrifice was a reminder that God is holy and we are not. The bloody, noisy slaughter of each animal confronted every Israelite with the truth that it was his sin that caused this animal's death. The violence, the blood, the horrible odors, and the repetition of it all was a prophetic cry for a Messiah Lamb. This bloody system would not end with a divine declaration of blanket acceptance; no, it would take a sacrifice to end this system of unending sacrifices.

You should feel a profound tension as you read through Exodus, Leviticus, and Numbers. This tension should stop you, get your attention, and make you uncomfortable. It is the tension that no one in Israel was able to escape. It is a tension we can't escape on our own either. It is the tension that sin introduced into the world. This tension is the mournful soundtrack of life in a fallen world. You hear it first in the garden as Adam and Eve are hiding from God. You know right away that something horrible has gone wrong. People made for relationship with God shouldn't want or need to hide from him. You can't look into that scene in the garden without concluding that something hugely significant is wrong that needs to be rectified, or life will never be what it was designed to be.

Here is the tension. How in the world can a perfectly holy God have communion with constitutionally unholy people? How will sinners ever be able to commune with the one for whom they were made? If relationship with God is at the core of human identity, meaning, and purpose, what kind of lost, insane life will human beings have without it? Will God bridge this huge, life-destroying sin gap, and if he will, how will he do it? This is where the tension intensifies. How will God extend his mercy to those he loves without compromising his holy justice? How in the world will mercy and justice ever work together? The answer is that sacrifices have to be made that satisfy the requirements of God's justice so he can extend the mercy of his forgiveness to sinners. The problem with the Old Testament sacrifices is that the satisfaction they supplied was sadly temporary. Clearly a greater, final sacrifice was needed for justification for sinners to be final and complete. The entire old system, with all of its blood and gore, was a daily cry for the final Lamb of sacrifice, Jesus. Let me summarize, with several points, what we learn as we observe the Old Testament sacrificial system.

1. The incredible, patient, and forgiving mercy of the Lord toward sinners.
2. The uncompromising holiness of God.
3. God's righteous anger with sin.
4. The inescapable seriousness of sin.
5. The inability of sin-flawed people to earn acceptance with God on their own.
6. The inadequacy of God's law as a means of achieving acceptance with him.

7. The inadequacy and temporary nature of sacrificing bulls and goats for sin.
8. The need for a once-for-all sacrifice that extends God's mercy without compromising his justice.

What needed to be done, no human being could do. What needed to be done, God would have to do in a triad of glorious miracles of grace: the incarnation of the Son, his perfect life and acceptable sacrifice, and his resurrection victory. It is only in the life, death, and resurrection of Jesus that the tension is ended. In Jesus God's perfect justice and forgiving mercy kiss. So a substitute was needed, a second Adam, who would live the righteous life that the first Adam sadly failed to live. It is important to note that the substitutionary work of Jesus Christ did not begin with his suffering and death, but with his birth. Every righteous thought and desire was for us. Every act of moral purity was for us. Every moment when Jesus resisted temptation was for us. His victory over the temptations of Satan was for us. His refusal to live in fear of the religious authorities was for us. It was vital that the second Adam establish a track record that was unstained by any sin of word, thought, desire, or action of any kind or at any time.

But the second Adam must do vastly more than the first Adam could have done. There is another way we needed for him to be our substitute. The second Adam came not only to be our righteousness, but also to be our sacrifice for sin. A payment for sin needed to be made that would once and for all satisfy God's requirement and allow sinners to be forgiven and to live at peace with God. The combination of his substitutionary obedience and his substitutionary sacrifice means that all who put their trust in him are justified, that is, they are fully and completely forgiven and able to stand before God as righteous. None of this can any sinner earn, deserve, or achieve on his own. The righteous life and the acceptable death of Jesus is the only means by which justifying grace can flow to sinners like you and me. Notice the clarity and the celebratory gratitude of the following passages when it comes to God's justifying mercy in Jesus Christ.

Therefore, since we have been justified by faith, we have peace with God through our Lord Jesus Christ. Through him we have also obtained access by faith into this grace in which we stand, and we rejoice in hope of the glory of God. (Rom. 5:1–2)

For while we were still weak, at the right time Christ died for the ungodly. For one will scarcely die for a righteous person—though perhaps for a good person one would dare even to die—but God shows his love for us in that while we were still sinners, Christ died for us. Since, therefore, we have now been justified by his blood, much more shall we be saved by him from the wrath of God. For if while we were enemies we were reconciled to God by the death of his Son, much more, now that we are reconciled, shall we be saved by his life. More than that, we also rejoice in God through our Lord Jesus Christ, through whom we have now received reconciliation. (Rom. 5:6–11)

For I decided to know nothing among you except Jesus Christ and him crucified. (1 Cor. 2:2)

All this is from God, who through Christ reconciled us to himself and gave us the ministry of reconciliation; that is, in Christ God was reconciling the world to himself, not counting their trespasses against them, and entrusting to us the message of reconciliation. Therefore, we are ambassadors for Christ, God making his appeal through us. We implore you on behalf of Christ, be reconciled to God. For our sake he made him to be sin who knew no sin, so that in him we might become the righteousness of God. (2 Cor. 5:18–21)

Yet we know that a person is not justified by works of the law but through faith in Jesus Christ, so we also have believed in Christ Jesus, in order to be justified by faith in Christ and not by works of the law, because by works of the law no one will be justified. (Gal. 2:16)

> But far be it from me to boast except in the cross of our Lord Jesus Christ, by which the world has been crucified to me, and I to the world. (Gal. 6:14)

There simply is no such thing as Christian theology that doesn't have a clear understanding of the doctrine of justification at its core. This doctrine creates the great differentiation point between Christianity and all other religions and irreligion. All other formal religions are built on some form of the theology that the "gods" are upset with human beings and need to be appeased. Each lays out some means by which you have to constantly work to quell the anger of God by your obedience to rules and offering of repeated sacrifices. Each is a system of fear, divine anger, and bondage to law out of which the believer never rises.

But even the irreligious are concerned with righteousness. Everyone wants to be right. Everyone wants to think he has a good track record. People tend to want to be accepted because they are good. What are you left with if you deny the existence of a holy God and his forgiving mercies? You are left with only yourself. You essentially have nothing more to trust than your wisdom, strength, and goodness. Your life is reduced to "Do right, good results. Do bad, bad things happen." It is a life burdened by the constant need to perform, the constant need to measure up, and the constant need to build self-convincing arguments for your goodness. It is an exhausting way to live that never works. The reality is that not only do we fall short of God's holy standards, but we fall short of our standards for ourselves. Not only do we break God's rules, but we consistently break our own rules.

The reason the doctrine of justification is so precious is that every human being desperately needs forgiveness. You don't enter into the glorious rest of justification by hoping in yourself, your efforts, your intentions, or your ability to somehow, someway, measure up to God's requirements. Imagine a gym with a forty-foot-high ceiling. Imagine I entered the gym with the intention of standing in the middle of that gym floor and jumping up and touching the ceiling. If you knew my purpose for entering that gym, you would say, "This is a truly insane or delusional man. It will never happen." Imagine further that you stand by the door and watch me begin to jump. You are overcome by the futility of what I am attempting and you feel sorry for me as I get more and more exhausted and further and further away from my goal. You would begin to think, "This man needs to admit his inability and give up. He will never do this. Whatever hope he had when he entered the gym and whatever hope is keeping him jumping, is false hope."

So it is with justification. The doorway to the warehouse of God's justifying mercies is hopelessness. Yes, it is true: when it comes to right standing with God, hopelessness is the doorway to hope. You have to abandon hope in yourself in order to run in the hope of humility and confession to God. This redeeming hopelessness ushers you into the Holy of Holies, the places where God dwells. It leads you to the mercy seat, where eternal, secure, and unshakable hope is found. It is not hope you have earned, but hope that has been earned by another and granted to you by grace. There would be no such thing as Christianity if there were any way that a human being could reconcile himself to God and stand righteous before him based on his own performance. If this were possible, the gospel would be a lie and the biblical narrative would not be needed. But the gospel is not a lie; it is the most essential and most glorious message ever written and spoken. In his righteous life and substitutionary death, Jesus has made it possible for us to be forgiven, accepted, and declared righteous by God. This is the ultimate good news.

But There Is More Good News

You can't do justice to the truth of God's justifying grace through the Lord Jesus Christ without considering one of the beautiful redemptive graces that attaches itself to this precious truth. Our justification is not just about our legal standing before God, but it is also about a brand-new identity as his child. Understanding this new identity is not only important to understanding the full implications of this wonderful truth, but it has implications for how you live your life. (I will have a lot more to say about this in the next chapter.)

This new identity can be summarized in two of the most important words in the Bible's redemptive vocabulary: *in Christ*. It is impossible to do biblical justice to the truth we are considering without talking about our union with Christ. This truth, that by grace we have been united to Christ, is a dominant theme in Paul's writing. He uses the phrase "in Christ" thirty-three times. Paul says that we were chosen "in him before the foundation of the world" (Eph. 1:4). By God's sovereign redemptive purpose, we were united to Christ before we took our first breath. It is an amazing thing to consider. It was not that we got smart, found Christ, and entered in. No, God placed us "in Christ" as a sovereign decision of his redeeming grace.

All of the graces of the gospel flow to us because we are in Christ. We are justified because we are in Christ. We are being sanctified because we are in Christ. We are loved as adopted children because we are in Christ. We are forgiven because we are in Christ. We have every need supplied because we are in Christ. We are objects of the Father's love because we are in Christ. We have eternal hope because we are in Christ. "Union with Christ is the fountainhead from which flows the Christian's every spiritual blessing—repentance and faith, pardon, justification, adoption, sanctification, perseverance, and glorification."[2]

Because of our union with Christ, we have new potential. One of the most encouraging passages in the New Testament is Galatians 2:20: "I have been crucified with Christ. It is no longer I who live, but Christ who lives in me. And the life I now live in the flesh I live by faith in the Son of God, who loved me and gave himself for me." Notice the three elements in this wonderful declaration that apply to all believers. First is a statement of *historical gospel fact*: "I have been crucified with Christ." We are united with Christ in his death and resurrection. This means that when Christ died, we died, and when Christ rose, we too rose to newness

2 Robert L. Reymond, *A New Systematic Theology of the Christian Faith*, 2nd ed. (Nashville: Thomas Nelson, 2010), 759.

of life. Jesus didn't die to purchase saveability. No, he took the names of all who were united to him to the cross with him. His payment for sin was our payment because we were united with him when he suffered and died on the cross.

Then there is a statement of *present gospel reality*: "It is no longer I who live, but Christ who lives in me." It is impossible with a few words to capture the extent of the glory of this statement and its implications for our daily living. Clearly, Paul is not saying that he is physically dead. If he were, he couldn't have written this. He is unpacking an amazing reality for every believer between the "already" of conversion and the "not yet" of homegoing. Paul is saying that because of our union with Christ, the life that now animates us, that is, ignites new thoughts, desires, and actions, is not ours; it's Christ's. The gospel is not a system of self-reformation. The gospel is about a union that rescues and transforms us. There is something more than a desire for change and a commitment to self-discipline that changes us. What changes us is the power of the risen Lord Jesus Christ that now resides inside of us. Because we are united to him, we are empowered by him to do what we could never have done before.

Finally, the passage ends with a *gospel commitment*: "The life I now live in the flesh I live by faith in the Son of God, who loved me and gave himself for me." Paul is saying that by faith he will live as if he actually believes that Christ lives within him. It is amazing to consider that being in Christ means that the power of the resurrection is now the power that animates our living. This is another provision of God's grace. Sin doesn't just leave us condemned, but it also renders us unable to be what God has designed us to be and to do what God has commanded us to do. In Christ we are empowered for a brand-new way of living.

In Christ, we now are accepted as the adopted sons and daughters of the Most High God. John says, "See what kind of love the Father has given to us, that we should be called children of God; and so we are" (1 John 3:1). The question is, "What kind of love does the Father give us?" The answer: "Adopting love." It would be amazing grace if God canceled our sentence of condemnation but kept himself separate from us. It would be wonderful mercy if he simply tolerated us. But it is only lavish grace that could take rebel enemies and welcome them as dearly loved adopted children. Now we live with all the rights and privileges of children of the Most High God. Elyse Fitzpatrick expresses the wonder of this.

> Our union with Christ may be summed up in these words: because the Father has immeasurable love for the Son, he has immeasurable love for us. He has immeasurable love for us because we are in the Son, part of him, one with him, married to him, part of the family. He looks at us as though we always were. When the Father looks at us, he doesn't scratch his head and wonder, "How did she get in here? What's he doing here?" No, he says, "This is my beloved daughter, my beloved son, in whom I am well pleased." All because we are in union with the Son he loves.[3]

The incalculable love the Father has for the Son now flows to us as his children, because we are one with Christ. This unity with Christ is also the foundation of a new culture of love and unity with one another. In his prayer for his disciples, and for us, Jesus makes this clear.

> I have manifested your name to the people whom you gave me out of the world. Yours they were, and you gave them to me, and they have kept your word. Now they know that everything that you have given me is from you. For I have given them the words that you gave me, and they have received them and have come to know in truth that I came from you; and they have believed that you sent me. I am praying for them. I am not praying for the world but for those whom you have given me, for they are yours. All mine are yours, and yours are mine, and I am glorified in them. And I am no longer in the world,

3 Elyse Fitzpatrick, *Found in Him* (Wheaton, IL: Crossway, 2013), 123.

> but they are in the world, and I am coming to you. Holy Father, keep them in your name, which you have given me, that they may be one, even as we are one. (John 17:6–11)

We could never create this unity on our own. We are one because we are one in Christ. We are in him and he is in us, and because this is true of you and me, we are united to one another as well. Being in Christ is the unique foundation of the unity of all who are in Christ. It is a unity that spans race, social class, gender, ethnicity, and geography.

Stop and think for a moment about what we have considered in this chapter. Think of the identity that is ours because of the amazing gift of grace that has given Christ to us. No longer aliens, no longer enemies, no longer condemned—but by grace we are in Christ, the children of God, objects of the Father's love, justified, forgiven, righteous, eternally loved, and united to God and to one another. The doctrine of justification and all the graces that attach to it is the best news sinners in this sin-scarred world could ever hear. What we could have never dreamed would be ours and what we have no capacity whatsoever to earn is now ours in Christ. We stand in the life-giving rain of justifying mercies, an eternal shower that nothing in heaven or on earth can ever stop. What better gift could ever be given than the gift of the person, work, and justifying grace of the Lord Jesus Christ? You should stop reading and celebrate for a moment.

18

Justification in Everyday Life

THEY STARTED THEIR RELATIONSHIP with hope, joy, mutual affection, and respect, and with a belief that this could be the lifelong relationship they both had longed for. It may seem cliché, but Rick and Maggie met at church. They sat in the same row of seats one Sunday and had a casual conversation. That was it—no sparks, no further plans. Two weeks later, to their surprise they landed in the same small group. A few weeks later they met for coffee. They talked and laughed and, before they knew it, two-and-a-half hours had gone by.

Rick and Maggie's first official date was at a Vietnamese restaurant, because they had discovered they both were pho lovers. The love of pho was one of many things they discovered they had in common. Picnics, movie nights, and trips to the shore became more and more regular. It wasn't long before they were inseparable and talking seriously about getting married. They were both established in the city, so no big move would be necessary. The plan was that after they got married, Maggie would give up her apartment and move into Rick's place. From a distance, this seemed like everyone's dream marriage.

But the couple that sat on the couch in my office had no joy. They looked like they were in more of a nightmare than a dream. They sat on separate ends of the couch, like the other person wasn't there. Rick and Maggie looked sullen and defeated. There was no warmth between them. Rick talked angrily about their relationship, like a man who had been deceived by a salesman into a bad deal. Maggie couldn't talk about it without crying. She was hurt like someone who had been betrayed.

At home they barely talked, and when they did it was only about their schedules, bills, and home maintenance concerns. And these brief conversations frequently dissolved into petty fights. Rick and Maggie, who once seemed to have so much in common, now lived in a constant state of cold war. Sunday morning worship and Wednesday evening small group were the only things they did together. In each situation, Rick and Maggie put on a happy face and gave nonanswers to probing questions.

As I listened to this couple unfold the sad state of their marriage and as I witnessed all of the hurt and anger that was the result, I kept thinking that what this marriage lacked was the gospel. Does my response to this suffering couple seem out of touch, too theoretical, or too preachy to you? Are you able to envision how the gospel of the justifying grace of Jesus could pull this couple out of the mire that they were stuck in? Are you able to see how the truths of the righteous life and substitutionary death of Jesus change everything when it comes to how we think about ourselves and the way we think about and relate to others? Can you think clearly about how this gospel of grace changes the way we handle the sin, weakness, and failure that are the inescapable experience of every marriage? Are you able to apply the doctrine of justification to the realities of your everyday life?

The gospel of justifying grace is not just a means of entrance into relationship with God and a guarantee of eternity with him, but it is also a brand-new culture to be lived right here, right now. The doctrine of justification changes everything—the problem is that thousands and thousands of Christians neither know nor understand this. I think that in our teaching, preaching, counseling, and discipleship we have often failed to trace out the implications of the "nowism" of the gospel of Jesus Christ.

In that office, as Rick and Maggie told their tale of marital woe, I listened to two people who did not know who they were and who had very little practical understanding of the magnitude of what they had been given in the justifying grace of God though his Son, Jesus. Sure, there were some places where they needed better communication skills and problem-solving strategies, but their problems rooted at a much deeper level. The way they communicated and the way they approached problems were symptomatic of something profoundly missing in the way they thought about themselves and their relationship. How could a Christian marriage be so free of hope, so lacking in grace, and so marked by constant judgment?

I want to answer this question by laying out the radical new life that is ours because of God's justifying mercies in Jesus. In order to do this I'll use 2 Peter 1:3–9 as a platform for understanding the new life that justifying grace provides for us.

> His divine power has granted to us all things that pertain to life and godliness, through the knowledge of him who called us to his own glory and excellence, by which he has granted to us his precious and very great promises, so that through them you may become partakers of the divine nature, having escaped from the corruption that is in the world because of sinful desire. For this very reason, make every effort to supplement your faith with virtue, and virtue with knowledge, and knowledge with self-control, and self-control with steadfastness, and steadfastness with godliness, and godliness with brotherly affection, and brotherly affection with love. For if these qualities are yours and are increasing, they keep you from being ineffective or unfruitful in the knowledge of our Lord Jesus Christ. For whoever lacks these qualities is so nearsighted that he is blind,

having forgotten that he was cleansed from his former sins. (2 Pet. 1:3–9)

This is the perfect passage for beginning to understand the right-here, right-now culture of the gospel that is ours because of the life, death, and resurrection of Jesus.

Second Peter 1:3–9 is a diagnostic passage. It is written to address and explain when something goes wrong in the life of believers. Here's the diagnosis: "For if these qualities are yours and are increasing, they keep you from being ineffective or unfruitful in the knowledge of our Lord Jesus Christ" (1:8). Peter is proposing that there are people who really do know the Lord and who have truly been rescued, forgiven, and brought near by his grace, but whose lives are ineffective and unfruitful. Their lives are not producing the expected harvest of the fruit of faith. Rick and Maggie's marriage lifestyle was clearly ineffective and unfruitful. Whatever they were thinking and doing wasn't producing the good fruit of unity, love, understanding, peace, hope, and joy. Their marriage was so unfruitful that I remember thinking, "There seems to be nothing Christian about this marriage."

Now, Peter's diagnosis begs a question: "How is it that a believer can have an such an unfruitful life?" The answer is in the passage. The people that Peter is addressing have ineffective and unfruitful lives because they lack qualities of character that produce good fruit. Peter lists these qualities: virtue, knowledge, self-control, steadfastness, godliness, brotherly affection, and love. When these qualities shape your actions, reactions, and responses to the situations and relationships of your daily life, the result will be a harvest of good fruit. You may be thinking, "I still don't understand what this has to do with the practical implications of the doctrine of justification." Stay tuned, because that connection is coming.

This passage leads us to yet another question: "Why do some Christians lack these essential character qualities?" Know that you and I have no ability whatsoever to work these qualities into our hearts and then into our daily living. If godliness could be produced in our own strength, the cross of Jesus Christ would not have been necessary. These qualities only ever come to us by means of God's grace. They are the right-here, right-now gifts of God's grace to us. So what is the answer to the question I have just posed? It is found in the next verse: "For whoever lacks these qualities is so nearsighted that he is blind, having forgotten that he was cleansed from his former sins" (1:9).

Peter is proposing that people like Rick and Maggie have ineffective and unfruitful lives because they are blind to the radical provisions of grace that are theirs as a result of God's justifying mercies. Quite apart from anything they could achieve on their own, their sins have been forgiven, and with this forgiveness comes a warehouse of glorious graces that can change everything for them and their marriage. Here's how Peter talks about the riches of God's justifying mercies in Jesus: "His divine power has granted to us all things that pertain to life and godliness" (1:3). What an incredibly glorious, mind-blowing, and hope-igniting statement. Let it sink in for a moment. As those who have been justified by grace, we now have every single thing we need to live a godly life between the "already" of our conversion and the "not yet" of our homegoing. We haven't just been forgiven (forgiveness is a glorious thing), and we haven't just been accepted (God's acceptance is an amazing gift), but we have also been richly supplied, right here, right now.

So, here's what happens to people like Rick and Maggie. They forget or maybe never knew who they are and what they have been given in Christ and, because they do, they don't pursue everything that belongs to them in Christ. Because of this, they put their trust in things they shouldn't trust, they give way to things they have the power to defeat, they hope in things that will fail them, and they settle for an ineffective and unfruitful life. And they repeat this pattern over and over again.

I think there are thousands of Christians who are stuck in a gospel-blind lifestyle and they don't know it. Some of them are angry, some of them are questioning their faith, some of them are hurting, some of them are depressed, and some of them feel paralyzed; but all of them have lost the joy of their salvation. Because they are blind, they don't get up in the morning determined to make every effort to get everything that is theirs in Christ. This is one of the reasons many of our churches, as communities of faith, are ineffective and unproductive as well.

So I want to unpack how the beautiful riches that are ours because of God's justifying grace in Jesus Christ change how we view ourselves, how we relate to others, and how we live in this broken world. God uses the truths of the doctrines of his word to change us, that is, to change how we think, what we desire, and how we live. Here are seven words that capture the new lifestyle that is propelled by the doctrine of God's justifying grace.

Humility

The doctrine of justification not only confronts me and you with how messed up we are, but it also confronts us with our complete inability to restore ourselves to any semblance of what we were meant to be. Humbly admitting the damage that sin has done to you is like standing in front of a once beautiful but now decayed and broken-down house with no understanding of how to restore it and no tools to do so. There we were, the destruction and decay of sin reaching to every part of our being, with no ability to help ourselves. There we were, enemies of the one we were made to have relationship with, and there was nothing we could do to make peace with him. As Paul says, "having no hope and without God in the world" (Eph. 2:12).

The doctrine of justification devastates self-glory. It puts a hammer to human pride. It makes a mockery of self-righteousness and the self-aggrandizing, self-justifying arguments that go with it. This truth destroys our pride in our power and our wisdom. It removes your ability to think that you have done something to be deserving. This truth requires you to confess that you have no power on your own to keep yourself from being without God and without hope. When you admit that what this doctrine says about you is true, humility results. And that is itself a gift of grace.

Pride is a source of sin out of which so many other sins and their bad fruit grow. Pride crushes compassion and sympathy. Pride makes it very hard for you to be patient and understanding. Pride makes you entitled and demanding. Pride never produces a willingness to forgive. Pride makes you judgmental and condemning. Pride makes you far more concerned about the sin of others than you are about your own. Pride is the enemy of self-sacrificing love. Pride makes you picky and easily irritated. Pride forces you to deny your wrongs and to shift blame to someone or something else. Pride makes it easier for you to complain than to give thanks.

Proud people don't tend to be peacemakers. Proud people don't suffer well. Proud people don't tend to be generous. Proud people tend to think they deserve what is comfortable and tend to hate what is difficult. Proud people envy the blessings of others. Proud people resist confession and are defensive when confronted. Proud people find winning more attractive than loving. Proud people are better at division than unity and create more enemies than friends. Proud people are always keeping score and tend to hold on to wrongs. Proud people thrive on being noticed, getting respect, and receiving acclaim. Proud people tend to see themselves as deserving the spotlight and thrive when on center stage. Proud people take credit for what they couldn't have produced on their own. Proud people demand loyalty, but will forsake you when they are not getting what they want from you. Proud people have to be right and need to be in control. Pride never has a good harvest. Much of the sin and bad fruit in our lives grows out of the soil of our pride.

So it is a grace to understand what the doctrine of justification says about you, who you were, what you deserved, and what your life would have been apart from God's justifying mercies. You can't say your hope in life and death is justifying grace and be proud and boastful at the same time. Pride crushes a believer's fruitfulness. One of the sweetest, most life-transforming fruits of the doctrine of justification is humility.

In their marriage Rick and Maggie fit Peter's description: nearsighted and blind. They lived forgetfully, failing to remember the humbling truth that justifying grace had rescued them not only from God's wrath but also from themselves. Because they forgot who they were and what they had been given, pride, subtle and not-so-subtle, infected every aspect of their marriage. Rick was self-righteous, seldom humbly admitting that he was wrong. Maggie was entitled and demanding, always finding a way to keep her desires front and center. For them, decision-making was a war for control. Forgetting God's grace, they seldom gave one another grace. Forgetting God's forgiveness, they failed to see the restorative beauty of confession and forgiveness. Here were two people who said they believed the gospel, but there was no gospel lifestyle in the marriage.

You cannot have a healthy marriage without humility. You cannot be a faithful, loving parent without humility. You cannot be an obedient child without humility. You cannot be a fruitful leader without humility. You cannot be a good neighbor, good citizen, or good worker without humility. Humility is one of the doctrine of justification's good fruits. Here again we are reminded that God gave us the truths of his word not just to inform us, but more importantly, to transform us. *Are you nearsighted and blind also? Has the truth of your justification produced in you the fruit of humility?*

Gratitude

Sin is self-centered. It causes us to be self-focused, self-absorbed, and self-obsessed. In 2 Corinthians 5:15, Paul says that Jesus came so that we would no longer live *for ourselves*. Because sin is self-centered, complaint is more natural for us than gratitude. Here again, the doctrine of justification is transformative. One of the beautiful fruits of this doctrine is a profound sense of gratitude. This is not gratitude because my day is going well, because people like me, because I am healthy, because I am affluent, because I am successful, because I have a big steak in front of me, or because my children don't publicly embarrass me. No, this gratitude transcends human situations, locations, and relationships. It is a gratitude that is not weakened by difficulty. This gratitude doesn't rise and fall with every rough patch of life.

You know that you are living out of the gospel of justification by grace through faith when you wake up in the morning and say to yourself,

"My marriage isn't all it could be, I have concerns about my children, and my finances worry me at times, but I am completely forgiven, and unfailingly and eternally loved. It is a love I didn't deserve and could not have earned. Jesus lived and died so that I would know this love even on my very worst day. I am loved!" Let your heart fill with gratitude that, because of what Christ did, you are an adopted son or daughter of the King of kings and Lord of lords. Stop to consider the reality that a holy God doesn't look on you as a Judge but with the loving eyes of a Father, because Jesus took your judgment on himself. How can you not be filled with life-shaping thankfulness?

Gratitude is a beautiful thing. You become grateful when you come to understand that who you are and what you have is not about what you have done, but what has been done for you. You know that the richest things in your life are not there because you are an achiever, but because by grace you are a receiver. Gratitude means you understand that your biggest blessings are gifts of love and not wages that you've earned. Gratitude is knowing that your biggest problem, sin, has been dealt with by the sacrificial generosity of another. Gratitude looks up and remembers.

People who are grateful for God's redeeming love tend to be joyful people. You won't find much joy in complainers. Grateful people, remembering their own need of rescue, tend to be kind, compassionate, sympathetic, and understanding. Grateful people remember what God has given them, and then in turn are generous, willing to make sacrifices in the service of others. People who carry gratitude for God's forgiveness with them through life tend to be willing to forgive, reconcile, and restore. People who remember that they are the recipients of God's patient mercy tend then to be patient and merciful. People who are grateful for God's amazing grace in Christ Jesus tend to be willing to give grace to others.

You can't put a value on the transformative power of gratitude. And you can't properly reflect on the doctrine of justification without walking away with a heart overflowing with it. Gone are the days of "I earned it, I deserve it, so I will boast about it." The doctrine of justification demolishes the old proud human meritocracy with all of its self-congratulatory delusions of grandeur. Paul says, "What do you have that you did not receive? If then you received it, why do you boast as if you did not receive it?" (1 Cor. 4:7). Vertical gratitude transforms not only your heart, but also how you respond in all of your horizontal situations and relationships.

Sadly, Rick and Maggie didn't live in light of Paul's words. Vertical gratitude did not protect and shape their marriage. Their conversations were colored by complaint. Rick wasn't patient and failed to respond to Maggie's weaknesses and failures with mercy. Maggie approached her relationship to Rick as one who felt deserving of, rather than grateful for, his love. She regularly threw up to Rick all the things she did for him, while she reminded him of all the things he failed to do. Together they seemed to always find more reasons to complain than to be thankful. It was an exhausting, discouraging, burdensome, and gospel-free way of living. Like every other child of God, Rick and Maggie had eternal reasons to be grateful. Gratitude would have transformed their relationship, but they had forgotten who they were and what they had been given in the justifying mercies of their Lord. *Has vertical gratitude transformed your heart and the way you respond in the situations, locations, and relationships of your daily life?*

Freedom

Here is another beautiful, heart-liberating, life-changing, and joy-producing fruit of the doctrine of justification. Justification by grace through faith really does set you free. The question is, "Do you carry that freedom into the everyday spaces of your life?" The justifying mercies of Christ set you free from the burdens of the law. Since Jesus perfectly measured up to every requirement of the law, we now have peace with God and full access to relationship with him even though, in this life, we will never measure up. Yes, we should determine to obey and we should resist sin, but we are freed from doing either as a means of achieving acceptance with God.

Justifying grace frees you from the paralyzing burden of guilt. No longer do we have to live in regret, dragging the heavy load of our past sins into our present and future. No longer do we have to hide in fear of the hammer of God's anger coming down on us. No longer do we have to do the burdensome work of denying, minimizing, and hiding our sin, working to make our sin feel in our hearts as less than sinful. No longer do we have to defend our righteousness when people near us lovingly confront us with wrong. Redeeming grace has freed us from these burdens.

No longer do we have to carry the burden of shame. Jesus shamed shame on the cross, so that we would no longer live in bondage to it. In the eyes of the one with whom it eternally matters, we are no longer stained, no longer dirty, and no longer scarred by sin. Because of justifying grace our record is spotless and we are righteous in God's eyes. We don't have to go slump-backed through life, protecting ourselves from onlookers as if we are rejected, unwanted, and unworthy. We are children of the King, his door is open, and we are welcomed. Shame died on the cross of Jesus Christ; why should we let it rule us any longer?

Justifying grace frees us from the burden of fear. Grace means we are no longer enemies of God, but his children. Grace means God is for us, and if God is for us, who can stand against us? Justifying grace unleashes on us an inexhaustible warehouse of divine blessings. Justifying grace means we are never left alone, never left to our own little bag of wisdom and strength, and never left to the few things we can control. Justifying grace means that God exercises his sovereign power not only for his glory, but for our eternal welfare as well. Justifying grace means we live under the unshakable security of God's provision and protection.

No matter where we are, no matter who we are with, and no matter what we are facing, the Lord Almighty is with us. Justifying grace means we awake every morning to new mercies that are form-fit for what we will deal with that day. Justifying mercies means that everything that would confound and confuse us is fully understood by and lives under the sovereign management of our Savior. Justifying grace ushers us out of the darkness of fear into the light and rest of the Father's care, where peace of heart is found and anxiety no longer haunts us. Freedom from the bondage of guilt, shame, and fear is ours in the justifying grace of the Lord Jesus Christ. We carry these burdens no longer because, as an act of justifying grace, Jesus has lifted them off our shoulders.

There was no marital infection more problematic for Rick and Maggie than fear. Fear of being the guilty one and the shaming that would follow motivated so much of their interactions with one another. They knew the power of inflicting guilt, and they were used to the sting of shame. One thing they shared in common was a fear of the next time the finger would be pointed at them and the power that would give the other person. You know you have lost sight of the gospel of God's grace and that your relationship is in trouble when fear has become a more powerful motivator than hope. You know your relationship is in trouble when hiding and defending are more regular than honesty and transparency. Rick and Maggie were tired of the cycle of fear, guilt, and shame, but they were blind to the fact that they were the ones keeping it going. They were blind to the fact that, in God's justifying mercies, they had been given everything they needed to live with one another in a very different way. *How much of your life is motivated by fear? Where it really matters, are you living in the freedom that is yours because you are a recipient of the blessings of justifying grace?*

Identity

We can hook the issue of identity (see chap. 18) to the doctrine of justification. Here is another place where it is important to remember that good scriptural theology doesn't just define for you who God is and what he has done, but it also redefines who you are as a child of God. One of the sweet blessings of God's justifying mercies is the new identity that is ours because we are in Christ—forgiven, adopted, and eternally loved children of God. We no longer have to search for identity, meaning, and purpose because we have these in Christ. And the thing that is so powerful about the identity that is ours as a result of God's justifying mercy is that nothing and no one can take it away from us. Here is the only place to find an identity that is not only heart-satisfying but also eternally stable. *In Christ*, forgiven, adopted, and eternally loved by the Father, *is* who we are and who we will forever be.

We are freed from having to be something. We are freed from having to prove we are worth something. We are freed from longing for something that will give us importance, prominence, or power. We are freed from being addicted to people's acclaim, respect, appreciation, and love. We are freed from letting accomplishments define us. We are freed from letting titles depict that we have worth. We are freed from asking cars, houses, and vacations to be markers of our identity. We are freed from the identity we get from political tribalism. We are freed from getting our identity from being in charge or in control. We are freed from needing to look strong, prepared, capable, and unafraid. We are freed from needing to hide our weaknesses and deny our failures. We are freed from putting on a public face as an attempt to hide what is actually going on inside. Because we don't get our value from how others respond to us, we are freed from bitterness and fantasies of vengeance when we are mistreated.

We are freed from the toxic identity anxieties that haunt so many of us, that get in the way of what we have been called to do, and that harm our relationships. One of the sweet blessings of God's justifying grace is how vertical identity frees us from horizontal identity chaos.

Sadly, for Rick and Maggie, identity was a huge issue in their marriage. When it came to identity, their marriage was a perfect storm. Although she didn't know it, Maggie had tied her identity and sense of well-being to her marriage. She always felt that she would not be complete until she was married. Her emotions rose and fell with however Rick was treating her on a given day. Rick, being a less-than-perfect man, would never be able to deliver the security of identity that Maggie was longing for. Rick had tied his identity to business success. He remembers his father saying to him when he graduated from college, "Now go out and make something of yourself." While Maggie looked to her marriage for hope, Rick's life was more and more dominated by his quest for career success. No career would ever provide Rick with what he was looking for. Their marriage would never work if Maggie moved toward Rick to find herself and Rick moved away from Maggie toward work to find himself. Vertical identity amnesia was wreaking havoc on their marriage, and they didn't know it.

Many believers, blind to what they have been given in Christ, run from relationship to relationship, job to job, location to location, and church to church searching for identity. Believers who don't understand the right-here, right-now blessings of God's grace spend themselves into hopeless debt in search of identity. Parents who fail to understand the "nowism" of the gospel of justifying grace put the burden of their identity on their children, a terrible burden for a child to bear. Pastors, forgetting the gospel that they preach, ask for ministry to give them identity and end up beaten down, discouraged, and burned out. Teenagers, unaware of the present benefits of the gospel of grace they have been taught, experience all kinds of anxiety and make all kinds of regrettable decisions in search of identity. Christian men, forgetting their vertical identity, feign strong personality, big muscle, and domineering, macho masculinity. Seminary students, who are at school to study the gospel, attach their identity to theological knowledge and biblical literacy. It is sad to think about how much gospel identity amnesia lives in the church, weakening its function and witness.

It is a sweet gift that in God's justifying grace we are blessed with the most wonderful and stable identity one could ever hope for. This identity will never fail us, shame us, or be taken away. Every horizontal identity will fail us somehow, someway. You can celebrate your inclusion among those who are in Christ, forgiven, adopted, and eternally loved. Be thankful you do not have to frantically search for identity anymore. Be glad that you don't have to ask people, places, experiences, and things to do for you what they were never meant to do. And resist the temptation to look horizontally for what you have already been given in the blessings of God's justifying grace in Jesus. *Where, right now, are you looking for identity? Could it be that there is trouble in your life because you are looking around for what you have already been given in Christ?*

Potential

One of the most exciting blessings of God's justifying grace is the new potential that is ours in Christ. With our justification comes new potential to say no to sin and yes to godly living. God doesn't just tolerate his justified ones and he doesn't just accept them, but he also does this incredible thing: he comes and lives inside of them. And with his presence, everything changes for us. God himself is the new potential of everyone who has received his justifying grace.

Consider how Paul talks about this in Romans 8.

> You, however, are not in the flesh but in the Spirit, if in fact the Spirit of God dwells in you. Anyone who does not have the Spirit of Christ does not belong to him. But if Christ is in you, although the body is dead because of sin, the Spirit is life because of righteousness. If the Spirit of him who raised Jesus from the dead dwells in you, he who raised Christ Jesus from the dead will also give life to your mortal bodies through his Spirit who dwells in you.
>
> So then, brothers, we are debtors, not to the flesh, to live according to the flesh. For if you live according to the flesh you will die, but if by the Spirit you put to death the deeds of the body, you will live. (Rom. 8:9–13)

This is a life-changing provision for every believer. With our justification comes the indwelling presence of the Holy Spirit, and with him comes resurrection power. We don't have to live according to the desires of the flesh. We can put to death the old life of being dominated by bodily passions and give ourselves to godly living in the situations and relationships of our daily lives. Philippians 2:13 says, "For it is God who works in you, both to will and to work for his good pleasure."

Because of God's justifying grace, we never battle the myriad of temptations in this fallen world on our own. The great victor battles on our behalf. We never war with the sin that still lives inside of us on our own. The Spirit wars on our behalf, even in those moments when we are too weak to do so. We now have the power to say no to sinful thoughts and desires. We now have the ability to say yes to every righteous thing God has called us to. We have been fully supplied for the spiritual battle that we will all face until we are on the other side, and the supply is God himself. The greatest gift of our justification is the gift of God himself.

This is why James is able to say without hesitation or qualification, "Resist the devil, and he will flee from you" (James 4:7). Satan flees not because of our power, but because of the presence and power of the one who now lives inside of us. The one who defeated him in his life, in his death, and at his resurrection now lives within us. Satan knows he is a defeated foe. So, when in the victor's strength we resist, he cuts and runs. This is the hope of every believer as we live in this world where temptation still haunts and indwelling sin still lives.

What could be more glorious, and at the same time more practical, than what we are considering right now? God Almighty living within us, empowering us in the face of temptation, enabling us to desire what is right, and providing for us the strength to do it. We are not just forgiven, not just adopted, not just eternally loved, but we are also given, in the presence of God within us, new potential for a brand-new way of living. There is no Christian life without the Spirit of the living Christ dwelling within us.

Rick and Maggie lived like they had no idea of the potential that was theirs as the children of God. A good marriage is a good marriage because people in that marriage say no. I don't mean they say no to one another. No, I mean they say no to themselves. They say no to raging emotions, to wrong thoughts, and to selfish desires, and they turn and go in a different direction. How is it possible to say no? It's possible because of the very blessing that we are talking about here, that is, the amazing blessing of God's powerful presence within us. If you want to destroy your life and relationships, all you have to do is indulge all of your thoughts and desires, go where they lead you, and do what they tell you to do. This is pretty much what Rick and Maggie did. They exercised little internal restraint, and in so doing, they decimated the love, hope, and joy of their marriage. *Are you living out of the new potential that is yours because of God's justifying grace? Where are you giving way to thoughts, desires, and temptations that you now have the power to resist? Where in your life and relationships do you need to exercise your power to live in a new way?*

Values

I know I have value problems. Things in my life rise to levels way beyond their true importance, and when they do, they capture my heart, control my thoughts and desires, and direct my behavior. I can lose sight of what is truly important, what is truly worth living for, and what will truly satisfy my longing heart. One of the benefits of God's justifying mercies is the power to clarify and reorient our values.

Think of what God did in order to deliver his justifying grace to you. Consider that he carefully ruled over the events of human history so that, at just the right time, Jesus would come. Consider the cost of Jesus leaving heaven's splendor to subject himself to all of the harsh experiences of life in this fallen world. Consider the unjust conviction, the horrible physical torture, the public pain and shame of the cross, and the rejection of his own Father, all of which Jesus willingly endured because he understood the eternal value of what he was doing on our behalf. Consider that God has ruled over every situation, location, and relationship of our lives so that we would be exposed to the reality of our own sin and the glorious offer of his forgiving grace. Consider that he gave us the ability to understand these truths and the power to believe them.

Consider that he has carefully ruled over the writing, delivering, and preserving of his word so that we could know him, trust him, and follow him. Consider the value of the gift of the Spirit to animate this new life that his justifying grace welcomes us to. Consider the value of all that

God has done to address the greatest plague of all, the one that infects us all and always leads to death: sin.

Rick and Maggie had lost sight of what was truly important in life and death. They argued over the trivial, and they fought for what was temporary. The things they treasured weren't nearly as valuable as they thought they were. They were a couple in desperate need of the values-clarification of the gospel of Jesus Christ.

Could there possibly be any treasure of more value than this? Is anything that exists, any possession, any person, any experience, any power, or any success, more valuable than the justifying mercy of the Lord and all of the rich blessings that flow from it?

The incalculable value of the treasure of God's redeeming reign is captured in two brief parables in Matthew 13.

> The kingdom of heaven is like treasure hidden in a field, which a man found and covered up. Then in his joy he goes and sells all that he has and buys that field.
>
> Again, the kingdom of heaven is like a merchant in search of fine pearls, who, on finding one pearl of great value, went and sold all that he had and bought it. (Matt. 13:44–46)

The kingdom of heaven is God's redeeming reign. These two parables present it as a treasure worth giving up everything for. It really is the treasure of treasures. Nothing compares in value to what our reigning Savior King has done for us. We have to go back again and again and remember again and again the value of God's justifying mercy and let it bless us with reoriented and clarified values. We need to resist letting the value of other things cause us to lose our gospel minds, tempting us to once again search for treasure as if we haven't already been given the greatest treasure that has ever been given. *What has risen in value in your heart and life way beyond its true value? Is there evidence in your life and relationships that you need to consider once again the values-clarifying truths of God's justifying grace?*

Defense

If you're the recipient of God's justifying grace, you can expect to be under attack. The Bible describes Satan as a roaring lion searching around for someone to eat next. It is a scary but vital warning. Although justifying grace has given us peace with God, the world we live in is not at peace. Spiritual war rages all around us. Even the most mundane moments are complicated by this spiritual war. There will be a day when this war will cease. On that day there will be no more temptation and there will be no more marauding enemy, but that day is yet to come. So today, we must live with eyes open and hearts ready to defend ourselves against both the ordinary and extraordinary attacks of the enemy.

There is no greater defense against the lies of the enemy, which are meant to weaken your faith and your resolve, than the truth of the doctrine of justification. Let me explain. Satan has two things in your life that he works with. First, he works with your ongoing sin, weakness, and failure. When you sin, failing to live up to God's clearly revealed standards, he comes close to you and says, "Maybe you are not one of God's children after all," or, "God must be so disappointed in you," or, "If God really loved you, wouldn't he help you right now to do what is right?" or, "Look at your life. Maybe everything you've believed is not as true as you thought."

But you have a powerful defense against these attacks in the doctrine of justification. Yes, you have been called to obey. Yes, you have been called to forsake everything, take up your cross, and follow your Savior. But the doctrine of justification tells you that your acceptance with God has not been nor ever will be based on the track record of your righteousness. Your acceptance with God, even on your worst, most foolish, and most rebellious day, stands on the solid rock of the perfectly righteous life and the complete penalty-paying death of the Lord Jesus Christ. When Jesus cried out on the cross, "It is finished!" he meant it. He had completed everything that needed to be done in order to secure your eternal forgiveness and acceptance with God.

There was then and there is now nothing left to do but to embrace that work by faith. Whenever Satan throws your unrighteousness at you, throw the perfect righteousness of Jesus back at him, and he will flee. He knows he is a defeated foe, unable to undo the completed work of Jesus on your behalf.

Yes, you should quest every day to live a more godly life. You should place yourself daily before the perfectly accurate mirror of the word of God, to see all of those places where you still need to grow in grace. But you cannot listen to any attack that devalues the righteousness of Christ, given over to your account, which connects the degree of your righteousness to your acceptance with God. You are eternally accepted not because you are righteous and worthy, but because Jesus is righteous and worthy on your behalf. When you fall short, confess your sin, commit yourself to repentance, and then get up and celebrate the eternal standing you have with God based on the righteous life and substitutionary death of Jesus.

There is a second thing that Satan will use to weaken your faith and your resolve. It is the mystery of God's sovereignty. In those moments when life is difficult and suffering is near, he will come to you and say, "Where is your God now?" or, "I thought God loved you. Would a loving God let this happen to you?" or, "Maybe God has abandoned you; maybe his promises aren't trustworthy after all," or, "Maybe God doesn't have the power to help you that he said he had." Once again, your best defense against these attacks is the doctrine of justification. Because of what Jesus has done for you, there is nothing in heaven and earth that can separate you from God's love. Difficulty in your life is never a sign of God's unfaithfulness, weakness, or neglect. Instead, these hard things become tools of redeeming love in your life.

I love how Paul ends his discussion of the suffering we will all deal with in this groaning world. Take time to drink in the words of Romans 8:31–39.

> What then shall we say to these things? If God is for us, who can be against us? He who did not spare his own Son but gave him up for us

> all, how will he not also with him graciously give us all things? Who shall bring any charge against God's elect? It is God who justifies. Who is to condemn? Christ Jesus is the one who died—more than that, who was raised—who is at the right hand of God, who indeed is interceding for us. Who shall separate us from the love of Christ? Shall tribulation, or distress, or persecution, or famine, or nakedness, or danger, or sword? As it is written,
>
> "For your sake we are being killed all the day long;
> we are regarded as sheep to be slaughtered."
>
> No, in all these things we are more than conquerors through him who loved us. For I am sure that neither death nor life, nor angels nor rulers, nor things present nor things to come, nor powers, nor height nor depth, nor anything else in all creation, will be able to separate us from the love of God in Christ Jesus our Lord.

What Paul has said is gloriously true. The life, death, and resurrection of Jesus guarantees, for all who believe, the inseparable, unfailing, inexhaustible, and eternal love of God. No matter what you may feel in any particular moment, you are being loved. No matter what you're suffering, you are being loved. No matter how confusing life may be, you are being loved. No matter how much you struggle with the things that are on your plate, you are being loved. On good days and bad, you are being loved. When life is easy and when it is hard, you are being loved. Nothing has the power to disconnect you from God's powerful redeeming love. When Satan throws God's apparent distance at you, throw God's inseparable love back at him, and he will flee. He knows he cannot break this inseparable bond.

Christian theology doesn't get any better than what we have been considering. The doctrine of justification doesn't just explain the means by which you have forgiveness and acceptance with God, but it also comes with a warehouse of right-here, right-now blessings that change everything about how you live your life and defend yourself against Satan's attacks. This doctrine is glory come to earth and into your life in the person and work of Jesus Christ.

• • •

Maybe you're wondering what happened to Rick and Maggie. Not only was their marriage harmed by their distrust of one another, but it was more foundationally harmed by their doubt of God. Not only had they succumbed to attitudes and behaviors that were damaging to their union, but they succumbed to Satan's attacks. When you come to doubt someone, you quit going to him or her for help. They had long since quit crying out to God for help. They had stopped running to his word for wisdom and encouragement. I knew they needed strategic marriage counsel, but they needed something more fundamental. This married couple desperately needed the gospel of the justifying grace of Jesus.

I knew I needed to open the doors for them to that warehouse of blessings that were theirs in Christ. I needed to help them remember once again who they were and what they had been given. And I needed to help them to understand what it looks like in a marriage to live with and relate to one another in light of these blessings.

Rick and Maggie came to me broken, angry, hurt, exhausted, and discouraged, and I gave them the gospel of redeeming grace. No, I don't mean that in an academic, theoretical sense. I introduced them to the culture, the identity, and the lifestyle that results when you walk the truth of God's justifying grace into your everyday life. Rick and Maggie listened and learned, they confessed and celebrated, and they began to live with one another in brand-new ways. Change wasn't instantaneous, but progressive change did happen, and although they don't have a perfect marriage, their relationship has been dramatically transformed.

I am persuaded that we shouldn't preach this doctrine of justifying grace just to unbelievers, but to believers as well. No matter how long you have known the Lord, you need to have your thinking, your identity, your values, and your behavior recalibrated and redirected by the radical view of life that flows from this core gospel truth. Has your life drifted like Rick's and Maggie's did? Over the years, have you lost your gospel mind? Do you live every day in light of who you are and what you have been given in the justifying grace of Jesus? Have the truths we have been considering captured your heart in a way that shapes your living? Do you frantically look horizontally for what you have already been given in the warehouse of blessings that are yours because of God's justifying grace? May we remember justifying grace and, in remembering, continue to be transformed by how deep it is, how wide it is, and how it reaches to every aspect of our lives.

19

The Doctrine of Sanctification

THOSE WHOM GOD has effectually called and regenerated, who have a new heart and a new spirit created in them, are further sanctified. God does this really and personally, through the virtue of the death and resurrection of Jesus Christ and by his word and Spirit living in them. For them, the rule of sin is destroyed, and their sinful lusts are more and more weakened and put to death. They are more and more alive and strengthened by saving grace to pursue true holiness, for without holiness no one will see the Lord.

Though this sanctification reaches to every part of their person, they will never be perfect in this life. Remnants of the corruption of sin will remain in every part of them. There is an ongoing war that will not be reconciled, the flesh fighting against the Spirit and the Spirit against the flesh.

In this war, the remaining corruption in them may prevail for a time, but through the continual strength of the Spirit of Christ, which sanctifies, their new nature will overcome, and so they will grow in grace, perfecting holiness in the fear of God.[1] See John 17:17; Acts 20:32; Rom. 6:5–6, 14, 19; 7:18, 23; 1 Cor. 6:11; 2 Cor. 3:18; 7:1; Gal. 5:17, 24; Eph. 3:16–19; 4:15–16; 5:26; Col. 1:11; 1 Thess. 4:7; 5:21–23; 2 Thess. 2:13; 2 Tim. 2:21; Heb. 10:10, 14; 12:14; 1 Pet. 1:2; 2:11.

Understanding the Doctrine of Sanctification

I remember that night vividly, like it happened this week. It was the moment when conviction of sin and saving grace exploded into my heart. I was a little boy, but I was compelled, by grace, to confess my sin and plead for the Redeemer's forgiveness. It was a heart-gripping, life-changing moment of spiritual rescue, far bigger, more glorious, and more transformative than I had any sense of at my young age. It was the beginning of the journey of grace that I am still on.

I've thought back on that moment hundreds of times. It is a specific and beautiful example of the magnitude and tenderness of God's redeeming love. Almighty God invaded a moment in time and reached into the heart not of a great hero or king, but of an inconsequential little boy. He drew that boy into his loving arms and made him his forever. I had little understanding that night of the magnificence of what had happened, but I knew I was a newborn, forgiven child of God. I knew that night that the burden of guilt, which had been building in me, had been lifted. Ten thousand years into eternity I will still be singing hymns of praise for that moment of grace.

As stunning and glorious as the first moment of redeeming rescue was, it was in no way all that God had for me. That night wasn't the culmination of God's work of redeeming grace in my heart and life; it was but the initial salvo of a lifelong process of redeeming grace upon grace. God is not satisfied with just declaring us righteous. That declaration is a glorious act of divine mercy, but this God of mercy wants more for us. He will not be satisfied until he has actually formed true righteousness in us. The process by which true righteousness is formed in us is called sanctification. *Sanctification is the process by which God actually makes us*

1 Author's paraphrase of the doctrine of sanctification as found in the Westminster Confession of Faith, chap. 13.

what he has declared us to be in Christ, righteous. This means our Savior is still at work saving us.

Here is where the doctrine of sanctification is humbling. The focus of the process of sanctification is not rescuing us from external evil, with all of its temptations, which is everywhere around us. The primary focus of sanctification is the ongoing, lifelong rescue of us from *us*. Although we have been forgiven, declared righteous, and adopted as God's children, the muck and mess of sin still remain in us. The doctrine of sanctification requires you to admit that you are deeply in need of help. It requires you to admit that your need of help is so profound that only divine intervention will be able to provide the help that you need. And it requires you to accept that your problem with remaining sin is so multilayered, pervasive, and expansive that it will take the rest of your earthly days to solve. The doctrine of sanctification is a rebuke to any kind of self-satisfied and passive Christianity. You are not good enough, you are not clean enough, you are not Christlike enough, and you do not have enough to solve these problems on your own. Sanctification declares to all believers that we are people still in need of what God's grace alone is able to provide for us.

No matter how long you have known the Lord, you still need his saving work acting upon your heart. No matter how much you have grown in grace, you still need to grow in grace. There simply is no such thing as a sanctification graduate. And even though God's truth is a powerful tool, our sanctification is not primarily about acquiring information. You can be theologically astute and biblically literate and be spiritually immature. Sanctification is about heart and life transformation. It is about character restoration. It is about being molded, by the power of God's saving hand, into the likeness of Jesus Christ. You will look the same, your natural gifts will remain the same, and your basic personality will be in place, but you will not be the same after years of sanctifying grace has done its wonderful work in you, because you will look more like Jesus than you did when you first believed.

So let's take a moment to examine God's process of sanctification. Like every other doctrine, sanctification is a bottomless pit of redeeming glory, too deep to be fully excavated in several pages. Because of this, my explanations will be selective and not exhaustive, but there are a few things I would like to highlight, examine, and clarify.

Grace

Although God calls you to give yourself to the labor of your own spirituality, the work of sanctification is *God's* work. The reading of God's word, prayer, the preaching and teaching of Scripture, the sacraments, public worship, and the ministry of the body of Christ are all tools of God's sanctifying grace, but they would not result in our sanctification without the God of saving grace using them with transforming power. We are no more able to sanctify ourselves than we are able to justify ourselves. For the progressive defeat of the sin that remains and our progress in spiritual maturity, we are completely dependent on our Savior.

Two passages are helpful reminders of what fuels our ongoing sanctification. In Philippians 2:12–13 Paul makes the two sides of the sanctification process clear: "Therefore, my beloved, as you have always obeyed, so now, not only as in my presence but much more in my absence, work out your own salvation with fear and trembling, for it is God who works in you, both to will and to work for his good pleasure."

Paul understands that, for us, our sanctification is a call to obedience and a call to run after everything that is ours in Christ; that is, to see every grace of our salvation applied to every aspect of our person and every part of our lives. But he wants us to know that our sanctification doesn't rest on our obedience, but on the powerful, ever-present, and always active saving grace of our Lord. So he says, "As you are obeying, running after all that is yours in Christ, are you holding on to the comfort and hope of knowing that God is at work in your will and desires, changing what you would have no power to change on your own?" You and I have been called to sanctifying work, but the burden of our sanctification does not rest on our shoulders, but on the infinitely capable shoulders of our Savior.

In another Philippians passage Paul says this about our sanctification: "I am sure of this, that he who began a good work in you will bring it to completion at the day of Jesus Christ" (Phil. 1:6). Notice Paul doesn't say, "I am confident that you will get your act together, take your salvation seriously, and obey as you have been commanded." No, when it comes to the sanctification of the Philippian believers, Paul looks to one place for confidence, that is, to the same Lord who chose, called, and justified them. Paul's confidence is in the surety that God would never abandon the saving work that he began.

Now here's why this is so terribly important. Yes, we are called to obey. Yes, we are called to take our salvation so seriously that we actively go after every aspect of that salvation, seeking to live it out in every dimension of our lives. But we have a problem. Because sin still lives inside of us, we tend to have fickle, wandering, and unfaithful hearts. Because sin still lives in us, there are times when the world outside of God's boundaries looks more attractive to us than it ever should. Because sin still lives inside of us, we get lazy and impatient, abandoning, for a time, commitments we have made. Because sin still lives inside of us, there is an ongoing war of worship in our hearts, pulling us back and forth between worship of God and worship of some created thing. Because sin still lives inside of us, there are moments when we allow ourselves to question God's goodness, faithfulness, and love.

Because sin still lives inside of us, if our sanctification—that process by which we grow in grace and take on the likeness of our Savior—were completely dependent on us, we would never be sanctified. This is why it was not enough for God to forgive us and adopt us; he literally has gotten inside of us by his Spirit, to continue to rescue us, restore us, and empower us between our conversion and our final homegoing. We all need the essential help of God's saving grace today as much as we needed it the first day we believed.

It may seem contradictory, but it isn't. In the Christian life, we are called to work and rest. We are called to never stop working out our salvation, never allowing ourselves to take it for granted, never permitting ourselves to become spiritually aloof or lazy, and never abandoning the spiritual disciplines to which we have been called. The Christian life is a welcome to the most wonderful work ever, the work of redemption. We are called to approach our new life in Christ with a spiritual work ethic. We are called to work.

But we are also invited to the sweetest Sabbath of rest our hearts have ever known (Heb. 4:9–11). This rest is the result of the completed work of Jesus on our behalf, and it becomes even sweeter when we understand that God has not just forgiven and accepted us, but he has also taken up residence inside of us. This one who is almighty in power, who cannot lie, and who will never abandon what he has begun is at work in us. He daily does in us and for us what we could never do for ourselves. He battles for us even when we don't have the sense to do so. He knows exactly what we need and what tools to employ to deliver it. As we work, he wields his grace, so that our work would result in our spiritual growth. Without his presence and ever-active grace, none of his children would grow in grace and into his likeness. Start every day praying for sanctifying grace and then, with a heart at rest, give yourself to the spiritual work to which you have been called.

Death and Life

Our sanctification really is a death and life process. These are the two essential, intertwined parts of God's ongoing saving process in the lives of his children. Sanctification is a death process. The sin that is still in us is progressively put to death. Imagine that you were given a brand-new home and it was beautiful in every way. Imagine your excitement as you open the door and walk from beautiful room to beautiful room. Imagine your gratitude and joy. Now imagine that for all of its beauty, there is a grave problem with this wonderful new house. A malevolent and deceitful killer lives there as well. However enticing his words may be and however harmless he may seem at times, he is out for one thing: to do you harm. He wants to rob you of your joy, destroy your trust in your benefactor, and fill you with fear. There is no good in him, his intentions are always evil, and he must never be trusted. Would you not do everything to get him out of your house? Would you ever consider finding a way to make it work for him to live there? Would you ever make room for him to do his evil work? Would you not do everything you could to rid yourself of his evil presence?

So it is with the sin that remains. Sin is a deceitful, malevolent, and seductive killer, still lurking in the corners of your heart. Sin is always harmful, always destructive, and never good. Sin is never something that you should find a way to live with. Sin is never an acceptable occupant in the home that is your heart. Sin must be destroyed. It must be eradicated. It must be put to death. There is no acceptable plan B. The goal of God's sanctifying grace is the final death of the sin that remains in us. Consider the words of Paul:

> For the mind that is set on the flesh is hostile to God, for it does not submit to God's law; indeed, it cannot. Those who are in the flesh cannot please God.
>
> You, however, are not in the flesh but in the Spirit, if in fact the Spirit of God dwells in you. Anyone who does not have the Spirit of Christ does not belong to him. . . .
>
> So then, brothers, we are debtors, not to the flesh, to live according to the flesh. For if you live according to the flesh you will die, but if by the Spirit you put to death the deeds of the body, you will live. (Rom. 8:7–9, 12–13)

Recall Paul's words earlier in Romans: "What shall we say then? Are we to continue in sin that grace may abound? By no means! How can we who died to sin still live in it?" (Rom. 6:1–2).

So, since it is not a spiritually rational option to be passive when it comes to the presence and destructive power of remaining sin, then the only option is to participate in the Spirit's work of putting it to death. How do we do this? I love Paul's words in 2 Corinthians 10:4–5: "For the weapons of our warfare are not of the flesh but have divine power to destroy strongholds. We destroy arguments and every lofty opinion raised against the knowledge of God, and take every thought captive to obey Christ."

Any thing, thought, desire, motivation, purpose, plan, attitude, or action that in any way, shape, or form opposes the knowledge of God and new life in his Son, must be destroyed. How? By the truth of God in his word, by humble honest confession, and by seeking the Spirit's help to turn away from everything that opposes God and his will. Sin must be put to death; there is no other option. We do not have the power to kill it on our own, but with confidence in the Spirit's presence and work, we take up weapons that have divine power and go about the work of hunting down and killing sin.

It is important to understand, however, that sanctification is not only about the death of sin, but also about new life in Christ. Colossians 3:1–4 is very helpful here:

> If then you have been raised with Christ, seek the things that are above, where Christ is, seated at the right hand of God. Set your minds on things that are above, not on things that are on earth. For you have died, and your life is hidden with Christ in God. When Christ who is your life appears, then you also will appear with him in glory.

In Christ we have been raised to newness of life, and because we have, Paul says we should "seek the things that are above." What does he mean? Paul is calling for us to live in active pursuit of all the new-life blessings that flow down to us from the throne of our risen and reigning Savior. Instead of pursuing the empty and temporary treasures and pleasures of this created world, Paul encourages us to run after the transformative, heart-satisfying, and eternal blessings that are ours in Christ. Paul reminds us that this is to be our foundational mindset, the gospel-rich worldview that changes the way we think about what is important in life and alters the way we live as a result. Celebrating our new life in Christ, we seek the things that are above. This is our "sanctification labor" until we are finally with our Savior in glory.

So in your friendships, seek the things that are above. At your university, seek the things that are above. In your marriage, seek the things that are above. In your sexuality, seek the things that are above. In your parenting, seek the things that are above. In your career, seek the things that are above. In your finances, seek the things that are above. In your thoughts, desires, and motivations, seek the things that are above. Each dimension of our lives provides an opportunity to run after, experience, and enjoy the unique new-life blessings that are ours as the children of God. As we do this, God meets us with sanctifying grace, convicting us, encouraging us, transforming us, and empowering us for his service. We seek what he has supplied in Christ, and the result is that we mature in his grace. A significant section of Scripture, the Epistles in the New Testament, were written to detail what it looks like to live this new life in Christ. They take this new-life reality into every area of life, with detailed explanations, applications, and instructions.

Sanctification really is a lifelong life and death process. Sanctification is the reign of sin progressively weakened in our hearts and the reign of the risen Christ taking greater control over us.

The Holy Spirit

God uses many tools of sanctification to continue his redeeming work in our hearts, but none of these tools have magical sanctifying power. A hammer in a carpenter's hand has no power in itself. Its ability to drive a nail into a piece of wood is entirely dependent on the will, muscle, and skill of the carpenter who holds it. So it is with all the tools that God uses to grow us in his grace and likeness; they have no power on their own apart from the powerful work of the Holy Spirit, who uses them to continue his work in our hearts and lives.

The Holy Spirit works to grow us in grace in the following ways.

The Spirit continues his life-renewing work in our hearts. In 2 Corinthians 4:16 Paul encourages us with the fact that, although our physical bodies are in the slow process of decay, our inner self is being renewed day by day. An important aspect of our sanctification is the Holy Spirit's ongoing life-giving ministry to us.

The Spirit blesses us with his ministry of the conviction of sin. There would be no grace of sanctification without the grace of conviction. Conviction of sin is not judgment, but rather our loving heavenly Father, through the eye-opening, heart-softening work of the Holy Spirit, is drawing us near so we walk closer and closer to him. With hearts that are still prone to wander, conviction of sin is one of the core blessings of God's sanctifying grace

The Spirit illumines God's word for us. Jesus said to his confused and fearful disciples, "When the Spirit of truth comes, he will guide you into all the truth" (John 16:13). The Holy Spirit continues to work so that we will have deeper and deeper levels of understanding of the truths of God's word. The Holy Spirit works through our study to teach us how to more practically and consistently apply the truths of God's word to our daily lives and relationships. As we commit to the study of Scripture, the Holy Spirit works to illumine our minds and enliven our hearts so that we are not just informed by what we have studied but transformed by it as well.

The Spirit empowers us to obey. Because of the crippling and weakening effect of sin, we are rendered unable to be what God designed for us to be and to do what God commands us to do. Because sin leaves us unable (as well as unwilling), we desperately need empowering grace. That grace comes to us in the person and work of the Holy Spirit. He lives inside of us, empowering us to take new steps of faith and obedience and gain new ground in our growth in grace.

The Spirit carries our cries to the Father. Life between the "already" and "not yet" is often so distressing and confusing that we don't know what is the "good" that God wants us to pursue. Because we don't always understand what God is doing and we are confused as to what we are supposed to do in response, we don't know what we should pray for. Be encouraged by Paul's words in Romans 8:26: "Likewise the Spirit helps us in our weakness. For we do not know what to pray for as we ought, but the Spirit himself intercedes for us with groaning too deep for words." Rather than critiquing the quality of our prayers, the Holy

Spirit carries our messy, confused groanings to the Father, carrying needs on our behalf that we are unable to put into words. In the middle of our sanctification, sometimes we won't know how to pray, but we do not need to be discouraged, because in those moments the Spirit meets us with intervening grace. When you don't know how to pray, pray anyway, believing that the Helper is near.

The Spirit reminds us that we are the adopted children of God. "Comforter" is a name that Jesus gave to the Holy Spirit during his final moments with his disciples. Life in this fallen world is hard. Sanctification is a rocky and twisted pathway up the mountain of God's grace. Our war with sin inside and outside of us is often discouraging and exhausting. In the middle of all of this, it is quite easy to forget who we are and what we have been given and, in forgetting, to lose our way. So comfort along the way is a sweet and necessary grace. God has given us his Spirit so that comfort is always near. He works in our hearts and minds to remind us that we are the children of God, and because we are, we are never alone and we are richly supplied. He comforts us by helping the eyes of our hearts to look through the dust and darkness of this fallen world and see the presence, power, and promises of our Redeemer once again.

The Spirit keeps us. All of the ministries of the Holy Spirit that we have been considering are God's means of protecting us, guarding and growing our hearts as we walk the long road toward the likeness of the Lord Jesus Christ. We are not just convicted, enabled, and comforted, but because we are, we are kept by the Holy Spirit's power. Our faith and obedience do not keep us along the way. God does, in the convicting, empowering, and comforting work of the Holy Spirit.

It really is true that there would be no such thing as personal sanctification if it were not for the presence, power, and constant work of the Holy Spirit. Be thankful today for the Holy Spirit's presence and power in your life. Be thankful for the redeeming good he brings your way. Be thankful that because he is in you, for you, and with you, you will continue to grow in grace.

Law

Your sanctification, that is, the process by which you continue to spiritually mature, is one place where you see God's law and God's grace work in beautiful cooperation. Saying that sanctification, like justification, is a work of redeeming grace does not mean that it works in opposition to the law. Law and grace do not exist in opposition to one another. God uses both his law and his grace in the lives of his people to rescue them from sin and to conform them to the image of his Son. Celebrating grace does not mean we denigrate God's law.

Think about the historical moment when God's law was given. God, in compassion for his chosen people, had heard their cries and had unleashed his almighty power to deliver them from four hundred years of slavery. But these former slaves had no idea how to relate to their Redeemer, how to live with one another, and how to live as they were created to live. So God, in an act of grace, gave them his law. His law was never a means of their achieving acceptance with him, but rather it was given to them because they already were his chosen people, the object of his love. The law, for the newly freed children of Israel, was a gift of grace.

So it is with our sanctification. The law functions as a tool of God's grace, in both the work of putting to death sin and the work of running after new life. How? First, if we are going to put to death sin, we need a clear understanding of what sin is and how it rears its ugly head in our daily lives. One of the primary functions of God's law is its ability to define and expose sin. Romans 7:7 captures this perfectly: "What then shall we say? That the law is sin? By no means! Yet if it had not been for the law, I would not have known sin. For I would not have known what it is to covet if the law had not said, 'You shall not covet.'"

We should be forever grateful for how clearly God has communicated his will for us in his law. It is a sweet grace to have a defined understanding of what is right and what is wrong in the eyes of our Creator. I don't think we thank God enough for his law and the tool of moral restraint it has been for us every day of our lives. It is a terrible thing to live your life in the middle of practical, ongoing moral confusion. God's law rescues us from the confusion of not knowing what is right and wrong and from the moral delusion of deciding for ourselves what is right and wrong. But there is even more to be thankful for here. We should be eternally grateful for how the Holy Spirit takes God's clearly communicated law and employs it to produce conviction in our hearts. The pain of conviction is a sign that sanctifying grace is at work in your heart. This conviction only ever happens when, by the Spirit's power, God's law and God's grace work in cooperation to move us toward maturity in Christ.

There is a second way God uses the law as a tool of sanctification in our lives. Without the law we would have no sense of what righteous living looks like. If we are called to say no to sin and yes to righteousness, then knowing what functional righteousness looks like is vital. Yes, because of the righteousness of Christ, given over to our account, we stand before God legally, or positionally, righteous. Sanctification is that process by which God works to make us functionally, or actually, righteous. Here's what the law does for us: it points us to what new-life living looks like. It defines for us what it practically means to no longer live for ourselves, but to live for the one who loved us and willingly suffered and died for us.

John says, "For this is the love of God, that we keep his commandments. And his commandments are not burdensome" (1 John 5:3). Sanctification is the process by which people who have lived lives shaped by the love of self, grow to become people whose lives are shaped by love for God. It is God's commandments that teach us what it looks like to love God functionally in every area of our lives. Remember that the Ten Commandments begin with commands to worship God alone. The rest of the commands define how the worship of God then shapes our living. So for the believer, God's commands aren't a burden. Grace has worked the love of God into our hearts, and if we love God, then we should naturally desire to please him in the way that we live. His commands define for us what God-pleasing living looks like. There is a way that obedience to God's commands is its own reward since, as we obey, we are being rescued from the deceitful destructiveness of sin and moving ever closer to walking in step with our Savior.

In sanctification, the law is a death and life tool. Both in the process of killing sin and in the process of running after a new life that is ignited by love for God, the law is an essential tool of God's sanctifying grace. If you are thankful for God's sanctifying grace, then you should love God's law, you should never see it as a burden to bear, and you should give thanks daily for how God uses it to continue the work he has begun in your heart.

Patience

If God's ultimate goal in our sanctification is "Be holy as I am holy," then you and I have a long, long way to go. I don't like to wait, and I suspect that you are like me. We don't enjoy long lines. We don't like to be told that dinner isn't ready yet. We get irritated when we have to wait for what seems like hours for a bank card service operator to answer. We don't tend to thank God for the opportunity to wait in traffic. We even get impatient when our computer fails to load instantaneously.

In sanctification, God invites you to wait. Your conformity to the likeness of Jesus Christ is a process and not an event. In the magnitude of his wisdom, God knew that this was the very best way. But we must remember that waiting is not just what we have to live with because God chose for our sanctification to be a lifelong process. No, waiting is a vital tool in the process of our growth in God's grace. When it comes to our sanctification, waiting is not about what we *get* at the end of the wait, but rather about what we *become* as we wait. In God's hands, waiting is a tool of becoming. It is much, much more than the price we have to pay in order to spiritually mature. Thank God for the wait. He is using it to change you.

Waiting, for the believer, never depicts God's absence, his passivity, a lack of care, or his unfaithfulness. Waiting is a sign that you are under the control of intervening grace, because if you had control, you would probably never wait.

> But they who wait for the LORD shall renew their strength;
> they shall mount up with wings like eagles;
> they shall run and not be weary;
> they shall walk and not faint. (Isa. 40:31)

As God works day by day, situation after situation, and in relationship after relationship to free us from sin and to renew us in his grace, may we wait with gratefulness and joy. As we gaze down the years, the road will seem rough and long to us, but we are not alone; the one who designed the road is with us, and each rock and turn is a tool of his grace.

• • •

God, who exercises his glory for our eternal good, planned not only to forgive us and adopt us as his children, but to also make us "partakers of the divine nature" (2 Pet. 1:4). It is an incredible thing to consider that God would love us so much that he would work unrelentingly until we finally bear the image of his Son. What could be better for us than to not only be restored to fellowship with him, but also to live in increasing righteousness and holiness? Sanctification is not a burden to bear but a good gift to celebrate. Yes, we experience difficulties and sacrifices along the way, but in the process, unwholesome and dangerous things die and good and wonderful things live. Along the way, love for the world weakens and love for our Lord grows. With each step of growth, idols tumble and true worship of God gains control. With every turn of the road, the allegiance of our hearts shifts a little more toward our Redeemer and his kingdom. And as we travel, we stop looking back at where we came from, and we fix our eyes longingly on our eternal home.

20

Sanctification in Everyday Life

I WAS IN ASIA visiting an art museum, as I often do when I travel. I walked around a corner and into a gallery that held a mesmerizing collection of paintings. I stopped at the doorway to take them in, and then went into the gallery for a closer look. From a distance each painting looked like undulating waves of gray on a pure white canvas. The waves had the illusion of being in motion, and the wave pattern on each painting was unique. Each painting shared the singular beauty of design that had come from the mind, the eye, and the hand of the artist. You knew right away that these stunning works of art had all come from the same creator.

After a few minutes of observation from a distance, I picked out one of the paintings that seemed especially interesting and walked over to it to get up close. When I got within inches of that canvas, I was blown away by what I saw. These weren't paintings, in the strictest sense of what that means. Those beautiful waves of color were created with ink. But here's what blew me away. Each canvas was covered in handwritten, numerically sequenced sets of numbers. There were thousands and thousands of numbers on each canvas, in hundreds and hundreds of rolls. The waves were created by the how darkly the artist wrote each number on the canvas and how close he placed each number to the next. The concept was mind-boggling, the composition was intricate and complex, the execution was exquisite, and the overall effect was exquisitely beautiful.

That the artist would take something so mundane as rows of little numbers and employ these to create such wonder almost brought me to tears. Then I looked around and saw eleven other canvases executed just like the one I had just examined. They all had those carefully placed rows of numbers. They all had that beautiful wave motion. I thought of the brilliance of the artist. I thought about the commitment it took to complete this process in just one painting, let alone twelve. And then I thought of how satisfying it must have been for the artist to walk into that gallery and see the beauty that had been created by him and him alone.

More than even those amazing paintings, our sanctification is the detailed work of a perfectly committed divine artist. In order for us to take on the beauty of the image of Jesus, that work must live in thousands of little moments in our daily lives. In the tiniest of increments, day after day after day, God transforms us from the ugly messes we were in our sin into the beautiful sons and daughters he saved us to be. He never gets bored, he never grows weary, he never is frustrated, and his commitment to complete his redemptive artwork never fades. Our Savior's canvases take a lifetime to complete, but he never forsakes the detailed work of his sanctification artistry. And he doesn't do this amazing work with only twelve of us, but with millions and millions of us over thousands of years of human history and in every place on the globe. He'll keep his hand to the canvas until we are as beautiful as he suffered, died, and rose again for us to be. There will be a day when we will walk into the greatest gallery ever to see the most detailed and beautiful work ever, now complete, and we'll spend the rest of eternity in wonder and celebration.

The attitude of wonder and amazement that gripped me that day in the gallery should grip us again and again and again between our conversion and our homegoing. In the small moments and grand dramas of our lives an artist is at work, creating the most beautiful image ever, the image of the Son of God. We are the canvas. Sanctification should never be seen as a hard load placed on your shoulders, when it is actually a beautiful display of redeeming grace that we are not only invited to see, but also welcomed to participate in. Let's consider what this sanctification artistry means for our daily lives.

There Is No Such Thing as Passive Christianity

If massive, long-term heart and life change is God's agenda between the "already" of your first moment of belief and the "not yet" of your entrance into your final home, then there is no room for a lazy, inactive, and undisciplined approach to the Christian life. The Christian life is a welcome to make *God's* purpose for you *your* daily life purpose. This means that God's work in and for you becomes your work as well. Your Christian life is about much more than regular church attendance, faithful giving, biblical literacy, theological knowledge, and occasional ministry. These are all very good things, but they are tools in the hands of a much deeper, more personal plan that your Redeemer has for you. What is that deeper plan? It is this: "Be holy as I am holy" (see 1 Pet. 1:16).

The Christian life is meant to be shaped by taking this plan seriously. We are not yet all that we have the potential to be in Christ. Sin still lives inside of us doing its ugly work. We are still susceptible to the seductive draw of temptation's call. We still have hearts that are prone to wander. We still have times when we want our own way more than we want God's way. We continue to have moments when we give way when we should resist, and resist when we should submit.

Who of us can take an honest look at ourselves and conclude that we are okay, no longer in need of convicting, empowering, and sanctifying grace? Would any of us be able to say that we are as holy as we need to be? Are any of us free of regret as we look back over the last month, the last week, or even yesterday? We can make only one honest conclusion as we scan our thoughts, desires, words, and behavior: we are people in the middle of an ongoing process. We all desperately need sanctifying grace.

Because we need sanctifying grace, we also need to actively use all of the tools of that grace, which God has provided. We should also be looking for how God will use the unexpected, unplanned, difficult, and unwanted situations in our lives to expose our need for growth and to grow us in his grace. I am persuaded that for most of us our problem in our spiritual lives is not dissatisfaction but satisfaction. I think we are all too easily spiritually satisfied. We become satisfied with a little bit of theological knowledge, a consumer's approach to our local church, a cursory devotional life, a little bit of money in the offering plate, a little bit better marriage, children who are a little more controlled, and some satisfying Christian friendships.

God wants so much more for us than we tend to want for ourselves. He wants us to actually become partakers of his divine nature. Let that phrase sink in. It means that right here, right now, you and I serve a dissatisfied Redeemer; he looks on us with eyes of love, knowing that we are not yet experiencing all that is ours as his children. His relationship to us is anything but passive. He is active in every moment of our lives to continue to form the likeness of his Son in us. His dissatisfaction is a call for us to be dissatisfied too. His constant sanctifying activity on our behalf is a welcome and a call for us to be active as well. His purpose is our purpose, his work is our work, and his goal for us needs to be our goal for ourselves.

Galatians 5 is particularly helpful here, as it lays out God's agenda for us.

> But I say, walk by the Spirit, and you will not gratify the desires of the flesh. . . . But the fruit of the Spirit is love, joy, peace, patience, kindness, goodness, faithfulness, gentleness, self-control; against such things there is no law. And those who belong to Christ Jesus have crucified the flesh with its passions and desires.
>
> If we live by the Spirit, let us also keep in step with the Spirit. (Gal. 5:16, 22–25)

Notice how this passage begins and ends. It starts with "walk by the Spirit" and ends with "keep in step with the Spirit." These two phrases communicate Paul's message that we ought to take God's sanctifying grace seriously. He essentially says, "The Holy Spirit is at work in your heart, so surrender your heart to the wonderful work he is doing in you and for you." And, "The Spirit has a destination for you, so determine to go where the Spirit is taking you." So what does this practically look like? It looks like having a life shaped by taking the fruit of the Spirit seriously. The Holy Spirit has been given to you to produce in you the spiritual fruit of your new life in Christ: love, joy, peace, patience, kindness, goodness, faithfulness, gentleness, and self-control. You and I have no ability to produce these beautiful things in ourselves; they are only ever the fruit of God's sanctifying grace. But we have been called to actively work *toward* what the Spirit is working *in* our hearts.

So you get up in the morning and you pray, "Lord, I am not as loving as your grace enables me to be. Please work in my heart to make me more loving, and please open my eyes today to all the opportunities you will give me to love others as you have loved me." Or, as you start your day, you say, "Lord, I know I don't live with joy because my heart is not filled with gratitude for all of the blessings that are mine as your child. Please help me to count my blessings today, and please give me the grace to express that joyful gratitude to those around me." Each fruit is a gift of God's redeeming grace, but it also is a goal for us to aspire to and to work toward. In each area of character that is the fruit of the Spirit, we are not yet all that God has purposed for us to be in Christ. Because of this, there is no room for lethargic, self-satisfied, consumerist, and passive Christianity.

The doctrine of sanctification is a call to a spiritual work ethic. No, we are not working for a greater acceptance with God. In Christ our acceptance is complete, but we are working out our salvation with fear and trembling (Phil. 2:12). So, in holy awe of the one who lives within us, working to radically change us, we make his work our life's work. And we do this with joy and not with grief. Where do we do this work?

Wherever we are. Each day, each situation, each location, each relationship, each new challenge, each trial, each situation, and each decision is an opportunity to take one more step on the road to the likeness of Christ.

The goal is clear. What is not clear is whether we will make God's goal the goal that shapes the way we live. Will we settle in to the typical passive Christianity, where our faith seems most vibrant during two hours each Sunday? Will we see our sanctification not as a burden to bear but as a glorious blessing of divine grace? Will we quest to be holy every day in everything we think, desire, do, and say in every situation and relationship of our lives? Will the pleasure of God mean more to us than momentary worldly pleasures? Will we joyfully give ourselves to the Spirit's process of sanctification until that work is needed no more? Or will we give way to a self-satisfied lifestyle that fails to take seriously what it means to keep in step with the Spirit? May God give us the grace we need to live in step with the Spirit.

The Church Is Essential

If you take God's change agenda seriously, making his sanctifying work your spiritual life work, then you will be thankful for the gift of the church. There is no such thing as a vibrant, ever-maturing, and ministry-oriented Christian life without the ministry of the local church. For the believer, the church exists because the lifelong process of progressive sanctification exists. I am persuaded that, for many Christians, their lack of understanding of the centrality of the work of sanctification to their Christian life has led them to be rather comfortable with a casual relationship to the life and ministry of their local church.

The ministry of the church is an important tool in the hands of the Redeemer to continue to advance the saving work he has begun in us. If you recognize in yourself the presence and power of remaining sin, and if you humbly acknowledge that you need to grow in Christlikeness, then you are confessing your need to take advantage of everything that the church offers you. The apostle Paul clearly captures for us the essential sanctifying ministry of the body of Christ.

> And he gave the apostles, the prophets, the evangelists, the shepherds and teachers, to equip the saints for the work of ministry, for building up the body of Christ, until we all attain to the unity of the faith and of the knowledge of the Son of God, to mature manhood, to the measure of the stature of the fullness of Christ, so that we may no longer be children, tossed to and fro by the waves and carried about by every wind of doctrine, by human cunning, by craftiness in deceitful schemes. Rather, speaking the truth in love, we are to grow up in every way into him who is the head, into Christ, from whom the whole body, joined and held together by every joint with which it is equipped, when each part is working properly, makes the body grow so that it builds itself up in love. (Eph. 4:11–16)

Think of how every ministry of the body of Christ contributes to the death and life process of your spiritual growth. We can't comprehensively explore everything that's in this passage, but Paul points out "sanctification needs," which are in the life of every believer, that are addressed by the ministry of the church. We all need to continue to grow in our knowledge and understanding of the things of God; we all need to mature in Christlikeness; and we all need to grow in our ability to recognize and defend ourselves against Satan's deceitful schemes. We all need the public teaching and preaching of the church, not only to mature us in our understanding of the truths of the gospel, but also to increase our ability to apply those truths to our daily lives.

We need to participate in public worship. We need to sing the truths of the gospel not only into our own hearts, but into the ears and hearts of one another. We need the public reading of God's word, always being reminded of its authority, sufficiency, and life-giving wisdom. We need the mutual-ministry fellowship of the body of Christ, constantly being reminded that our walk with God is a community project and that we have been called to live with one another in the fellowship of self-sacrificing love. We need the example, wisdom, rebuke, and encouragement of mature brothers and sisters who understand how to live as children of God in this fallen world.

We need the church's call to give sacrificially, to stand for justice and mercy, and to proclaim the gospel of grace so that we learn practically what it looks like to forsake our little kingdom of one and give our lives to the greater work of the kingdom of God. We need the counsel of seasoned and trained Christians to help us deal with the brokenness of sin and suffering that touches all of our lives. We need the faith-strengthening experience of the sacraments, being reminded again and again that our hope rests on the person and work of the Lord Jesus Christ. No ministry of the church is a luxury, because no member of the church is fully sanctified.

So if you take your ongoing sanctification seriously, don't just be thankful for your church, don't just be a casual attender; give yourself to your church. Joyfully participate in all of its public and private ministries, sacrificially support its work, be active in ministries that don't target you but address the needs of others, develop solid mutual ministry relationships, find ways to use your gifts there, and don't let the imperfection of your church discourage you. Remember, your church is populated by people just like you; that is, people who are in the middle of God's process of sanctification and who still have a long way to go. The importance of the church in God's work of growing us in grace is stated clearly and powerfully by Paul in 1 Timothy 3. If the church is the pillar and foundation of the truth by which God sanctifies us, then there is no growth in grace without the impact of its life and ministry on our hearts.

> I hope to come to you soon, but I am writing these things to you so that, if I delay, you may know how one ought to behave in the household of God, which is the church of the living God, a pillar and buttress of the truth. (1 Tim. 3:14–15)

Sanctification Gives Marriage, Parenting, and Friendship a New Model and Purpose

Sometimes God's plan is a mystery and sometimes it is confusing, but as a rule, what God has planned for us is different than anything we would have planned for ourselves. So it is with marriage, parenting, and friendship. Why would God put these comprehensive and personally demanding relationships in the middle of the world's most important incomplete process (sanctification)? Wouldn't it have been better to get us fully sanctified first? I mean, what do you think is going to happen when you put a sinner next to a sinner, in a fallen world and in an intense personal relationship? In all of our relationships, we have all experienced the messy disappointment of God's plan, since none of us has been in a relationship free of disappointment.

The only way to understand God's plan for our relationships is to understand that he has a much better purpose for those relationships than that they would be a means of us experiencing relational bliss. If God's sole purpose for our relationships is our comfort, pleasure, and ease, then he is a massive failure. In truth, God's ultimate goal for our relationships is that they would be powerful and effective tools in the death and life work of sanctification.

What God wants our relationships to promote is something profoundly more beautiful than temporal personal happiness. Yes, we should find joy in these relationships, but God's purpose is much bigger than our happiness; he desires our holiness. Relationships where people are committed to growing in Christlikeness become more serving, more loving, more forgiving, more understanding, and more unified, and because they do, the people in them become happier.

It is in the messiness of a sinner living with or alongside another sinner that our sins of heart and hands get exposed. It is in the burden of living with a less-than-perfect person that we learn to love as Jesus loved. As we learn what it means to give grace to another person, we come to understand and esteem more deeply the grace that we have been given

These relationships expose the selfishness and rebellion of our hearts, and in so doing, they expose the depth of our need for everything that is ours in Christ. The mess of these relationships is God's mess. It is not a divine mistake, but rather a divine intention. God knows who we are and the world we are living in, he knew whom we'd be living with, he knew the trials that this would bring, and he knew he would use all of it to continue to form in us the character of our Savior. God's ongoing redeeming work in us sanctifies our relationships, calling them to a higher purpose than horizontal relational joy.

But the doctrine of sanctification does something else for our relationships; it blesses them with a much better model. I'm afraid many Christians have a piecemeal, moment-by-moment, how-are-things-going-today way of evaluating their relationships. Am I happy today? Did we fight today? Did I win today? Did I feel loved today? How do I keep that conversation from becoming contentious? And the questions go on and on.

Many people treat their relationships as series of helpful, happy, or hurtful moments. They don't have a long-term model or the patience and perseverance that such a model would require. If our marriage, parenting, and friendships are significant tools in the hands of the one who is constantly at work shaping us into the image of Jesus Christ, then we should have a progressive sanctification model for those relationships. Because we are people in process, our relationships are in process. Here's what I mean. Because we are less than perfect but have the potential for significant change, our relationships will be less than perfect but have the potential for change. And because personal change is not an event but a process, change in our relationships will tend to be a process as well. Because God is understanding, patient, and sympathetic when we are weak and when we fail, we should be the same with one another. If God doesn't throw our need for growth in our faces, then we should never do that with one another. If God is unwilling to give up on us in the slow process of personal transformation, then we shouldn't give up on one another either.

So, in any moment of marriage our ultimate goal should not be momentary peace, but rather that this moment would help us take another step in making the character of Jesus the character of our marriage. The goal of parenting isn't doing everything you can in a particular moment to get your child to do what you want him to do. No, your goal should be that you would take yet another step in responding to your child as

Christ would and taking yet another step in helping this child to know who he is and how much he needs the wisdom and grace of the Savior. The goal of friendship is not to finally find the kind of friends you've longed for, but to see those relationships as God's means of promoting long-term spiritual good in them and in you.

If our relationships are a tool God is actively using to transform us from what we are to what grace gives us the potential to be, then our relationships need to be characterized by the self-sacrifice of patience and perseverance. If we are all people in the middle of a long-term process, then we need to be kind, tenderhearted, sympathetic, and understanding with one another. If, in the process of sanctification, God forgives us again and again, then we should do the same with one another. If, when we fail, God picks us up again, offering us the grace of fresh starts and new beginnings, then we should do the same with one another. If, in this long process, God's hope for us never wanes, then our hope for one another shouldn't fade either.

Yes, there are relationships on this side of eternity where, because of the betrayal of sin, the trust is so terribly broken that there is no way of continuing on, but for most of us, the doctrine of sanctification provides the only productive model for how a sinner can live with another sinner in this broken world. It provides a way for us to understand the messiness all of us experience; it give us a goal to work toward; it provides us with an essential process mentality; and it holds before us character qualities that are vital for these relationships to thrive. The doctrine of sanctification gifts us with a new purpose and a new model for all of the principal relationships of our daily lives. You probably won't get what you hoped for and dreamed about in your relationships, but you'll get something infinitely better; you'll get what God promised.

The Doctrine of Sanctification Promotes the Sanctity of Everything

Think with me for a moment. If God is working his ongoing work of salvation in every situation, location, and relationship of our lives, then everything is sacred. If God uses everything in our lives as tools of his heart- and life-transforming grace, then we constantly live on holy ground. If God uses even the smallest of circumstances in our lives to move us closer to the likeness of Jesus Christ, then even the smallest moments are spiritually significant. Our entire existence is made holy and sacred because the Redeemer is not only present, but he is doing his holy, sanctifying work, even when nothing seems holy about a particular moment.

If we are God's children and objects of his constantly active sanctifying grace, then there is no secular, unholy, just-normal-whatever moments in our lives. We have no divide in our lives between the secular and the spiritual. There is no moment when God is separate from us. There is no situation where he is inactive. There is no regular day when deeply spiritual things are not going on. God's redeeming grace never goes on hiatus. His sanctifying love never takes a break. Everything is spiritual. Everything is sacred. Everything has Godward direction. Everything has redemptive significance. Everything.

I am not arguing that we should be morosely serious all of the time. I am not suggesting that you shouldn't enjoy a wonderful meal or a hearty laugh. Go shopping, go fishing, go to a game, take a hike, permit yourself a good nap, watch a good cooking show, listen to some good music, or read a good book, but as you do that, remember who you are, who your Lord is, and the process you are in because of his redeeming grace. Don't act like some things don't matter or like most of your life is mundane and unimportant. Your Redeemer works miracles of redemption in the midst of moments when it seems not much of significance is happening. Because of who you are as his child, because of who he is as your Redeemer, and because of what he is doing in and for you, your life is lived in sacred spaces.

I am afraid that many of us live God-forgetful lives. What I mean is that other than when we are participating in something that is obviously spiritual, like a public worship service, prayer, or our times of personal devotions, we live in a state of functional spiritual amnesia. In so doing, we fail to live with a consciousness of the incredible identity that is ours as children of God, the amazing reality that God actually lives inside of us, the storehouse of blessings that is ours, and the profoundly important redemptive process that is ongoing in our hearts and lives. Because we don't carry around with us a consciousness of God and his work on the ordinary day, we don't make his purpose our purpose and his work our work. We tend to be serious about our sanctification when something overtly spiritual is going on, but outside of that, not so much.

But holy work is going on everywhere and all of the time. Sanctifying grace makes your marriage sacred. Sanctifying grace makes your parenting holy. Sanctifying grace makes your job holy ground. Sanctifying grace makes your home a sacred space. Sanctifying grace makes your sexual life a holy thing. Sanctifying grace makes your use of money a sacred endeavor. Your life as a neighbor, your participation in politics, your moments of leisure and entertainment, your finances, your diet and physical health, and the plans you have for your life are all made holy, because in all of these places sanctifying grace is operating. Note the way Paul uses the example of our physical bodies (because he has been discussing sexual immorality) to remind the Corinthian believers of the sacred nature of everything in our lives: "Or do you not know that your body is a temple of the Holy Spirit within you, whom you have from God? You are not your own, for you were bought with a price. So glorify God in your body" (1 Cor. 6:19–20).

Paul has just placed your Savior right in the middle of your sexual life (1 Cor. 6:16–18). Of course he is there, because he is in you and you are in him. By grace, you and your Savior are bound together, and by grace you are the object of his redeeming presence and work even when you are having sex. But Paul pushes the envelope further and reminds us that not only sex but everything in our lives belongs to the Lord, for his purpose and his use. He paid the ultimate price to make us his own. There is nothing in our lives that belongs to us for our purpose and our using. We bring glory to God when we live with him in view—wherever we are, whatever we are doing—and when we seek to make God's redeeming purpose for us the purpose that shapes the way we think about and approach everything in our lives.

Think of the holy ground you live on every day. Before the foundations of the earth were laid in place, God claimed you as his own. He wrote the history of the world, so that at the right moment, the Savior would be born in Bethlehem. Jesus took on your humanity, subjected himself to the hardships of this fallen world, lived a perfect life, died an acceptable death, and rose again, conquering sin and death. Jesus did all of that with you in mind. He wrote every period of time, place, location, situation, and relationship into your story, so that you would hear the gospel of his grace. He worked conviction into your heart, gave you ears to hear the truth, and gifted you with the ability to believe. He gave you his word and moved inside of you, by his Spirit. He poured down the blessing of his promises on you and will never leave you. He rules your life with your continued salvation in mind, using everything at his sovereign disposal to move along the work of his transforming mercies. There is never a moment when you aren't the object of redeeming love and sanctifying grace. The gargantuan, sovereignly directed plan of redemption has placed you on the ground you now stand on. From eternity past to eternity future, your life has been claimed as holy ground.

How can you consider this without falling to your knees in awe, gratitude, and worship? How can you not keep the eyes of your heart constantly open to the operation of God's sanctifying grace? And how can your living not be shaped by understanding that every aspect of your life is made sacred by sanctifying grace?

Difficulty Is a Primary Sanctification Tool

You have probably never heard anyone say, "I had three of the easiest years of my life, and I learned so much and changed so much." In passages too numerous to mention here, the Bible confronts us with the fact that the things we would like to avoid in our lives are the very things God uses to produce the most good in us and through us. We struggle with seeing difficulty, in the hands of God, as a tool for massive spiritual good, because all of us still struggle with a particular form of idolatry. In 2 Corinthians 5:15, Paul says that Jesus came so that those who live would no longer live for themselves. He is positing that the DNA of sin is selfishness. You see that in the sin of Adam and Eve in the garden. Their disobedience was about love of self, replacing love of God in their hearts. The core idol of idols is the idol of self. This idol places us on center stage and causes our lives to be shaped by what we want, how we want it, where we want it, when we want it, and whom we want to deliver it. I suspect that this will be hard for you to read, but I am persuaded that the idol of self is far more influential in our choices, words, and behavior than we tend to think.

If selfism is still with us because sin is still in us, then there is another idol that we will tend to serve. It is the idol of comfort. I imagine that you are like me; that is, that you tend to think that a good life is a comfortable life. We get irritated, impatient, and angry at even minor difficulties. Long lines make us mad. Having to listen to an overtalkative person makes us impatient. A day when we don't feel great causes us to grumble and complain. We complain when it's cold, when it's hot, when it rains, when the sun is too bright, or when it gets dark too early for our liking. We grumble if our food is too hot, too cold, too salty, or not seasoned enough; we complain if the portions are too big, if we're still hungry, or if it's not the kind of food we like. We get mad when the weaknesses of our spouse make our life messier, when our children demonstrate that they really do need our parental care, when our neighbors are less than what we would like them to be, or when the dog seems to always do the irritating things dogs do.

Sadly, we spend many of our days being dissatisfied with our lives, because we are not getting our comfortable way. Is it any wonder, then, that we would have a hard time being thankful that the difficulties in our lives are a primary tool of God's transforming grace? As long as self is in the center, we will struggle with anything that is uncomfortable. So, when it comes to the sanctifying power of difficulty in the hands of God, we need to do two things. First, we need to humbly *confess* that we often treasure our comfort more than we treasure sanctifying grace. We cannot long for redeeming grace and curse difficulty at the same time. That's like hiring someone to build you a house and then requiring him to leave his tools at home. God will fulfill his redemptive promises to you through the tool of uncomfortable situations that you would have never chosen for yourself. When it comes to his work of sanctification, what he gives you is always infinitely more valuable than what he takes. Stop reading for a moment and humbly confess your love of what is comfortable, and then pray for the grace to love God and his redeeming work more.

Second, we need to *remember* the cross of Jesus Christ. I find myself, in my speaking, writing, and personal life, going back to this theme again and again. The cross of Jesus Christ teaches us a powerfully encouraging truth: God is able to bring the very best of things out of the very worst of things. This is one of the miracles of his redeeming grace. What could be worse in all of human history than the unjust conviction, torture, and execution of the one perfect man (Jesus) who ever lived? What could be better than the final penalty-paying, life-giving sacrifice of Jesus? What seemed a massive public defeat was, in fact, the divine victory of the ages. On the cross Satan wasn't winning; no, the cross was his doom. From this very bad moment, plotted and executed by evil men, grace upon grace flows to all who believe. The cross reminds us that God brings rich, beautiful, and eternal spiritual good out of bad things.

So because sin still lives in us, the work of sanctification still goes on, and because it does, suffering will enter our doors. These hard moments are never a sign that God has forsaken us, but rather an indication that his transforming grace is at work. For this reason, we can look difficulty in the face and be thankful, not for the pain of difficulty but for what God will produce in us and through us by it.

Your Devotional Life Is Not a Duty but a Tool

In the over four decades that I have been in ministry, I have spent thousands of hours counseling troubled, depressed, fearful, angry, hurting, beaten-down, and confused Christians. It has not been a burden, but a huge personal blessing. I have been chosen to see God's hand at work in struggling people's lives, up close and personal. I have seen the darkness of depression begin to lift. I have seen people begin to be freed from addiction's hold. I have seen marriages restored and families reunited. I have seen people who doubted God's goodness come to rest in his care. Not every ending was a happy one, but I am thankful that I have witnessed rescue, restoration, new life, fresh starts, new hope, and new beginnings over and over again.

What does this have to do with how one's personal devotional life is a powerful tool in God's work of sanctification? One of the troubling themes that popped up again and again as I got to know the believers that God sent my way was how few of them had regular habits of personal worship. Now, let me be clear here. I am not arguing that the trouble in their lives was caused by their lack of personal study and worship. Nor am I suggesting that personal worship would have ended their emotional and spiritual trouble. But I am suggesting that because of the absence of regular personal study and worship, many of my counselees lacked the personal growth and preparedness for trouble that regular personal worship produces. Regular personal worship won't free you from the personal trouble of heart, mind, and soul, but it will surely alter the way you journey through those troubles.

I am convinced that spending time each day in scriptural meditation and worshipful prayer is a powerful tool of sanctifying grace in the hands of our faithful and loving Redeemer. Permit me to list how the regular habit of personal worship contributes to God's ongoing work of personal heart and life transformation. Daily study of God's word, worship, and prayer will result in the following:

- A deeper knowledge of the nature and character of God.
- A clearer understanding of how God works.
- An ever-deepening love for and trust in him.
- A deeper willingness and commitment to surrender your life to him.
- A deeper knowledge of yourself as sinner, sufferer, and saint.

- A deeper understanding of the life you have been called to as a child of God.
- A deeper and more practical grasp of the truths of God's word.
- A clearer and more practical understanding of the gospel of Jesus Christ.
- A deeper awareness of the nature of sin and temptation.
- More regular patterns of conviction of sin, confession, and repentance.
- Being better prepared for spiritual warfare and Satan's attacks.
- Becoming more and more thankful for God's presence, power, and promises and the blessings of being loved by him.

If you are committed to make God's purpose of personal transformation the work you give yourself to as his child, then you will see the discipline of personal study, worship, and prayer not as a spiritual burden, but as a loving welcome. Here is an invitation to be a daily participant in the most wonderful work that has ever been done, the rescuing, forgiving, and transforming work of redeeming grace. Here I am welcomed to sit at the feet of my Father, to experience his love once again, and to take in his wisdom again. Here I am welcomed to look at myself in the perfect mirror of Scripture, seeing myself with clarity and accuracy. Here I am invited to humbly confess my sins, weaknesses, and failures, without fear of being mocked or rejected. Here I am taught how to war against sin and how to defend myself against the enemy's attacks. Here I am encouraged, comforted, and strengthened. And here I am given reason for facing my day with faith, hope, and courage.

Make regular personal worship one of the nonnegotiable habits of your life, knowing that the invitation to commune daily with God is not only a tool of his sanctifying grace, but it is a sign of your Savior's love for you.

The Doctrine of Sanctification Is a Rebuke to Progressive Christianity

I have a confession to make. I spend a bit of time every day reading my Twitter feed. No, I never participate in the aggressive, cancel-culture back-and-forth that Twitter has become known for. I do, however, follow a cross section of Twitter sites that give me a wide-ranging picture of what is happening in our culture and in the church at this moment. I think this habit is important to what God has called me to do. This daily time on Twitter has been both encouraging and stimulating and discouraging and disheartening.

There are clear, courageous, loving, and hopeful gospel voices on Twitter that make me think and give me joy. But many voices there make me wonder what has happened to us and cause me great concern for the church of Jesus Christ that I love so. What should concern anyone who takes their faith seriously, and specifically God's call to "be holy as I am holy," is the rise of *progressive Christianity*. These voices are all over social media and provide the content and perspective of several very popular books.

Alisa Childers, who has written very helpfully about progressive Christianity, lists five identifying characteristics.[1]

1. There is a lower view of the Bible. The Bible becomes less than the authoritative word of God from cover to cover. It gets reduced to *containing* the word of God. When we replace *is* with *contains*, guess who decides which part of the book is God's word and which isn't?

2. Feelings are emphasized over facts. Feelings, opinions, and personal experiences are valued more highly than divinely revealed objective truth.

3. Essential Christian doctrines are open for reinterpretation. The Bible gets reinterpreted on hot-button issues like homosexuality and abortion and on doctrinal issues like the virgin birth and bodily resurrection of Jesus and the existence of a literal hell.

4. Historic terms are redefined. God's love is redefined, sin becomes less or different than what the Bible presents it to be, and the inspiration and authority of Scripture are redefined.

5. The heart of the gospel message shifts from sin and redemption to social justice. There are profoundly important biblical commands for the people

1 Based on Alisa Childers, "5 Signs Your Church Might Be Headed toward Progressive Christianity," *Alisa Childers* (blog), May 8, 2017, www.alisachilders.com. Used by permission.

of God to be agents of God's mercy, defending the cause of the oppressed. But the core message of Christianity, the gospel, is that because of our sins, Jesus came and lived a righteous life, died a substitutionary death, and rose again, giving us new life and reconciling us to God.

What you end up with is something that does not look at all like the Christianity that has been written about, defined, and explained by Christian theologians for generations and held dear by believers throughout the ages. The elements of progressive Christianity, which Childers lays out, mean that this is another gospel, one that lives in contradiction and opposition to the true gospel of Jesus Christ, which is clearly and expansively laid out in Scripture.

What does this have to do with progressive sanctification? Everything! In progressive Christianity the goal of the Christian life is for you to be happy, feel fulfilled, be comfortable with yourself, and love others in whatever way you feel is best. Accepting yourself as you are replaces confession of sin, and self-fulfillment replaces working out your salvation with fear and trembling. The authority and glory of God are replaced with the authority and glory of self. Progressive Christianity is a seductive rewriting of our faith that plays to our temptation to put ourselves in the center and make life all about our wants, needs, and feelings. It does this while presenting itself as a better reading of what the Bible teaches than what the church has taught throughout its history.

The doctrine of sanctification reminds you that your acceptance with God is only ever based on the person and work of Jesus Christ, while it calls you to forsake everything to follow Jesus, committing yourself to make his holy transforming work in you the work that shapes everything in your life. The doctrine of sanctification calls you to rest in God's grace, while it calls you to a life of surrender and obedience, never complacent and never passive between your conversion and your homegoing.

Because in the doctrine of sanctification God calls us to "be holy as I am holy," it is a rebuke to any kind of pseudo-Christian, me-centered, you're-as-good-as-you-need-to-be, quit-saying-you're-sorry, don't-be-judgmental, and sleep-with-whomever-you-want lifestyle. This new way of interpreting the gospel has no doctrine of sanctification and no call to holiness, and because it doesn't, it is an alien gospel, dangerously distinct from the gospel that has been so lovingly revealed by God in his word. So be aware of whom you read, be aware of how the gospel of Jesus Christ is being defined and explained, and reject any gospel that puts human comfort in the place of the glory of God and his holy claim on every aspect of your life.

If you are a parent, prepare your children, who will surely be exposed to the voices of this different gospel. If you are a pastor, talk about this with your people, many of whom spend many hours every week on social media. Discuss this with your friends. If you are a university student, listen carefully and examine what you are being taught in your student ministry. Above all, thank God for his glorious grace in Jesus and for how his call to be serious about holiness rescues you from the one thing you can't escape on your own: you.

The God who created us and saved us by his grace knows us better than we know ourselves and desires for us what is much, much better than anything we would have desired for ourselves. The holiness he calls us to is a gorgeous expression of everything humanity was intended to be. It is beautifully depicted for us in his Son, God in the flesh, the Lord Jesus Christ. His call gives us dignity and purpose, something that is worth living for far more than the goals we would have set for ourselves. It brings humility to how we live and a tender, loving beauty to our relationships. It calls us to a life of moral commitments, without being arrogant, judgmental, and condemning of others. The doctrine of sanctification is not a joy-killing burden to bear, but a welcome to a beautiful life where surrender to the plan, purposes, and call of God really does become the doorway to true happiness and rest of heart.

21

The Doctrines of the Perseverance and Glorification of the Saints

THOSE WHOM GOD has accepted through his beloved Son, has effectually called, and are being made holy by his Spirit, will not finally fall away from grace, but will persevere in that grace until the end. They will be eternally saved.

The perseverance of the saints does not depend on their own free will, but upon God's unchangeable choice, which flows from the free and unchangeable love of God the Father; from the effectiveness of the merit and intercession of Jesus, from the Spirit who lives inside of them and the seed of God, planted in them, and from the nature of the covenant of grace. From all of these comes the certainty that they will persevere.

However, because of the temptations of Satan and the world, because of the corruption of sin remaining in the saints and their neglect of God's means of preserving them, they may fall into sins, continuing in those sins for a time, incurring God's displeasure and grieving the Holy Spirit. Because of this, some of the saints' blessings and comforts may be taken away, their hearts hardened, their consciences seared. This hurts and scandalizes others and brings temporary judgment on them.

After death, peoples' bodies decay and return to dust, but their souls live forever. They neither die nor sleep, but return to the God who gave them. The souls of righteous people are made perfectly holy and are received in the highest heavens, where they behold the face of God in light and glory, waiting for the full redemption of their bodies. See Gen. 3:19; 2 Sam. 12:14; Pss. 32:3–4; 51:10, 12; 89:31–32; Eccles. 12:7; Isa. 64:5, 9; Jer. 32:40; Mal. 3:6; Matt. 26:70–74; Luke 16:24; John 10:28–29; 14:19; 17:21–24; Acts 13:36; Rom. 2:10; 5:1–11; 8:11, 16, 30; 9:16; 1 Cor. 2:7; 11:32; 15:50–55; 2 Cor. 5:1–8; Eph. 1:18; 4:30; Phil. 1:6; Col. 1:27; 2 Thess. 2:14; 2 Tim. 2:10–19; Heb. 2:10; 6:17–18; 12:23; 1 Pet. 1:7; 4:19; 5:10; 1 John 2:19; 3:9; Jude 6–7.[1]

Understanding the Doctrines of Perseverance and Glorification

Your ability to imagine is an important part of your faith. Let me explain. For the believer, imagination is not the ability to conjure up what is unreal, but rather, it is the ability to see what is real but unseen. We are called to "see" God's saving grace, his cleansing blood, his Spirit, living inside of us. We live with the "sight" of the storehouse of blessings that are ours as the children of God and the magnificent and glorious future that is ours by grace. God, in mercy, gives us eyes to "see" what sin normally blinds our eyes from seeing. Imagination is a vital part of his gift of faith to us.

So imagine with me being given a gift that can never be taken away, one that will never grow old, wear out, break, stop functioning, or lose its value. We are used to things decaying. Regardless of the seeming invincibility of youth, our physical bodies eventually grow weak, frail, and old. The new car that even smelled new soon becomes the used car that you're thinking of trading in for a newer model. If you've had a car accident, the body may have been repaired, but your car will never be quite the same. Similarly, the most amazing athlete doesn't stay amazing

1 Author's paraphrase of the doctrines of the perseverance and glorification of the saints as found in the Westminster Confession of Faith, chaps. 17 and 32.1.

forever. Either injuries diminish him or age weakens him, but his skill and power will surely fade.

Our relationships don't last forever. Sometimes sin causes a swift dramatic end or slowly eats away at trust until there is no relationship left. Sometimes death separates us. Most of the time, other things in life separate us. Think of all your friends over the years with whom you now have little or no contact. Hopes and dreams die. Jobs and careers don't last forever. Once-vibrant churches become empty religious monuments to a spiritual community that is no more. You'll outlive the puppy you just brought home, and the blossoms in your garden will turn brown and fall to the ground.

We are so used to the fading away of so many things in our lives, we are so used to things breaking or not working as intended and then shopping for a replacement, that it's hard for us to imagine a gift that cannot be taken away or ever fade, but rather becomes more beautiful. It's hard for us to imagine a gift that doesn't disappoint as the years go on, but rather fulfills its promise to bless us with unprecedented glory. It's hard for us to grasp with our imaginations what saving grace is able to do, because it is unlike anything we have ever experienced in our lives.

This chapter is meant to give you eyes to see the wonder of God's saving grace. We want to look at the wonder of its keeping power (perseverance of the saints) and the wonder of its final blessing (glorification of the saints). It is my hope that our awe of God's gift of saving, keeping, and ultimately victorious grace would ignite not only worship in your heart, but also a life of joyful surrender, obedience, and service to the giver of this wonderful gift.

Perseverance of the saints describes for us the process by which God keeps every one of his adopted children, and glorification describes the final blessing of his keeping power.

The Perseverance of Everyone Who Is Saved

From the outset of seeking to understand the magnitude, comfort, and practicality of this doctrine, it is important to understand that the foundation of our perseverance is love. It is the power of love that keeps us, but here is what is essential to understand: it is not our love for God that keeps us to the end, but God's unshakable love for us. To unpack the doctrine of perseverance is really to meditate on the nature, the work, and the power of the love of God for his own.

Romans 8:28–39 is incredibly helpful here.

1. God's redeeming work in the heart and lives of his children is unstoppable. When it comes to the perseverance of the redeemed, Romans 8:29–30 is an airtight, says-it-all passage: "Those whom he foreknew he also predestined. . . . Those whom he predestined he also called. . . . Those whom he called he also justified, and those whom he justified he also glorified." This unbreakable chain of grace will complete its work in the life of each and every person who has placed his or her trust in Jesus. True love does not quit; and so it is with the most perfect expression of love, the saving love of God in Christ Jesus.

2. God exercises his sovereignty for the redemptive good of his children. "All things work together for good, for those who are called according to his purpose" (Rom. 8:28). Since the context of these words is God's unshakable redemptive commitment, then they should be understood in that light. Here is where ultimate comfort is to be found. The one who is in control of everything is right now exercising his control over everything for the redemptive good of his people. And as the verses that follow declare, he will not stop delivering the goods of salvation to his children until they are with him and like him in glory.

3. Along the way, God will supply everything his children need. Since what Paul has just written in Romans 8:28–30 is true, Paul asks these rhetorical questions: "If God is for us, who can be against us?" and "He who did not spare his own Son . . . , how will he not also with him graciously give us all things?" (8:31–32). If God spared nothing to bring us to himself, and if our future is secure by the power of his love for us, does it make any sense at all to think that he would abandon us along the way? Embedded in the surety of our perseverance is the promise of God's faithful provision. He who gave us his Son and secured our destiny will provide everything we need between our justification and our glorification. The sacrifice of his Son is our guarantee of that commitment.

4. No one can bring a charge against God's children. But Paul is not done unpacking the security that is ours because of God's redeeming love. He states, again by means of rhetorical questions, that no one has the right to bring condemning charges against those whom God has justified in Christ Jesus. The evil doubts, the condemning guilt, and the spiritual anxiety the enemy assaults your heart with are bogus and false. The Judge of all things has made a final moral judgment, based on the righteousness and sacrifice of Jesus, that we are forever forgiven, forever accepted, and forever righteous in his eyes. The charges against us have been dropped forever. Hold your justification card in the face of the condemner and walk away. The ultimate Judge has made a final judgment. It is over and done, the courtroom is closed, the lights have been turned out, and the door has been locked. We no longer live before the condemner's bench, but rather in the Father's house.

5. Nothing can separate God's children from his love. Here is the final argument Paul makes for the perseverance of the saints. Yes, they suffer in this groaning world; yes, there are times they don't even know how to pray; yes, they live with the condemning attacks of the enemy; and yes, they wander and stray, but nothing in heaven or on earth can ever separate them from the love of God in Christ Jesus (Rom. 8:35–39). There is nothing as powerful as his redeeming love, and it is that love that keeps his children to the end. You are his children, not first because you believed, but because he placed his love on you. He doesn't love you because you believe; no, you believe because he loved and is loving you. In the end, our perseverance is the result of the love of God being poured down on us through the person and work of the Lord Jesus Christ. This lover doesn't woo and walk away, his words of love are not empty talk, his commitment doesn't weaken when we fail, and he will keep every one of his promises until the end. We are secure in his love.

This beautifully encouraging passage in Romans echoes what Jesus said in three important perseverance passages in John. In John 5:24 Jesus says, "Truly, truly, I say to you, whoever hears my word and believes him who sent me has eternal life. He does not come into judgment, but has passed from death to life." Could the implications of this declaration by Jesus be any clearer? If you have placed your trust in Jesus, God's judgment of you is your spiritual past, but has no place in your spiritual present or future. The one who said these words was on his way to the cross, where he would take the judgment of all who believe on himself. He would pay their penalty, so that they would be able to stand forever before God without fear of his judgment. If you have placed your trust in Jesus, you have passed from death to life. There is no spiritual death on the path before you. Down the road, for everyone who has believed, is life, glorious eternal life. Your death dilemma was forever solved by the death of Jesus for you. So your spiritual story will never be about the drama of death but about the blessings of new and eternal life.

However, the glorious encouragement of the certainty of the final security of the salvation of every true believer should never result in a Christian lifestyle that is lazy, casual, and lacking in serious devotion and obedience. We are kept by the power of the redeeming love of our Father, but he uses regular means to accomplish this miraculous work. The Redeemer has spoken: "He does not come into judgment, but has passed from death to life." His declaration is the seal of our perseverance.

Jesus also spoke about perseverance in John 6:37–40:

> All that the Father gives me will come to me, and whoever comes to me I will never cast out. For I have come down from heaven, not to do my own will but the will of him who sent me. And this is the will of him who sent me, that I should lose nothing of all that he has given me, but raise it up on the last day. For this is the will of my Father, that everyone who looks on the Son and believes in him should have eternal life, and I will raise him up on the last day.

Jesus has just declared that he is manna, the bread of God sent down from heaven. Then he says something that should be an enormous encouragement to anyone who is struggling, as a Christian, through the hardships and temptations of this fallen world. There is no metaphor or mystery to these words. They are direct, and their meaning is clear. First he says, "It's the Father who gives you to me and whomever the Father gives to me, I will never cast out." You and I come to Christ because of the Father's initiative, and we are kept by the Savior's will and power. It is God who draws us and it is God who keeps us. Salvation is of the Lord.

Then Jesus doubles down on his declaration. "I will lose nothing of what the Father has given me, so those who believe in me, I will raise up on the last day." Sovereign grace calls us, draws us, and keeps us. This is where our hope rests as we persevere from our moment of first belief until we see our Savior face-to-face. We do not give the spiritual life to our dead hearts that enables us to believe, and we do not have the independent spiritual power to keep ourselves to the end. God really is our refuge and strength.

One additional passage in John pointedly speaks to our perseverance.

> My sheep hear my voice, and I know them, and they follow me. I give them eternal life, and they will never perish, and no one will snatch them out of my hand. My Father, who has given them to me, is greater than all, and no one is able to snatch them out of the Father's hand. I and the Father are one. (John 10:27–30)

Jesus has just declared himself to be the Good Shepherd. What a beautiful word picture capturing his love for, commitment to, and protection of his children (sheep). Even in the middle of this word picture, the words of Jesus are unmistakably clear. It is not hard to understand what "they will never perish" and "no one is able to snatch them out of my hand" mean. You and I persevere because we are held, by grace, in the Father's sovereign, omnipotent hand. No one has taken or will ever take anything from our heavenly Father that he hasn't chosen to give away.

What these passages teach us is that the power that keeps us is the power of the Lord. Our salvation is initiated by him, continued by him, and finalized by him. If we had the power to do any of this, the intervention into the world of divine grace would not have been necessary. And if the stability and continuance of our salvation rests on our shoulders, then the Christian life becomes a scary, fearful, and anxiety-laden existence. With sin still inside us and with hearts prone to wander, we would never be sure, always trying to earn and secure our place and never quite sure that we have. But these passages are clear; every part of the process of our salvation rests on the will, power, love, and grace of the Lord. We rest because the Good Shepherd will keep every one of his sheep forever.

Although the teaching of Jesus is clear, this passage leaves us with two questions. First, if what we have just considered is true, then does it make any difference how we live? Does the doctrine of the perseverance of the saints mean that casual, lazy, and consumerist Christianity is okay? If we're this secure, why not enjoy the pleasures of sin for a bit? There is no indication anywhere in Scripture that the keeping power of God gives you license not to take his call, wisdom, and commands seriously between the "already" of your conversion and the "not yet" of your homegoing. In fact, the Bible teaches the opposite. It tells us that God exercises his keeping power through the vehicle of regular means. You are not kept because you have regular personal worship, but your Savior employs that regular habit to keep you. You are not kept because you are faithful in participating in the gathering of your church for public worship and teaching, but God uses that commitment to keep you. You are not kept because you commit yourself every day to live inside of the boundaries of God's commands, but God uses that discipline to keep you. You are not kept because you abandon your kingdom and give yourself to the work of God's kingdom, but God employs that surrender to keep you. God does the extraordinary work of keeping us until the end through the ordinary means of the regular habits of the Christian life. Consider the following.

> Do you not know that in a race all the runners run, but only one receives the prize? So run that you may obtain it. (1 Cor. 9:24)

> And let us not grow weary of doing good, for in due season we will reap, if we do not give up. (Gal. 6:9)

> For you have need of endurance, so that when you have done the will of God you may receive what is promised. (Heb. 10:36)

> Therefore since we are surrounded by so great a cloud of witnesses, let us also lay aside every weight, and sin which clings so closely, and let us run with endurance the race that is set before us. (Heb. 12:1)

> I am coming soon. Hold fast to what you have, so that no one may seize your crown. (Rev. 3:11)

These are but a few of the many passages that say that the way you live as a believer matters. And one of the reasons it matters is that God uses your commitment to endure, with all of its regular habits of faith, as a tool to keep you by his power. So you work, you fight, you resist, you obey, you confess, you repent, you worship, you study, and you do it all over and over again. None of these disciplines would be enough to keep you forever in the Shepherd's fold, but each is a tool the Father uses to keep us to the end. No, the doctrine of perseverance doesn't teach us that the way we live doesn't make any difference. It calls us to the very opposite.

The second question is, "Then what do we say about believers who fall away?" We've all seen both well-known public people and people near to us deny the faith and walk away. It's painful to watch, and, if this dynamic is misunderstood, it can cause you to question your own potential to persevere. We know people whom we would have called true believers—some even mature believers and some we looked to as our leaders—who seemed to not only know the word of God but who also seemed to love the Lord, who say they no longer believe and no longer call themselves Christians. Does this mean that we can fall away too?

This question requires discussing two groups of people. The first group are those who wander away for an extended period of time but return.

Because we have hearts that are not yet fully purified from the corruption of sin, we will all have moments when our thoughts and desires wander outside of God's boundaries. For some of us, this will mean a moment of disobedience in attitude or action, followed by confession and repentance. For others, those initial sinful desires will lead us away from God's path for an extended period of time. I have counseled many parents whose children wandered from the truth for years and returned to the beliefs of their youth. Sometimes a spouse has drifted away for a period but later returned.

If people we know and love have professed faith and lived it out for a period and then forsook the faith, we should not give up on them, we should not stop praying for them, and we should not shut the door of the welcome of grace to them. We pray because God is able to do in their hearts what we would never be able to do. We should pray for remembrance, for conviction, for a softening of the heart, for confession, and for a return of a longing for God and the fellowship of his people. As they wander, we should do nothing to compromise God's truth and his call, while at the same time extending to them the same patient grace that God has given us.

Then there is a second group of people. Writing about them is much more heartbreaking to me. There are people who seem to know the Lord, seem to celebrate his grace, seem to love God's word, seem to love Christian fellowship, and seem to be giving themselves to a life of obedience to and service of God. They may become prominent members of the body of Christ, they may even have had some years in vocational ministry, but tragically they forsake the faith and never come back. Has the Father failed to keep them? Has the Good Shepherd lost one of his sheep? Is our salvation not secure?

Three passages in Scripture directly address this second group of people. In explaining his famous parable of the seed, which pictured how people receive the word, Jesus talks about the seed that fell on rocky soil.

> As for what was sown on rocky ground, this is the one who hears the word and immediately receives it with joy, yet he has no root in himself,

> but endures for a while, and when tribulation or persecution arises on account of the word, immediately he falls away. (Matt. 13:20–21)

When Jesus says, "he has no root in himself," he means the word of God had not taken root in the soil of his heart. It had not produced true transforming faith; that is, the bondage of sin in the heart had not been broken by grace. There had not been a shift in the deepest allegiances of the heart from service of self to surrender to God. The Spirit had not actually taken up residence in the person's heart, empowering and transforming him. If the word has not taken root in your heart, you aren't one of God's children, though you may seem to be for a period of time.

On another occasion, in words of hard warning, Jesus adds to our understanding of this second group of people.

> Not everyone who says to me, "Lord, Lord," will enter the kingdom of heaven, but the one who does the will of my Father who is in heaven. On that day many will say to me, "Lord, Lord, did we not prophesy in your name, and cast out demons in your name, and do many mighty works in your name?" And then will I declare to them, "I never knew you; depart from me, you workers of lawlessness." (Matt. 7:21–23)

It is important for us to hear these words: "Not everyone who says to me, 'Lord, Lord,' will enter the kingdom of heaven." This includes people who have seemed to do "mighty works" in the Lord's name. Why won't they enter the kingdom of heaven? Jesus's answer is clear: "I never knew you." This means these people were never sheep in the Great Shepherd's flock. They were never the adopted children of the Father. For all of their seeming righteousness and mighty works of ministry, they were never a part of the community of the redeemed. If the Savior doesn't know you, then you are not one of his children. It is heartbreaking to consider, but not everyone who is a member of a visible local church is, in fact, a member of the invisible church, God's eternal household.

In his first letter, John addresses the group we are considering with brief but very clear words: "They went out from us, but they were not of us; for if they had been of us, they would have continued with us. But they went out, that it might become plain that they all are not of us" (1 John 2:19). John's words are a good summary of the two passages we previously considered. Why do people forsake the faith and never come back? The answer is, because they were not true believers.

Many things can masquerade as true faith. A person may love the intricacies of theology but not love the Lord. A person may love being part of the loving community of faith but not actually be a person of faith. A person may love the process and prominence of a ministry position but not have surrendered his heart to the lordship of Jesus Christ. A person may enjoy the experience of public worship while not having given his heart and life to the worship of the Lord. Not everyone who appears to be a person of faith is a person of faith. "They went out from us, but they were not of us" is the sad answer to the question, "If God keeps us to the end, why do some fall away?"

How do we respond to this group of people? The answer is, the same way we respond to the first group. Thankfully, we do not have the ability to see into people's hearts. This would be a burden we could not bear. But because we do not have this ability, we need to respond to those who have forsaken the faith with *hope* in the drawing, convicting power of God, with the same *grace* that God extended to us, with *words* of tender warning, with the Savior's *love,* and with patient and with perseverant *prayer*. As we do this, we receive their wandering away not as an occasion for us to be proud, but as a warning to us to continue to run after the grace that has run after us.

Yes, the Lord will exercise his almighty power to keep his own, but that does not mean we should be lazy or take our faith for granted. The God who goes to extraordinary lengths to keep his children uses ordinary means to do so. So we make those means the constant habits of our lives until we are on the other side and do not need to persevere any longer.

The Final Glorification of Everyone Who Is Saved

God will complete his work in us. We will be finally and fully redeemed. Everything that Jesus lived and died for will live in us. The work of the fundamental transformation of our hearts will be completed. We will finally, in every way, be made in the likeness of our Savior. There is glory coming that is beyond any glory we have ever experienced or imagined. There is an end to God's saving work. The great celestial orchestra will be in full crescendo as the fully glorified children of God march into their final home. They will receive a crown, but all the praise, worship, and celebration will be directed at their Savior, as they begin to sing glory songs to him that will never end.

It is hard to wrap our limited little brains around what glorification actually means. We have spent our lives around flawed people. Even the most mature and noble among us have their nobility nicked, scratched, and dented by sin. From birth to death, flawed is our everyday normal. Flawed thoughts, flawed desires, flawed attitudes, flawed words, flawed actions and reactions, flawed decisions, flawed love, flawed relationships, flawed worship—this is the human community we are accustomed to. Only as we observe Jesus during his brief journey on earth do we get a glimpse of what our flawless future will look like. The incarnated and then resurrected Jesus is the clearest prophecy of our future glorification.

In the time we are now living in, between our conversion and our homegoing, there is a seeming contradiction and tension between what God has declared us to be (righteous) and what we actually are (not quite righteous, actually). Only in our final glorification will this tension of the ages be finally and forever resolved. God calls us to live patiently in the middle of this tension, celebrating what we have been declared to be but humbled by what we actually are. We have to humbly admit that hypocrisy lives everywhere; it's in us and around us. The only place hypocrisy doesn't live is in the heart of God and his fully glorified children. So God calls us to hold on to the promise that he will complete what he has begun, as he blesses us with the grace to do so. We don't stop looking to Jesus, with expectancy tempered by patience, holding on to the promise that we will be like him.

Here is what glorification means: "Beloved, we are God's children now, and what we will be has not yet appeared; but we know that when he appears we shall be like him, because we shall see him as he is" (1 John 3:2). There is no better single-phrase summary of what glorification means than these five words: *we shall be like him.*

All of God's grace-adopted children will finally be like him. That flawed husband, struggling with sexual sin, will be like him. That young person, fighting temptation at her university, will be like him. That disgruntled businessman will be like him. That guy cursing at traffic will be like him. The disgruntled wife, who is envious of what her friend has, will be like him. That pastor, who has lost his passion for ministry, will be like him. The seminary student, who has confused theological knowledge with spiritual maturity, will be like him. That couple, who have spent their way into deep life-altering debt, will be like him. That person, crippled by anxiety, will be like him. Because all of these people are true children of God, their futures are bright. The seeming contradiction between who God has declared them to be and how they now live will be broken once and forever. The struggle will end because they will finally be what justifying grace declared them to be: righteous. What a stunning hope to hold on to. It's hard to live in the middle, with all of its struggle and disappointments. That's why it's important to hold on to the surety of our glorification. Live now amongst the flaws with future flawlessness in view.

What it means to be glorified has two dimensions. First, there would be no such thing as the completion of our redemption without the final funeral of sin. We all hate funerals because they confront us with death and final separation, but this is one funeral to look forward to and celebrate. Sin will die. If you are God's child, waiting for you on the other side of the death of sin is a glorious eternal life. Imagine life without the seduction, stain, deceit, destruction, and death that sin rained upon humanity. Imagine life without daily spiritual warfare. Imagine the final defeat of the devil and all the forces of darkness. Imagine being finally free of sin's burden and bondage. The corrupting power of sin will die. It seems too good to imagine, but that day is coming; the death and resurrection of Jesus Christ is our guarantee.

Consider the words of Revelation 22:3: "No longer will there be anything accursed, but the throne of God and of the Lamb will be in it, and his servants will worship him." Sin brought with it the curse of separation from God, the curse of condemnation, and the curse of death. In our final home, because there is no more sin, the curse will be forever broken. When Revelation says "no longer will there be anything accursed," you know that sin has finally and forever been eradicated. Without the death of sin, there would be no such thing as the final glorification of all who are saved. As the glorified children of God, we will sing these words with joy unlike anything we have experienced before:

> "O death, where is your victory?
> O death, where is your sting?"
>
> The sting of death is sin, and the power of sin is the law. But thanks be to God, who gives us the victory through our Lord Jesus Christ." (1 Cor. 15:55–57)

So as we live in this world where sin still does its ugly work inside and outside of us, we live with the promised defeat and death of sin in mind. We refuse to give up hope and to give way to what Christ defeated and will finally destroy. What does it look like to live with the final defeat of sin and death in view? In the same passage quoted above, Paul answers this question. "Therefore, my beloved brothers, be steadfast, immovable, always abounding in the work of the Lord, knowing that in the Lord your labor is not in vain" (1 Cor. 15:58). Living in light of the final death of sin means living a life of courage and hope. It means standing strong against the seductive voice of temptation. It means refusing to move when evil beckons. It means refusing to live for things that will soon pass away. It means giving your time, strength, resources, gifts, and energy to things that have eternal significance. It means understanding that you have been called to the Lord's work. And it means understanding that nothing you do in the Lord's name is ever a waste of your commitment and time. Living with the final victory in view means living a life of victory as you wait for that final victory.

But there is more. What the Bible says about this second aspect of our glorification seems too good to be true. This glory is so gloriously glorious that no one would have the guts to make it up. But here's the biblical promise. Not only will sin die, but we will be perfected in holiness, taking on the true likeness of Jesus, and we will reign in glory with him forever. With stunning clarity and confidence Peter says that we will "become partakers of the divine nature" (2 Pet. 1:4). Let those words sink in. No, you and I won't be God, but we will be godly in the fullest sense of what that word means. Paul not only says that we will appear with our Savior in glory (Col. 3:4), but he also says that there is waiting for us "an eternal weight of glory" (2 Cor. 4:17). In Romans 8:18 Paul says, "For I consider that the sufferings of this present time are not worth comparing with the glory that is to be revealed to us." The glory of this future glory is so glorious that it will overwhelm all the moments of pain we have experienced as we suffered along the way. Paul says, "For this light momentary affliction is preparing for us an eternal weight of glory beyond all comparison" (2 Cor. 4:17).

Like our sanctification, our glorification is a death and life process. Our glorification means the final death of sin and the curse that it carries and the radically new life of sharing in both Christ's likeness and his glory. We will no longer need to glance over our shoulder or into our hearts to protect ourselves from sin's evil work. And we will no longer carry the sadness and struggle of living in an inglorious world, broken by sin. We will be taken up in glory, to share forever in the glory and the reign of glory of our triumphant Lord and Savior, Jesus Christ. There could be no better end to the history-spanning work of redemption than what I have just described.

So we persevere, with eyes on the glory that is coming, knowing that perseverance doesn't keep us but that we are kept by our Savior's power. On those days when sin haunts us, when our kids resist us, when our marriages seem cold, when we feel like aliens at our university, when we are sick and physically weak, when our job is a daily burden and our church disappoints us, we stand firm, not because life is easy but because our future glory is secure. We keep doing those things that our Lord has called for us to do, remembering that they are his means of drawing us close and keeping us safe. We face each day knowing that even though right now few things seem secure, one thing is absolutely secure: "We shall be like him, because we shall see him as he is" (1 John 3:2).

22

Perseverance and Glorification of the Saints in Everyday Life

MY LIFE HAS BEEN a long, long journey. The valleys have been dark and deep, the mountaintops high and exciting, and the sun often behind clouds. I have walked through deserts with mouth parched and sand in my eyes. I have taken drinks from cool rivers and rolled around in lush green pastures. At times I have prayed for rain and at times I have prayed for it to stop. Sometimes it seemed like I walked for days, only to find myself back at the same place again. I have experienced cold winters that made my soul shiver and burning-sun summers that heated up my heart. Sometimes I have been weak and weary and sometimes strong and ready to go. I have been knocked down and wondered if I could get up, and I have been picked up and carried when my strength failed.

I have been taken places where I never intended to go and guided away from where I planned to go. I have matured along the way while my immaturity continues to be exposed. I have witnessed sin's tragedies and experienced redemption's glories. I have come to understand that I am a soldier in a great spiritual war and that I never fight alone or in my own strength. I have reconciled with the fact that I have a lot to offer but that none of it is from me, belongs to me, or is to bring the focus on me. I have known heartache and have been surrounded by love. As I look down the road ahead, I often find it hard to wait, while the Lord calls me to be patient.

I could not have written my own story. I had no accurate vision of tomorrow, let alone any idea of where I would land and what I would be doing. I no longer have any doubt about who is the author of my story, who designs every chapter and rules every turn of the plot. I know that with all the valleys, deserts, rivers, and mountain peaks, there is nothing random about my journey. I am the object of miraculous and glorious grace. I know I would be nothing, I would have nothing, and I would have offered nothing if it were not for that grace. My story is one of divine rescue and many divine interventions. I once thought that the goal was that I would know truth, but I have come to understand that the goal is to surrender everything I am and have to the God who stands at the epicenter of what is true. I have come to live with a deep sense of privilege, that I have been chosen to have grace shower down on me, shower after shower after shower.

But not every day is filled with motivation, satisfaction, and gratitude. I face weary and disheartening days. Sometimes life in this groaning world seems too complicated, too stressful, and too difficult. I have moments when I lose my gospel sanity, throw my hands up in the air, and want to scream. Sometimes hard work doesn't work and the hurt of misunderstanding seeps into my heart. I have faced days of physical sickness, when I didn't think I could get out of a chair and the spiritual attacks were debilitating. And there have been times when more was accomplished in my weakness of spirit and body than on my stronger days. In all of this, I have come to understand that I was not just pushing my way forward, but I have been carried along.

I have not just been accepted; I have been loved. I have not just been loved; I have been inhabited. I have not just been inhabited; I have been empowered. I have not just been empowered; I have been transformed. I have not just been transformed; I have been kept. And I have not just been kept; I will be glorified. This is the plotline of my life. Nothing has been for naught. Every twist and turn and every high and low has been formed by the unrelenting power of divine grace. Every bit of it, even the confusing and painful things, are pieces of a puzzle, that, when assembled, says, "Blessing."

So, today, I give myself to the call, commands, and wisdom of the author of my story. I know that what he calls me to is his means of rescuing me from me, drawing me near and keeping me safe. Although I live in mundane little moments of surrender, in those moments he exercises almighty power to keep me. There will be moments of confusion, celebration, and tears to come, but by his grace I will follow, knowing that whatever dark valleys I am led through and however twisted the road ahead may be, there is incalculable glory to come.

But this is not just my story—it is your story as well. If you are God's child, the confusing, multipiece puzzle that is your life spells "blessing" too. You too haven't just fought your way forward, for you too have been carried along. In all of your belief, study, surrender, obedience, and sacrifice, you too have been kept by God's power. Even though the days may seem mundane and repetitive, you are being taken somewhere that is glorious beyond anything you have experienced or have the power to imagine. Like me, you aren't writing your own story. It is being written by another, and he is the definition of wisdom, power, and grace. Like me, you will face what is discouraging and disheartening, but nothing you face is for naught. The author of your story never writes a throwaway chapter. Every word on every page of your story is placed there by divine wisdom and grace. As is true in my life, every call and command from your Lord is a grace. He empowers his commands to keep you. You simply cannot understand your story without embedding it in the larger story of redemption.

So here's what we all need to do. We need to embed everything that is happening right now in the context of the truths that we are considering.

This triad of God's call for you to persevere, his promise to keep you, and the glory that is at the end should be an interpretive tool by which you make sense out of the situations, locations, and relationships of your life. This is what this chapter is meant to help you to do, so you don't get lost along the way, go your own way, or lose sight of the glory at the end of the way.

The doctrines of perseverance and glorification are not just important theological insights. They have been revealed to us so that between the "already" and "not yet" they would form for us a way of living. Remember, belief is not just a matter of mental assent but also a way of living. If you don't live what you believe, then you probably don't believe it in the biblical sense of what *belief* means. So let's trace the real-life implications of the doctrines of perseverance and glorification with seven words.

Motivation

If I were to view a video of the last two months of your life and observe you with family and friends, at work, in moments of leisure, in your private and public moments, and as you performed the mundane tasks of everyday life, what would I conclude motivates you? Scripture teaches us that human beings are purpose-oriented, goal-oriented, and value-oriented. Words in the Bible like *worship*, *treasure*, *idol*, and *prize* point us to the truth that we are all living for something. At the level of our hearts, there is always a reason for what we do. For example, there are things that you do and say in your marriage that are your means of getting out of that marriage what is important to you. The same could be said of parenting and friendship. The way you invest your free time, the things you do in your private moments, and the way you handle your money are all shaped by what is important to you. We are all motivated all of the time by something.

The doctrines of perseverance and glorification provide for us a constant and transcendent motivation for everything in our lives. Often, whether we are aware of it or not, we are motivated by things that are too small, too self-focused, and too temporary. For example, when I angrily threaten my child, I am hoping that fear will get him to pick up his toys. When I loudly complain about how late dinner is, I hope my volume and tone will motivate my spouse to start preparing it earlier. When I honk my horn in traffic, I am hoping to motivate the drivers in front of me to move aside or drive faster. It's easy to reduce your life down to petty little moments of motivation and satisfaction.

But we have been saved by grace for something far bigger and better than this "what can I get out of the moment" way of living. We have been drawn into the family of the King of kings, the Creator and Ruler of everything. We have been indwelt by his Spirit and made wise by his word. He actively protects and empowers us by grace. We have been called to give ourselves to the work of his eternal kingdom. And we walk toward a destiny that is secure. We cannot allow ourselves to live for what is small and temporary, when we have been drawn by God into what is huge, glorious, and eternal.

The doctrines of perseverance and glorification provide the big-picture motivation that every child of God needs. Let's use marriage as an example. Your marriage is a sacred place; it is holy ground, because it is one of the locations where God calls you to patiently follow him by faith (persevere) and where God is exercising his keeping power. You see, every command God gives you as a husband or wife is profoundly more than God's plan for a happy marriage. Every one of those commands is a means by which God draws you near and keeps you safe.

Following his commands in your marriage requires that you surrender your agenda to him. Everything he calls you to requires you to lay aside what you want and what you think you need for what God says is better. Each command provides not only a hedge of protection around your marriage but, more importantly, a wall of protection around your heart. And God not only blesses you with his protective commands, but he also empowers you with the desire and the power to keep them. In so doing, he is keeping you by the power of his wisdom, presence, and grace.

Your marriage is where the high and holy work of redemption continues to take place. The same is true of every other relationship and location of your life. The doctrines of perseverance and glorification expand our visions to see something more than the need, problem, desire, or expectation of the moment. It gives us a way not to ignore these things, but to look at them through the lens of God's lovingly protective presence and power. These doctrines remind us that God has invaded our lives by his grace, that he is present and active, that he will allow nothing to separate us from his love, and that he will exercise his power to keep us to the end.

Where do these glorious things take place? The answer is, in the mundane moments of our daily lives. And what does God use to keep us? He uses ordinary means to do his extraordinary redeeming work. In this way those little moments of life are anything but mundane, because they are the places where God tirelessly works to draw us near and keep us safe. The space between the "already" and the "not yet" is made sacred because it is the holy ground where redeeming grace continues its eternal work.

In those moments we should require our motivations to be ruled by things that are transcendent and eternal, rather than things that are small and temporary. So we make God's work our work. Since he is keeping us, we determine that we will persevere in keeping his commands, in choosing what he says is of value, and in surrendering our hearts to something bigger than our little self-focused momentary longings. Along the way, that life of surrender is also a life of rich blessing. A marriage where the husband and wife have laid down their selfish cravings for the greater agenda of their Lord will be a more joyful, peaceful, unified, loving, and understanding marriage.

Future glorification is also meant to motivate us in the here and now. Endurance in the transcendent and eternal things to which God calls us is hard. There are costly sacrifices along the way. Sometimes it looks like the bad guys are winning. It can seem as though obedience simply isn't paying off. Suffering, at times, clouds our sense of God's presence and activity. So it is vital for us to keep our eyes on the guaranteed glory that awaits us. What I have described is precisely what Psalm 73 is about.

Asaph, in the middle of his journey, had lost his way. Here's how he describes it. "My feet had almost stumbled, / my steps had nearly slipped" (v. 2). Why? "I was envious of the arrogant / when I saw the prosperity of the wicked" (v. 3). What does he mean? "Behold, these are the wicked; / always at ease, they increase in riches" (v. 12). Then he complains, "All in vain have I kept my heart clean / and washed my hands in innocence. / For all the day long I have been stricken / and rebuked every morning" (vv. 13–14). Asaph is saying, "What has my obedience gotten me? They don't obey you, and their life is easy. I obey, and my life is hard."

Here's how Asaph describes himself in the midst of this struggle: "When my soul was embittered, / . . . I was brutish and ignorant; / I was like a beast toward you" (73:21–22). What was the turnaround for Asaph? What changed his perspective? Notice what he says: "You guide me with your counsel, / and afterward you will receive me to glory" (v. 24). He says he realized that the lives of the wicked were like a brief dream that disappears when you wake up or a vapor that quickly evaporates (v. 20). Asaph deals with his hardship and suffering by keeping his destiny in view. Glorification becomes his motivation.

What if someone promised you the perfect place to live, in a more beautiful location than you had ever seen or imagined, with every single one of your needs met and where you would be surrounded by relationships of love forever? What if that person told you that you would need to surrender what you now have, that the journey would be long, and that there would be sacrifices and suffering along the way, but at the end the glories that have been pictured for you would be yours? What if someone promised that when you become weak and disheartened, someone would be there to encourage and strengthen you, so you could continue the journey?

What if this person said that there is a place in this gloryland prepared just for you? What would you say and do as you compared the small bag of things you have now to the unprecedented beauty of the gift laid before you? Wouldn't you say, "I'll take that journey"? Wouldn't you be willing to make those sacrifices? Wouldn't you, in moments of discouragement, when you are about to lose your mind, picture those promises again, remember the glory, and press on? Would anything stop you?

Welcome to the journey that is the Christian life. Yes, you are called to a life of surrender. You are called to endure, and you will face suffering and sacrifices along the way, but a guaranteed glory is awaiting you far beyond anything you would be bold enough to ask for or have the capacity to imagine. I ask you again: "In your friendships, at your university, at your job, in your marriage, as a neighbor, in your church, or as a parent, what motivates you?" Have you shrunk your motivation to what is small and temporary, when the doctrines of perseverance and glorification point you to the fact that you have been chosen to be part of what is transcendent and eternal?

Commitment

As I have traveled around the world, experiencing the church in many cultures and fellowshiping with God's people despite language barriers, I have been both overjoyed and concerned. It gives me joy to see God's work in cultures around the world, but I have been again and again concerned with how the average Christian is responding to God's work. Let me explain. I have had many conversations with sincere believers who, on the surface, seem hungry and alive, but who, under the surface, lack a deep, life-shaping commitment to their faith.

It has become clear that what many believers rely on to fuel their Christian life is Sunday mornings, Christian blogs and social media sites, cursory morning Bible reading, and popular Christian books. Rather than living as disciples of Jesus Christ, in the truest sense of what that word means, they have the regular habits of a Christian consumer. However, embedded in the doctrines of the perseverance and glorification of the saints is a call to a commitment to do all that is necessary to mature and to endure to the end. These doctrines call us to pursue all of the tools that God has blessed us with that draw us near to him, keep us safe, and employ us in the greater work of his kingdom.

It is possible to be a consumer of Christian stuff (books, music, conferences, Sunday gatherings, etc.) and not be committed to your own spiritual growth and perseverance. It is possible to consume Christian things, but not have a lifestyle that is shaped by taking your own perseverance and the path toward your glorification seriously. Sure, it is good to read a solid gospel devotional every morning. If I didn't think so, I wouldn't have written one. But it needs to be said that a several-minute gospel reading every morning is very different from being a disciplined and committed student of the word of God.

A student of the word of God will study to develop a high level of biblical literacy. A student of the Bible will study to understand the flow of the gospel narrative that is the core theme of Scripture. A committed student of God's word will study to know, understand, and be able to apply the core doctrines of the Bible. A student of Scripture will study so he can defend himself against internal and external attacks on his faith. A serious student of the word of God will study so he can share his faith with fluidity, humility, practicality, and joy.

The doctrines of perseverance and glorification also call each of us to a committed life of prayer. I think that many of us reduce our prayers to a brief prayer in the morning, asking for help in time of trouble, and prayer before a meal. Sadly, many of us do not view prayer as a powerful tool in God's hands, meant to keep us near and safe, to guard our hearts from sin, to grow us in our affection for our Savior, and to engage us in the history- and geography-spanning work of God's kingdom. If we don't see prayer that way, we will tend to see it as a spiritual practice of last resort. If nothing else works, then we pray. Scripture says that the prayer of a righteous man is "powerful and effective" (James 5:16 NIV).

Prayer is real live communion with the King of kings. It is being invited into the Holy of Holies, that place where the Spirit carries our groanings to the Father. Prayer isn't just praying about the work of the Lord; it is doing the work of the Lord. There are so many things that need to be done that we have no power whatsoever to do. Prayer carries these things to the one who has both the power and the willingness to do the gospel work and produce the gospel fruit that no human being could ever do or produce.

In prayer we cry out for what we cannot do for ourselves. We pray for eyes that see what our sin-blinded eyes would never see without divine intervention. We pray for real heart surrender and lasting heart change. We pray that God would rescue us from ourselves and gift us with the desire and the power to fight temptation. But we don't just pray for ourselves; we intercede on behalf of others and for the health and growth of the church. We carry to our Father real people who are struggling with real and significant things. We bring to God the specific needs of his church. In so doing we are following the Lord's example, praying that God's name would be revered and that his kingdom would come and his will would be done, right here, right now, where he has placed us. In prayer we close our hearts off to the worship of the world and give ourselves to the worship of our Father in heaven.

The kind of prayer I have been describing isn't done in a few minutes on a busy morning. It takes time, discipline, and commitment, but it should never be burdensome. Prayer is a loving welcome by the Savior King to be part of the most important thing you could give yourself to, redemption.

I could write about many more things that should be regular commitments of a disciple of Jesus Christ, one who takes his perseverance and future glorification seriously. Scriptural study and prayer are just two examples. But I want to alert you to one thing. If you are not investing time in the foundational commitments, habits, and disciplines that these doctrines call you to, other things in your life will fill up those places in your heart and in your schedule. We all stay busy. Our schedules are full and we are exhausted at the end of the day. We have to do certain regular everyday things just to maintain our physical, economic, and relational health, but are all of those necessary commitments shaped by one transcendent commitment? How much time and energy are we investing in our own growth in God's grace and our own perseverance? You cannot properly unpack these encouraging doctrines without uncovering in them a call to commitment, that is, an invitation to make God's work in and for you the spiritual work that you become committed to as well.

Hope

Every human being does it. Most often we are unaware that we are on this constant and unending search. Everyone digs through the mound of the situations, locations, relationships, and experiences of their existence, searching for hope. We all look for reasons to continue, for reasons to be encouraged, and for strength for the task at hand. Life is hard, filled with the unplanned, the unexpected, and the unwanted. Since we are not in control, our lives often seem out of control. People fail us, but also we fail ourselves. Dreams capture us, but evaporate into disappointment. Plans build, but often don't work out as we hoped. Even our churches often turn out to be less than we hoped they would be. In a fallen world it is impossible to successfully avoid the disappointments of life.

He was one of the most hopeless people I have ever met. To be honest, this man discouraged me. He was utterly alone, alienated from his family and without even one friend to call. He hated his work, feeling robbed of his potential by corporate politics. He called himself a corporate basement dweller. He despised the neighborhood he lived in. He would have never chosen to live there, but it was all he could afford. He talked of how joyless the day was when he moved into his house. Every room in that old row house seemed to accuse him of being a failure.

A deep abiding despondency resided in him. You could see it in his posture and hear it in his voice. He had quit putting effort into anything, so his house was messy and in ill repair and his diet was whatever was convenient. The smallest obstacle would stop him and then leave him with self-hatred because he was so easily defeated. The first time I met with him, I had difficulty getting him to talk at all, but when he did, he told me that he didn't know why he decided to talk to me because he knew this would prove to be a waste of time, like everything else in his life.

I helped him tell his story, from earliest memory until the present. I got to know him and his world better than anyone in his life ever had.

I got to know his family, his school experiences, his long list of disappointing relationships, his painful work life. I learned what his hopes and dreams had once been and how every dream had vaporized. For hours we journeyed through his history, his thoughts, his desires, his anger, and his despondency. And he kept coming back because I was the first person who listened—really listened—to him and after I heard it all, I didn't forsake him. I loved him. He was hard to like, and being with him was like being enveloped in a dark cloud. He was not only massively discouraged, but he was also obstinate and unyielding. He shot down every quasi-positive thing I said. But the longer I was with him, the more I loved him and the more my hope for him increased.

My love for him and my hope for him kept building because as we talked, I kept thinking again and again of a biblical description from a powerful New Testament passage: "Remember that you were at that time separated from Christ, alienated from the commonwealth of Israel and strangers to the covenants of promise, *having no hope and without God in the world*" (Eph. 2:12). It hit me as he told his long, sad story that there was no God in it at any time or any place. It was perhaps the most godless story I had ever heard. It was the cosmos devoid of the divine, reduced to people, places, and things, all of which had failed to deliver anything worth living for. Whenever I encounter this passage, I am struck by Paul's spiritual equation, "no God, no hope."

No human being was ever meant to live this way. Living a godless existence not only robs you of the deepest, most encouraging, and most faithful form of hope that you could ever find, but it also robs you of your humanity. By the Creator's design, the very nature of who we are is connected to the very nature of who God is. In this way, the existence of God becomes the most important interpretive tool for making sense out of ourselves. Everything in life will disappoint us in some way, and so when we rest our hope on those things, our hope will fail us too.

I had hope for my friend precisely because he was so hopeless. He didn't have much that he loved, much that held on to his heart, or precious things he was unwilling to forsake. He was ready to discover where true, faithful hope was to be found, and find it he did. It took a while for all those old depressive habits of thought, with all of their negative interpretations, to be replaced by a God-centered way of interpreting life but, step-by-step, that change did take place. Don't get me wrong: I didn't ever ask him to deny reality. But I taught him how to look at the most painful realities through the lens of the presence, activity, power, and promises of God. I don't mean to be trite, but I gave him gospel glasses to wear and told him to never take them off again.

You may be wondering what all this has to do with the truth of the perseverance and glorification of the saints. The answer is found in a gospel crescendo at the end of 1 Peter. It is one of my favorite hope passages in all of Scripture. I have run there again and again for encouragement: "And after you have suffered a little while, the God of all grace, who has called you to his eternal glory in Christ, will himself restore, confirm, strengthen, and establish you. To him be the dominion forever and ever. Amen" (1 Pet. 5:10–11).

This is a perseverance and glorification passage. Peter is tying hope to a God who is at work and will complete his work. All of the things Peter has called believers to do and all of the hope they are to have as they do them are tied to this God and his unrelenting commitment of grace to his own. Notice that Peter doesn't give an unrealistic, overly rosy view of life. There is no denying reality here. He acknowledges that the saints will suffer, but also that even in the darkest of moments there is someone wonderful at work, doing something eternally important that will end in glory. There is no better rock of hope than God's enduring work and its final culmination in glory. Suffering isn't ultimate; God is. Discouragement isn't Lord; God is. Failure doesn't rule; God does. Weakness isn't King; God is. And hope in his work now and the stunning beauty of what is to come will never disappoint you.

Here's the question: Do you interpret your life this way? When life disappoints, where does your heart go and where does your mind land? Do you look at your life through the lens of Peter's gospel glasses?

Confidence

This song was the ultimate gospel earworm, written by Andraé Crouch. Now, this is not one of the great hymns of the faith, but I love it for its street-level understanding of the roots of confident living.

When trouble is in my way
I can't tell my night from day
That I'm tossed from side to side
Like a ship on a raging tide
I don't worry, I don't fret
My God has never failed me yet
Troubles come from time to time
But that's all right, I'm not the worrying kind because

I've got confidence
God is gonna see me through
No matter what the case may be
I know He's gonna fix it for me

Job was sick so long
Till the flesh fell from his bones
His wife, cattle and children,
Everything he had was gone
But Job in his despair
He knew that God still cared
Sleepless days and sleepless nights
But Job said that's all right because . . .

Some folks wonder how I smile
Even when I'm goin' through trials
They say, "Andraé how can you have song
When everything is goin' wrong"

But I don't worry I don't fret
My God has never failed me yet
Trouble's coming from time to time
But that's all right,
I'm not the worrying kind because . . .[1]

Notice the rock of Crouch's confidence. It's not his education, his musical gifts, his ability to move an audience, his public acclaim, or even his biblical understanding. No, he is not the person that gives himself confidence.

We look up to confident people, people who are aware of who they are and what they are able to do. We love the stories of tough people who walk confidently into tough places and accomplish amazing things. Because we all want to be confident, we all love a hero story, and we like it even better if it's the story of an unlikely hero. We all like to think that in tough and important moments, we would rise to the challenge with confidence too.

But the Bible teaches us that the unshakable reliability of independent self-confidence is a delusion. None of us is so strong as to be incapable of being defeated. None of us has that power. None of us has that control. In the face of the high towers of human difficulty, we all know in our heart of hearts that we're pretty small. Even the strongest of people are weak when it comes to the most significant dilemmas of life.

So, where is confident living to be found? Again, the truths we are now considering (echoed in Andraé Crouch's confessional lyric) point us in the one and only right direction: "God is gonna see me through." That's right, Andraé, he will, to an unimaginably glorious end. So, small and weak as we are, prone to moments of foolishness, sometimes following and sometimes failing, during moments when our hearts are in tune and moments when they wander, we have the best reason for confidence ever. It transcends the boundaries of human wisdom, authority,

1 Andraé Crouch, "I've Got Confidence," copyright © 1969 Bud John Songs (ASCAP) (adm. at CapitolCMGPublishing.com).

and strength of righteousness. It is greater than our greatest giftedness or skill. It's confidence for the parent seeking to be God's ambassador in the lives of their children. It's confidence for the student, feeling alone at a huge university. It's confidence for the elderly woman, who deals with the weaknesses of old age every day. It's confidence for the successful businessman as he resists the materialism and pride of power that is all around him. It's confidence in the face of sexual temptation. It's confidence when life is hard and God is distant. It's confidence when nothing around you or inside of you encourages confidence.

The doctrines of the perseverance and glorification of the saints preach to us of the presence and unrelenting redemptive activity of our Savior. Our confidence is not in our commitment to God, but in his commitment to us. So we get up every morning and we say with Andraé Crouch, "I've got confidence, God is gonna see me through." Is this how you approach your days?

Fearlessness

We all wish we could say, "Therefore we will not fear though the earth gives way, / though the mountains be moved into the heart of the sea" (Ps. 46:2). These words are the definition of fearless living, even in the face of cataclysmic occurrences. Who wouldn't want a life that is fear-free? Did you notice the significant word that begins the verse? It points us to where fearless living is found. The word is *therefore*. Fearless living is always based on something. There is something that you know and understand about yourself, someone else, your life, or the situation that you're in that removes your fear. It is always, "I am unafraid because ________." So the "therefore" of Psalm 46:2 points us back to 46:1: "God is our refuge and strength, / a very present help in trouble." There is the reason every child of God can live a life that is not bent, twisted, distorted, and directed by fear.

The Christian life should not be a fear-filled existence. We should not live in constant doubt as to whether we are God's children or not. We should not be wondering if we've sinned too much or gone too far.

We should not be anxious when we think about God or about how God looks on us. We should not always be looking for ways to prove ourselves to God, to prove our faith, allegiance, and commitment. We should not read the warnings of Scripture as if they were predictions of our condemnation. We should not live with the terror of our own potential apostasy.

Yes, we should take our faith seriously. Yes, we should commit to obey. Yes, we should give ourselves to Bible study and to prayer, to the worship and fellowship of the body of Christ, and to the missional work of the kingdom of God. But none of these things should be motivated by fear of God's wrath falling on us if we fail to do them. An active, committed, and courageous Christian life should be motivated by the surpassing joy of knowing that God has taken us as his own, that nothing can separate us from his love, and that he will carry us into the glory that he has promised us. This is the kind of fearless living that the doctrines of the perseverance and glorification of all believers welcome us to.

We should not be crippled by horizontal fear either. The same Lord who is relentlessly at work to bring us to the final glorious end of our salvation also rules over every situation, relationship, experience, and location of our lives. Our Savior is in charge of all the things that would confuse us, dishearten us, or frighten us. Yes, we will suffer along the way, yes, we will experience sadness and loss, and yes, we will be weary and weak, but we will never be alone. The Lord Almighty walks this journey with us, and he will not let anyone or anything get in the way of the success of the most significant process in the universe, redemption. Everything he ordains for us, he is present in with us. No circumstance will be the end of us or will defeat him. If we live, we will be blessed with knowing he is in us, for us, and with us. If we die, we will be with him and like him in glory. Fear is defeated by his presence, power, promises, and grace. The doctrines of perseverance and glorification stand as reminders that this is true.

As I was writing this chapter, I came across the words of Moses as he was preparing Israel to cross over the Jordan into the land that God had promised, but which was filled with enemy nations. There is encouragement for all of God's people anytime and anywhere in these words.

> For what great nation is there that has a god so near to it as the LORD our God is to us, whenever we call upon him? And what great nation is there, that has statutes and rules so righteous as all this law that I set before you today?
>
> Only take care, and keep your soul diligently, lest you forget the things that your eyes have seen, and lest they depart from your heart all the days of your life. Make them known to your children and your children's children—how on the day that you stood before the LORD your God at Horeb, the LORD said to me, "Gather the people to me, that I may let them hear my words, so that they may learn to fear me all the days that they live on the earth, and that they may teach their children so." And you came near and stood at the foot of the mountain, while the mountain burned with fire to the heart of heaven, wrapped in darkness, cloud, and gloom. Then the LORD spoke to you out of the midst of the fire. You heard the sound of words, but saw no form; there was only a voice. And he declared to you his covenant, which he commanded you to perform, that is, the Ten Commandments, and he wrote them on two tablets of stone. And the LORD commanded me at that time to teach you statutes and rules, that you might do them in the land that you are going over to possess. (Deut. 4:7–14)

The question that begins this passage could be asked of all of us. Who has had a god so near as our God is to us? We are not afraid, because God is near. Like the children of Israel we have seen God unleash his power on our behalf. He has exercised his power for us, not just to defeat physical earthly powers but to defeat the ultimate power of sin and death. We have heard his holy voice in his word, speaking words of wisdom, life, and grace. He has pulled back the curtain of mystery for us and shown us his will and his ways. He has revealed to us our deepest problem and its only cure. And he has spoken to us in the person, words, and work of his Son. He has promised to keep us to the very end. And he has given us his commands to draw us near and keep us safe, and to teach us what it means to follow him by faith. What people has a god that is so near, so wise, so loving, so powerful, so faithful to the work he has begun, like our God?

May the obvious answer to this question shape the way we approach our relationship with God and our journey through this fallen world and toward our final destination. When fear approaches, may we not look at ourselves or our circumstances for hope and courage, but may we look up and remember, "God is our refuge and strength, / a very present help in trouble." We will persevere to the glorious end because our Lord will persevere in his redeeming work until it is complete.

Sacrifice

Everybody makes sacrifices for something. We'll sacrifice our leisure, time, money, and energy to exercise our way to better health. We'll sacrifice the enjoyment we have in certain kinds of food in order to lose weight. We'll sacrifice the pleasure we get from material things so we can work our way out of debt. These are all pretty positive sacrifices, but some of our sacrifices are not so positive. A father will sacrifice the time he should spend with his family in order to climb up the career ladder. A man or a woman will sacrifice the health and trust of their marriage for a few minutes of sexual pleasure with someone other than their spouse. We'll sacrifice our ability to contribute to the work of God's kingdom so we can spend more of our money on possessions and pleasure.

Embedded in the doctrines of the perseverance and glorification of the saints is a call to sacrifice. Yes, it is God who assures, by the power of his protecting grace, that he will keep you to the end. Yes, it is God who assures that his saving work ends in you being made like Christ and you reigning with him in glory forever. But one of his tools in assuring that these things happen is his call to forsake everything and follow him by faith.

> Now great crowds accompanied him, and he turned and said to them, "If anyone comes to me and does not hate his own father and mother and wife and children and brothers and sisters, yes, and even his own life, he cannot be my disciple. Whoever does not bear his own cross and come after me cannot be my disciple. . . . So therefore, any one of you who does not renounce all that he has cannot be my disciple." (Luke 14:25–27, 33)

This passage does not teach that we should go out and treat our families hatefully. It does not tell us that our Lord is going to take everything away from us. It is about the commitment of our hearts. We should love our Lord so much and we should be so committed to participating in the work he is doing in and for us that we are unwilling to let anything get in the way of our joyful commitment to our Lord and his work, even the people nearest and dearest to us. This passage is a call to sacrificial living for the sake of our own redemption and for the glory of our Redeemer.

So we joyfully sacrifice our own free time or our desire to express our anger in order to bring up our children in the nurture and admonition of the Lord. We sacrifice our leisure in order to have the time and energy to participate in the mission of our local church. We say no to that promotion because it will take time away from essential spiritual disciplines that we have committed ourselves to. We say no to entertainment that tempts us to think about and desire things that God says are wrong. What Jesus is calling us to in this passage is a refusal to let anything get in the way of our pursuit of everything that he is working on right now in us and everything that he has promised is ours to come.

So since you are going to make sacrifices in your life, why not make the best sacrifices ever? Why not sacrifice now for what you will enjoy forever? Why not let go of some temporary pleasures for eternal glory? Why not let go of what stunts your spiritual growth for what God will use to grow and mature you? Why not forsake love of the world for love of your Father in heaven? Why not forsake what cannot satisfy you now for what will satisfy your heart forever? Why not surrender the thoughts and desires of your heart to the one who will only ever call you to and lead you toward what is good? Why not run from the temptation of all the bad sacrifices that this fallen world throws at you and make the best sacrifices you could ever make? And why not pray for grace to be willing to forsake everything to follow the one who has promised you more than you could ever ask or have the ability to imagine? The doctrines of perseverance and glorification really do call you to make the best sacrifices that you could ever make, sacrifices that end in unimaginable eternal glory.

Perspective

It is easy to lose perspective. It is easy to let things in our lives rise in levels of importance way beyond their true importance, claiming the thoughts and desires of our hearts and controlling the way we make decisions and live our lives. Your marriage is important, but there are things in your marriage that can rise above their true importance and begin to shape the way you behave there. Your education is important, but there are things in your life at your university that may become more important than they should be. Your job is essential, but you will have to fight letting your goals become more important than they actually are, causing you to make choices that you should not make.

In the doctrines of the perseverance and glorification of all who are saved, God blesses us with eternal perspective. These doctrines are meant to live in our hearts with such authority and with such glory that they keep us from losing our gospel minds. These doctrines are meant to help us journey through this fallen world, with all of its seductive voices and beckoning idols, with a constant sense of what is truly important; that is, what is worth giving our lives to.

Winning that argument is not as important as you might think it is at the time. Doing anything to get the love of that person is not as important as it may feel. Getting those high grades at your university, no matter what, may not be as important as it seems to you. Buying that next thing you've convinced yourself you need may not be as important as you now think it is. Having that pleasure now, no matter what it costs, may be more dangerous than important. In the fight of faith between the "already" and "not yet" we need perspective. These doctrines bless us with the constant reminder of what is truly important right here, right now, and for all of eternity. May that perspective give us perspective, keeping our hearts focused and our lives moving, step by step, toward the glory that is to come.

• • •

Like every doctrine we have considered together in this book, the doctrines of perseverance and glorification lead us to the cross. On the cross Jesus took our rejection so that nothing ever again would separate us from the Father's love. On the cross Jesus made the ultimate sacrifice, so that every sacrifice he calls us to would be for our rescue now and our glory to come. On the cross Jesus suffered, so that as we suffer with him now, we are progressively formed into his likeness and will someday reign with him in glory. Jesus died so that he would not only live in us now, but so that we would live with him forever. So with the cross behind us and glory in front of us, we press on. We submit to his call, we resist the enemy, we follow him by faith, we fight to endure, and we do it all with joy, knowing what we have been given and looking forward to what is to come.

23

The Doctrine of Eternity

GOD HAS APPOINTED a day when he will judge the world. This will be a righteous judgment by Jesus Christ, who has been given the power to judge by God the Father. On that day, not only will the fallen angels be judged, but also all persons who have ever lived on the earth. Everyone will stand before the throne of Christ the Judge, to give an account of their thoughts, words, and actions, to be judged according to what they have done, whether good or evil.

The reason God appointed this judgment day is to show the glory of his mercy by the eternal salvation of those he has chosen and to show the glory of his justice by condemning those he rejected, who are wicked and disobedient. After his judgment, the righteous will be given everlasting life and will receive the full and refreshing joy that comes from the presence of the Lord. The wicked, who do not know God and do not obey the gospel of Jesus Christ, will be thrown into eternal torment. They will be punished with everlasting destruction from the presence of the Lord and from the glory of his power.

Christ wants us to be fully persuaded that there shall be a day of judgment, both to deter everyone from sin and to comfort the godly in adversity.

He has kept that day unknown to us, so that we would shake off worldly security and always be watchful. We don't know what hour the Lord will come, but we should always be prepared to say, "Come Lord Jesus, come quickly, Amen."[1] See Eccles. 12:14; Matt. 12:36; 25:21, 32–46; Mark 9:48; 13:35–37; Luke 12:35–40; John 5:22–27; Acts 17:31; Rom. 9:22–23; 14:10–12; 1 Cor. 5:3; 2 Thess. 1:5–10; 2 Tim. 4:8; Jude 6; Rev. 22:20.

Understanding the Doctrine of Eternity

You are about to read something that will seem extreme, but it is essential and true. Without the doctrine of eternity, there would be no such thing as the gospel of Jesus Christ, let alone any such thing as gospel hope. If there is no future where justice is meted out and where the drama of sin and death is finally resolved, then none of the doctrines that we have considered are worth our attention. You cannot read your Bible without feeling the tension of the drama between a holy Creator God and his unholy creatures. The blood, guts, dirt, smoke, and stench of this drama are splashed across every page in Scripture. People weep and creation groans, waiting for a final resolution. As the earth anxiously waits, the sad music of a world gone bad drones on. We listen for this music to reach a final crescendo, but it still drones on.

Because of the person and work of Jesus, the people of God wait with hope, but all of their waiting, all of their striving, and all of their hoping is for nothing if there is no such thing as final judgment and the forever that follows. You would go crazy if you read a seven-hundred page novel, bursting with tension and drama, only to find out that the author never wrote the last chapter. Luella, my dear wife, hates it when we have invested two hours in a movie that ends without any resolution to all the plot questions that it put before us.

Everyone cries out for eternity—they just don't know it. The little boy who is choking back his tears because he has been bullied is crying out for eternity. The wife who is devastated by her husband's adultery is crying out for eternity. The old man who is dealing with the pain, weakness, and lone-

1 Author's paraphrase of the doctrine of eternity as found in the Westminster Confession of Faith, chap. 33.

liness of old age is crying out for eternity. The pastor who has ministered long with little fruit is crying out for eternity. The lonely teenager who just wants to be understood and accepted is crying out for eternity. The worker who has been reamed out by his boss once again, for reasons he doesn't understand, is crying out for eternity. The hungry homeless man is crying out for eternity. The black man who had another door of possibility shut to him because of his race is crying out for eternity. The couple who just discovered their car has been stolen is crying out for eternity. Somehow, someway, we all know in our hearts that this is not the way it is supposed to be. Somehow, someway, we all long for a better world.

Everything we have believed, given our hearts to, and invested our lives in as the children of God requires a final resolution, so the doctrine of eternity is essential. Without this truth, Christianity is simply not the Christianity we gave ourselves to. Understanding this doctrine is vital if you want to understand your faith and apply it to your daily life. I will discuss the doctrine of eternity in two sections: the doctrine of eternity and the righteous, and the doctrine of eternity and the unrighteous. By righteous, I mean those who, by grace through faith, have been covered by the perfect righteousness of Jesus

The Doctrine of Eternity and the Righteous

I want to anchor my explanation of the doctrine of eternity and the righteous in one passage, 2 Peter 3:11–13.

> Since all these things are thus to be dissolved, what sort of people ought you to be in lives of holiness and godliness, waiting for and hastening the coming of the day of God, because of which the heavens will be set on fire and dissolved, and the heavenly bodies will melt as they burn! But according to his promise we are waiting for new heavens and a new earth in which righteousness dwells.

What is so important about this passage is that it not only tells you things that every believer needs to know about eternity, but it also tells you that these things should form the way you live right now. The doctrine of eternity is a truth that not only gives us future hope, but it should also become for us a hermeneutic for the way we make sense out of our lives right here, right now. This is important because the way you make sense out of your life then shapes and directs the way you live your life. The doctrine of eternity is a foundational Christian interpretive tool. It should define the way you think about your past, your present, your future, yourself, God, and meaning and purpose. Without this truth as a structural part of your thinking, you will not make proper sense out of your life.

Before I interact with this vital passage, I want to place it in its larger moral/theological context. This context is important for understanding the full import and practicality of this passage. First, the Bible declares that human beings are worshipers (see Rom. 1:25). I am not talking about worship in the formal religious sense, but in the practical, everyday, and motivational sense. Everybody worships something; that is, something is always ruling our hearts, and what rules our hearts will exercise control over our words and behavior. This passage is about worship in light of eternity.

Second, the Bible warns us about the selfishness of sin. In fact 2 Corinthians 5:15 tells us that Jesus came so we would no longer live for ourselves. Yes, it is true that the DNA of sin is selfishness. This passage is a selfishness of sin passage. Will I live for my glory or for the greater glory of God? Third, this passage is a spiritual warfare passage. Scripture confronts us with the reality that on this side of eternity, all of life is spiritual warfare. These verses in 2 Peter 3 are about how to be a good soldier in that war until the final victory and our passage into the final kingdom where that war is no more.

I want to outline this passage and our discussion with three practical directions: *live eschatologically, wait actively, embrace God's promise.*

Live Eschatologically

"Since all these things are thus to be dissolved, what sort of people ought you to be in lives of holiness and godliness . . ." (2 Pet. 3:11). Notice the structure of this verse, "Since . . . what then?" It is an "if/then" sentence. If these things are true, then this is how you should live. The very structure of the sentence tells you something important about Peter's understanding of the doctrine of eternity. For Peter, the doctrine of eternity is not a distant, abstract, isolated, or impersonal point of Christian theology. It is impossible for Peter to think of this truth in that way. For Peter, this truth presses in on his daily life. It tells him what's important, and in light of what's important, how he is to make decisions, act, and react at street level. He has just said the most incredible, unusual thing—something that is so far out of the bounds of our normal thinking that it takes our breath away.

Peter has just said that everything around us, all those things that locate and orient us, all of the physical things that occupy and entertain us, every single thing in this created world, will be burned up (2 Pet. 3:10). Look around right now; everything that you are looking at will be gone. None of it is permanent. It will all evaporate in the searing heat of a final display of the glory of God's power. Let this sink in. It will all, every bit of it, be gone forever. Every building, every mountain, every stream, every lush garden, every animal, every monument, every tree, every limestone cliff, every sea creature, every sandy shore, every wardrobe of fine clothes, every car, every highway, every place of solace or amusement, yes, every physical thing will be burned up. It's hard to find a more stunning statement in all of Scripture. None of the things we tend to think will always be there are permanent. This physical world is not ultimate. God is ultimate, and he will bring all these things to a final and spectacular end.

It is because of his heart of grace that God lets us know what is going to happen to this place that has been our physical home. He graces you with a knowledge of then, so that you can know how to live now. If someone could look in the future and tell you for sure that a tech company you are about to invest in is going to have a spectacular blowup and fail, you probably won't make that investment. If someone knew that a certain heating system would eventually blow up and burn down your house, then you wouldn't purchase that system. God lovingly tells us what we would have no way of knowing or imagining, but which is vital to understand for our present living.

Let's return now to Peter's question, "Since this is true, what sort of lives should we live?" If all of this is going to burned up, by God's plan and his power, it makes no sense whatsoever to live for the physical glories of the created world. It is an act of spiritual insanity to attach my identity, my meaning and purpose, and my sense of well-being to what will be gone in an instant. Why would I invest my life energies in those things? You see, God has hardwired you and me for glory. We love and are motivated by glorious things. There are only two kinds of glory, the glory of God and sign glory. Sign glory is any glorious created thing. I call it *sign glory* because every glorious thing in creation was designed to be a sign that points us to the inestimable glory of the one who made it. So we are either giving our hearts to and investing our lives in the glory of the physical creation or in the glory of God.

No, I am not saying that you shouldn't enjoy a good steak, a fine piece of music, a great movie, or a beautiful garden. I am not saying that you shouldn't be dedicated in your job or be committed to success in your career. We are talking about what rules your heart and controls the way you live your life. Peter says that in light of the incendiary end of everything around us, it only makes sense to live right here, right now for the greater eternal glory of God. Now, how in the world do we do that? How do we resist letting the physical pleasures of this created world dominate and control us? Peter's answer is in the second part of verse 11, "in lives of holiness and godliness." The way we live for the glory of God is by obeying his commands, surrendering to his will, and living inside of the boundaries of his plans for us.

God's commands are not burdensome. They have been given to us not only for his glory but also for our good. His commands fit within the boundaries of what he has planned for us, for his world and for the eternity that is promised to his children. There is no greater blessed life and no greater heart-satisfying existence than to get up every day committing yourself to keep God's commands. And in living this way for God's glory, you free yourself from bondage to other glories. If physical pleasure is temporary and God's glory is eternal, then the only sane way to live is to commit yourself to godliness. You do this in your marriage, living for the honor of God and not for the glory of getting your own way. You do this in your parenting, pursuing not what you want for or from your kids but what God has called you to do as his ambassador. You do this in your career, not being obsessed with how high you can go but driven by the glory of God in everything you do and say in your career. You do this at your university, focused not just on grades but on living a godly life in a challenging place. You do this in all of the situations and locations of your daily life. Eternity doesn't just tell you what is going to happen in the future, but it also tells you the best, wisest way to live right here, right now.

Wait Actively

In the Bible, waiting is not a meaningless, purposeless pause, forced on us by the control of another. One of the reasons we don't like to wait is that waiting immediately confronts us with the fact that we are not in control. Something or someone is causing us to have to wait. For Peter, waiting is not inaction but a call to action. We are not called to just sit around patiently until the end. No, there are things that we are called to do because of the end that is surely to come. Peter says, ". . . waiting for and hastening the coming of the day of God, because of which the heavens will be set on fire and dissolved, and the heavenly bodies will melt as they burn!" (2 Pet. 3:12). One word in this verse should jump off the page for you. This word points to the significance of actions that you take as you wait. It's a word that makes your choices, words, and actions sacred. For Peter, waiting is a calling to holy activity, activity that has eternal consequence. Peter doesn't just say that we should wait patiently; he says, "waiting and *hastening*" the coming of the final day of the Lord. If this final cataclysmic day is already written into God's book, how in the world can anything I do or say right now make any difference at all? We tend to think that the end is the end and, until the end, what we do doesn't really matter. We tend to think we're small and don't have much power and control, and we wonder how in the world can anything we do hasten the day of the Lord?

Here is where it is vital to remember that, in his sovereignty, God determines not only what will happen, but the means by which it will happen. I dealt with this extensively in the chapters on the doctrine of God's sovereignty. Peter is saying that the eternity-focused activity of God's people, as they wait for that final day, is a means that he has ordained to bring that day about. He has chosen us to be a tool to bring about what he has ordained. This means that what we do and say right now really does have eternal significance. This is a call to eternity-envisioned action, action that God has ordained to really make a difference. The cries of longing of his people hasten his return. The prayers of God's people hasten his return. The kingdom commitment and work of his people hasten his return. The evangelism of God's children hasten his return. We wait, knowing that how we wait and what we do as we wait are means by which God brings our waiting to an end.

Embrace God's Promise

Every human being is searching for paradise, but there is no paradise in this fallen world. Wherever we look, our hope and dreams for paradise always disappoint us. Nothing seems to fulfill our golden dreams. Nothing is as good as we wished it would be. Nothing works as we hoped it would. We stumble through the world as a company of dissatisfied dreamers, hoping the next dream will come through for us. We do this because paradise was written into our hearts. We do this because we were hardwired for eternity. So Peter says, "But according to his promise we are waiting for new heavens and a new earth in which righteousness dwells" (2 Pet. 3:13). Wow, what a power-packed collection of words!

Peter is reminding us to live like we really do believe that there is one sitting on the throne of the universe who makes promises that are never broken. There is one who always comes through. There is one who always does what he has promised he will do. There is one whose words are always faithful and true. There is one who doesn't change his mind, take another direction, or turn his back on those who are waiting. There is one who never gets bored, never gets tired, and is never too busy to do what he has promised. There is a promise maker who is unlike any promise maker we have ever encountered anywhere else in our lives. He is fully able to keep every one of his promises because he rules all of the situations and locations where those promises need to be delivered. The promised game has forever changed, because onto the field has come the Lord of lords. And what he says will come true because no one can question him, no one can get in the way of his will, and no one can stop his hand. No one.

So what is his sure and secure promise? It is a promise of something unbelievably beautiful after the great fire. It is so sweet to know that the fire is not the end. How discouraging would it be if what God had called us to ended in an inferno, with darkness to follow? But the fire at the end is not the end. There is something so far out of the field of our experience and so distant from anything that we can imagine that it is hard to wrap our brains around it. The promise is that after the end, God is going to give us a new home. No, we won't be floating on clouds and playing golden harps. He is going to give us a new heaven and a new earth. This one will not be like the one that we have been accustomed to living in. What will make it radically different from the broken world we live in is that it will be a place where righteousness will dwell, unchallenged forever.

Righteousness doesn't just mean that the new heavens and new earth will be inhabited by a holy God and people who are now partakers of his divine nature; that is, fully formed into the image of his Son. It means that everything will be righteous. Everything will be in its proper place, doing perfectly what it was meant to do. We have no experience of everything being righteous; that is, everything in its God-ordained place, perfectly doing what God designed it to do. Yes, it is true, nothing will ever be out of place again, fail to do its part again, or ever break again. Nothing will rebel against the Creator's plan. It will be uninterrupted peace and harmony forever. The Bible has a name for this: *shalom*. The shalom that was shattered in the garden will be restored forever, never to be broken again. Perfect righteousness will reign forever and ever. This is glorious glory.

So the doctrine of eternity assures you that God will fix everything that sin has broken. It tells you that right now you should live with that promise in mind. It warns you of the impermanence of physical things. It preaches to you of the eternal importance of the way you live as you wait. And it promises you an end that is far more glorious than anything you would have dared hope for.

Even with all of this, however, this doctrine still presses something more in on us.

The Doctrine of Eternity and the Unrighteous

We tend not to like to talk about hell, that place of eternal punishment, but we should. I want to tell you why it is practically important to do so. We all long for the final defeat of evil. We all cry out for a world where there is no more injustice. We all long for perfectly righteous justice to finally and forever win. Injustice haunts us everywhere we are. It's there in that moment when a frustrated dad takes his bad workday out on his family. It's there in moments of partiality, when the favored person gets what another person deserves. It's there in countless moments of racial injustice. It's there in acts of thievery and violence. It's there in a corrupt court system, corrupt politics, and corrupt government. It's there when bitterness and vengeance tear a family apart. It's there in ethnic hatred and terroristic acts. It's there every time we look down on someone who is different from us. Injustice lives on the school playground, in our homes, in government, in the corporate world, and wherever sinful human beings fail to act, react, relate, and lead with love.

Hell tells us that evil will be defeated. Hell tells us there will be a righteous judgment. Hell tells us evil will be punished. The Bible is very clear; there will be a final judgment, and there is a real place of ultimate punishment called hell. It is important for us to face this topic. God has revealed to us the truth of the dark side of eternity because he loves us.

I want to anchor our discussion of eternity and the unrighteous with a Jesus teaching, recorded in Matthew 25:31–46:

> When the Son of Man comes in his glory, and all the angels with him, then he will sit on his glorious throne. Before him will be gathered all the nations, and he will separate people one from another as a shepherd separates the sheep from the goats. And he will place the sheep on his right, but the goats on the left. Then the King will say to those on his right, "Come, you who are blessed by my Father, inherit the kingdom prepared for you from the foundation of the world. For I was hungry and you gave me food, I was thirsty and you gave me drink, I was a stranger and you welcomed me, I was naked and you clothed me, I was sick and you visited me, I was in prison and you came to me." Then the righteous will answer him, saying, "Lord, when did we see you hungry and feed you, or thirsty and give you drink? And when did we see you a stranger and welcome you, or naked and clothe you? And when did we see you sick or in prison and visit you?" And the King will answer them, "Truly, I say to you, as you did it to one of the least of these my brothers, you did it to me."
>
> Then he will say to those on his left, "Depart from me, you cursed, into the eternal fire prepared for the devil and his angels. For I was hungry and you gave me no food, I was thirsty and you gave me no drink, I was a stranger and you did not welcome me, naked and you did not clothe me, sick and in prison and you did not visit me." Then they also will answer, saying, "Lord, when did we see you hungry or thirsty or a stranger or naked or sick or in prison, and did not minister to you?" Then he will answer them, saying, "Truly, I say to you, as you did not do it to one of the least of these, you did not do it to me." And these will go away into eternal punishment, but the righteous into eternal life.

What is striking about this passage is that Jesus is telling us that everyone lives a Godward life. It is impossible not to respond to God in some way because he literally is the environment in which every human being lives. You can't get up in the morning without bumping into God. We could not exist without the exercise of his providence. We would sink into the hopeless insanity of unbridled depravity if it were not for his restraining grace. He sustains the systems of our bodies, and we use the gifts he has given to do our work. To be human is to be created for Godwardness. You either acknowledge his existence and bow in surrender or you deny him and go your own way. His dominance in our lives and in the world around us really does make denying him a moral outrage.

So you are either responding to God in humble surrender and devotion, trusting in the grace of his Son and living with him in view, or you are denying his existence, taking your life into your own hands, repudiating his commands, and writing your own rules. Jesus is declaring that everyone who has ever lived has responded to him in some way. You worship and serve him or you worship and serve yourself. You trust his grace or you tell yourself you have no need of grace. You work to please him or you work to please yourself. You live in a regular state of Messiah-consciousness or Messiah-denial. You are either a sheep or a goat; there is no moral ground of comfortable neutrality.

Jesus says that in the final judgment, he will separate the sheep (those who have trusted him and his grace, followed him by faith, and done his work) from the goats (those who have denied him and his call on their lives). The righteous will be ushered into the everlasting life and the perfect righteousness of the new heavens and new earth, and the unrighteous into everlasting punishment. Let's be clear, the final judgment is about how you have responded to God, and there are only the two possibilities (as we have seen and as Jesus made clear). The place of punishment is an actual place, hell. It is described this way in Revelation 20:15: "And if anyone's name was not found written in the book of life, he was thrown into the lake of fire." Matthew 25:41 calls it an "eternal fire." Revelation 20:10 talks of the devil being thrown into "the lake of fire and sulfur" and then says, "They will be tormented day and night forever."

It is simply impossible to gloss over what the Bible teaches about the final judgment and the eternal punishment of hell. If you take this teaching out of your Bible, the gospel simply loses its power. If there is no final judgment of and punishment for sin, then the law was not necessary and the cross of Jesus Christ is not needed. If there is no final judgment and punishment for evil, sin is not so sinful after all and God is not as holy as he declared himself to be. Without the final judgment of and punishment for sin, there is no need for Jesus to live a perfectly righteous life and take our punishment on himself. If there is no final judgment, you can sin without consequence and you have no need for forgiving grace. If you deny the final judgment and the final place of eternal punishment, you are left with a Christianity that has no gospel in it. You are left with empty religion, devoid of meaning and hope.

Because we are reticent to think and talk about hell, I want to do my best to describe hell's hellishness to you. I am going to do this by lifting a rather long section from my book *Forever: Why You Can't Live without It*.[2] This excerpt is from a chapter called "The Dark Side of Forever." In preparation for writing about the final judgment and hell, I came across this passage again, and after reading it, I knew I could not write a better description of the horrors of the eternal torment of hell than what I wrote in *Forever*. There are three things that together create the hellishness of hell.

> *1. Separation from God.* I don't know if I can provide the graphic description that everlasting separation from God requires, but I will try. Not enough has been written about this horror. It would be an existence far beyond any darkness that any human being has ever experienced. Every person, believer or unbeliever, benefits from the presence, power, and grace of God, for God's presence is what holds

2 Paul David Tripp, *Forever: Why You Can't Live without It* (Grand Rapids, MI: Zondervan, 2011), 60–62.

the world together and gives the world its order, beauty, and regularity. The sun that warms you and the breeze that cools you are signs of God's presence. The fact that you have water to drink and food to eat are the result of God's presence and control. God gives you breath and strength every day. He sustains your mental, emotional, spiritual, and physical capabilities. Even though we often are unaware of it, he guides and protects us every day. He sends the rain, he nurtures the flowers, and he is Lord over the storm. The regularity of all that makes up our existence as human beings and makes living possible is the result of his presence and his care. And he gifts us with all of these daily blessings that make life work even though we do not deserve them.

Imagine what would happen to the world if for just one moment God would withdraw his presence and his power. Everything around us would explode into utter chaos, and we would lose all ability to be the beings we were created to be. Now imagine the horror of the eternal chaos of living in a place completely separate from the presence, power, and grace of God. Imagine being in a place where nothing is what it was created to be; where there is no order, beauty, or rationality; where emotions have descended into unspeakable darkness; where there is nothing on which you can depend; where everything is completely broken and will never be restored; where every day is a horribly bad day and will never be followed by a better day; where beautiful things have become monstrous things; where everything and everyone is bent, twisted and distorted; where everything you lay your eyes on is a horror and there is no escape. Imagine the awfulness of God saying, "You have wanted to live separate from me your entire life, so you will now live in that state forever." Imagine the hell of separation from God.

2. Inhumanity. We were not created as independent, self-sufficient human beings. We were designed to live in a loving, worshipful, and dependent relationship with God. We are God's image bearers, designed to reflect his likeness. Our humanity reaches its fullest and most beautiful expression when we are living in close communion with the one who made us. Our humanity really is connected to his presence. The Bible describes the damage sin has wreaked on us in the present world this way: "They have become filled with every kind of wickedness, evil, greed and depravity. They are full of envy, murder, strife, deceit and malice. They are gossips, slanderers, God-haters, insolent, arrogant and boastful; they invent ways of doing evil, they disobey their parents; they have no understanding, no fidelity, no love, no mercy" (Romans 1:29–31).

Consider how far this description is from the beautiful human beings God created in the garden of Eden. The King James Bible translates "no love" as "without natural affection." This is a description of the progressive loss of one's humanity. Those who persist in sin against God begin to lose the humanity of heart, the sensitivity of soul meant to protect and restrain every human being. They quit feeling things that human beings are meant to feel. Their hearts become hard and uncaring. What Paul is describing in this passage is prevalent in this present world. It is happening while God still exercises the restraint of his protective, providing, and order-producing grace. Imagine what human beings would become if every dark impulse was given free rein because the presence of God was totally withdrawn. Imagine living in a place where no good thing resides in anyone's heart. If nothing that makes human life human life can exist apart from the presence of God, what would happen if God was completely absent? Now imagine living in this state of dark inhumanity forever, and you are getting close to understanding one of the singular horrors of hell.

3. Unending Torment. Because it is so easy for us to minimize our unfaithfulness to the relationship with God for which we were created, and because we daily step over God's boundaries, the torment of hell stands as a warning and protection for us. To come close to understanding the unending penalty for sin, we must stand at the intersection of the perfect holiness and justice of God and the enormity of the evil of sin. Our problem is that we have a perverse ability not to see sin for the huge evil that it is. In fact, we have the ability to look at sin and not see it as sinful at all. When we do this, we are in grave danger.

> The fact that we think eternal punishment is harsh and makes God less than fair demonstrates how far we have strayed from the biblical understanding of how evil evil is and how gloriously holy God is. Those who will experience eternal punishment will not do so because of an occasional breaking of God's law, but because of a lifelong, moment-by-moment rebellion against their Creator, a consistent desire to be in God's place, and an unyielding rejection of God's offer of rescuing and forgiving grace. Perhaps the biblical description of the torment of hell is one of the only accurate mechanisms we have been given to weigh the magnitude of the sinfulness of sin.

• • •

The doctrine of eternity is essential to our faith. The glories of the new heavens and new earth are laid out for us so that we would live with the comfort of knowing that God will keep all of his promises to us, that he will fix everything that sin has broken, and that we will finally be made like the Son, no longer with our backs bent over with the burden of remaining sin. The horrors of hell are laid out for us as a loving warning from a perfectly holy but tenderhearted heavenly Father. He wants us to understand the Godwardness of everything we do, the seriousness of sin, and the moral consequence of rejecting his authority, repudiating his law, denying a need for his grace, and living as we please.

So, in grace, God lets us eavesdrop on eternity and, as we do, we either hear celebratory songs of worship and victory or we hear the screams of those in torment. He lets us in on the future in order to draw us close and keep us safe until the end. And he knows that we will live as we were designed to live only when we live with the inescapable reality of eternity in view.

24

Eternity in Everyday Life

IT IS SO EASY and it feels so natural to live for the present. It is so easy to fall into a shrunken-world existence where everything is dominated by the needs, wants, opportunities, or fears of the moment. I am afraid that in the busyness and intensity of daily life, many of us completely lose sight of the future. Do you spend your money with forever in view? Do you use your computer with eternity in focus? Does the future shape the way you live in your marriage? Do you invest your time and energy like a person who really does have destiny in view? Would anybody around you conclude that eternity is in your thinking, that it really matters to you? Does the existence of a forever sculpt the way you approach your sexuality? How does eternity affect the way you do your work or approach your career? Does eternity make a difference in the way you live in the present?

The inescapable reality of eternity as a significant part of our culture's worldview has been stolen away. You will hear no reference to eternity on cable news. You won't see forever references in culturally significant social media sites. There are no courses at your local university on the impact of eternity on philosophy, politics, and the sciences. There are no books in the self-help section on Amazon on the topic of the family and eternity. What the Bible says is surely to come has been cut out of both the philosophical and popular cultural conversations. As a culture, we have concluded that eternity doesn't matter or doesn't exist at all. There are almost no cultural voices coming from influential cultural institutions that will reinforce your belief in eternity or help you to understand what it means to live in light of it.

So that is what this chapter is about. Remember, the theme of this book is that true belief is always lived. Faith is never just something you do with your mind, but it is always also a commitment of your heart that changes the way you live your everyday life. What does it look like to live in light of eternity? What follows is a beginning answer to this question.

I want to anchor this chapter in a passage we have looked at briefly already. This passage is an Old Testament case study about what happens to the life of a believer when he loses sight of eternity. It demonstrates graphically how it is nearly impossible not to lose your gospel mind when you fail to live with eternity in focus. I think Psalm 73 has never been a more important passage than it is for us today. It speaks to the anger, angst, and discouragement in many of us. It addresses a question that burdens and disheartens many of us. Why does it seem like so many ungodly people prosper, while so many believers seem to have such a hard time? Why does it sometimes seem like my commitment and obedience are for nothing? Where have all the promises of God gone? Where is God in all the chaos? Psalm 73 lives in the gap between the "already" and the "not yet," the very place where all of us live. If you're not going to lose your gospel mind, you need to make Psalm 73 a very familiar friend.

> Truly God is good to Israel,
> to those who are pure in heart.
> But as for me, my feet had almost stumbled,
> my steps had nearly slipped.

For I was envious of the arrogant
  when I saw the prosperity of the wicked.
For they have no pangs until death;
  their bodies are fat and sleek.
They are not in trouble as others are;
  they are not stricken like the rest of mankind.
Therefore pride is their necklace;
  violence covers them as a garment.
Their eyes swell out through fatness;
  their hearts overflow with follies.
They scoff and speak with malice;
  loftily they threaten oppression.
They set their mouths against the heavens,
  and their tongue struts through the earth.
Therefore his people turn back to them,
  and find no fault in them.
And they say, "How can God know?
  Is there knowledge in the Most High?"
Behold, these are the wicked;
  always at ease, they increase in riches.
All in vain have I kept my heart clean
  and washed my hands in innocence.
For all the day long I have been stricken
  and rebuked every morning.
If I had said, "I will speak thus,"
  I would have betrayed the generation of your children.
But when I thought how to understand this,
  it seemed to me a wearisome task,
until I went into the sanctuary of God;
  then I discerned their end.
Truly you set them in slippery places;
  you make them fall to ruin.
How they are destroyed in a moment,

> swept away utterly by terrors!
> Like a dream when one awakes,
> O Lord, when you rouse yourself, you despise them as phantoms.
> When my soul was embittered,
> when I was pricked in heart,
> I was brutish and ignorant;
> I was like a beast toward you.
> Nevertheless, I am continually with you;
> you hold my right hand.
> You guide me with your counsel,
> and afterward you will receive me to glory.
> Whom have I in heaven but you?
> And there is nothing on earth that I desire besides you.
> My flesh and my heart may fail,
> but God is the strength of my heart and my portion forever.
> For behold, those who are far from you shall perish;
> you put an end to everyone who is unfaithful to you.
> But for me it is good to be near God;
> I have made the Lord God my refuge,
> that I may tell of all your works. (Ps. 73)

Asaph is pretty graphic as he describes what he was like when he failed to live with eternity in view. He says, "My feet had almost stumbled. . . . my soul was embittered." He envied the arrogant. "I was pricked in heart, I was brutish and ignorant; I was like a beast toward you." This is a troubling picture of the spiritual and emotional impact on us in the present when we fail to make sense of our lives with eternity in view. You cannot properly understand the moment that you're in unless you are making sense of it in light of what is to come. The terrible spiritual tension that Asaph is experiencing as he is trying to understand himself and others, with all of its envy and discouragement, is resolved only when he begins to look at the very same things with eternity in view. I want to expand on the themes of this passage as we seek to understand what eternity-focused living looks like.

Determine to Fight Eternity Amnesia

Forgetting the warning and the hope that come from what is to come never produces anything good in your thinking or in your living. Here is the impact of eternity amnesia on your life in the present. (I am using material here that I have adapted from my book *Forever.)*

Unrealistic expectations. If you fail to keep eternity in focus, you will ask the present world to be for you and do for you what it never can. We will tend to want the here and now to behave as only our final destination can. Our disappointments are always connected to our expectations. If you live a life that is shaped by unrealistic expectations, you will live a life burdened by disappointment at every turn. Eternity reminds us that this broken, groaning world will never deliver to us that paradise that our hearts long for. *Do you live with unrealistic expectations of people, places, and things?*

Too much self-focus. You and I were created to live with something more than this present moment in view. We were designed to live for something bigger than the pleasure, comfort, and happiness that this moment can give us. We were made to live for something vastly bigger than ourselves, with a much longer view than this moment provides for us. Eternity confronts us with something that is very important. If you're going to experience any satisfaction and contentment, you have to keep this in view. Eternity requires us to face the fact that we are not in charge, that we don't write our own stories, and that the spotlight on center stage is on someone else. The culmination of the story requires us to face the reality that every chapter along the way has been written for the glory of another. Eternity confronts us with the fact that our lives move and turn according to the will of another and that his will will be done. The got-to-have-it-now-or-I-won't-be-happy self-obsession of our culture never produces peace of mind and heart. It never results in contented living. Eternity calls me to look beyond my momentary hopes and dreams, wants and needs, and opportunities and difficulties. *Does self-focus (your wants, needs, plans, and feelings) exercise too much power over the way you live your life?*

Wanting too much from people. When we lose sight of eternity in our relationships, we will constantly be asking the people near us to deliver to us the paradise our hearts long for. The people around us have no ability to deliver to us the perfect love, the unblemished righteousness, the constant peace, and the freedom from trouble that we will only ever experience when we're on the other side. Right here, right now, you won't have paradise children, you won't marry a paradise spouse, and you won't have a paradise boss, a paradise neighbor, paradise friends, or a paradise pastor. Looking to others to give us what they will never be able to give only ends in frustration, anger, disappointment, conflict, and division. *Do you expect from people what they will never be able to deliver?*

Desiring too much control or struggling with too much fear. Many of us swing back and forth between fear and control. Fear grips and controls too many of us, so to protect ourselves from the things we are afraid of, we want way more control than we will ever have over the events and people in our lives. In our eternity amnesia, we feel like life is passing us by, like we will never get those things for which we longed, or that we will be saddled with things we never wanted to face. Those unfulfilled longings and unwanted troubles don't announce to us that we've been forgotten and that life has failed us. No, they remind us that we were designed for another, better world. Sturdy peace in this world is found only when we live with the world that is to come in view. *Are you too focused on control? Is fear more of a motivating fact in your life than it should be?*

Doubting the goodness of God. I think many of us struggle at street level to hold on to our belief that God is good, because some things that he brings into our lives seem to be anything but good. If you don't understand God's agenda for you and his world, you will end up questioning his character. Unless we remember that God's promises to us will reach their final fulfillment only in the world that is to come, we will feel as if God has made promises to us that he did not intend to keep. What is really happening is that God is giving us a taste of his good gifts in the here and now so we will keep hungering for the full experience of them that is waiting for us in eternity. *Do you find yourself questioning the goodness, faithfulness, and love of God?*

Becoming more disheartened than thankful. Sadly, many of us are disappointed, not because God has ignored us or failed us in some way, or we have suffered much, or because the people around us are less than perfect, but because we approach life with the hope that it will deliver things that we will enjoy only in eternity. Our disappointment reveals more about our own eternity amnesia than it does about God or the people and things around us. Only when you have eternity in view and accept the fact that this is not your final destination can you approach everything in your life with biblical realism. *Is it more natural for you to complain than to be thankful?*

Lacking incentive and hope. All of the things that I have just described work to weaken our motivation and hope. This world is not an unending cycle of dashed hopes and evaporating dreams, but because of God's plan it is marching toward a moment when everything that is broken will be finally and completely restored. This gives you reason to get up in the morning and press on with all of the things God has called you to do. Sure, you will face hardships in your life, things that you never thought you would have to deal with, but the doctrine of eternity reminds you that this world is not all that there is. Every broken, bent, twisted, and decayed thing will be restored. Everything you now struggle with will be fixed. Eternity gives you a reason to continue even when nothing in your life seems to be working as it should. Greet your feeling of futility with the truth that what you're experiencing right now is not permanent. *Does life seem futile to you? Do you go through times when you struggle with motivation and hope?*

Tendency to deny consequences. One of the important functions of the doctrine of eternity right now is that it requires us to face the fact that life does have consequences. You cannot live however you want to live, do whatever you want to do, and make whatever decisions you want to make without any consequences. There is life after death, there is a final judgment, and there is a place of eternal punishment. The doctrine of eternity presents us with the ultimate consequence, and because it does, it infuses our lives right now with a moral seriousness that you can find no other way. Yes, there is a day of reckoning that no one will be able to escape. Eternity reminds you that how you live really does matter. *Are there times when the denial of consequences makes it easier for you to step over God's boundaries?*

Recognize Eternity's Gift of Values Clarification

By God's design we are value-oriented, goal-oriented, purpose-oriented, and importance-oriented beings. We are all living for something, in pursuit of something, or in the service of something. There are things in our lives that we value, and things that have little value to us. There are things that we say we value, but that we don't invest in in the way that you would expect if we valued them as much as we say we do. There are things in our lives that rise in levels of value way more than their true value, and when they do, they begin to control our thoughts, desires, words, and actions. Your life is shaped by what you value. If you want to know what you truly value, consider where you tend to invest your time, energy, gifts, and money.

The doctrine of eternity is an enormous help when it comes to our struggle of values, because it teaches us what is truly valuable and worth living for. Eternity blesses us with ultimate values clarification. Go to Revelation, and listen to the voices that are on the other side. What is the subject of their celebration? It's not wealth, power, grand palaces, people's acclaim, success, or achievement. No, the constant focus of the celebration is the Savior and his faithful and victorious grace. We need the values clarification of eternity because we so easily lose our sense of what's important. For some of us this means that we spend way too much time, energy, money, and worry on our lawn. Thousands of dollars and hundreds of hours are invested fighting weeds and producing the green that has become so important to us. Is your lawn more important to you than it should be? Or maybe you're the husband who has invested too much on your man toys. You don't need to invest any more in guns, tennis rackets, fly rods, or golf clubs. Have you spent so much time using your collections of toys that you don't have the time you should to spend with your wife and children? Do you spend too much time and energy on your appearance? Perhaps you have too much makeup and too many outfits in your closet. Are your true values revealed by the fact that you spend more time on your appearance than you do on your daily personal time of worship? Maybe you're a university student and keeping up with social media has become far too important. Having a voice in the endless conversation means too much to you, and scrolling to the next site eats too much of your time. Yes, we all can benefit from the values clarification that the doctrine of eternity blesses us with.

How is it that the doctrine of eternity clarifies our values? I suggest eight ways.

1. The existence of eternity immediately tells me that I have been designed with bigger concerns than a right-here, right-now focus on my wants, needs, and feelings. If there is a such thing as eternity, then whatever I want, whatever it is that I think I need, and my feeling of the moment must be understood and evaluated in light of what is to come.

2. The existence of eternity tells me that since this is not a destination but a preparation for a final destination, the goal of this moment is not to use my resources to turn now into as much of paradise as I can afford. If there is no such thing as eternity, then it makes sense to grab as much personal pleasure and comfort as you can get, because this life is all you have. But if there is an eternity, then it means that my life is not about just the pleasures of the moment, but more significantly about the destination that is to come.

3. The existence of eternity tells me where and when my only true satisfaction will be found. Eternity confronts us with the fact that the ultimate in personal happiness, joy, fulfillment, and satisfaction will never be found in the created world of people and things. Eternity invites us to understand that the highest of human pleasures are found in a person,

the Lord Jesus Christ. When he is at the center, when he is my reason for everything and I am living in complete surrender to him, then I will know unfettered joy and contentment of heart. The doctrine of eternity exposes the lie of materialism for the deceit that it is. It constantly reminds me that material things will not satisfy the longings of my heart, because whether I realize it or not, those deep longings are really for God.

4. The existence of eternity tells me what I should be investing my resources in. It tells me what will bring me the greatest return. Jesus told his followers to invest in a purse that would not wear out. Paul pleaded with his readers to "seek the things that are above" (Col. 3:1). Some things provide temporary pleasure but soon fade away. But there are investments you can make with your time, energy, and money that will last for all of eternity. The doctrine of eternity calls for us to have long-term values and to invest in things that have more than quickly fading fruit.

5. The existence of eternity clarifies my values by alerting me to what is truly important. As I said earlier, our lives are always shaped by naming some things as important and other things as unimportant. It is vital to get this function right. How sad it would be to invest your life in things that turned out to be not so important after all.

6. The existence of eternity tells me the danger of giving way to the temptation to worship the creation and not the Creator. We all live in the middle of a daily worship battle. There is a constant battle for what will rule our hearts, and in so doing, control the way we live. Our hearts are either being ruled by love for and worship of the Creator or by something in the creation. The glory of our final home will be that finally the Creator will be in his rightful place in our hearts, never to be replaced by anything ever again. The highest joys of the human existence are found when the Creator is in his rightful place as King in our hearts.

7. The existence of eternity assures me of the grace I need to fight the values battles that will wage in my heart. In this struggle of values, we are never alone, because the King of kings has invaded our lives by his grace. He never sends us into battle without going with us. He never calls us into battle without providing us with the right weapons. And he fights

for us even in those moments when we are too discouraged, too weak, or too foolish to fight for ourselves. If God has graced me with a place with him in eternity, then he will also give me all the grace that I need along the way. The doctrine of eternity reminds me that embedded in the promise of future grace is the guarantee of present grace.

8. The existence of eternity gives me hope when I get my values completely wrong. It is a hope not based on my track record, but on the grace and goodness of my Lord. There will be moments when you and I will lose sight of what's important. Our hearts won't always love what is best. But eternity reminds me that my ultimate hope is not in my getting it right, but in the one who always got it right and always did what is right. My ticket into the glory of eternity was not purchased by my right values and obedience, but by Jesus's perfect life, substitutionary death, and victorious resurrection. Because this is true, I can run to him now with my values failures and know I will find his mercy and grace. The doctrine of eternity reminds me that with all of my wanderings, he will keep me to the end and welcome me into my final home to live with him forever.

Live with a Preparation, Not Destination, Mentality

For most of us the problem is not that we intentionally deny the truth, but rather that in the busyness of life, we live thoughtlessly. Because we are focused on the endless stream of momentary needs and events, those urgent things that press on us every day, we fail to live up to what we say we believe. The beautiful truths, which are meant to encourage, warn, motivate, and guide us, get lost in the fog of the everyday. So we fear when we should have courage, we are disheartened when we should have hope, or we lack motivation when we have glorious reasons to press on. Some of us struggle with our faith because theological thoughtlessness keeps us from experiencing the beauty of what God is for us, has taught us, and has planned for us. God hasn't failed us, our theology hasn't failed us, but we have often failed to remember the most gorgeous body of truth that the human heart could ever embrace.

So it is with the doctrine of eternity. Remembering this truth will not only protect you from a lot of heartache, but it will guide you as you walk the path to the forever that God has promised you. One of the most important things that this doctrine does is remind you that this is not your final destination, but rather a preparation for the final destination that is to come. Preparation is hard. It takes commitment, discipline, endurance, and a constant eye on the prize that is to come. In the hands of an all-powerful and ever-present Redeemer, everything in your life is used to prepare you for the forever that is to come. In the hands of God, there is no wasted drama, no useless moments, or anything that was meant for nothing. The time between our conversion and our homegoing is not wasted waiting. No, it has been planned by God so he can continue his work of transforming us. He knows we are not ready yet for what is to come.

Athletes know that preparation is not as exciting as the game, but it is essential. They expect preparation to be repetitive, tiring, and painful, but they also know that it changes them. The problem is that many of us don't have the athlete's mentality, so we carry all kinds of unrealistic hopes and dreams as to what this moment will be, only to be disappointed again and again. Rather than living with a preparation mentality, in our theological thoughtlessness we fall into living with a destination mentality. We live as if this is all there is, loading the bulk of our hopes and dreams into this moment. This way of living never produces good fruit. It is the seedbed for hopelessness, anger, relational brokenness, doubt of God, and a whole catalog of other temptations. If you live with a destination mentality, you'll ask people, places, and things to be what they will never be on this side of eternity, and the results of this are never good.

But if you live with eternity in view, remembering that this is not your final destination but rather a time of preparation for your final destination, you will not be surprised when things don't work as they should, when people are less than perfect, when your dreams don't unfold as you expected, or when hardship comes your way. You'll know that when difficulty comes, you are being molded by the hands of the divine artist into something progressively more beautiful and more fit for what is to come. Yes, you'll still experience the pain of suffering and loss and you'll still get tired, but you won't experience pain without hope, exhaustion without motivation to continue, or hardship without joy. This is clearly not designed to be our final destination; to live like it is only makes every hard thing even harder. No, this is a time of loving preparation for the glory that has not only been promised to us but also purchased for us by the willing sacrifice of our Savior.

Find Contentment and Hope in Delayed Gratification

It is a very difficult but important thing that every parent tries to teach her children. It simply doesn't come natural for them, so lots of instruction is needed. Every child needs to understand the reality of and the value of delayed gratification. Little children ask fifteen minutes into a day-long road trip if you're almost there yet. A child will go out and check for plants in the garden the day after the seeds were planted. They haven't yet learned the simple truth that, by God's design, most good things don't happen in a moment. The doctrine of eternity is a doctrine of delayed gratification. God's promise is sure, but so is the reality that he has chosen for us to wait. We don't disappear into the glory of eternity the moment we first believe. The slowness of the march from the garden of Eden to the new heavens and new earth, which is so graphically chronicled in Scripture, confronts all of us with how naturally impatient we are. We like results to come quickly, and when they don't, we get antsy and irritated.

The Bible teaches us that the investments we make, with eternity in view, in the little moments of our lives will have a return that will last for all of eternity. In fact, you and I should read all of the principles and promises of Scripture through the lens of delayed gratification. Take Proverbs for example. How should we understand the promises of the proverbs? The more you study Proverbs, the more it becomes clear that the entire redemptive narrative is embedded in every proverb. Understanding this is the only way to make sense of the practical life wisdom that we find there.

Let's take this proverb for instance: "A soft answer turns away wrath, / but a harsh word stirs up anger" (Prov. 15:1). There is no doubt that in this proverb God is calling us to a calmness of character and faith in the face of another's anger. But in this proverb, is God promising that every time we respond to an angry person with quiet calm, we will immediately turn off his or her anger? Although this is a wise way to respond to an angry person, in the right here, right now, soft answers don't always de-escalate the anger of the other person. So what good is the proverb? This is where the lens of delayed gratification is helpful. Rather than this proverb being a mechanical guarantee, it is a wisdom call to live with eternity in view. When I respond with quiet calm in the face of anger, I am living in a way that is consistent with the divinely appointed move of the universe. The meek will inherit the earth! The meek Messiah will win! All the angry voices will be silenced as every knee bows and every tongue confesses that Jesus is Lord. What the proverb promises *will* happen; it may not be right when you would like it to happen, but it will come. And living in a way that is consistent with what is to come will always bear good fruit in your heart and life. Every proverb is written with eternity in view, so every proverb calls us to live within the principle of delayed gratification.

In fact, because we are on a slow march to the glory of the new heavens and new earth, delayed gratification is a significant element to true biblical faith. Hebrews 11 makes this very clear.

> These all died in faith, not having received the things promised, but having seen them and greeted them from afar, and having acknowledged that they were strangers and exiles on the earth. For people who speak thus make it clear that they are seeking a homeland. If they had been thinking of that land from which they had gone out, they would have had opportunity to return. But as it is, they desire a better country, that is, a heavenly one. Therefore God is not ashamed to be called their God, for he has prepared for them a city. . . .
>
> And what more shall I say? For time would fail me to tell of Gideon, Barak, Samson, Jephthah, of David and Samuel and the prophets—

> who through faith conquered kingdoms, enforced justice, obtained promises, stopped the mouths of lions, quenched the power of fire, escaped the edge of the sword, were made strong out of weakness, became mighty in war, put foreign armies to flight. Women received back their dead by resurrection. Some were tortured, refusing to accept release, so that they might rise again to a better life. Others suffered mocking and flogging, and even chains and imprisonment. They were stoned, they were sawn in two, they were killed with the sword. They went about in skins of sheep and goats, destitute, afflicted, mistreated—of whom the world was not worthy—wandering about in deserts and mountains, and in dens and caves of the earth.
>
> And all these, though commended through their faith, did not receive what was promised, since God had provided something better for us, that apart from us they should not be made perfect. (Heb. 11:13–16, 32–40)

These are the things that are said of the people of God who have gone before us. Faith is having a life that is shaped by holding tightly on to the promises of God, because you are living with eternity in view. So even though God's promises aren't fully fulfilled in the here and now, you don't abandon your hope in those promises. Why? Because you are living with their full future fulfillment in view. And you know that the final fulfillment, in the new heavens and new earth, of all that God has promised will make every moment of waiting, every moment of enduring, and every moment of investing worth it.

Delayed gratification helps you to live in your marriage with a patient and hopeful heart. It helps you to keep doing the good things as a parent that God has called for you to do, even when you don't see much fruit in your children. It keeps you from demanding that all of your relationships need to be comfortable or that your work life is always gratifying. It helps you to be happy investing your money in things that have an eternal return, rather than spending it all on present pleasure. The doctrine of eternity reminds me that God will keep every one of his promises, but it also reminds me that, even though I will get tastes of fulfillment along the way, there may be a long wait between my investment in those promises and God's final fulfillment. There simply is no such thing as true biblical faith that is not content with delayed gratification. There is reason for hope. It is not in the rapidity of the fulfillment of God's promises, but in the faithfulness by which he keeps moving us to the glorious end that is secure because he promised it to us. So with eyes on eternity, we believe, we invest, and we wait.

Commit Yourself to Gospel Stubbornness

Eternity calls you to stubborn faith. No, not stubborn in the sense that you demand your own way or refuse to follow God's way when it is uncomfortable for you. There is a sanctified, God-glorifying form of stubbornness that, with an eye on eternity, refuses to give way to cynicism, refuses to give way to hopelessness, and refuses to quit believing, obeying, and resting in God's promises no matter what. If you're going to be a contributor in the body of Christ, you will need sanctified stubbornness. If you want a peaceful, loving, and harmonious marriage, you better exchange selfish stubbornness for sanctified stubbornness. The only way not to lose your mind and your cool when you're dealing with stubborn children is if, with eternity in view, you stubbornly continue to do the ambassadorial things God has called you to do. If you want to avoid the nasty tit for tat that often infects our relationships, you are going to have to stubbornly refuse to give way to the temporary buzz of winning or having your own way. If you want to avoid debt and do good things with your money, you'll need to stubbornly resist spending for the moment and commit to investing in things of eternal value.

Stubborn faith refuses to live for self, refuses to live for the moment, and refuses to step over God's wise and loving boundaries. Stubborn faith keeps focusing on eternal glory rather than letting today's choices be dominated by present and temporary gain. This is exactly the kind of stubborn faith that 1 Corinthians 15:58 calls us to: "Therefore, my beloved brothers, be steadfast, immovable, always abounding in the work of the Lord, knowing that in the Lord your labor is not in vain." If there is a second resurrection, with a glorious eternity to follow, then this is the only kind of faith that will serve you well between the "already" and the "not yet."

Let's be honest here: sinful stubbornness is more natural to us than God-centered and eternity-focused stubbornness. As long as sin lives in us, we will be tempted to say no when we should say yes and yes when we should say no. There are times when God calls us to move and we refuse to move, and times when he is calling us to be steadfast and we are all too easily moved. But here is the good news. The risen Lord Jesus, whose resurrection makes our steadfastness worthwhile, is with us in our stubbornness struggle. He meets our weakness with his grace. He blesses us with new mercies every morning. He walks with us through trouble. In love, he stubbornly refuses to let us go. His stubborn commitment of grace makes our sanctified, eternity-embracing stubbornness possible, and that's a very good thing.

Keep Watching the Trailer

I think one of the greatest inventions in modern media culture is the movie trailer. It gives you enough of a taste of the essence of the plot and characters of a movie that you are able to decide whether you want to watch it or not. Sometimes Luella and I decide we want to go to a movie, so I will get out my iPad and watch movie trailers until I find the one that grabs my interest or that I think Luella will enjoy. Now, in the movie world sometimes trailers are a bit of a lie. They show you the two gripping moments in an otherwise dull movie to make you think it is action packed, so you will buy tickets. About thirty minutes into the film you know that you have been taken. So you sit irritated through a film that doesn't really interest you just to get your money's worth.

The doctrine of eternity is the ultimate trailer. But it is way more than an invitation to escapist entertainment for a few hours. No, this trailer welcomes you to a brand-new way of living, where everything you do is done with eternity in view. It calls you away from shortsighted faith. It pulls you back from living for momentary pleasures that soon evaporate. It warns you not to live for your own glory, but for the glory of another, a glory that you will someday share face-to-face. What this trailer encourages you to give yourself to is far more glorious than the trailer is able to display for you.

The thing about the eternity trailer is that it doesn't give you just a glimpse at the main characters and key points in the plot. No, this trailer gives you the complete origin-to-destiny redemptive narrative, it helps you to know the hero of the story intimately, it tells you how to live in light of the amazing drama of salvation, and it describes to you the glorious glory of the final chapter. It is the only trailer that has the power to change the way you think about yourself, about God, about meaning and purpose, about right and wrong, about others, and about everything else in your life. It is not only heart-engaging, it is also heart-transforming.

But here's the problem: everything in the eternity trailer is counterintuitive. It introduces us to a story that none of us could have ever written, even in our most imaginatively creative moment. And the eternity that is the final chapter of the story challenges us to think way beyond the little boxes of meaning that we often use to make sense out of our lives. So here's what you and I have to do. We have to keep watching the eternity trailer over and over again. You won't find it on Netflix, but you will find it starting with the first page of Genesis and propelling you to the last chapter of Revelation. You and I have to dive into this narrative day after day. We have to have our thinking, our desires, our hopes, and our living expanded to the size of eternity, or we will live the shrunken lives that always result from theological thoughtlessness.

Eternity calls us to live for things that are grand, transcendent, and glorious even as we live in the middle of the muck and mud of a broken and sin-scarred world. Eternity welcomes us to live with hope even when nothing around us seems to be working as it should and we are simply not strong enough or sovereign enough to initiate the changes that are necessary. Eternity invites us to live with the author and hero of the story in view, even though we can't physically see him or hear him now. Eternity warns us not to fight for things that don't matter in the long run, but to invest our time, energy, and money in things that have eternal consequence. The eternity trailer is designed by God to be transformative. There is nothing so different from what you're experiencing now as eternity is, so there is nothing that should focus your thinking more than eternity should.

God has given us the trailer. It's ours not just to casually think about, but to take in and consume, knowing that although things around us may seem to stay the same, by God's grace we will change and the way we live will change. We just have to keep watching the trailer.

• • •

We have come to the end of the most deeply moving book I have ever written. I'm not talking about what I have written, but rather about the amazing truths God has revealed to us. My goal has been to help you consider, understand, and apply these truths to the place where you live and to your relationships with the people who are there with you.

Over the last few months I have scaled the towering heights of divine revelation, and I am incredibly grateful to have done so. I have meditated on the wisest, most beautiful truths the human mind could ever consider. I have walked through the deepest and darkest valleys of human lostness, thankful for how the darkness has alerted and warned me. I have seen the smile on God's face, the healing touch of his finger, the incredible might of his power, the tender mercy of his heart, the fathomless depth of his wisdom, the searing force of his anger, the boundless expanse of his love, and his unstoppable march to ultimate victory. All of this has been displayed for me through twelve majestic but simple and practical core doctrines of our faith.

The journey hasn't always been easy. As I approached each new doctrine, I felt like I was getting ready to free-climb a ten-thousand foot rock face. Each time it seemed daunting, and I felt unable to do justice to the glorious truth that loomed with majesty before me. But I wasn't free-climbing, nor was I climbing alone. God climbed with me, and the rope of his word held me fast. With each doctrine, I had to deal with my own conviction as I was confronted with the fact that I too have gaps between what I say I believe and the way I live. But each moment of conviction was met by the grace of the cross, because the very doctrine of the word of God, when properly understood, leads you there. Each doctrine is shorthand for the narrative of his person and his victorious redeeming work. As I near the end of this book, I know that I needed to write it, not just for you but for me as well, so that together we may live inside of the most transformative body of truth that has ever been revealed for the human mind to consider.

Near the end of my writing an old hymn kept coming to mind. I would find myself humming it without deciding to. I googled this hymn, and as I read the lyrics carefully again, I decided that it would be the way I would end this book. May we view the word of God and its doctrines as this hymn does and may the prayers of the last verse be our prayer as well.

Your Word is like a garden, Lord;
with flowers bright and fair;
and everyone who seeks may pluck
a lovely cluster there.
Your Word is like a deep, deep mine;
and jewels rich and rare
are hidden in its mighty depths
for every searcher there.

Your Word is like a starry host;
a thousand rays of light
are seen to guide the traveler,
and make his pathway bright.
Your Word is like an armory,
where soldiers may repair,

and find, for life's long battle day,
all needful weapons there.

O may I love your precious Word,
may I explore the mine,
may I its fragrant flowers glean,
may light upon me shine.
O may I find my armor there,
your Word my trusty sword;
I'll learn to fight with every foe
the battle of the Lord.[1]

1 Edwin Hodder, "Your Word Is Like a Garden Lord," 1863, in *Trinity Hymnal* (Suwanee, GA: Great Commission Publications, 1990), no. 139.

General Index

Scripture Index